Nationalism and Internationalism in the Post-Cold War Era

The tension between nationalism and internationalism has been a major feature of world politics since the end of the Cold War. Based on a Nobel symposium, this collection brings together an international selection of acclaimed authors from a wide variety of academic disciplines. The book combines focused case studies and more theoretically based material to critically examine the post-Cold War political landscape. Subjects covered include:

- changing interpretations of the nation–state and nationalism
- the growing prominence of transnational organizations
- technological changes in information, communication and transport
- multiculturalism and citizenship
- ethnicity and religious identity in African, Indian, Bosnian and Polish nationalism
- the growing global significance of Islam

This outstanding volume is an invaluable resource for students of Politics and International Relations, as well as all those interested in the interplay between nationalism and internationalism in the modern world.

Kjell Goldmann is Professor of Political Science, **Ulf Hannerz** is Professor of Social Anthropology and **Charles Westin** is Director of the Centre for Research in International Migration and Ethnic Relations. The editors are all based at Stockholm University, Sweden.

Nationalism and Internationalism in the Post-Cold War Era

Edited by
Kjell Goldmann, Ulf Hannerz
and Charles Westin

London and New York

First published 2000
by Routledge
11 New Fetter Lane, London EC4P 4EE

Simultaneously published in the USA and Canada
by Routledge
29 West 35th Street, New York, NY 10001

Routledge is an imprint of the Taylor & Francis Group

© 2000 edited by Kjell Goldmann, Ulf Hannerz
and Charles Westin

Typeset in Baskerville by
Florence Production Ltd, Stoodleigh, Devon
Printed and bound in Great Britain by
TJ International Ltd, Padstow, Cornwall

British Library Cataloguing in Publication Data
A catalogue record for this book is available from the
British Library

Library of Congress Cataloging in Publication Data
A catalog record for this book has been requested

ISBN 0–415–23890–0 (hbk)
ISBN 0–415–23891–9 (pbk)

Contents

Contributors

Arjun Appadurai is Samuel N. Harper Professor in Anthropology at the University of Chicago where he is also Director of the Globalization Project. He was one of the founders of the journal *Public Culture*. Of his books *Modernity at Large* (1996) is his most recent.

Fredrik Barth has most recently held chairs at Emory University, the University of Oslo, and Boston University. *Balinese Worlds* is the most recent of his many books on the Middle East, South and Southeast Asia, Papua New Guinea, and anthropological theory.

Rainer Bauböck is a Senior Researcher at the Austrian Academy of Sciences, Research Unit for Institutional Change and European Integration, and at the universities of Vienna and Innsbruck. He is the author of *Transnational Citizenship: Membership and Rights in International Relations* (1994) and co-editor of the recently published *Blurred Boundaries: Migration, Ethnicity and Citizenship* (1998).

Kjell Goldmann is Professor of Political Science at Stockholm University and was Dean of the Faculty of Social Sciences 1987–96. His most recent book is *The Logic of Internationalism: Coercion and Accommodation* (1994). He is a contributor to a *New Handbook of Political Science* (1996).

Liah Greenfeld is University Professor of Sociology and Political Science at Boston University. She is the author of *Nationalism* (1992), a forthcoming volume tentatively entitled *The Spirit of Capitalism: Nationalism and the Origins of Economic Growth*, and other books.

Ulf Hannerz is Professor of Social Anthropology at Stockholm University and a past president of the European Association of Social Anthropologists. His most recent book is *Transnational Connections* (1996).

Stanley Hoffmann is the Paul and Catherine Buttenweiser University Professor at Harvard University, where he has taught since 1955. He was the Chairman of the Center for European Studies at Harvard from its creation 1969 until 1995. His most recent book is *World Disorders: Troubled Peace in the Post-Cold War Era* (1998).

Kalevi J. Holsti is University Killam Professor of Political Science at the University of British Columbia, Vancouver. He is a past president of the Canadian Political Science Association and of the International Studies Association. His most recent book is *The State, War, and the State of War* (1996).

Ali A. Mazrui is Professor and Director of the Institute of Global Studies, State University of New York at Binghamton. He is also a Professor at the University of Jos, Nigeria; Cornell University, Ithaca, NY; and School of Islamic and Social Sciences, Leesburg, Virginia. Among his many books on African and international affairs are *Cultural Forces in World Politics* (1990), and the latest *The Power of Babel: Language and Governance in Africa's Experience* (1998), co-authored with Alamin M. Mazrui.

Seteney Shami was the founding chair of the Anthropology Department at Yarmouk University, Jordan. She was director of MEAwards at the Population Council's regional office in Cairo and is now program director for the Middle East at the SSRC in New York. She is co-author of *Women in Arab Society: Work Patterns and Gender Relations in Egypt, Jordan and Sudan* (1990) and co-editor of *Population Displacement and Resettlement: Development and Conflict in the Middle East* (1994).

Yael Tamir teaches at the Department of Philosophy, Tel Aviv University. She is author of *Liberal Nationalism* (1993) and editor of *Democratic Education in a Multicultural State* (1995). Since 1999 she has been the Minister of Absorption in the Israeli government.

Jerzy Tomaszewski is Professor at the Institute of Political Studies, Warsaw University, and Director of the M. Anielewicz Center for the Study and Teaching of the History and Culture of the Jews in Poland. He is author of *The Socialist Regimes of East Central Europe: Their Establishment and Consolidation 1944–67* (1989) and other works on central and Eastern Europe.

Katherine Verdery teaches at the University of Michigan, where she is the Eric R. Wolf Professor of Anthropology and faculty associate of the Russian and East European Studies. Her most recent books are *What Was Socialism, and What Comes Next?* (1996) and *The Political Lives of Dead Bodies: Reburial and Postsocialist Change* (1999).

Joseph H. H. Weiler is Manley Hudson Professor and Jean Monnet Chair at Harvard University. His most recent book is *The Constitution of Europe: Do the New Clothes Have an Emperor and other Essays on European Integration* (1998).

Charles Westin is Professor of Migration and Ethnicity Studies at Stockholm University and Director of the Centre for Research in International Migration and Ethnic Relations. He has recently edited *Racism, Ideology, and Political Organization* (1998).

Acknowledgements

This book is based on contributions to a Nobel symposium held at Stockholm University on 7–10 September 1997. We acknowledge the generous support of the Nobel Foundation. Special thanks are due not only to the paper givers but also to those who served as discussants during the symposium and made invaluable contributions to the deliberations: John Breuilly, Barry Buzan, Robert E. Goodin, Louk Hagendoorn, Robert O. Keohane, and Stanley Tambiah. Ingrid Nordling was an excellent symposium administrator. Mark Graham and Ebba Hedlund assisted with the final editing of this volume.

K.G.
U.H.
C.W.

Introduction

Nationalism and internationalism in the post-Cold War era

Kjell Goldmann, Ulf Hannerz and Charles Westin

Real wars should perhaps have a single, dramatic ending; but when did the Cold War actually end – with the signing of the world's first treaty on nuclear disarmament in 1987, with the crumbling of the satellite regimes in East or Central Europe in 1989, or with the dissolution of the Soviet Union in 1991? The understanding that this war was indeed over perhaps did not come immediately to either participants or spectators. But then soon enough, the commentaries and the forecasts for the coming era began to appear. History had 'come to an end', there was a 'new world order' – yet there were also the threats of a future 'clash of civilizations', or even a 'coming anarchy'. Bipolar opposition had inhibited the expression of both nationalism and internationalism, it appeared; this no longer seemed to be the case.

Whatever we count as the end of the Cold War, some years have now passed since then, and it should be possible to discern some of the features of the world's post-war political landscape, actual or potential. This volume, originating with a Nobel symposium held in Stockholm on 7–10 September, 1997, brings together prominent representatives of a variety of disciplines in discussing the parts played by nationalism and internationalism and by the interrelations between the two in the shaping of that landscape, and in considering what recent experience may imply for established theory about these matters.

In this Introduction we hope to draw together themes from the contributions in a way which both offers an overview of central concepts and issues and does justice to the diversity of viewpoints coexisting and tangling with one another in a lively interdisciplinary field. To organize this diversity, it may be useful to consider first what goes into the title of the volume. We begin with the latter part, 'the Post-Cold War Era', and the issue of how to characterize that period.

Obviously, a restrictive reading of the term might involve a focus on changes immediately relating to the decline and dissolution of the Soviet Union, the disappearance of Walls and Iron Curtains, and the shift away from a global bipolar power structure and a nuclear arms race. These changes are a prominent concern in the volume and are dominant topics in several chapters.

More broadly, however, one might take 'the Post-Cold War Era' to mean ' the present', the 1990s, or perhaps 'the future', the early twenty-first century. As a more neutral and inclusive term of periodization, this could allow us to attend more generally to other phenomena and tendencies of current history: the changes in the world market economy, and the strengthening of regional units (especially the European Union); technological changes involving not least information, communication and transportation; the growing prominence of international and transnational organizations; in a word, much of what tends to be labelled 'globalization', and which may or may not be related to the fact that the Cold War has ended. Such a more generous usage may be helpful, among other things, in drawing attention to the interplay between, on the one hand, events and processes more directly linked to the ending of the Cold War and, on the other hand, those which have other contemporary mainsprings.

Third, as a matter of historical facts on the ground, perhaps there is yet another facet to the notion of a 'Post-Cold War Era'. This is a period in which we may find ourselves paying renewed attention to matters that tended to be neglected while the Cold War was still going on: other conflicts dispersed around the world, other possible dividing lines. To paraphrase our contributor Kalevi Holsti, there was, in the period preceding ours, an 'intellectual myopia' caused by the Cold War.

And then finally, to theorists and philosophers, a 'Post-Cold War Era' may simply be one where, having come out of the shadow which deep political, ideological and military divides and an ever-present risk of a nuclear holocaust may throw over intellectual activity, one can allow oneself to think more freely about other (possibly Utopian) ways of organizing and governing humanity.

We believe that our readers will find all these ways of thinking about what is 'after the Cold War' represented – singly or in combinations – in the chapters which follow. With regard to the first part of the title, 'Nationalism and Internationalism', we would note that we might also have used the plural form, nationalism*s* and internationalism*s*. There would have been a couple of reasons for this. One is that what has been conceived of as nationalism as well as internationalism has varied in time and space to the extent that even finding the common denominators may present some difficulty. In so far as several of the chapters are closely and explicitly concerned with recent periods in particular countries or regions, while others perhaps more implicitly draw on fairly generalized Western European or North American understandings of nationalism or internationalism, this is one dimension of variation. But we need also take into account the differing emphases of disciplines. Political philosophers with normative preoccupations may strive towards impeccable formulations of nationalism or internationalism; some political scientists and political historians may be dealing with nationalist and internationalist ideologies and policies within a relatively autonomously defined political field; many anthropologists, sociologists and members of some other disciplines are more inclined to see nationalist and internationalist ideas and practices as embedded in broader social and cultural orders and entangled with other kinds of allegiances – and also perhaps more ready to accept that in their everyday forms, nationalisms and internationalisms may be fragmented, situationally shifting, and internally inconsistent.

Programmes, conditions and processes

Such relative emphases hardly work out as a clear-cut division of labour among the disciplines. We can also map some of the diversity of approaches and assumptions along other lines, however, with some overlap with the tendencies just mentioned. Generally in the social sciences, and among our contributors, there is a certain mixture of engagements with '-isms', '-ities' and '-izations' – with programmes, more or less steady states (in the sense of physics rather than politics) or conditions, and processes. It may be useful to pay some early attention to terminologies and usages here.

As terms are constructed, we often recognize easily enough which is which. Sometimes, indeed, matching terms of all three types occur, in a way which should make obvious what is intended: modernism, modernity, modernization; globalism, globality, globalization; internationalism, internationality, internationalization. Yet as in the latter cases, one of the terms can be in more widespread use than the others and may expand into what one might think ought to be the referential turf of the others. At other times, a term which in principle could exist along such lines may never have been coined or may have some other or more restricted use, while another term occupies the conceptual space that could have been involved. Moreover, let us bear in mind that the '-izations' do not refer to all kinds of processes but to processes of increase: becoming more global, becoming more modern, becoming more international. Presumably, all 'steady states' of social and cultural phenomena could also be examined in processual terms, involving maintenance or reproduction.

We should be aware, then, that usage in the social sciences (or, for that matter, in everyday lay language) is not entirely transparent in this area of concern. We have not attempted to impose conceptual conformity on our contributors, and it is not our purpose here to advocate a particular definition of each actually or potentially existing concept. It may be useful, none the less, to indicate some of the choices that may need to be made in the interest of precision and to identify where, as we understand them, our contributors place themselves in relation to such a conceptual map.

With regard to our central terms, nationalism and internationalism, it would appear that they have frequently been used to denote events, actions, developments, and maybe structures, on the one hand, and principles, doctrines, arguments and even broad states of mind, on the other. Formal definitions are generally of the latter type, and it may be useful to reserve the '-isms' for programmes rather than conditions or processes. The distinction is crucial, since programmes and processes need not go together. In particular, the process of the internationalization of politics results to some extent from the pursuit of a programme that is nationalist rather than internationalist: far-reaching integration is currently advocated all over Europe in terms of the need to retain the essence of one's national identity, to regain a degree of control over one's national affairs, and to gain for one's nation an increased influence over international affairs. This has been a leading principle of the foreign policy of countries like Belgium and the Netherlands for many years. It has been argued in Sweden in terms of a presumed difference between 'formal sovereignty', which may be given up in favour of 'real sovereignty', the real thing. The Irish pride themselves on the international standing they have gained for their country as a result of EU membership. An even more telling example is the eagerness of the post-Communist governments in Central and Eastern Europe to join the EU; Europeanism goes hand in hand with 'the national value of Hungarianism', as it has been put (more about this in Goldmann 1997). It is clear that the -ization is one thing and the -ism another.

Assuming that we are dealing with a programme, there may be reason to raise the further question whether the nationalist or internationalist features of the programme hinge on goals, on means, or on a combination of goals and means. There is a tradition of regarding internationalism as the advocacy of international interdependence and institution-building for the sake of international peace and security – not as the advocacy of international interdependence and institution-building for any purpose, nor as the advocacy of anything that may bring international peace and security. It is also common, however, to denote an interest in international cooperation as internationalism regardless of purpose. Furthermore, when it comes to US foreign policy internationalism denotes the opposite of isolationism and may differ rather considerably from internationalism in the sense of a programme for international peace and security.[1] By the same token, nationalism may be defined as the pursuit of political sovereignty or autonomy for the sake of one's national identity, that is, as a principle for state formation (Gellner 1983: 1; Hobsbawm 1990: 9; A. D. Smith 1986: 129); it may also be defined as the pursuit of sovereignty or autonomy for any purpose, however, or as the pursuit of anything that may be supportive of one's national identity, or even as the pursuit of anything regarded to be in the national interest (Breuilly 1993: 2). In this case too, there may be a tradition of defining the concept in terms of a particular means – ends relationship (sovereignty for the sake of identity) but there is no lack of other usages. Nothing is correct and nothing is incorrect, except perhaps confusion.

Assuming again that we are dealing with a programme, a further question pertains to the meaning of 'programme'. The choice here is between a narrow definition in terms of principles for action and a broader interpretation of 'programme' as a conceptual framework, a way of thinking, a state of mind. An internationalist in the former sense is eager, say, to strengthen the United Nations; an internationalist in the latter sense is one who thinks about matters in global terms. Similarly, a nationalist in the former sense is opposed, say, to supranational organization; a nationalist in the latter sense is one who sees everything from the point of view of his or her own nation. In the literature on both internationalism and nationalism the concepts seem mostly to be used in the narrow rather than the broad sense, but there is neither consistency nor clarity on this score either.

Finally, we may have to decide whether to conceive of nationalism and internationalism as varying on a scale from moderate to radical or to specify a threshold for what is to be regarded as nationalist or internationalist. For example, phenomena such as the demand of the Saami minority in northern Scandinavia for recognition of specific territorial rights, or the Danish 'no' to the Maastricht Treaty, may be seen either as reflections of moderate nationalism or as differing from nationalism. By the same token, watching MTV or taking an interest in the Olympics may or may not represent internationalism. It seems clear that a threshold is often assumed; it is not always precisely defined.

Among the contributors to this volume, Kalevi Holsti is inclined to conceive of nationalism and internationalism as processes. Internationalism to him means integration and nationalism means fragmentation. Otherwise, the authors generally come down on the side of programme-oriented conceptions of both internationalism and nationalism.[2] This is mostly implicit as regards the former concept: whereas several authors have much to say pertaining to internationalism as a programme for peace and security (see below), they tend to take this interpretation of the concept for granted. The concept of nationalism has posed more of a challenge, it appears. Rainer Bauböck, in citing Gellner's (1983:1) standard definition of nationalism as 'a theory of political legitimacy, which requires that ethnic boundaries should not cut across political ones', places himself among those viewing nationalism in programmatic terms. Stanley Hoffmann adopts a more elaborate version of the notion of nationalism as programme when defining it – after describing it as 'this protean phenomenon' – as an ideology for the promotion of the nation's integrity and uniqueness, or even its world mission or superiority over others. Hoffmann, in contrast to Gellner and Bauböck, appears to see nationalism as a matter of degree; this is related to his defining it in terms of a variety of objectives rather than as merely a programme for political sovereignty. Arjun Appadurai goes somewhat beyond the conception of nationalism as a programme in the narrow sense in emphasizing the unique commitment he thinks nationalism entails – the willingness to kill and to die 'for the good of a plainly artificial collective form' – and in focusing attention on the 'puzzle of full attachment'; here, obviously, there is an implicit notion of a threshold that is fairly high. Liah Greenfeld takes the further step of defining nationalism as 'the foundation of our social consciousness, the cognitive framework of our perception of reality' and as 'the framework of today's characteristic identity'.

So much for the variety of ways in which our most central concepts can be defined, and have been defined by the contributors to this book. Next we shall consider how nationalism and internationalism relate to neighbouring concepts such as ethnicity and globalization. Then two classical issues will be surveyed in the light of the present contributions: primordialism versus constructionism in the analysis of nationalism, and the validity of internationalism as a programme for peace and security.

Multiple relations: religion, ethnicity, globalization

The scholarly interest in nationalism, we may remind ourselves, was revitalized across several disciplines in the late Cold War era, beginning in the early 1980s. Among the major works of that period were Ernest Gellner's *Nations and Nationalism* (1983), Benedict Anderson's *Imagined Communities* (1983), and Anthony D. Smith's *The Ethnic Origin of Nations* (1986). Eric Hobsbawm's *Nations and Nationalism since 1780* (1990) may also be seen as belonging to this generation of studies. It is worth taking note again of some of the arguments and assumptions of these writings.

Before the principle of nationalism had done its work, Gellner argued, an ethnographic map would look like a painting by Kokoschka, with a 'riot of diverse points of colour' showing 'great diversity and plurality and complexity' and 'ambiguous and multiple relations' (1983: 139). A later map, organized by nations, would show very little shading, neat flat surfaces clearly separated from each other, and little overlap or ambiguity; more like a painting by Modigliani.

Yet this should perhaps be seen as an achievement of the past, for Hobsbawm concluded his book by suggesting that as the history of the late twentieth and early twenty-first century was to be written, nations and ethnic groups would be seen as mostly retreating before a new supranational restructuring. It was a development which he looked upon with favour. One sign that the national phenomenon was declining was indeed the progress historians had recently made in studying it: 'The owl of Minerva which brings wisdom, said Hegel, flies out at dusk. It is a good sign that it is now circling round nations and nationalism' (Hobsbawm 1990: 182–3).

In the post-Cold War era, nationalism in some number of places seems to have entered a new day (suggesting, at worst, that Minerva's owl has been at least temporarily grounded?). And turning to Gellner's metaphors from art, several of the contributors to this volume – Appadurai, Bauböck, Greenfeld, Holsti, Mazrui, Shami, and Weiler are among the obvious instances – seem to paint pictures which are not very Modigliani-like: divided allegiances in many places continue to entail overlaps, ambiguities and clashes. There is recurrent mention in the chapters to follow of the conflicts between Hutu and Tutsi in Central Africa, and between Orthodox, Catholic and Muslim Bosnians. The work of the 'principle of nationalism', after all, seems not yet quite done, or is becoming undone.[3]

Nationalism and internationalism, complex notions in their own right, thus often appear in one connection or other with a number of other phenomena or concepts: ethnicity, multiculturalism, religion (sometimes of the varieties characterized as 'fundamentalist') on the one hand, transnationalism and globalization on the other, to take the most prominent examples. Sometimes the relationship between nationalism and internationalism, on the one hand, and ethnicity and related concepts, on the other, may be fairly clearly one of competition, at other times one of coincidence and support. Yet in other instances the links may be more complicated.

In their chapters, Fredrik Barth and Ali Mazrui dwell on issues of religious allegiance – Barth in analysing the enigmatic relationship of Islamism to nationalism and internationalism, Mazrui in discussing (apart from ethnicity) the part of Islam and Christianity in recent African politics and international relations. Jerzy Tomaszewski also touches on questions of religion in his discussion of post-World War II Polish nationalism, while Appadurai refers to Hindu–Muslim conflict in India. In our comments here, we may need to consider more extensively questions of ethnicity and globalization, and their place in the contributions to this volume.

There is widespread agreement among our authors that contemporary states only rarely have a population made up of a single ethnic group. Most of the authors, however, appear to take the notion of ethnicity for granted, and avoid going into definitional problems here. Liah Greenfeld, however, suggests that the main feature of an ethnic identity is that it is ascriptive and appears to go as far as to imply that all ascriptive characteristics (even eye colour) objectively constitute ethnic categories, although not all of them are in fact accorded 'cultural significance'. While the details of this view may not importantly influence her continued line of argument, we suspect that many scholars would be in some conceptual disagreement with her here. In line with what seem to be current conventional assumptions, we are inclined to reserve the term ethnicity for groups and group identities that are in fact recognized in social life on the basis of a mixture of perceived cultural and social inheritance.[4] On the one hand, that is to say, an ethnic identity is 'passed down': you have the identity of your parents and ancestors, and this tends to make ethnicity a matter of lay understandings of kinship and biology. On the other hand, one tends to recognize ethnic membership in terms of particular behavioural markers, which are interpreted to signify a shared and more or less enduring group culture (including, at different times and in different places, religion, language, customs, and so forth). We can easily discern the potential of ambiguity and arbitrariness in such an understanding of ethnicity; but then we should remind ourselves that those popular understandings to which we apply the generalized scholarly label 'ethnicity' may be variable and that the handling of ethnic identities and classifications in social life often involves dealing with degrees of opacity. It would appear that on the whole, the ways in which ethnicity is referred to in subsequent chapters is not in conflict with the view of it just sketched.

Such a view, one might note, implies that there is no simple relationship between ethnicity and cultural diversity. There can be considerable cultural diversity within an ethnically homogeneous population; conversely, members of ethnic groups who mark themselves off from each other socially may share a great deal of culture, in the sense of meanings and practices. Such a distinction between culture and ethnicity, however, is not always upheld in popular, political, or even scholarly discourse. 'Multiculturalism', a prominent concept of the post-Cold War era, to a large extent does not refer to just any cultural diversity but to diversity organized by ethnicity. (Moreover, while as an '-ism' the term could for the sake of clarity be restricted to a programme of supporting cultural diversity, of one kind or another and in one way or another, it is clear that it is sometimes used to refer to cultural diversity as an existing state of affairs as well.[5])

The English language lacks a widely accepted single noun for denoting the collectivity of people to whom we would apply the adjective ethnic. The French *ethnie* has been adopted by A. D. Smith (1986) and is also used by Stanley Hoffmann in this volume, but generally it has not caught on. The more common 'ethnic group' has the possible drawback of entailing an underestimation of scale – one may tend to think of 'group' in terms of 'small group' (face-to-face interaction, or common interests or purpose) – yet despite such shortcomings, we shall use it here, turning next to the triangular relationship, again problematic, between ethnicity, nation, and state.

Certainly the conceptual distinction between 'nations' and 'ethnic groups' is often blurred. We assume, however, that not all ethnic groups will readily be seen as nations and that not all nations are defined in ethnic terms. Some time ago, Barth (1975: 15) rather provocatively introduced an aboriginal group he had studied, the Baktaman, as 'a nation of 183 persons occupying a tract of mountain rain-forest near the centre of New Guinea', but no doubt the more common tendency is to reserve the term 'nation' for larger and more organizationally complex units than the Baktaman; in the context of politics, we also expect them to show both a will and a capacity for governance.[6] When Mazrui gives an estimate of 1,500 to 2,000 ethnic groups in Sub-Saharan Africa, and Holsti offers the higher figure of 3,000 for the continent as a whole, we may remind ourselves of the relative arbitrariness and context-dependence of such classifications and enumerations generally, but we may also note that we would be less inclined to accept that nations can be counted in such numbers. Some ethnic groups, then, are more likely to qualify as nations than others.

On the other hand, it is a commonplace that the relationship between nation and state is also problematic. The tendency to refer to just about any state as a 'nation' (or 'nation–state') is strong, even in instances where the claim seems dubiously grounded by any criterion; for as Benedict Anderson suggests in *Imagined Communities* (1983: 12), nation-ness may be 'the most universally legitimate value in the political life of our time'. Yet what we witness again and again are attempts to make state, nation and ethnic group coincide as closely as possible, not only at a level of rhetoric but as a matter of organizational fact. As Holsti puts it: 'The only "permanent" solution to the "natural" country idea is either moving populations or moving frontiers.' By no means referring to a new phenomenon, the post-Cold War era has familiarized us with yet another term for one such solution, 'ethnic cleansing'. The term 'nationalism', protean as it is, can be made to stand for such programmes as well, or for less consistent, systematic or violent varieties of xenophobia. In his chapter on Polish nationalism, placing the post-Cold War scene against the background of a longer post-World War II historical period, Jerzy Tomaszewski argues that anti-Semitism has maintained a fairly continuous presence in Polish politics. He also notes the hostility to Romanies, again noticeable in Central and Eastern Europe in the post-Cold War period. And we likewise get a glimpse, in Tomaszewski´s chapter, of the fact that in the Communist period, anti-Semitism, designated as anti-Zionism, could put in an appearance as a form of internationalism, too.

It may indeed have become a rather widespread view that multicultural, multiethnic states are naturally and inevitably troubled, by internal conflict, domination, and general unease. Let us note again, then, that we are more likely to hear of the bad news than the good news (or of conditions which are not held newsworthy at all). Holsti points out that most people in such countries seem to live together peacefully – 'through a variety of formal and informal arrangements, pragmatically developed over long periods among people who understand that for ordinary commerce and lives to work, coexistence is the only low-cost alternative'. Mazrui's notion of the 'ecumenical state', in which various ethnic and religious groups work out a formal and informal political *modus vivendi* is an example.

Obviously the state apparatus can have a role here. Multiculturalist public policies, as institutionalized in Canada and Australia, while differing in many respects, have the common aim of acknowledging ethnic and cultural diversity and managing its strains and tensions. The basic idea is that ethnic identity, or membership of or identification with any cultural group, should under no circumstances serve as an obstacle for people to exercise their social, political, and constitutional rights; it should not prevent them from enjoying full access to societal institutions, or to participate in society as equal, worthy members. In other words, state multiculturalism here is about equal opportunities, the rule of law, and the respect for human rights.[7]

The engagement of the state with ethnic diversity is not always benign, however, as Holsti points out, noting Hitler's Holocaust, Stalin's Ukrainian massacres, and the Turkish annihilation of Armenians as examples. Arjun Appadurai, in his discussion of 'predatory nationalisms', makes a similar point: the latter thrive where 'ethnicist criteria of being and belonging become primarily tied to the procedures, rewards and spoils of the state-apparatus'.

Ethnicity and religion have been interrelated in a variety of ways with nationalism and internationalism for a long time. Globalization in the sense of relations over long distances can also be seen as extending far back in human history, with intercontinental trade, forced or voluntary population movements, and political colonialism as conspicuous ingredients. Much of the ethnic and cultural diversity which characterizes various territories in the present is the enduring result of long-distance migrations that occurred centuries ago. In the 1950s and 1960s, 'nationalism' was a term probably most frequently used synonymously with anticolonialism in Asian and African contexts.

Even so, globalization has tended to be unevenly distributed in time and space, and it would appear hard to deny that the recent easy access to vastly improved communication and transportation facilities has allowed a considerable overall acceleration of globalization, which thereby becomes a complex social, cultural, political and economic phenomenon, with a technological infrastructure of jet planes, television, telephones, fax and electronic mail. In its current intensity, then, it may belong more peculiarly to the late twentieth century, and thus to the period in which we are especially interested here.

Globalization is a multifaceted notion. In one frequent usage, it refers especially to the increasing integration of global markets in recent decades. This complex of economic tendencies is referred to in this volume particularly by Katherine Verdery in her analysis of nationalist and internationalist strategies and idioms in post-1989 Romania, where she suggests that the end of the Cold War was largely a consequence of the new relationships of state socialist economies to global capitalism.

According to a broader conception, globalization refers to the more general growth of interconnectedness across national and continental borders which has been particularly salient in recent times (Robertson 1992). A wide range of actors and groupings are visible on this increasingly cohesive world arena: global corporations, international organizations (many of them part of the United Nations apparatus), religious movements, human rights organizations, occupational groups, dispersed family groups, and so forth. It is worth pointing out that not all such collectivities and structures need to be large-scale phenomena in themselves, even as they are geographically extended. In the aggregate, however, they create a highly intricate and internally diverse web of global interconnections.

It is likewise worth noting that globalization in this sense should not be equated with global homogenization. While the activities of many global businesses as well as international organizations do point in such a direction, there is room for the reproduction of considerable social and cultural diversity, as well as for the generation of new cultural forms, within the interconnected global structure.[8] Moreover, many groups tend to react to increasing, and possibly threatening, interconnectedness by demarcating their own boundaries more sharply, socially and symbolically. This fact is rather out of line with Hobsbawm's prophecy of a decline of nations and nationalism, but currently exemplified by a variety of groupings, variously oriented toward cultural protectionism, cultural fundamentalism or xenophobia, at local, regional, or national levels, around the world. In this volume, in his discussion of the chauvinist Shiva Sena movement in Bombay, Arjun Appadurai provides an example of this tendency. One might add that Samuel Huntington (1993, 1996), in his controversial 'clash of civilizations' argument to which several of our contributors refer, takes such identity politics to the highest global level. (The 'Huntington thesis' could also be taken as an example of attempts to get away from the 'Cold War myopia' referred to earlier. If civilizational divides are as deep and enduring as Huntington argues that they are, they ought to have deserved some attention from scholars of international relations between 1945 and 1990 as well.)

Even as some groups may identify themselves more self-consciously with a locality as a result of globalization, others become more deterritorialized; and this has not least been conspicuously true with regard to some ethnic groups and even some 'nations'. In the second half of the twentieth century migration has created new diasporas, in addition to the old ones, and at the same time new means of communication allow their members, far apart in geographical space, to remain more closely in touch. Diasporas involve roots as well as routes (Clifford 1994). In the post-Cold War period, some diasporic groups have been able to renew their linkages to what were for a long time largely inaccessible homelands – Estonians or Armenians, for example, or the Circassians returning, from Jordan and elsewhere, to visit ex-Soviet Caucasus, as described in Seteney Shami's chapter. (There was an Iron Curtain in the Middle East and Central Asia as well.) Shami's discussion of the Circassians as well as the Chechenyans – a group hardly known to many outside the Soviet Union and the Middle East before the 1990s – contributes vividly to a view of 'diversity and plurality and complexity' as characteristic not just of some prenationalist past, but of the current map of nationalism and ethnicity.

Central as the notion of globalization may have become, there are contexts in which the use of the term occasionally seems a little hyperbolical. Perhaps it ought to be restricted to structures and processes which are indeed global, or at least, transcontinental, in their reach. The terms 'transnational' and 'transnationalization' have also come into widespread use in a largely overlapping sense, and should perhaps be preferred as we refer to more limited regional cross-border phenomena.[9] But then, as we tend to use them to describe what is more exactly 'trans-state', they can create ambiguities of their own. Diasporas may be transnational in the sense of extending across state borders (containing populations which may regard themselves as nations in their own right), but then they may also insist on being nations of a sort themselves. Ali Mazrui's discussion of the expansive political role of the Tutsi in the Central African region could also be taken as an example of a transnational phenomenon, but again, if one accepts for the moment that the arbitrary boundaries drawn in Africa at the beginning of the colonial period now delimit entities that should be termed nations. Moreover, we could observe that 'transnationalism' seems quite frequently to be used, at least in some disciplines, more as a state of affairs or a process than as a programme – perhaps the form 'transnationality' should be promoted here.[10]

Primordialists and constructionists

'Nationalism' and 'internationalism', Katherine Verdery writes in her chapter on post-Communist Romania, are not so much opposing doctrines as elite idioms employed to marshall allies in fields of power. On the surface, then, there may be '-isms', programmes, but as we develop this theme we discover that these are used rather more as dressing for other purposes.

This view relates to a cluster of issues touched upon by a number of our contributors. On the one hand, there is a contrast between what is described as 'primordialism' and 'constructionism' (or 'situationism', or more narrowly, 'instrumentalism'). This contrast may be drawn in the case of ethnicity as well as nationalism. On the other hand, there is in the case of nationalism a distinction between two major types which may be denoted by various terms but often as 'ethnic' and 'civic', respectively.

The notion of primordiality seems to have been brought effectively into the scholarly vocabulary for contexts such as ours by Clifford Geertz (1963: 109ff.).[11] Primordial attachments, according to Geertz, 'are seen to have an ineffable, and at times overpowering, coerciveness in and of themselves'. He suggests that they are of six major kinds: assumed blood ties, race, language, region, religion, and custom. (Ethnicity is not explicitly included as such on this list, but the term was not yet in much use in the early 1960s, and several of the other items are close to it.) These are attachments which, again in Geertz' words, 'seem to flow more from a sense of natural – some would say spiritual – affinity than from social interaction'.

Among our contributors, Greenfeld and Mazrui appear to use the notion of primordiality, presumably more or less in Geertz' sense, without much worry. For Mazrui it is perhaps a convenient term to bring together ethnicity and religion, the two entities he is concerned with, in a largely organizational mode. Greenfeld gets closer to defining a primordialist position for herself as she compares nationalism to the great religions and suggests that it today 'forms the foundation of our social consciousness, the cognitive framework of our perception of reality'.

In popular discourse, certainly, the tendency to resort to ideas of primordiality in explaining not least distant, unfamiliar conflicts is quite pronounced. 'Tribalism' and 'ancient hatreds' are thus seen to underlie many outbreaks of violence in the post-Cold War period. It may, however, be another characteristic of the times we are in that several other contributors are more inclined to distance themselves from any view they would think of as primordialist; Holsti, for example, in his discussion of ethnic conflicts and state involvement. Indeed, it may now be that 'primordialist' (like 'essentialist', a related notion) is more often a label researchers will critically attach to each other than one with which they will personally identify, while lay beliefs about premordiality are seen as a resource elites may use for political mobilization.

It seems reasonable to raise the question here to what extent the primordialism in question has its locus in lay beliefs or in the minds of scholarly observers. One could note, for one thing, that even Geertz, who has figured so prominently in the spread of the notion of the primordial, does not embrace it wholeheartedly: 'By a primordial attachment is meant one that stems from the 'givens' – or more precisely, as culture is inevitably involved in such matters, the assumed 'givens' – of social existence.' It 'seems to', 'is seen to' – again and again, a certain distance. And then Geertz (1963: 114) points out that 'in the enduring structure of primordial identifications', some may be latent but lie ready to take explicit political form under 'the proper sorts of social conditions'. The question, after all, turns out to be one of how primordiality is constructed, and when, why, and to what degree it is mobilized.

Between 'primordialists' and 'constructionists' in the scholarly world, then, there is perhaps a continuum rather than a real polarity, depending on the way they see attachments as being formed; on the way they think about the kind of control culture exercises over people, or people over their culture; on what they believe about the relationship between politics and culture; and on how far they insist on pushing the inquiry into the 'assumed givens'. Possibly primordialist theorizing may find a real home of its own in socio-biology, but otherwise it seems to be in considerable part a question of accepting a version of the sociologists' Thomas theorem – 'when people define something as real, it is real in its consequences'. On the other hand, committed constructionists may raise questions about just why things get defined as real, may ask further questions concerning who stands to gain from maintaining them or from mobilizing them under particular circumstances, and may be sceptical toward the history of supposedly time-less identifications.[12] It is with the middle kind of question that construc-tionism tends to get more specifically instrumentalist. Yet under such circumstances, one should note that in order for one party in a situation to be able to manipulate 'primordial attachments' successfully with some particular political or material ends in mind, it would seem that there must be another party which is more receptive to the primordial claims and arguments. That is to say, the analysis may have to acknowledge, or assume, an interaction between different stances toward primordiality in its constructed forms. Analyses of conflicts in ex-Yugoslavia in terms of elite political entrepreneurship often entail this kind of argument.

The issue of primordialism is approached most directly in two of the contributions to this volume. It was a common impression in the wake of the Cold War that nationalist forces had been let loose across post-Communist Europe. The Cold War – this was commonly thought – had kept national or ethnic conflicts frozen in the Soviet-dominated bloc. Now a thaw had occurred and hence old conflicts had reappeared; the return of history this was called. The so-called deep-freeze theory, with its strongly primordialist overtones, is effectively rejected in two of the chapters to follow. Jerzy Tomaszewski shows that in spite of their proclaimed inter-nationalism, the Communist rulers in East Europe had played on national sentiments and traditions to mobilize public support. This is a familiar theme from the literature on nationalism, as indicated already. John Breuilly (1993: 93), for example, has reminded us of three functions that an ideology can perform – coordination, mobilization, legitimation – and has shown in detail how nationalism has been used for such purposes in a variety of contexts. Tomaszewski demonstrates that this was also the case in Eastern Europe, despite the fact that the rulers here purported to represent internationalism. Katherine Verdery's argument that references to both nationalism and internationalism in post-Communist Romania were employed to legitimize property interests also gives precedence to the instrumental over the primordial. There seems to have been neither freeze nor thaw in East Europe: nationalism and its sibling, ethnicity, evidently were put to political use both during and after the Cold War. Again, too, there is Holsti's suggestion that the perception of the emer-gence or re-emergence of ethnic or national conflict may be an intellectual myopia caused by the Cold War itself.

The contrast between what we here term 'civic' and 'ethnic' nation-alisms (with the American case as the most prominent instance of the former) comes up in other ways and with somewhat varying terminologies in other chapters. In Hoffmann's more elaborate set of distinctions, 'cosmopolitan liberal nationalism' may be the most ideal-typically civil variety. Greenfeld argues that 'individualistic nationalisms' can only be of the civic variety. Appadurai enters an argument with Jürgen Habermas and the latter's notion of constitutional patriotism, which we take as a version of civic nationalism. In Appadurai's view, the purely civic variety of nationalism is less likely to build up that 'surplus of affect' which is 'more libidinal than procedural'. Weiler scrutinizes the recent appearance of a concept of European citizenship and discusses its relationship to national citizenship. His conclusion is that if the latter in Europe has an ethnic, 'organic–cultural', tendency, European citizenship should be, in a complementary fashion, modern, rational, civilizatory.

Hobsbawm (1990: 12), in his book referred to above, argued that 'no serious historian of nations and nationalism can be a committed political nationalist', for 'nationalism requires too much belief in what is patently not so'. Presumably, he would extend this claim to include scholars in other disciplines as well. Whatever may be the case, we may indeed not have any strongly committed nationalists among our contributors here. On the other hand, we may perhaps sense here and there a measure of respect for the phenomenon. And while the preference may be for the more civic varieties, there is some recognition that they may entail a certain cultural deficit – there is less accumulated symbolic density, and consequently there is less of what Appadurai describes as 'full attachment'. One discerns a relationship here between an existing state of affairs, or ongoing cultural process, on the one hand, and the legitimacy of a programme, on the other. We can see that what ethnic nationalisms can draw on is to a large extent the kind of primordial attachments just referred to above (appropriately demystified for scholarly purposes).

Yet ethnicity itself is not the only source of symbolic density in nationalism. Other types of primordiality enumerated by Geertz may coincide with it. Among scholars sometimes labelled primordialists, there is often an emphasis on shared history or shared territory as major factors (which constructionists such as Hobsbawm are inclined to subvert). In recent times, there has been a considerable interest among anthropologists and scholars of popular culture in showing how everyday life, the media, and new public events – even trivia such as national beauty queen contests – keep contributing to the growth of national symbolic density in the present (see e.g. Hannerz and Löfgren 1993, 1994; Billig 1995). Appadurai, in his contribution here, draws attention to a much more disturbing alternative source: state violence. If we must accept that symbolic density is an asset of nations, we must hope for more benign kinds of 'cultural engineering' – to use a notably constructivist term once coined by Ali Mazrui (1972: xiv). Finally, as far as these kinds of bases of '-isms' are concerned, one may want to ponder the fact that there seems so far to be less cultural density in internationalism.[13]

The future of internationalism

The end of the Cold War was commonly taken to have paved the way not only for nationalism but also for internationalism. There was now, many thought, a uniquely favourable occasion for putting ideas about internationalist peace-building into practice. Immanuel Kant's *Zum ewigen Frieden* became *à la mode*. Long-lasting, even if not eternal, peace seemed a realistic expectation at least as far as Europe was concerned.

The assumption that the end of the Cold War made Kantian internationalism a relevant consideration is not questioned by any of the contributors to this volume. What we find instead is a discussion of its implications from a variety of perspectives. Papers such as these would not have been written if the avoidance of nuclear war between the East and the West had remained a chief concern. They presume that it has now become a meaningful task to discuss the outline of a new kind of international order for the next century.

Stanley Hoffmann distinguishes between two spheres of conflict, the traditional inter-state and 'a huge sphere of intra-state conflicts, some of which result from the clash of competing nationalisms . . . while others are the effects of the disintegration of weak, artificial or corrupt states'. There is a tension here between four universally recognized norms, he argues: sovereignty, national self-determination, democracy and human rights. The gap between the likely and the desirable is, in his view, huge. What is likely is either collective non-intervention or a modicum of humanitarian intervention. Hoffmann advocates the latter, and not only when the UN Security Council has found international peace and security to be threatened, but also when fundamental human rights are violated inside states. This necessitates an international police force, he believes. Internationalism is still in its infancy in this regard, but sovereignty has been turned from an absolute to a conditional norm and should be seen to provide a country with legitimate security from external aggression and interference 'only insofar as it respects internationally recognized human rights, and the kind of international obligations that a treaty establishing a global system of criminal justice . . . might establish'.

Hoffmann offers a moderately internationalist programme striving to take what he calls practical politics into account, Yet he 'has few illusions that even [these] rather non-utopian suggestions . . . will be carried out in the near future'. One reason is the survival of the national idea. The European Union shows how much can be achieved by liberal democracies, Hoffmann suggests, but it also shows 'the limits of cosmopolitanism'. Here again Weiler's consideration of the relationship between Eros (the national) and Civilization (the supranational) provides an unusual perspective on the tension between the national idea and cosmopolitanism that Hoffmann has in mind. Crucially, Weiler writes, the idea of a community of states is not meant to eliminate the national state but to 'create a regime which seeks to tame the national interest with a new discipline'. Supranationalism does not seek to negate the interplay of national differentiation and commonality but to 'diminish . . . the importance of the Statal aspects of nationality . . . as the principal referent for transnational human intercourse'. Individuals are invited to see themselves as belonging to two demoi, one based on 'organic–cultural identification and belongingness' and the other on 'transnational affinities to shared values which transcend the ethnonational diversity'. This, and Weiler's somewhat playful suggestion that we would be better off thinking about 'differentities' rather than single, one-dimensional identities, is reminiscent of Appadurai's scrutiny of the assumption of the modern system of nation–states that space, cultural identity and distributive politics should be contained in formally equal, spatially distinct, isomorphically enveloped entities requiring 'full attachment'. In its place, Appadurai suggests that one could envisage a global politics admitting a heterogeneity of overlapping forms of governance and attachment.[14] Perhaps this is an understanding of nationalism and internationalism for which Georg Simmel, with his attention to 'the web of group affiliations', could stand as an intellectual ancestor?

Hoffmann and Weiler remain within the framework of internationalism in the moderate sense of a programme for peace and security without world government (Goldmann 1994: 4), for building a 'half-way house . . . between systems of governance based on principles of anarchy and those based on hierarchy' (Holsti 1992: 55–6), for international interdependence and institution-building on the basis that 'the development of the nationalities can only favour international interests as a whole by guaranteeing variation and richness' (Lange 1919: XX). This is one of the most successful political ideas of the twentieth century. Radical internationalism in the sense of a world state has always been politically marginal but is the object of Yael Tamir's contribution. Tamir sets out to show that the case against the formation of a global state is not compelling and that the idea of a global state deserves to be taken more seriously than ever before. The global state she envisions, however, is one that 'imposes a thin layer of human rights and leaves a wide range of autonomy to the different groups to govern their own lives and coordinate a wide range of exchanges between themselves'. Such a global state would intervene in the autonomy of groups 'only in order to stop oppression and protect human rights'. This, interestingly, is not dramatically different from Hoffmann's 'practical politics' and 'non-utopian suggestions'. It seems as if the gap between the utopian and the non-utopian is diminishing in the wake of the Cold War.

The internationalist programme, as it may be called, has always been conceived as a programme for peace and security at the inter-state level. Two contributors to this volume take the step of applying it to intra-state problems or, if you wish, to the reduction of conflict between nations rather than between states. Holsti does this very explicitly. Intra-state internation conflict has always posed a problem for internationalism, he reminds us; what he calls the Bentham hypothesis – trade and communication between peoples will promote empathy, mutual understanding and friend-ship – has always seemed difficult to reconcile with the fact that conflict, including inter-nation conflict, has been common within states. Holsti considers the evidence, indicates that there is a tendency to take note of failures but not of successes, shows that much intra-state conflict does not result from ethnic hatred but from governments playing the ethnic card to further their own agendas, and concludes that when we look at the majority of post-1945 states, 'Bentham's observations and expectations seem to be emerging as the normal rather than the exceptional.'

Rainer Bauböck focuses on secession. He discusses the arguments for and against a right to secede and concludes that a federal solution will often be preferable to either centralized government or the break-up of the state. The federation, however, must guarantee collective rights, other-wise secession may be justified anyway. Note the similarity between Bauböck's federation, Tamir's global state and Hoffmann's non-utopia: in all three cases it is a matter of pluralism within a common institutional framework with powers that are only limited. To advocate such a compro-mise between anarchy and hierarchy may be to pronounce a politico-philosophical truism, but it is interesting to see that you may arrive at this quintessentially internationalist insight from such different directions. The internationalist programme for peace and security would seem to gain additional support from these contributions as well as from Holsti's empir-ical results. The problem, as Hoffmann suggests, is one of implementation rather than effectiveness.[15]

The layout of this volume

As we are acutely aware, our attempt in these introductory comments to sketch some of the more prominent issues discussed by our contributors can scarcely do justice to their individual empirical, conceptual and theo-retical richness. For similar reasons, we doubt that there is any manner of grouping them which will not somehow violate their multidimension-ality. We have, however, ordered them into four parts which we hope our readers may find a useful for purposes of overview.

Part I, 'Commitments and Contexts: Ethnicity and Religion' includes the three chapters by Greenfeld, Mazrui and Barth. In different ways, each of these emphasizes the fact that nationalism is embedded in social and cultural contexts where other major allegiances may at some times align themselves with it, and at other times compete with it or otherwise subvert it.

In Part II, 'The Iron Curtain rising', the chapters by Tomaszewski, Verdery and Shami take us to some particular areas of the world very directly affected by that Cold War territorial divide identified by Winston Churchill's metaphor: Poland, Romania, the Caucasus. These chapters focus on particular national, international and transnational situations and linkages, and illuminate several major developments of the transitional period, against their respective historical backgrounds.

We have placed the chapters by Appadurai, Holsti and Weiler in Part III under the rubric 'Attachments and Arrangements'. One of Appadurai's main concerns is with the problem of exclusive, 'full attachment' to particular imagined communities, and the connection of such attachments to collective violence; towards the end of his chapter, he suggests a differently organized global politics, permitting a heterogeneity of cross-cutting rather than monopolistic attachments. As we have seen, Holsti, likewise engaging with the issue of nationalism and violence, points to the involvement of the state in recent internal conflicts, and concludes that left to themselves, varied communities in an internally diverse society tend to work out arrangements for peace, exchange and collaboration. Weiler, in scrutinizing the problem of loyalties in an increasingly integrated Europe, seems to suggest a particular mode of dividing loyalties. With this group of chapters, we seem to move from an inspection of particular recent and ongoing processes to more programmatic, even somewhat Utopian formulations for world organization.

Finally, in Part IV entitled 'Images of World Order', with the chapters by Hoffmann, Bauböck and Tamir, this more normative stance is developed in ways which, as we have suggested, seem to converge on a combination of pluralism with a limited common institutional framework. And so here we perhaps face the best promise of the post-Cold War Era.

Notes

1 Rosenau and Holsti, in a study of US elite attitudes in about 1980, distinguished between 'Cold War Internationalists' and 'Post-Cold War Internationalists'. The objects of the former were to 'maintain alliance commitments; keep up with the Soviets militarily and respond to their efforts to extend their influence in the Third World' whereas the object of the latter was to 'promote a multiplicity of economic and political institutions to facilitate movement toward world order and away from confrontation' (Rosenau and Holsti 1983: 379). Only the latter qualifies as internationalism in the sense of a programme for international peace and security. See Goldmann (1994: 2–5) for a consideration of various definitions of internationalism as programme.

2 Katherine Verdery makes a point of rejecting definitions of nationalism and internationalism as doctrines or programmes in favour of regarding them as 'idioms utilized in political struggles' and as 'political rhetorics'. This, however, is a matter of the seriousness with which a position is advocated rather than of its substantive contents.

3 One prominent recent work on nationalism, Rogers Brubaker's (1996) study of the relationships between nationalising states, minorities and external homelands in Post-Communist East and Central Europe, also focuses on such complex relationships.

4 We follow here the argument set forth by Barth (1969) in a statement which has been highly influential in studies of ethnicity for the last few decades.

5   Some additional comments on condition/process/programme distinctions may
    be in order here. 'Ethnicity' clearly belongs to the condition, 'state-of-affairs'
    side as far as the primordialist interpretation is concerned. The terms 'ethnifi-
    cation' and 'ethnicization' do not seem to be in frequent use, yet it makes
    perfectly good sense to conceive of a process through which identities are made
    ethnic, as for example in primary and secondary socialization. An accepted term
    for the process of making ethnic, in the sense of ethnic group emergence, is
    'ethnogenesis'. Obviously a programmatic side to ethnic identity promotion must
    also exist, so that a term 'ethnicism' could be applied; Appadurai indeed uses
    the adjective 'ethnicist'. Ethnic cleansing, to which Appadurai, Bauböck,
    Greenfeld, Hoffmann and Holsti refer, may be regarded as an extreme instance.
    In some contexts ethnicism has been used as an equivalent to racism.
6   According to Østerud, it is a common denominator of the wide variety of concep-
    tualizations that a nation is by definition a perceived *political* community (Østerud
    1997a: 169).
7   While this human rights vision may be in accordance with other policies for
    dealing with cultural diversity resulting from immigration (Israel's absorption
    policy, or the traditional US assimilation ideology), proponents of radical multi-
    culturalism maintain that it represents a new approach. Rex (1985) makes a
    useful distinction between the public and private domain, uniformity and diver-
    sity of practices, equal and differential rights. He identifies four possibilities: (1)
    equal rights in the public domain, diversity of cultural practices in private or
    communal matters; (2) equal rights in the public domain, uniformity of cultural
    practices in private or communal matters; (3) differential rights in the public
    domain, diversity of cultural practices in the private or communal domain; (4)
    differential rights in the public domain, uniformity of cultural practices in private
    and communal matters. Multiculturalism, as Rex envisages it, recognizes cultural
    and ethnic diversity in the private spheres but insists on equal rights in society
    at large – different but equal, as the slogan goes.
8   The view that international organizations have a major part in diffusing a 'world
    culture' is interestingly proposed for example by Meyer *et al.* (1997). On glob-
    alization and diversity, old and new, see e.g. Appadurai (1996a) and Hannerz
    (1996).
9   When 'transnational' and 'international' are distinguished from one another, the
    latter term tends to be reserved for contexts where nations, or rather states, are
    themselves involved as actors, whereas 'transnational' activities and relationships
    involve a wide range of border-crossing actors and phenomena. See Keohane
    and Nye (1977: 25) for an oft-quoted distinction between interstate and trans-
    governmental relations, on the one hand, and transnational relations, on the
    other.
10 Basch *et al.* (1994: 7), for example, define transnationalism as 'the processes by
    which immigrants forge and sustain multi-stranded social relations that link
    together their societies of origin and settlement'.
11 Anthony D. Smith's influential work on the ethnic origin of nations basically
    harks back to a moderately primordialist position. Smith (1986) argues that
    ethnicity is at the kernel of nations and nation building. Ethnicity represents a
    kind of proto-nationalism. For Gellner (1983), on the other hand, ethnicity is
    of little importance for explaining the origins and rise of nations. Ethnicity may
    be exploited, and even created, to pursue national policy objectives, but the
    origins of the national project must be sought elsewhere. Smith has later char-
    acterized his approach as one which 'balances the influence of the ethnic past
    and the impact of nationalist activity' (1995: 19).
12 We may remember that Hobsbawm's and Ranger's tellingly titled *The Invention
    of Tradition* (1983) appeared at the same time with some of the books that

revitalized the study of nationalism, and had a considerable influence on the latter.

13 Note here, however, Hannerz' (1996: 81ff.) argument, to a degree polemically aimed at some of Anthony D. Smith's statements, that transnational experiences may be building up a greater symbolic density; conceivably these could be turned into an internationalist resource.

14 See also Appadurai (1996a: 158ff.).

15 Goldmann's (1994) conclusion about the effectiveness of the internationalist programme for peace and security is that global peace is not to be expected from institution-building and interdependence, but that the situation in post-Cold War Europe is more likely to be conducive to successful internationalist peace-building, since in Europe the institutions are stronger, the network of cooperation tighter, and democracy the prevailing form of government. He thus shares Hoffmann's view that even modest change is unlikely to occur at the global level in the foreseeable future.

Part I
Commitments and contexts

Ethnicity and religion

1 Democracy, ethnic diversity and nationalism

Liah Greenfeld

The meaning of 'ethnicity'

The purpose of this chapter is to examine the logical connections and the historical pattern of relationship between nationalism, ethnicity, and democracy. The exercise must begin with a set of definitions, and I want to start with what appears to me the most misunderstood and inadequately defined phenomenon among the three. What do we mean when we speak of 'ethnic diversity'? On the face of it, the term refers to nothing more than a plurality of ethnicities within a society, or the existence in it – in the words of the director of the United Nations Research Institute for Social Development – of 'physical and cultural differences, [such as] those of religion, language, and race'.[1] In this sense, 'ethnic diversity' is both ubiquitous and innocuous. The physical and cultural differences covered by the term 'ethnicity' – language, customs, religion, territorial affiliation, and physical type – represent various ascriptive characteristics, often perceived as 'primordial' or inherited. All of us have ascriptive characteristics: our eyes are a certain color we have not chosen; we have certain, genetically determined, complexions; our families, cities, and neighborhoods into which we are born often have their specific traditions, accents, and even dialects. These ascriptive characteristics necessarily differ from those of many others within our society, and as a result, no society can be characterized as lacking ethnicity or ethnic diversity.

Nevertheless, in some societies we do not notice this diversity, and therefore consider them 'homogeneous', while in others such diversity is distinctly (and often painfully) visible. This is so not because there is less diversity among individual members of one society, so far as their ascriptive characteristics are concerned, than of another, but because the same measure of diversity may be *perceived* differently. Not every society attaches cultural significance to ethnicity and ethnic diversity and regards them as the core of its members' fundamental identity. Very few societies before the modern age, if any, did so. When a *modern* society does not attach cultural significance to the ethnicity of its members and does not regard it as the foundation of their identities, the identities that are cultivated are rather civic, they have to do with one's acceptance of the values of one's society and achievement in their framework. In this case, ethnic diversity is highly unlikely to have any political significance. Many modern societies, however, do attach to ethnicity great cultural significance and, whether or not they explicitly regard ascriptive characteristics as the essence of their members' identities, allow it to become an important political force.

Cultural significance attached to ethnic differences is rarely proportionate to their 'objective' magnitude. Very often these differences are minimal or virtually non-existent, but, when perceived as culturally significant, they are magnified – often to the point of being turned into a cultural rift that cannot be bridged, which, among other things, makes ethnic violence a possibility at any given moment and peace always unstable and precarious. An example of such minimal differences, magnified and turned murderous by cultural significance attached to them, is former Yugoslavia, and in particular Bosnia. The differences between Serbs, Croats and the so-called 'Bosnian Muslims' are mostly in the imagination. These three groups of Southern Slavs belong to the same race and look the same; they speak Serbo-Croatian – the same language; their religion, which has been made so much of recently, cannot, in practice, be used to distinguish between them, because overwhelming majorities in each of them are (or were until the eruption of the recent conflict) non-believers. These facts are overlooked because the identities of Serbs and Croats have been traditionally defined as ethnic identities (and since they cannot envision the world any other way, they necessarily define as ethnic the identities of members of the third group, the descendants of Slavic Muslims in Bosnia). The definition of an identity as ethnic presupposes a belief that a person's inclinations, attitudes, and behavior are determined ascriptively, by the group to which one is born, which, in effect, means genetically – that they are given, so to speak, in the blood, and though they can be hidden or suppressed, cannot, under any circumstances, really be changed. In other words, one is a Serb, a Croat, or a Bosnian Muslim every moment of one's life and in everything one does, whether one is aware of this or not.

Parenthetically, one should note that the glorification of ethnic diversity under the name of 'multiculturalism' in immigrant societies such as the United States or Australia, while mostly peaceful in its consequences, has similar cognitive implications. In the absence of social countercurrents (which, in these cases, is an extremely important proviso), cultural perspectives which emphasize ethnic identity discount the individual as an independent social actor and the bearer of rights and subordinate him or her to the group to which he or she *objectively* (namely, in terms of one's ascriptive characteristics and irrespective of one's will) belongs. Such a celebration of ascriptive characteristics denies the individual the freedom of choice and the right to self-determination, and make an accident of birth, if not a census category, destiny.

'Democracy': definition

By contrast, 'democracy' in Western discourse refers to the cultural and political perspective which asserts the primacy of the individual over the group and affirms individual liberty as an inalienable right and a reflection of an inherent ability. Of course, this term is also ambivalent. I have discussed this ambivalence in an earlier article on a closely related subject, 'Nationalism and Democracy'.[2] Connoting in general the idea of popular sovereignty, I argued there, the word 'democracy' is used to describe political structures that have very little in common, apart from the fact that in all of them, evidently, democracy is seen as an important value. In many cases, this universal approbation is the only reason for adopting the concept of democracy: it is a manner of collective self-validation. The countries that have the word 'democratic' in their formal titles – such as Democratic and Popular Republic of Algeria, People's Democratic Republic of Ethiopia, or Democratic People's Republic of (North) Korea – would hardly be considered model democracies by Western standards. Neither, obviously, would the no-longer-existing German Democratic Republic, so called to distinguish itself from the other, apparently insufficiently democratic, Germany to which it now joined. In their turn, Western democracies, referring to themselves as 'liberal' or 'constitutional' democracies, have been – until a couple of years ago – consistently called 'formal' and 'false' by people in 'people's republics' all over the world, the true democracy in the eyes of the latter being 'socialist' democracy.

Which of these democracies ('socialist' or 'bourgeois', 'liberal' and 'constitutional' or 'social' and 'economic', 'organic', 'guided', 'new', or 'high') are true, and which are false, is fundamentally a question of semantics. But the decision as to which of them to adhere to is, obviously, not. It is a matter of the gravest consequence, with profound implications for every sphere of social life. In the modern world, the political character and social structure of a society depend not on whether it is 'democratic' or not – for every one among the two hundred or so nations of the globe today, including absolute monarchies and dictatorships more modern in character, accepts the principle of popular sovereignty and claims to be or to aspire to become democracies – but on the specific definition of 'democracy' and the *meaning* of popular sovereignty in that society. This is an important point which has not been given the attention it deserves. Adherence to the 'ideals of democracy', profession of a desire for 'democratic reforms' in the end of the twentieth century place societies in question in the end of the twentieth century, no more. As abstract notions of 'truth' and 'justice', which take on different, often contradictory, meanings in different social contexts, adherence to 'democracy' tells us nothing about the character and aspirations of a people. Were this recognized, there is no doubt that recent transformations in East European societies and particularly Russia would have appeared to us in a very different light.

The euphoria with which the news of the upheaval was in fact met in the West, and in the United States, in particular, should be attributed to the lack of such recognition.

Obviously, the joy of the Western nations over the prospective 'democratization' of the world (specifically, of formerly Communist countries) was aroused, not by the apparently increasing popularity of the word at the time; neither, one would hope, was it caused by the prospect that from then on societies previously subjected to self-appointed rulers would choose their despots in an orderly fashion. It was caused, rather, by the naïve presupposition that 'democracy' everywhere meant 'liberal' or 'constitutional' democracy, that, in every language, democratic incantations were a sign of awakening to the idea of human rights – the respect for the individual, so characteristic of the West.

For, to return to the point made earlier, it is this respect for the individual as the basis of the principle of popular sovereignty, not the principle as such, and not the 'democratic procedures,' which lies at the foundation of *liberal and constitutional democracy* (that democracy, the prospects of which, presumably, are of interest to the participants in this project, and appears in the title of this chapter). The idea of popular sovereignty, as was mentioned above, forms the basis of legitimacy in every modern polity and can be interpreted in many ways. The procedures are the tools through which the principles of liberal democracy are implemented, but, as with other tools, they may be used for the implementation of other principles as well. It is possible to import the procedures without at the same time importing the principles that first brought them into being since they do not themselves constitute liberal democracy, but merely enable it to function. Thus both the general principle of democracy and the formal democratic procedures can coexist with different political regimes (authoritarian and liberal), and with different social and economic structures (egalitarian as against rigidly stratified – whether ethnically, culturally, politically, or economically – societies; capitalist as against socialist economies). The idea of the human rights, in distinction, favors, and is, therefore, associated with a particular type of political, social, and economic structure – liberal, egalitarian, and capitalist. The idea of the human rights implies the equality of all mature individuals under the law which guarantees to each of them the enjoyment of certain inalienable rights, specifically the right of self-determination or liberty. This right is exercised through majority rule, but only as a result of the 'freely given consent' of the minority (that is, a group whose *opinions* are in a minority), with human rights setting limits to the power of the majority.

It follows that, as principles of human association, ethnic diversity and (liberal) democracy are contradictory. Logically, it is impossible to attach great value and importance to ethnicity and ethnic diversity without encroaching on the human rights of the ethnically diverse individuals. Rights of communities and rights of individuals cannot be ensured in equal measure; either the former or the latter must become subordinate. When formulating public policy to deal with ethnic diversity and to promote liberal democracy, it is very important constantly to keep in mind which one of these two sets of rights – often antithetical in their consequences as well as logical implications – one wants to uphold. Plainly put, cultural validation and empowerment of ethnic identity and ethnic diversity endanger liberal democracy. However heretical in the current political climate this may sound, the best way to assure that such democracy will thrive within *ethnically diverse populations* may be by rejecting the principles of ethnicity and ethnic diversity and, instead, encouraging civic identities and commitment to pluralism, or diversity, of a civic nature.

Nationalism and its general implications

The question arises: why, given the contradictory character of the ethnic and liberal democratic agenda, are the two nevertheless so often perceived as allies and even aspects of each other? The source of this misconception appears to be the substitution of a direct connection for an indirect one. The investment of ethnic diversity with cultural significance and liberal democracy are indirectly related because both are the products or corollaries of nationalism. Ultimately, the misunderstanding of the relationship between these antithetical principles is rooted in the misunderstanding of nationalism.

At the end of the twentieth century, nationalism remains at least as powerful a force in our lives as it was a century ago. The claim that the fundamental cultural patterns have not changed during the course of a century may arouse some resistance and the evidence of such continuity, however ubiquitous and palpable, may strike us as surprising. We have become accustomed to rapid technological change and to the idea that change in general is a normal, and predictable, part of social life. It no longer threatens our image of order, but represents an integral element of it. Yet there is nothing surprising in the tenacity of nationalism. Cultural frameworks which define historical epochs, as nationalism defines modernity, change slowly, and in the life of an historical type of society, which modern society is, a hundred years is not a very long time. We can estimate the life-expectancy of nationalism by comparing it to other order-defining cultural frameworks, such as the world's great religions. The widespread notion that nationalism is the modern religion may be misleading if used, as commonly it is, as a strict definition; it then obliterates conceptual distinctions between nationalism and religion and obscures the nature of both. It is, nevertheless, fully justified as a metaphor which helps us to see the functional equivalence of the two. Like the great religions of the past, nationalism today forms the foundation of our social consciousness, the cognitive framework of our perception of reality. Seen against the record of the great religions' historical longevity and continuous vitality over centuries of political, economic, and technological change, the recognition of this functional equivalence may give us a more accurate idea of nationalism's projected life span and pace of development than would our experience with food-processors or word-processors, whose ever-changing models seem to be the chief inspiration for our model of ever-changing reality.

Like the great transcendental religions in earlier historical periods, nationalism also forms the framework of today's characteristic identity – national identity. This identity, which reflects the cognitive framework provided by nationalism and the image of the social order implied in it, differs in several important respects from identities fostered by religious cultures. To begin with, nationalism is secular. It locates the sources of ultimate meaning, law, and authority, which religious consciousness identifies with transcendental forces, in this world, specifically, in social reality. (This, among other things, implies attribution of moral significance and purpose to history, and thus encourages the idea of social progress, to which, chiefly, we owe our predisposition to expect and welcome all manner of change. The 'end of history' euphoria, as well as our inclination to interpret social and political transformations as positive, generally, and the readiness to see advances in technology as signs of profound social and political transformations, are explained by this.) An earthly community, the nation, becomes the supreme object of loyalty.

This community has several unique characteristics. It is seen as the bearer of sovereignty, and membership in it, or nationality, ensures the fundamental equality (equality in regard to the fundamental, defining characteristic) of all who qualify for it. The related principles of popular sovereignty and of the fundamental equality of membership represent the definitive principles of national consciousness and have significant implications for the nature of political and social processes in communities constituted by such consciousness, nations. All polities that define themselves as nations or polities that claim membership in the community of nations, without being defined as nations themselves (such as empires: for example, the Russian and Austro-Hungarian empires at the beginning of this century, and the Soviet Union at the end of it) adopt an impersonal, legal-rational, or *state*, form of government which, in principle, has a representative character. The authority it exercises emanates neither from itself, nor from transcendental sources beyond the nation, but from the nation. And this principle applies equally to polities which are representative democracies in actual fact and to modern dictatorships which dispense with representative institutions. What allows for such differences in the implementation of the same principle are the differences in the definition of the nation, which I shall address below. The principle itself, however, materially affects the experience of politics and life, in general, in modern societies, adding to it dignity unknown to those who, in principle, could not see themselves as represented in the power wielded over them and even theoretically speaking had no share in it. It is this, in principle, impersonal and representative character of political authority in nations, which permits openly authoritarian regimes to insist on their democratic character. Modern tyrants may sincerely believe in the ideals of democracy, which, in most cases, are identical with the ideals of nationalism as such.

The most important structural implication of nationalism is an implication of the principle of equality of membership and the inclusive character of national identity, which has to do with the change in the nature of social stratification. In distinction to pre-national social formations, nations – or modern societies – develop open, or class, systems of stratification, based on achievement, rather than ascription, with individual, rather than family, as the unit, and transferable properties, such as money and education, rather than birth, as the basis of status distinctions. Though achievement may be variously defined and education and wealth ascribed different relative importance, all societies defined as nations accept social mobility as in principle legitimate and allow considerable, though different, rates of mobility in practice. This, in principle open, nature of stratification also, obviously, has a tremendous effect on the experience of life in modern societies. On the one hand, it makes each and every one of us the maker of one's destiny, increasing our sense of control and empowerment and adding excitement to life, which, by definition, becomes less predictable. On the other hand, by making life less predictable, it creates an inherently anomic, and thus stressful, environment, oppressing us with choices which must be made and the responsibility for our success or failure, and depriving us of the sense of security and peace of mind which come with predictability.

Every modern society experiences dignity and empowerment to a degree unknown to any society before it, and every modern society to a degree heretofore unknown suffers under conditions of pervasive anomie and disorientation. This is what the experience of modernity is, and it is directly related to the structures of the state and class stratification, in turn directly related to the twin principles of nationalism which provides the cognitive framework of modernity – popular sovereignty and fundamental equality of national membership. The presence of these principles allows us to define as nationalisms otherwise quite dissimilar systems of ideas and sentiments. The differences among them, which are reflected in the often dramatic differences in the interpretation and institutional realization of the two principles and, as a result, in their effects on the human experience, deserve as much attention as do the similarities.

Types of nationalism

The tendency of most theories of nationalism to treat it as a uniform phenomenon does not correspond to its reality. Every particular nationalism in some respects differs from every other and, optimally, its adequate

understanding requires attention to all such differences. Much of the variation in the institutions and fortunes of nations, including variation that
is historically most significant, can none the less be related to differences
in the definition of the nation and the criteria of membership in it,
according to which one can distinguish three *types* of nationalism. The
nation can be defined either as a composite entity, an association of individuals, or in unitary terms, as a collective individual. The former definition
gives rise to *individualistic* nationalisms. Individuals, in the framework of
nationalisms of this type, are believed to be inherently free and equal,
their liberty and equality seen as a reflection of their humanity, rather
than of nationality, as their *human* rights; consequently, the principles of
popular sovereignty and fundamental equality of membership are regarded
as natural laws. Interpreted in such individualistic fashion, these principles are realized in social and political institutions which safeguard these
rights. These are the institutions we identify with liberal democracy.

The definition of the nation in unitary terms as a collective individual
generates *collectivistic* nationalisms. In this case, the essential properties of
the individual members of the nation are believed to be communicated
to them and determined by the nation. Sovereignty becomes an attribute
of the nation itself – it is implied that individuals enjoy freedom if they
are members of a sovereign (that is politically independent) nation; their
equality is equality *in nationality* – no institutions are required to ensure it,
and no contradiction is perceived between the principle and openly inegal-
itarian structural arrangements. As a collective individual, the nation is
seen as a moral being in its own right, possessed of its own will, needs,
and interests, which are independent of the wills, needs, and interests of
the individuals who compose it. Since it is believed to be a higher moral
being, a natural object of their loyalty, the interests of the nation, in case
of discrepancy, always take priority over the interests of the individuals,
whose rights, in so far as they are acknowledged at all, can always be
legitimately sacrificed to the good of the nation. Since the will and the
interests of the nation do not reflect the wills and interests of its members,
the nation's goals are not to be sought in the voice of the majority, which
may not be aware of them. This presupposes the need to decipher the
will of the nation independently of the expressions of popular opinion
and an ability to do so on the part of a certain elite, whose special qualifications establish fundamental inequality between its members and the
rank and file of the nation. For these reasons, collectivistic nationalisms
tend to generate more rigidly structured societies than individualistic
nationalisms do; they also tend to promote authoritarian political regimes,
which, in distinction to premodern forms of collectivism, commonly manifest themselves as forms of socialism, communism and socialist or popular
democracy.

As to the criteria of national membership, they can be *civic* or *ethnic*.
The definition of national identity in civic terms presupposes the equation

of nationality with citizenship, in which case it becomes, in principle, a matter of individual choice and commitment, the primary object of which is a specific set of rights and duties, or, in other words, a social contract. Such nationality may be acquired and lost; it is conceivable that one would exchange one national identity for another or even decide to live without nationality at all. Ethnic criteria of national identity, in distinction, imply that nationality is viewed as an inborn characteristic, genetically transmitted and essentially unalterable. They imply that one has one, particular, nationality as one has one, particular, sex. The technical possibility and instances of sex change at the end of the twentieth century in certain parts of the world may make this comparison somewhat problematic. But they are likely to reinforce the presumption of the immutability of national identity in the framework of ethnic nationalisms. Ethnic nationalists recognize that some perverse individuals may try to change their nationality (in most cases, it is their original nationality which is believed to make them perverse in the first place), but such attempts are regarded with disgust as unnatural and are trusted to end in failure. The cases of sex change in the West (elsewhere it is not an option), accomplished with the help of advanced technology, may well be taken as an additional proof of the perverse nature of the Western society as a whole, as it is viewed as the incarnation of evil, and thus serve as a reaffirmation of the ethnic worldview.

Owing to the logical and moral primacy of the individual in the constitution of individualistic nations, individualistic nationalisms can only be civic. The definition of the nation in unitary terms, on the other hand, allows for the existence of both civic and ethnic varieties of collectivistic nationalisms. Whether the criteria of national identity adopted are civic or ethnic in such a case depends on the historical context of the formation of a particular nationalism and the qualities emphasized as reflective of the nation's individuality, spirit, or uniqueness. If nationalism develops in the atmosphere of collective self-confidence and against the record of visible and generally recognized achievement, nationality is likely to be defined as civic. The choice of ethnic criteria, on the other hand, is usually related to a pervasive sense of backwardness and collective inferiority, which suggests an emphasis on inner, ascriptive characteristics, on natural qualities, inherent in one's very being, rather than what one does, and concealed from the outsiders. The combination of collectivistic and civic elements in a national consciousness creates a problematic, ambivalent type of nationalism, which may develop (as in France) as two, co-existing but irreconcilable, national traditions, grounded in contradictory principles. Ethnic criteria of nationality, in distinction, reinforce the immanent tendencies of collectivistic nationalism. Ethnic and collectivistic nationalisms consistently subjugate the individual to the collectivity and consistently reject the notion of individual freedom as both unrealistic and immoral (redefining, as I mentioned, the concept as national freedom from foreign domination). The principles of collectivistic ethnic nationalism are directly opposed to those of individualistic civic nationalism and, consequently, of liberal democracy, which individualistic civic nationalism implies. These two types represent the extremes of the modern ideological continuum, two alternative modern worldviews, whose confrontation has been the major source of political conflict throughout the twentieth century. The representation of this conflict during the Cold War as a conflict between two universalistic ideologies, communism and liberalism, concealed from view its actual sources. Communism, however, only camouflaged ethnic nationalism of which it was, to start, a particular expression.[3] The abandonment of the camouflage could not and did not signify the victory of liberal democracy over its antithesis and, as becomes increasingly clear, was misinterpreted as the end of the hostilities.

The appeal of ethnic identity

The first (and in some cases only) stage in the formation of ethnic nationalism is a form of cultural and moral relativism. Inspired by a sense of collective inferiority and resentment against societies (or social groups) perceived to be morally and culturally superior, the architects of such nationalisms begin by insisting on the plurality and equality of (national) 'cultures'. The fact of plurality is taken as a sign of its necessity and value (according to the principle 'the concept of existence and perfection is one and the same').[4] Originally it is attributed to the will of God, when God is replaced by Nature – to the great Idea behind or inner purpose of the latter. Like species of life, different nations form irreplaceable (and, therefore, equally valuable) elements of a great mosaic that reveals and testifies to glory of Providential/Natural design. Thus, this plurality – every nation, every people, every culture – must be preserved.

In some cases (those of larger, more powerful, and better positioned societies or groups, but not exclusively) this transvaluation of values, which allows for a redrawing of the cognitive map and alleviation of the sense of inferiority, is quickly carried to the second stage. A new moral absolutism replaces relativism, substituting for the equality of national, 'ethnic' communities a new hierarchy, which reflects the degrees of proximity to the redefined absolute (with the ethnic community of the redefiners inevitably ending up on top). Measured by the new standard, the previously inferior nation becomes superior; it is also determined that only some nations (for instance, only 'historical' nations)[5] must be preserved, while others may as well perish; in certain cases, in fact, they must perish, for they embody principles antithetical to the Idea and interfere with the providential design.

German nationalism, from the vocabulary of which I draw some of these terms,[6] is likely to be more familiar to the reader than some others. It offers the most dramatic example of ethnic nationalism in action, and for this very reason may not be accepted as a representative example. Other examples, however, may be easily found, such as Russian nationalism before, during, and after communism, or 'black nationalism' in the United States. The latter would be commonly discussed in terms of 'ethnic politics' and under the rubric of 'ethnicity', rather than 'nationalism'. But 'ethnicity' is the guise under which ethnic nationalism appears in the discourse and the reality of civic nations.

By the end of the nineteenth century ethnic nationalism was already the most common type of nationalism in the world, leaving the two other types, both of which preceded it historically, far behind. Our century was the century of its undisputed ascendancy, with almost every new nation – and this century witnessed the birth of many nations – assuming the ethnic form. The prominence of 'ethnic' issues in the life of the pre-eminent liberal democracy and their importance in the international law (for instance, in the conventional interpretation of the 'right to self-determination') testifies to its pervasiveness in the modern consciousness. Our very confusion with regard to nationalism and ethnicity, our inability to distinguish between different types of nationalism (dramatically different in their implications) and to perceive the close similarity between the ideologies of ethnic identity and ethnic nationalism, shows how natural it has become for us to think in terms of ethnic nationalism, how unproblematic, how legitimate its vision appears to us.

The source of the greater appeal of ethnic nationalism, as compared to the two forms of civic nationalism, is its ability to provide superior psychological gratification. It limits individuals' freedom, and by the same token relieves them of responsibility and offers a sense of tangible order, the universal human need for which free society, where one may choose one's identity, leaves only imperfectly fulfilled. It is natural, what with the stress of anomie and the disconcerting indeterminacy of one's reality, to yearn for the comfort of the regulated world where one is never allowed more than what one can accomplish and where one's dignity is ascribed to one as a national birthright and assured by the membership in the dignified community irrespective of one's accomplishments. The experience of modernity, in other words, created as it is by nationalism, favors ethnic nationalism.

What are the prospects of liberal democracy in light of these considerations? One cannot say. The openness of the social system does not allow predictions, and social scientists make bad prophets. So far, liberal democracy – that is, individualistic civic nationalism – has persevered, despite the strides made by its ethnic rival and despite the widespread psychological predisposition for ethnic nationalism. In fact, individualistic nations represent the most enduring and stable of all modern polities; their citizens remain firmly committed to them (as demonstrated by the exceptionally low rates of emigration from them) and they appear to be exceptionally successful in recruiting new members through immigration.

On the other hand, the inroads of ethnic nationalism – in the form of demands for 'ethnic diversity' – in individualistic civic nations are of fairly recent date: they are a phenomenon of the last half century only. It is too early to assess the effect this may produce on the character of original national identity – and on liberal democracy. One claim one can make with certainty is that our future, ultimately, depends on the nature of our collective commitments and if we, as a society, commit ourselves to the political ideal of 'ethnic diversity', antithetical to liberal democracy, we shall weaken liberal democracy at home and dim its prospects abroad.

Notes

1   Dharam Ghai, Director, United Nations Institute for Social Development, 'Opening Statement' at the International Seminar on Ethnic Diversity and Public Policy, United Nations, New York, 17 August 1994. Mr Ghai retired as director in early 1998.
2   Greenfeld (1993), pp. 327–9 are reproduced in this section with minor modifications.
3   My argument in regard to Communism as a camouflaged ethnic nationalism was presented in Greenfeld (1985).
4   The principle, common to German Romanticism, is here presented in Goethe's formulation (Pascal 1967).
5   A Hegelian phrase adopted by Marx and Engels. See Talmon (1991).
6   See the discussion of German Romantic nationalism and in particular Adam Müller in Greenfeld (1992).

2   Transnational ethnicity and subnational religion in Africa's political experience

Ali A. Mazrui

The two most powerful primordial forces operating in Africa are ethnicity and religion. Ethnicity defines the basic social order; religion defines the basic sacred order. Ethnicity creates the solidarity of shared identity; religion creates the solidarity of shared beliefs.

In the context of Sub-Saharan Africa the words *ethnic group* and *ethnicity* are now used to replace the old concepts of 'tribe' and 'tribalism'. In Africa south of the Sahara there may be between 1,500 to 2,000 ethnic groups. Arab Africa is more homogeneous outside the Sudan. In Arab Africa north of the Sudan the smaller ethnic groups include the Nubi, the Berbers, and in a religio-cultural sense, the Copts.

While ethnic groups in Africa are in their hundreds, it is arguable that there are only three religious traditions – the indigenous, the Islamic and the Christian. The religions of the different ethnic groups are much more similar than their languages. It is therefore possible to conceptualize their sacred beliefs as constituting one single religious tradition – the indigenous legacy.

If there are hundreds of ethnic groups, and only three basic religious traditions in Africa, one is tempted to conclude that ethnicity in Africa is a divisive force, while religion is potentially unifying – especially since the other two religious traditions in Africa, Christianity and Islam, are worldwide fraternities. Christianity and Islam are also doctrinally universalist.

This chapter will explore the relationship between ethnicity, religion and the balance between unity and fragmentation in Africa. How do primordial forces affect contemporary politics and the struggle for national and regional integration? Let us look more closely at the interplay between primordiality and statecraft, between religion and ethnicity, between domestic forces and international repercussions.

Parochial religion and transnational ethnicity

At one level Christianity and Islam are indeed universalistic religions; and this should therefore have the effect of transnationalizing the politics of its adherents in Africa. Muslims of one African country, for example, should find areas of political solidarity with Muslims in another African country. On the other hand, ethnicity (in the sense of 'tribalism') appears to be a case of subnational identity. It should therefore be a parochializing force rather than a transnationalizing tendency in Africa.

But there are occasions in Africa's experience when the roles of religion and ethnicity are reversed. In such situations, it is ethnicity which becomes a transnational and Pan-African force – while Christianity and Islam become parochializing and fragmenting to the nation. The most dramatic recent case of transnational ethnicity has been the impact of the Tutsi on the whole area of the Great Lakes in Africa. The Rwanda Tutsi who were in exile in Uganda formed an army of their own and became the Rwanda Patriotic Front. As exiled Tutsi, they staged their own invasion into Rwanda in 1994. This was in the middle of the Hutu genocide against the Tutsi in Rwanda, following the shooting down of the plane of President Habariyamana in April 1994. The Rwanda Patriotic Front entered Rwanda from Uganda not to perpetrate carnage but to pursue conquest. With remarkable discipline they resisted the temptation of committing countergenocide against the Hutu. Instead they went for the capital city, Kigale, and succeeded in capturing it. To all intents and purposes, their triumphant operation established a new Tutsi-led political order in Rwanda.

Two years later, the indigenous Tutsi of Zaire (as it was then called) were being harassed by the authorities and the armed forces of Zaire. The local Tutsi were being treated as if they were immigrants from Rwanda, when in fact most were indigenous to Zaire. They decided to resist – and proceeded to form a fighting force. To their surprise they were militarily successful against the official security forces of Zaire. The victory whetted the appetite of the resisters, and a wider rebellion against the Mobutu regime in Zaire was born.

As the rebellion gathered momentum, it attracted more and more discontented groups of Zaire to join it. Most significantly it attracted Laurent Kabila, originally from Shaba province of Zaire. Kabila captured the leadership of the movement, and the rebellion culminated in the capture of the capital city, Kinshasa, in May–June 1997. Kabila became president of the renamed Democratic Republic of Congo.

But before all this, there was Yoweri Museveni, who had captured power in Uganda in 1986. Ethnically he was from the Bahima, close ethnic cousins of the Tutsi. The exiled Rwandans in Uganda had helped him capture power. After 1986 it was 'pay-back time'. Museveni wanted to help exiled Rwandans find their way back home. As a Ugandan 'Tutsi' he helped create the Rwanda Patriotic Front which then captured power in Rwanda. The new configuration of the Rwanda–Uganda coalition helped the Tutsi of Zaire to start the rebellion which culminated in the overthrow of the 32-year-old dictatorship of Mobutu Sese Seko, in faraway Kinshasa.

However, new conflicts were unleashed under the succeeding regime of Laurent Kabila. Rwanda, Uganda and Congolese Tutsi remained united but this time against Kabila.

What the story of the Great Lakes since 1994 has revealed is that Pan-Tutsiism can be a *transnational* force. It has helped to change the history of Uganda, Rwanda and the new Democratic Republic of Congo quite significantly. This is quite apart from the unsettled role of the Tutsi of Burundi, a country which is still profoundly divided against itself.

Ethnic conflict *within* countries between the Hutu and the Tutsi continues to be a horrendous and bloody experience. But Pan-Tutsiism as a solidarity movement demonstrates that it can be a region-wide liberalizing force. Uganda, Rwanda and Congo have moved closer to liberalization than they were before the Tutsi-Hima factors helped to transform them.

Certainly the rebellion against Mobutu Sese Seko was neither purely national nor indeed exclusively ethnic. The rebellion against Mobutu was region-wide and almost Pan-African. In addition to help from Rwanda and Uganda, the Kabila movement was also aided by such other countries as Angola, though the ethnic configurations here were different. The conclusion to be drawn from all this is that ethnicity in Africa is not only a fragmenting force within countries; it can also become a transnational or supranational force linking one country to another.

Paradoxically, Christianity and Islam are sometimes *parochializing* forces in Africa. This has certainly been the case in Nigeria (Africa's largest country in population) and Sudan (Africa's largest country in territory). In Nigeria, among the three largest and politically most important ethnic groups, almost all Hausa are Muslims; almost all Igbo are Christians; and the Yoruba are split between Christians and Muslims. Islam has reinforced Hausa identity and its differentiation from non-Muslim groups; Christianity has reinforced Igbo identity and its differentiation from non-Christian groups. It seems almost certain that the Hausa would have felt less 'different' from their non-Muslim neighbours had the Hausa never been Islamized. And perhaps the Igbo would have felt less culturally 'superior' to their neighbours had the Igbo never been Christianized by Europeans. The conclusion to be drawn is that Christianity and Islam, although universalist religions in doctrine and proselytizing ambition, have had parochializing consequences in certain African situations.

This is certainly also the case in Sudan, where the fact that the Southern region is basically non-Muslim has sharpened its differentiation from the more Islamized and Arabized North. The fact that the Southern political leaders have been disproportionately from the small Christianized minority within the South has contributed further towards deepening the cleavage between North and South. Once again Islam and Christianity – far from creating 'universalist bonds' among people – have only resulted in aggravating regional and ethnic sectionalism.

Models of church–state relationships

With regard to the relationship between church and state more institutionally, Africa has experienced approximately four models. One model is a *theocracy* in which a country has an established church – state and church institutions have been interlocked. Ethiopia before the revolution of 1974 was, to all intents and purposes, a Christian theocracy. The imperial monarchy traced its origins to King Solomon of the Jews and had links with the Ethiopian Orthodox Church. Nearly half the population of Ethiopia was not Christian at all. This sharpened the distinction between Christian Ethiopia, on one side, and Muslim and traditionalist Ethiopia, on the other.

Sudan since 1983 has been another kind of theocracy – this time an Islamic theocracy. It began with the Presidency of Ja'afar Numeiry who attempted to base the Sudan's legal order upon the *Shari'a* (the Islamic law). Numeiry was overthrown in the wake of popular demonstrations in 1985, and Sudan even experimented briefly with a revived multiparty system with Sadeq el-Mahdi as Prime Minister. But the Islamic laws (the so-called September laws) were not abolished. When the military returned to power under General Umar Hassan Ahmad Al-Bashir, the Sudanese state moved even more deeply into Islamization. This process also resulted in sharper differentiation between Northern and Southern Sudan.

Another model of relationship between religion and politics in Africa is based on the concept of a *religious nation* rather than a *religious state*. While Ethiopia before 1974 and Sudan since 1983 have been religious states, Zambia in the 1990s has officially declared itself a religious nation. With effect from President Frederick Chiluba's presidency, Zambia is officially a 'Christian nation'.

Ironically, President Chiluba's predecessor as Head of State, Kenneth Kaunda, was in many ways a more religious figure than Chiluba, and was descended from a more clerical family. But Kenneth Kaunda preferred to stick to the concepts of both a secular nation and a secular state. Chiluba's declaration of Zambia as officially a 'Christian nation' immediately marginalized the millions of followers of African traditional religions and followers of syncretic movements. It also marginalized the one million Muslims and the thousands of followers of the religions of South Asia (such as Hinduism). Christianizing thus had the effect of narrow-mindedness and parochialization.

On the other hand, Chiluba's declaration of Zambia as a 'Christian nation' has attracted more Western militant evangelical missionaries – sometimes even at the expense of the older Anglican and Catholic traditions of Zambia. Once again Christianity has been fragmenting rather than universalizing.

The third model of relationship between religion and politics in Africa is that of the *ecumenical state*. In this case, there is neither a state religion nor is the state completely separate from religious institutions. What distinguishes an ecumenical state is its readiness to accommodate the different religions through official institutions, or official processes, or both.

Outside Africa, Lebanon has been the ecumenical state *par excellence*, in which the entire constitutional order has been based on power-sharing among the different religious denominations. The President has been a Maronite Christian; the Prime Minister a Shiite Muslim; the Speaker of the House a Sunni. And the seats of the legislature have been allocated according to the different denominations.

In Uganda in the 1970s, President Idi Amin Dada experimented with the ecumenical state within which the government was supposed to be the arbiter and referee between Catholics, Protestants and Muslims. But Idi Amin's Uganda was, in other respects, too disorderly and tyrannical to accomplish a credible ecumenical state.

A *de facto* ecumenical state is Senegal. Its population is 94 per cent Muslim – a higher percentage than the Muslim population of Egypt. And yet in the first twenty years of its independence, Muslim Senegal had a Roman Catholic president, Leopold Sedar Senghor. Among African countries, Senegal is a relatively open society. President Senghor had many political opponents who called him by such epithets as 'lackey of France', 'political prostitute', or 'hypocrite of Negritude'. What the critics seldom called him was *kafir*, or infidel. In other words, his religion was almost never held against him. Leopold Senghor had worked out a special relationship with the *Marabouts* and other religious leaders of Muslim Senegal. The political process was *de facto* ecumenical.

To comprehend the scale of the Senegalese achievement, we need to compare it with the record of the United States. Although the United States has been a secular state for two centuries, it has only once strayed away from the Protestant fraternity in relation to the presidency. We are not even sure that Catholic John F. Kennedy did indeed win the majority of the popular votes, especially since there were irregularities in the balloting in Illinois. But whatever the electoral figures, Kennedy did become the first and only Roman Catholic President of the United States.

American Jews have done extremely well in the country, and have penetrated every institution of power to some extent or another. But American Jews have not even tried to capture the White House. They have wisely decided that a Jewish candidate for the presidency would provoke so much Christian fundamentalism and anti-Semitism that they would lose the gains they have made as a community in influence and power since the end of World War II. The Jews have left the US presidency alone. Now there are as many Muslims as Jews in the United States. Yet a Muslim president of the United States is still a mind-boggling prospect in this constitutionally secular state.

And yet little Senegal had a Christian president in an overwhelmingly Muslim society. Senghor was succeeded by Abdou Diouf, a Muslim. Yet

Diouf's First Lady was Roman Catholic. How many Western politicians would make it to the position of head of government or head of state if their spouses were Muslims? What all this means is that Senegal has developed a *de facto* ecumenical state long before any Western country approached such a degree of religious broadmindedness.

Malawi seems to have a Christian majority. And yet in 1994 Malawi elected its first Muslim president – another case of African liberalism in sharp contrast to the West. But Malawi cannot really be described as an ecumenical state, since there are no interlocking arrangements between the state and religious leaders as there are in Senegal. Malawi could be described, however, as a more convincingly *secular state* at the level of the presidency than almost all Western countries. No Western state is capable of electing a Muslim president or prime minister in the foreseeable future (except in such Muslim-majority countries as Bosnia, Albania and Turkey).

Tanzania seems to be a half-way house between a secular state and an ecumenical state. Without any constitutional stipulation, the country seems to be leaning towards a system of *religious alternation* of the presidency. It began with a Christian president (Julius K. Nyerere). He was succeeded by a Muslim president (Ali Hassan Mwinyi), who in turn has now been succeeded by another Christian president (Benjamin Mkapa). It seems very likely that the first president of the twenty-first century will once again be a Muslim. Tanzania's stability may be at risk if that does not happen.

The fourth model of relationship between religion and politics in Africa is indeed the *secular state* – but sometimes more complex, and sometimes more genuinely secular than anything achieved in the Western world. The great majority of African states try to be secular – but combined with a readiness to accommodate not only *ethnic arithmetic* (a quantified balance between ethnic groups) but also the *sacred calculus* (a compromise with the demographics of religion).

The secular state of Sierra Leone elected its first Muslim president in 1996 – President Ahmed Tejan Kabba. His government was overthrown in a military coup in May 1997. Muslim-led Nigeria offered to intervene militarily in Sierra Leone to restore the democratically elected government to power. Was the Nigerian government acting on behalf of the Economic Organization of West African States (ECOWAS) in this military venture? It seemed strange that a military government like that of Nigeria should seek to defend democracy in another country. And yet Africa has witnessed reverse situations before – Western democracies seeking to defend military dictatorships. If one had a choice, it is better to see a military regime defending democracy (as in the case of Nigeria and Sierra Leone) than to see a democracy defend a military government (as the United States and France had often done in the past, in defending Mobutu Sese Seko's military government).

The struggle continues in Africa to contain ethnicity as a subnational force without neutralizing its potential as a Pan-African supranational force.

The triple heritage of religion in Africa is alive and well – indigenous, Islamic and Christian. What is often overlooked is that the indigenous religious forces are the most ecumenical – promoting the spirit of 'live and let live' in the spiritual domain.

Parochial ethnicity and transnationalizing religion

The reverse situation, of ethnicity as internally divisive and religion as transnationally unifying, has also been part and parcel of the African experience. Indeed, Sub-Saharan Africa's worst civil wars have been fundamentally ethnic – including the Nigerian civil war (1967–70); the war for the independence of Eritrea (1962–92) and the Angolan civil war (1974 into the new 21st century).

On the other hand, conflicts in North Africa have tended to be religiously inspired rather than ethnically focused. This includes the civil war in Algeria which has been going on since the military aborted the 1992 elections to prevent an electoral victory by the Islamists (the Islamic Salvation Front). By the year 2000 over 100,000 people had been killed in the dirty and indiscriminate Algerian conflict.

Also religiously focused is political violence in Egypt, at two levels – the struggle of the Islamists against the pro-Western government of President Husni Mubarak and in favour of a more Islamically oriented Egypt; and the tension between Muslims and the minority Coptic Christian Church.

If civil wars in North Africa are mainly religiously inspired and civil wars in Sub-Saharan Africa are mainly ethnically inspired, Sudan once again falls in between, exhibiting features of both ethnicity and sectarianism. The fundamental divide between Northern Sudan and Southern Sudan is ethnic and cultural – but this ethnocultural divide has been reinforced by the fact that the North is much more Arabized and Islamized, and the South is partially Christianized. In this and many other respects, Sudan illustrates the contradictions of both Arab Africa and Sub-Saharan Black Africa.

The religious aspect of the Sudanese conflict has had international consequences. In the first Sudanese civil war (1955–72), the Southern side successfully presented itself internationally as a victim of an Islamic *jihad* from the North. Efforts of the Khartoum government to promote and teach the Arabic language in the South were portrayed as efforts at forced conversion to Islam. Government take-over of missionary schools (which had been happening all over Africa regardless of religion) was condemned as a strategy of Islamization.

In reality the Sudanese government's policy in the South from 1955 was an attempt at national integration through a *language* policy rather than a religious policy. The idea was to integrate and develop the South through the Arabic language (the most widely spoken language in the country) rather than continue with the primacy of the English language as a medium of instruction, as most Christian missionary schools had chosen to do.

But the wider world seldom drew any sharp distinction between a language policy of Arabicization and a religious policy of Islamization. The first Sudanese civil war was thus widely regarded as a religious confrontation between a Muslim government in Khartoum and Christian liberation fighters in the South. Fortunately, negotiations in Addis Ababa in 1972 were at last successful in bringing that particular conflict to an end.

It was the second Sudanese civil war which began in 1983 which was more clearly provoked by a new religious policy of Islamization from Khartoum. Beginning with the regime of General Ja'far Numeiry and later sustained more thoroughly by the Government of General Umar Hassan Ahmad Al-Bashir and the ideological leadership of Hassan Turabi, Sudanese regimes attempted to construct an Islamic state. The religious policy became transnationalized when the Sudan in the 1990s saw itself as an international revolutionary force, and supported liberation movements elsewhere. Sudan's critics saw its Islamic regime as a supporter of international terrorism.

More purely ethnic conflicts elsewhere in Africa were also tempted sometimes to use the religious card, either to win support for themselves or to demonize their enemy. The population of Eritrea is a mixture of Christians and Muslims. But sometimes in the course of Eritrea's war for independence, the Islamic card was used to win support from the Arabs in Eritrea's struggle first against the Christian theocracy of Haile Selassie and later against the Marxist–Leninist atheism of Mengistu Haile Mariam in Addis Ababa.

In their struggle to create the separate state of Biafra, the Igbo of eastern Nigeria often used the religious card to win sympathy for themselves as 'Christians', and to demonize the Federal Government of Nigeria as 'Muslim-dominated'. The Biafran propagandists often tried to portray the North–South divide in Nigeria as a Muslim–Christian divide. Such a characterization of the North–South divide was a distortion – but it was a good propaganda ploy in the competition for support in the Western world.

When Idi Amin (a Muslim) was in power in Uganda (1971–9), the ethnic strifes in the country were often externally portrayed as Muslim versus Christian struggles. In reality, those conflicts were fundamentally 'tribalistic' – Kakwa versus Acholi; Nubi versus Langi; Nilotics versus Bantu; the Baganda against their rivals.

On the other hand, Idi Amin's expulsion of Israelis from Uganda in 1972 did win him many friends in the Arab world. Indeed, Amin's breaking off of diplomatic relations with Israel a year before the 1973 October War in the Middle East made him a pathbreaker in the new Afro-Arab solidarity against Zionism. Idi Amin set a precedent for Africa's break with Israel in 1972, which was followed by almost every other African state the following year, in the wake of the October war.

A pro-Arab orientation in Idi Amin's foreign policy from 1972 onwards was one of the few consistent aspects of his regime. The Arab world was not ungrateful. Libyan troops briefly tried to save him when the Tanzanian army invaded Uganda in 1979 – and then the Libyans decided to go neutral after a while. Tripoli and later Riyadh gave Idi Amin comfortable political asylum with his entourage, after he was ousted from power by Tanzanian troops in 1979. Idi Amin is still a guest of the Saudi Royal House as a political refugee.

Domestically the convulsions within Amin's Uganda were indeed mainly ethnic, regional and 'tribalistic'. The religious divide was third or fourth in importance. But in foreign policy the Islamic factor was more important than it was domestically. From 1972 onwards Idi Amin's foreign policy was increasingly influenced by Pan-Islamic considerations.

The nature of the civil conflicts within Africa may be categorized as either politically primary or politically secondary. A politically primary civil war, for example, is one which seeks to redefine the boundaries of the political community. Civil wars which are secessionist or fundamentally separatist are politically primary in this sense. The Nigerian civil war (in which the Igbo tried to create an independent Biafra) was therefore politically primary. It sought to redefine the boundaries of the political community. This is also true of the 30-year war for the independence of Eritrea (1962–92). On the other hand, the 1997 conflict in Zaire (now Congo) was basically secondary. The ideals and goals of the Kabila movement were not separatist. The goal was to capture power in Kinshasa and to create a better political order.

The civil war in Mozambique was also basically secondary since it entailed no major secessionist or separatist tendencies. It was at best a clash of ideologies and personalities. A secondary civil war is concerned not with changing the boundaries of the political community but with redefining the goals of the political community, or enlisting new leadership.

Sudan has had two phases. The first Sudanese civil war, with the Anya Nya in the South (1955–72) was fundamentally secessionist and was therefore primary. It concerned the boundaries of the political community. The second Sudanese civil war (from 1983 onwards) was led by the rebellion of John Garang in the South. Garang was not after the separatist ideal of a new country of the South. His aim was to democratize and secularize Sudan as a whole. The second Sudanese civil war has been, on the whole, secondary since 1983 (despite the presence of a few individual secessionists both North and South).

South Africa: the racial war that never was

There was a time when South Africa seemed destined to experience one of the bloodiest examples of primary civil wars – an actual racial war appeared inevitable. After all, everywhere else in Africa where there had been a large white minority there had been severe bloodshed before full majority rule was realized. Kenya experienced the Mau Mau War (1952–60); Algeria experienced its war of independence (1954–62); Rhodesia and Angola had their equivalent conflicts. Since South Africa had the largest white minority of them all, how could South Africa possibly avert the same blood-stained fate?

But one particular difference turned out to be more relevant than many people imagined. The whites of South Africa identified themselves with Africa but not with the Africans. The Afrikaners especially were passionately loyal to the African soil (the land) but not loyal to the African blood (the indigenous people).

In contrast, the whites of colonial Algeria were loyal neither to Africa nor to the Africans. Their loyalty was to France. They owed no special allegiance to the soil of Africa except as a means of livelihood. They certainly owed no loyalty to the blood of the indigenous peoples. They attempted to turn Africa into an extension of France. Similarly, the whites of Angola attempted to turn their part of Africa into an extension of Portugal. This is in contrast to those whites of South Africa who identified themselves with the African soil so much that they called themselves Afrikaners, and thus even attempted to appropriate the name 'Africans' for themselves. White Rhodesians were simply too British, many of them enjoying dual citizenship right through Ian Smith's Unilateral Declaration of Independence (UDI). Of all the whites of Africa, perhaps only the Afrikaners had evolved a mystical relationship to the African land. The Afrikaners mixed their sweat mystically with the African soil, but did not mix their blood spiritually with the African people.

How did South Africa avert a racial war in the twentieth century? One reason was indeed cultural – this was the simple fact that the Afrikaners were half-way towards Africanisation through a marriage between the Afrikaner *soul* and the African *soil*.

A second reason why South Africa has averted a racial war in the twentieth century is essentially a division of labour between Black political power and white economic privilege. The White man said to the Black man: 'You take the crown, and I will keep the jewels!' The Black man was to acquire the political crown, while the White man retained the economic jewels. In many ways, while political apartheid was ending, economic apartheid is still intact. The best land, the best mines, the best jobs, the best shops and commercial opportunities, are still overwhelmingly in white hands or under white control. The challenge for the post-Mandela South Africa is how to dismantle economic apartheid without causing widespread economic and social havoc.

While most people are convinced that South Africa has indeed averted a primary civil war in the twentieth century (White versus Black), can we be complacent about averting it in the twenty-first century if economic apartheid remains intact? The twenty-first century may not have the moral leadership of the rank of Nelson Mandela. It may still have the valuable resource of the marriage between the Afrikaner soul and the African soil.

But this brings us to the third reason why South Africa has averted a racial war in the twentieth century. This concerns Africa's short memory of hate. Cultures vary considerably in their hate-retention. The Irish Catholics have high retention of memories of atrocities perpetrated by the English. The Orange Order among Irish Protestants insist on celebrating every year the victory of Protestant William of Orange over Catholic James II at the Boyne and Aughrim in the 1690s. The Armenians have long memories about atrocities committed against them by the Turks in the Ottoman Empire. The Jews have long memories about their martyrdom in history. On the other hand, Jomo Kenyatta proceeded to forgive his British tormentors very fast after being released from unjust imprisonment. He even published a book entitled *Suffering Without Bitterness*.

Where but in Africa could somebody like Ian Smith, who had unleashed a war which killed many thousands of Black people, remain free after Black majority rule to torment his Black successors in power whose policies had killed far fewer people than Ian Smith's policies had done? Nelson Mandela lost twenty-seven of the best years of his life. Yet on being released, he was not only in favour of reconciliation between Blacks and Whites. He went to beg White terrorists who were fasting unto death not to do so. He went out of his way to go and pay his respects to Mrs Verwoerd, the widow of the architect of apartheid. Is Africa's short memory of hate sometimes 'too short'?

What saved South Africa from a primary civil war in the twentieth century? It was a convergence of those three forces. The mystical relationship between the Afrikaner soul and the African soil, the Black African's short memory of hate, and the historic bargain which conceded the political crown to Blacks and kept the economic jewels to Whites at least for a while.

Political violence: primary and secondary

The distinction between primary conflict (boundaries of a political community) and secondary (goals of a political community) is not necessarily a measure of the violence generated by either. Yes, we do start from the premise that a civil war which is a battle about breaking up a country (like the American Civil War of the 1860s) is more fundamental than a civil war about which ideology prevails or which leaders triumph (like the Spanish Civil War of the 1930s). And yet it is possible for a secondary civil war about ideology and 'who rules' to generate much more violence than whether a country survives as one.

The worst case of genocide in Africa occurred in Rwanda in 1994. And yet the Hutu–Tutsi confrontation in Rwanda and Burundi has almost never been about secession – it has been much more often been about 'who rules'. The genocide of Rwanda in 1994 was, in our terms, a case of secondary political violence, however horrendous the scale.

The civil war of the 1990s in Algeria is secondary in our sense, since it is neither secessionist nor separatist in any sense. But the Algerian war has been internationalized in a big way. The violence in Algeria has spilt over into France, partly because the government in Paris was seen as being supportive of the anti-Islamist regime in Algiers. And because the borders of the European Union are now more fluid and open to nationals of its member countries, violence involving Algerians in France is a matter of concern to France's European neighbours as well.

Algeria's own Arab neighbours fear a different kind of spillover – not the spread of direct Algerian violence (as has happened in Paris) but the spread of politicized Islam among Moroccans, Tunisians and other North Africans. Morocco and Tunisia especially fear the 'contagion effect' of militant Islam in their own populations.

Just as the Algerian war of independence (1954–62) had a greater impact on Europe than any other African anti-colonial war, so Algeria's confrontation between militant Islam and militarized secularism may be pregnant with implications for France and Europe as a whole. The Algerian war of independence changed the course of French history in a number of decisive ways. It put so much pressure on the French political system between 1954 and 1958 that eventually France itself hovered over a civil war. Only one man could save it – Charles de Gaulle, who was persuaded to emerge from retirement in a new hour of crisis.

The Algerian war and Charles de Gaulle convinced France at long last that the Fourth Republic was not working. The Fifth Republic was born after a referendum. In this way, ironically, the Algerian war helped give French governments greater stability under the new Constitution.

Because the Algerian crisis had helped to bring Charles de Gaulle back into power, the impact on European and world history was wide-ranging. Under de Gaulle, France pulled out of the military wing of the North Atlantic Treaty Organization; France kept the UK out of the European Economic Community for the rest of the 1960s; France pursued more vigorously an independent nuclear military policy; and France gave political independence to almost all its African colonies within two or three years of de Gaulle's assumption of power. Algeria itself became independent in 1962. If the Algerian war of independence was so multifaceted in its impact on Europe and the world, will the Algerian civil war which started in the 1990s also turn out to be pivotal internationally? The war is certainly being watched closely in varied capitals of the world, far and near.

While the big universalizing issue of the war of independence was the dilemma between Algerian self-determination and French sovereignty, the big universalizing issue of the civil war since the 1990s is the dilemma between the dream of an Islamic democracy (aborted in 1992 by the military) and the rival dream of a liberal secular democracy (preferred by the secular political parties of Algeria).

With regard to the two religious struggles in Egypt since the 1990s, one is clearly secondary and the other is semi-primary. The struggle of the Islamists to replace Husni Mubarak with an Islamic constitutional order is secondary in our sense, since no separatist or secessionist issues are involved. However, the tension between Islamic militants and the Copts has features which are semi-primary since the tensions often imply profound unhappiness about Copts and Muslims being citizens of the same country. Of course, most Egyptians are religiously tolerant and would 'live and let live'. But there are extremists among both Muslims and Copts who regard it as a tragedy that they share the same country. It is in that sense that this particular religious tension in Egypt is semi-primary and culturally 'separatist'.

Of the two Egyptian struggles, the secondary one against Husni Mubarak has had wider international ramifications. While the Algerian Islamist struggle has spilt over into France, the Egyptian Islamist struggle has spilt over into the United States. Rightly or wrongly, some have even seen a direct connection between Islamist threats to Nobel Laureate Neguib Mahfouz in Egypt, on one side, and the blowing up of the World Trade Center in the United States, on the other. Political violence in Egypt evolves into political terrorism in the United States, according to this view. Once again it is hard to draw a sharp line separating religion as a divisive force domestically from religion as an international force in world affairs.

Conclusion

I have sought to explore in this chapter the complex relationship between Africa's two most powerful primordial forces – religion and ethnicity – and how they have affected the political process. In particular, I have emphasized the balance between integration and fragmentation, and between domestic forces and international repercussions.

Most Africanist scholarship has examined politicized ethnicity in Africa as a problem for national integration. This chapter has raised the question of whether ethnicity is sometimes unifying region-wide. On the other hand, there are assumptions in the popular mind about the universalism of either Christianity or Islam or both. This chapter has raised the question as to whether Christianity and Islam can sometimes be parochializing forces. If so, under what circumstances?

Oversimplistic observers tend to divide the world between countries which are secular and countries which have an established church. This chapter has discussed the third category of the ecumenical state in Africa

– sometimes displaying greater religious liberalism (as in Senegal) than the West has as yet achieved. Senegal is a Muslim country which accepted a Roman Catholic President for twenty years.

We have also distinguished primary civil wars (disputing the boundaries of the political community) from secondary civil wars (disputing the goals or leadership of the political community). Countries which are torn by a primary civil war are probably at a lower level of national integration than countries which are quarrelling about goals or 'who rules'.

However, the scale of violence is not necessarily commensurate with the distinction between primary and secondary. In a single year, more people died in small Rwanda, in a secondary civil war, than died in three years of civil war in Nigeria, with nearly fifteen times the population of Rwanda. Yet the Nigerian civil war (with a lower casualty rate) was secessionist and therefore primary.

The complexities of Africa's social and political experience continue to unfold. Primordial forces of ethnicity and religion intersect with processes of new identity formation and enlargement of political scale. Out of the tumult and anguish, out of tension and tribulation, a new face of Africa is bound to emerge – bruised but hopefully unbowed.

3 Are Islamists nationalists or internationalists?

Fredrik Barth

Clearly, what is generally now referred to as 'Islamism' is becoming a current of increasing importance in the political life of many Arab and other Middle Eastern countries, and in world politics. It is less clear what are the wellsprings of Islamism in Middle Eastern populations, and what may become the movement's long-term impact on national and international developments. I believe that even to begin to answer such questions we must look well beyond the arenas of institutionalized national and international politics. We need to know much more about the world constructions within which Islamism exists, and its role in the subjective lives of those who embrace it. Only on that basis can we hope to trace the dynamics that determine its present and future national and international roles. But to recognize this is to recognize how daunting my brief for this symposium is, both in complexity and scope. To reduce the diversity of political contexts slightly, I will focus mainly on the Arab Near East. But even within this frame, I can only provide a sketchy picture, one that presents a sprawling argument of part substance, part theory, and part pure guesswork.[1] If the text seems to lead through a long detour, I do, towards the end of my argument, provide some answers directly addressing the question in my title.

Fundamentalism

I shall retain the word 'fundamentalism' as a general label for the Islamist current. In this, as indeed in my characterization of its main conceptual elements, I follow the Syrian philosopher and sociologist Sadik Al-Azm (1993). Al-Azm explicitly argues for its character as fundamentalist, and also its probable historical connection with similar currents in Christian thought. He shows how the very concept 'fundamentalism' figures in the Islamists' own discourse (e.g. in usages such as *al-Usuliyya al-Islam*, from *usuli/usus* 'foundation', and *Usul-al-Din*, 'the Fundamentals of Religion', see Al-Azm 1993: 96). The term thus would seem to carry very appropriate connotations for a way of thought that seeks to recapture and apply in the contemporary world the fundamentals of Islam.

As a first step to analyse its conceptual relations to ideas of nationalism and internationalism, it is notable that the terminology used by the Islamist fundamentalists seeks carefully and categorically to distinguish its character and goals from those of Arab nationalist movements. These latter, secular movements have frequently adopted religious concepts and imagery in their rhetoric; and the Islamists' response to this fact has been to seek out other words for their programs and visions so as to mark the difference. Thus, for the evocation of ideas of revival and awakening, the early anti-colonialist and nationalist party of Syria/Iraq pre-empted the label *Ba'ath* Party ('Resurrection Party'); consequently, the fundamentalists have had to adopt another term: *Ihya*, 'revival', for their cause. Where nationalists speak of *Yakazah*, 'awakening', fundamentalists choose a different word, *Sahwa*, for the same concept. Where in Arab socialist rhetoric 'internationalism' is referred to as *Al Umamiyyah*, fundamentalists in turn speak of *al'Alamiyyah*, 'worldism', for their global vision (cf. Al-Azm 1993: 98ff.). Neither nationalist nor internationalist associations appear to be acceptable to them.

How do Islamists describe their own program? Very clearly as a return to fundamental Islam, and in aggressive counterpoint both to secular and nationalist ideas. Thus Saleh Sirriyah, the leader during the Islamist attempt to seize the Egyptian Military Academy in Heliopolis in 1974, condemns as an apostate anyone who believes in 'materialism, existentialism, pragmatism, democracy, capitalism, socialism, patriotism, nationalism, and internationalism' (ibid.: 106). Why not democracy? Because God alone is sovereign. Why not patriotism, nationalism? Because national unity in the Arab Near East was forged in an anti-colonial struggle for independence that united Muslim and Christian Arabs under the slogan 'religion belongs to God, while the fatherland belongs to us all!' (ibid.: 107). Why not internationalism? Because the traditional concept in Islamic thought for a larger world of law and peace is one that is neither linked with any explicit concept of nationhood and statehood, nor to a liberal idea of an all-embracing, global tolerance: it simply contrasts the ideally expansive and all-inclusive *Dar-al-Islam* 'Land of Islam' to the surrounding and peripheral *Dar-al-Harb*, 'Land of War/Chaos'.

Islamism is of course a thoroughly modern articulation of ideas, but it resonates with a large array of older Muslim themes and modes of thought. I have known a more archaic version of this kind of world as an ethnographer working among Afghan/Pathan peoples in the border areas of the North-West Frontier Province of Pakistan (Barth 1959, 1985), culturally closely related to the present supporters of Taliban fundamentalist rule in Afghanistan. The then 'Tribal Areas' of the frontier are inhabited by Muslims often characterized as both 'fundamentalist' and 'fanatical' in the older literature. Implacably opposed to infidel rule during colonial times, they remained effectively unvanquished by the British Indian Army through a series of violent confrontations led by *ad hoc* religious leaders of *jihad*, 'holy war'. This world was in fact mostly stateless, organized partly in acephalous political systems, partly in authoritarian but weak mini-states. But none the less, these were not anarchic or chaotic communities: Hobbes was wrong to imagine that a population not subject to a state would be in a continuous condition of 'Warre'. The tribal areas, on the contrary, made up a strikingly sophisticated society of people who knew and practised the Rule of Law in its Islamic form, but largely without the benefit of repression by a state system. It composed a cosmopolitan population well informed about the larger world. Its Muslim scholars travelled widely and served widely dispersed followings. Men in search of employment and trade similarly wandered through large regions, and were familiar with diverse cultures and forms of society. In citing this ethnography, I simply wish to emphasize the deep historical roots and the wide regional distribution of the basic conceptual premise of Islamist fundamentalism: that an ordered society and the rule of law derive not from the existence of the state, but notionally vice versa; and that their source is God and 'Islam', in the literal sense of submission to God, not any worldly sovereign.

Wellsprings

For God, in the fundamentalist conception, has instituted the complete and eternally valid civil laws needed for the good society. Thus through the very constitution of a Muslim as a person who has submitted to God, a well-ordered society is also instituted. Political order, in this view, arises not from people's collective attachment to demarcated states, parties, movements, or groups; it arises from each Muslim's personal, existential and moral commitment to the religion of Islam.

Given that these conceptions of the relationship between law, society, and religion should be widely shared among Muslims, we cannot expect them to translate directly into particular political positions, such as a specifically fundamentalist party within a national electorate. Though they provide an important premise for fundamentalist conceptions of politics, they do not in themselves provide the basis for a political faction. In searching for the wellsprings of Islamism, we need to identify other specific ideas, views, and circumstances that make a person gravitate towards fundamentalist positions, views that are general and pervasive enough so they would provide relatively ubiquitous wellsprings for a growing current of opinion and a broad basis for potential popular support. This indicates that we may need to search for ideas and positions that are not explicitly political, but rather more broadly salient in contemporary popular experience.

That leads me to the crux of my thesis: the wellsprings of contemporary Islamism are found, I will argue, not in any grassroots appeal of a political position within the configuration of forces that today makes up each separate Muslim state, nor in a widespread popular appeal of particular macro-political national or international agendas: they are located much more broadly in a general sense of disquiet among many Muslims about their present lives and the world they are living in. In this sense, Islamic fundamentalism is a spiritual awakening before it is a political movement. The recent swift and deep changes in the parameters of existence for most Muslims have led to *a crisis of meaning and propriety* in ordinary life, particularly by reducing normative certainty and patriarchal authority. In reinstating moral absolutes and relegitimizing parts of a more familiar traditional order, fundamentalism serves to counteract this crisis by enhancing normative certainty, reallocating domestic authority to men, and regulating the management of women's sexuality. It is these domestic empowerments and what they promise of improved self-images and strengthened domestic order in the lives of ordinary persons, not any inherent appeal of fundamentalist macro-political programs, that nourish Islamism as a popular movement.

Such a fundamentalist 'revival' or 'awakening' does not appeal equally to all, whether young or old, male or female, affluent or poor. But let us look more closely at the trade-offs, as they might appear to variously positioned persons in Middle Eastern societies, between life as now experienced and the life promised by fundamentalism.

First, the general parameters of change. All areas of the Muslim Middle East have undergone a profound modernization over the last half century. For many of its people, it is certainly not urbanization as such that is new but the particular forms of contemporary urbanization, and the ubiquitous impacts of global markets, mass media, and secular education. The expanding market has intensified the characteristic capitalist tension between subjective appetites or needs, and the person's means within a monetized economy. The resultant consumerism makes individual social identities increasingly contingent on the person's participation in material consumption. Ordinary lives have been further changed by the reduction of sexual segregation. Many traditional forms of sociality in public space have disappeared, and new (monetized) forms of entertainment have appeared. Many arenas of life have become privatized while households/families have grown smaller and more isolated. The growing diversity of ideas and ideologies in media, public education, and public discourse merely multiply the fields of ambiguity and uncertainty, within the family as in public life. Most of these changes are familiar enough in the life of any Western person; but in the Middle East they have taken place even more swiftly and recently, allowing major elements of the older forms of life and identity to linger in personal memory and experience. This can make for an all the more poignant sense of change, and of loss.

A rejection of these changes and a return to older patterns of life would appear most clearly attractive to older men of moderate or limited means. It would secure them an authority determined by gender and seniority within the family, and also enhance their identity in local civil society by making it much less dependent on consumption, competitive economic success, and exceptional education. But these gains should not only be understood as enhancing the arbitrary powers of elderly men: it also provides these men with the normative answers to cope better with their responsibilities, and to acquit themselves as husband and fathers with greater integrity and certainty. Adherence to fundamentalism thus lends dignity and respectability to their lives.

To middling and younger men, something is lost in having to submit to seniority; but in return a trajectory leading to patriarchal authority seems secure and not too distant. Meanwhile, a husband's control – and moral authority – in relation to his wife devolve on him immediately at marriage or even at betrothal: his first small legitimate imperium is thus established quite early in life. And what are the alternatives? The bankruptcy of modern permissiveness in the form of the playboy role model is probably fairly obvious to many, besides its being attainable only by the limited few that belong in the economic elite. Greater dignity can be achieved, and the frustrations of most ordinary lives reduced, by an enhanced moral certainty about one's own choices and actions in following religious precepts. And in a situation of political confrontation, resistance, and violence, fundamentalist young men, as fighters for the cause, can gain a dramatically enhanced experience of self-value and importance in the eyes of others – one that is not obtainable by any normal means.

For women, the attractions of a return to traditional Muslim constraints would seem less clear. The young unmarried women who by choice or under duress turn to fundamentalism must no doubt shelve the heady dreams of freedom, equality, and a transformed life that fired some of their seniors. On the other hand, the more modest gains actually achieved by emancipated older women, who would be known and familiar to younger women and might serve them as role models, may yet not seem to embody goals entirely out of reach for a woman embracing fundamentalism: higher education is still possible, and a position of some influence is conceivable to the more ambitious. More importantly, obvious gains by adopting a fundamentalist position take the form of greater protection, safety, and indeed enhanced trust in circles of same-gender friendship; while the insecurities and normative uncertainties of cross-gender relationships are reduced. Presumably, clear norms and constraining contexts for the management of a young woman's own sexuality may be welcomed by many with relief, at least in some phases of maturation. Thereby also, the prototypical threat in Muslim thought – of *fitna*, scandal and chaos – is backgrounded.

For a married women, these considerations will be less salient, but not entirely absent, and an enhanced normative certainty and the authority to exercise it over other women, and children, are certainly part of what fundamentalism can offer older women. Moreover, a partnership with a man who can construct an identity for himself that incorporates greater dignity, assurance, and responsibility may not be without its compensations for a wife. Thus for women, as for men, a life of greater normative certainty, founded on religious precepts, may prove both easier to live and more satisfactory to experience than the greater contingency and ambivalence that come with modernism an secularism.

My thesis is: these are the things that fundamentalism is primarily about among its sympathizers and supporters. If so, how would we find these features reflected in the patterns of popular recruitment to the Islamist movement? And in turn, how is the Islamist *political* agenda constructed, within the nation and internationally, on the basis of such a membership?

The Islamist constituency

In trying to form a picture of the existing constituency of Islamist fundamentalism, we battle under a severe impediment in that empirical evidence is limited and journalistic interpretations are abundant. The media flood us with a rather poorly informed, externalist and Western discourse, which cannot but affect even the native Middle Eastern commentators, and too readily allows us to see what we have been instructed to look for. So here is one of those parts where guesswork, intuition, and limited bits of informed hearsay take over in my argument.

I believe it is important to distinguish between three levels of Islamist membership: the leadership; a broader cadre of local opinion leaders; and a mass of supporters and sympathizers. As implied by my sketch of the movement's wellsprings, this third category is no doubt large in all Middle Eastern nations; but its degree of active engagement will depend strongly on the particular history of mobilization, confrontation and conflict within each country. Basically, public engagement in Islamism arises from two main sources. On the one hand, it is stimulated by a person's general dissatisfaction with the decay of religious and moral values, the deterioration of community life, and the corruption, exploitation, and arbitrary uses of power among the secular state's public officials and institutions – in that sense, it is already somewhat politically oriented in being disenchanted with the existing power structure. But equally important, it caters to the personal interests of many people: by its promise to institute a clear and conservative framework within which to battle the growing complexity of daily life, and as a way of shoring up the authority of persons who feel they have the right or the duty to exercise control in their close family and social circle. This can be seen as a more private pay-off by political alignment with the fundamentalists.

Observers with some grassroots contact tell us that the broad base of fundamentalist support and sympathy is found mainly among lower middle class and lower class persons, often with rural backgrounds. Large numbers of them are presumably of older or middle age, and they are drawn from both sexes. Contrary to what has frequently been imagined in the media, the fundamentalists' appeal is more limited among the victims of severe poverty, since the battle for survival among such depends on greater pragmatism, and their hopes to win any form of socially recognized dignity have already been irretrievably shattered.

On the second level, among the cadre of opinion leaders, are found proportionately more younger people as well as older. They need not be enrolled in any formal fundamentalist organizations, but they generally signal their orientation in their form of dress, and among men often by growing beards. Their influence is exercised within pre-existing social networks of family, neighbourhood and workplace, and takes the forms of personal example, activism, criticism, argument, and sometimes violence. Again according to locally informed observers, such person tend to be middle or lower middle class, often with better education and higher intelligence than others of their family and background, and often suffering from frustrated ambitions. Presumably, it is among young men of this category that secret cells are also most readily recruited.

Finally, in the highest leadership category of such a broad popular movement we should be prepared to include a large and diverse range of leaders, and not focus only on a small number of stars. This multi-echeloned leadership group will be composed of persons who have advanced through the intermediate level described above, and of course includes numerous Muslim divines and religious students. Even at this level, it does not seem to be the case that the Islamist movement coalesces in anything like a tight, unified organization: it remains decentered and multiple in its roots and branches. Its direction and policy are determined by the formation of shifting coalitions, to which different levels of leaders bring their personal followings, broader public authority and influence as well as, for some of them, secret cells of militant and terrorist groups. It would seem that these latter groups are based on strong internal discipline but little effective control by the higher, coalition-based factions. The militant cells may be quite small, and patterned or derived from three somewhat different historical models: the Muslim Brotherhood's 'Special Apparatus',[2] the Palestinian resistance organizations, and the veterans of the recent Afghan war.

Among Islamists in general, most if not all members are also subjectively very much part of the modern world, and cherish most of its technologies and ideas: there is no marked element of 'nativist' rejection of modernity generally. Indeed, the appeal and vitality of the movement may be significantly spurred by the failure of governments to deliver their secular promises of modern prosperity and rights to a broad sector of their population. This failure, and the corruption, arbitrary force, and self-seeking exploitation that permeate so many secular regimes, can fire fundamentalist indignation when contrasted to the integrity of the religious ideals of fundamentalism. The various voluntary social services, welfare services, and medical facilities run by fundamentalist organizations in poor urban neighbourhoods serve to demonstrate this tact and commitment. Fundamentalists seem to be united in their belief that a true practice of religion will put the contemporary world right, not that the experienced and potential benefits of modern life need to be forsaken.

Thus, the constituency of the Islamists is probably rather wide and heterogeneous, composed of persons with orientations ranging from spiritual to practical, conservative to Messianic, compassionate to terrorist. This diversity indeed accurately reflects a diversity represented in the Koran itself, as the fount of fundamentalism: the Koran embraces a positive valuation of both civilization and simplicity, individual responsibility and submission; it shows a practicality in its design of civil and person law, a graphic violence in its instituted punishments for misdeeds and crimes, and a transcendental conception of martyrdom and holy war.

Parameters for a political agenda

What transforms these widespread personal and moral orientations into an organized political force? Basically, the formulation of a political agenda, and a collective organization to execute such an agenda. But if I am correct that a political agenda, in the stricter sense, is not an integral part of the Islamists' appeal to their supporters, how is that agenda determined and what may be its thrust? I suggest that we should not naïvely try to derive such an agenda from a logical analysis of fundamentalist first principles, or even the rhetorical or dogmatic statements made by the Islamist leadership. It would be methodologically sounder, if possible, first to analyse the actual patterns of social transactions whereby political agendas are indeed decided. In attempting this, we may observe that certain parameters are laid down by circumstances, other features are emergent results of the political dynamics whereby factions are mobilized and opponents engaged.

First, let me suggest four important parameters. Nearly everywhere, fundamentalism exists (1) *in opposition* to the existing regime, within states that give little scope to the free play of political parties.[3] This allows an Islamist political movement, at least for a while, to draw sustenance from a very wide range of dissatisfactions with the existing regimes among people, without being committed to particular, specified programmatic alternatives.

The wider historical context also entails that fundamentalists are committed to an (2) *anti-Western* political position: the current hegemony of the West – whether seen as representing Christianity, materialism, or ex-colonial and superpower dominance – cannot be in accord with Islamist visions. The persistent Western policies favouring Israel (and to variable extent policies elsewhere, as towards Iraq, Bosnia, and Iran) have consistently served to exacerbate a legacy of anger and bitterness. Local discourses give varying salience to these themes, but they draw on deep grievances and passions, and the fundamentalists inflame them, often as challenges to the national governments' submissive or pro-Western policies.

Other parameters influencing the Islamist political agenda are structural rather than substantive. I have described a leadership and a structure of authority that is multicentric and fragmented; one might also expect it to be particularly (3) *fractious*. That will be so because its sources are in large part intellectual, ideological, and scholarly, grounded on divine truth as represented in a complex and evocative holy text. This provides endless sources of possible doctrinal and interpretational division, and the movement is only secondarily held together by tactical and organizational forces since it, like the very concept of the Muslim state, springs from foundations in belief, and not vice versa.

A further structural feature is (4) *the option of violence*. It is important to state explicitly that there is no militant doctrine generally valid in Islam. The concept of *jihad*, 'holy war', is, as all religious concepts, amenable to multiple interpretations, ranging from an inner spiritual battle against irreligious tendencies within the person to an overt militant activity in the world to defend Islam against its enemies. None the less, there are certainly clear historical precedences for the political use of militancy and violence in periods of Islam, from the battles fought under the leadership of the Prophet, through the Assassins of the Middle Ages, to contemporary practices. There is also a textual body in the Koran that promises eternal bliss for martyrs who die in such battles, without clear indications as to the social institutional context whereby such action needs to be legitimized. This means that Islamists can readily draw on the use of violence as one fundamental option of political action.

This is especially important in the political context of opposition to regimes that do not allow the free expression of public opinion. Violent resistance in such contexts, as we see in a variety of situations around the world today, has clear and distinctive properties. It gives conspicuous attention and voice to resistance, even on the part of single or very small groups of people. It is nearly impossible even for the strongest regime to prevent. And it engages the regime in an exchange of moves that presents the two opposed parties as somehow conceptually equal, no matter how unequal their actual powers may be.

The shaping of political action

These parameters constrain but do not determine what the national (not to speak of the *inter*national) political agenda of the Islamists will be. And the wellsprings I have identified for the movement hardly add much constraint to its choice of policies: unlike, for example, a Green Party, which will be committed by the nature of its constituency to a particular kind of agenda, the Islamist leadership is left rather free to shape its national policy. Within the broad parameters sketched above, I expect Islamist political agendas in different Middle Eastern nations to come about as an aggregation of the chain of local episodes of religious, moral, and political debates and accusations; an accumulating history of political manoeuvres within a volatile field of rivals and opponents; and the effects of occasionally fateful regime actions or countermoves. There is little evidence that political positions are developed within some central Islamist command structure as strategic blueprints derived from ideological premises, or indeed that, if formulated, they would prove to have marked effects within the movement or much stability over time and in changing contexts. Since the leadership level among Islamists is fractious and divided, we need above all to acknowledge each separate leader's need to act tactically, in a field of continuous political entrepreneurship. In such a situation, the first necessity for every leader would be to establish and cultivate the viability of his particular relationship to his faction and following, from one day to the next. Whoever fails to reproduce his political enterprise will lose his place as a leader. Thus only he who maintains his appeal to a particular constituency, or manages to replace it by other followers in a shifting field of allegiances, will retain his status within the leadership.

In such an entrepreneurial context, a diversity of dissimilar political enterprises will coexist. Where one leader maintains his following by organizing welfare services in a locality, another does so by spiritual influence among religious students through skilfully deploying his gift for theological debate, while a third may concentrate on building and supplying a small cell of young militants. On this level, transactions become more specific. The spiritual leader offers teaching and training, prestige, and a swifter upward career to his disciples in return for more dedicated students, verbal citation and support, and theological authority. Leaders of secret cells, on the contrary, must provide military training and equipment, enhanced self-images and a mystique of *jihad* and 'the art of death' (cf. Commins 1994: 146) in return for secrecy, submission to commands, and willingness to take risks. And other enterprises, such as the welfare-providing agencies, again depend on other transactions. A distinctive field of mobilization for all factions is provided by the large settlements of expatriate workers in Europe, such as Algerians in France and Turks in Germany, where Islamist activists are freer to recruit and can draw also on the dissatisfactions generated among the less successful or otherwise frustrated members of these populations.

Each leader is a potential player in coalition forming with the others; but the joint policies at which such coalitions are able to arrive will be eternally contingent, provisional, and pragmatic. Within the broad parameters noted above as (1)–(4), the Islamists' political agenda emerges as the sum, or rather the volatile vector, of such a play of forces, and not as a set policy. And through the counter-efforts of each state and regime, by their responses and actions, a *perpetuum mobile* effect is introduced into the whole field, whereby the relative successes of different enterprises and different strategies are constantly changing.

A great deal of ethnographic fieldwork, ranging from the back streets of Cairo and the halls of Al-Azhar University to the Bekaa valley, would have to be pursued with a sceptical and open mind to test or substantiate this model. And if it has some validity, the aggregate picture would probably prove complex indeed, and might not add up to a much clearer image of the movement as a whole.

For perhaps this contingency and instability reach all the way up into the highest levels of the Islamist movement. That would explain why even its highest leadership and policies appear so opaque: because even the currently most influential among the leaders are not in a position to articulate enduring, definitive political agendas or emerge with claims to authority to speak for the movement as a whole, without thereby jeopardizing the very coalitions that they lead. In this they seem very different from the Qaddafis, Saddams, Nassers and Arafats of secular, nationalist movements, particularly once such figures have been able to seize the organizational apparatus of a regime, no matter how unstable. In contrast to nationalist or ethnic movement, the leadership of fundamentalist movements seems to remain eternally elusive. It is true, Islamists in opposition and under police pursuit obviously cannot be public figures in any straightforward way; but there does not even appear to be mythology of central, charismatic leadership among Algerian Islamists, Muslim Brotherhoods or other fundamentalist factions. The Ayatullah Khomeini admittedly burst on the scene as a supreme leader with an agenda – but he did so only as he seized control of a state structure and even then he remained rather inscrutable. One could argue that the opacity of Islamist political goals may be merely an artefact of media ignorance and incomprehension – but such a media-created world becomes our globally shared reality and cannot but shape also local perceptions and local events as well as perceptions in the larger world. But beyond that, I believe there are structural features and identifiable processes at work affecting the Islamist movement that would produce this opacity in agenda and leadership. Most importantly, I would point to the basic transaction that establishes the relationships between fundamentalist leaders and their popular base: the exchange of domestic empowerments to followers in return for their political support to a rather wide latitude of options and actions by the leadership.

Conclusion

If this picture is true, it would be foolhardy to predict Islamist positions and future policies. My conclusions are thus mainly negative, but contain some possibly useful theoretical and analytical caveats. The Islamists can neither be characterized as nationalists nor internationalists in their political outlook, for two main reasons. They probably lack the institutional structure that would enable them today to embrace such long-term, stable political agendas as these concepts imply. Equally important, the very concepts of 'nationalism' and 'internationalism' are inappropriate for the analysis of the world that they inhabit. Though we are all ultimately very much part of one global political field, a political analysis of Islamism based on concepts that are developed in debates that are pursued in the context of contemporary European politics will prove to be so historically specific, value-laden, and full of ethnocentric assumptions that they cannot usefully illuminate a political current that moves in so different a conceptual world.

Can I suggest any better way to analyse contemporary fundamentalist currents in the Arab Middle East, and identify and even predict the policies of Islamists? My attempt to model the processes that might be involved in the shaping of such policies is not very helpful, since it calls for a rather detailed analysis, and depends on data that are probably not available. Given the Islamists' organizational form and the range of ideas, in its present position of opposition it might move either towards compromise or an escalating confrontation and violence; a greater fragmentation into national agendas or a Messianic, expansive internationalism within Islam. Very much obviously depends on the particular history of action and counteraction with national governments. In the unequal battle with a regime's repressive powers, terrorism is an ever-present countermeasure; and such an escalation, if adroitly pursued, can result in rallying to militancy much of the presently pacific popular support. But the vast majority of fundamentalists basically want *both* moral revival and economic progress; so the ebb and flow of material expectations, and popular perceptions of who is responsible for frustrating them, will inevitably also play a major role.

Notes

1   For data and judgements, I draw mainly on my experience in the Middle East from 1951 till today, including periods of anthropological fieldwork in several localities. Second hand, I have benefited from my wife Unni Wikan's fieldwork and familiarity with Cairo over more than twenty-five years, and also from countless conversations and discussions with colleagues from the Middle East, or from elsewhere but with deep knowledge of the Middle East. Since these inputs have been so diverse and long-lasting, there is no way I can acknowledge my debts more precisely. For misunderstandings and misinterpretations, on the other hand, I must take the full responsibility.
2   The Special Apparatus composed an inner cadre of shock troops, first established during the 1930s, who were especially trained in religion, law, first aid, and weaponry. They reportedly were enrolled by taking an oath of secrecy on a Koran and a pistol (Mitchell 1969: 203ff.).
3   Among Arab states, it might be argued that Saudi Arabia is an exception, built as it is on the foundations of the fundamentalist Wahhabi movement of Arabia in the eighteenth and early nineteenth centuries, closely associated with the Saudi dynasty (see, e.g. Zubaida 1993: 10ff.). However, the emergence of the

Saudi state in the twentieth century depended directly on military action and resulted in an absolute dynastic regime; to the extent that Islamism currently is a popular movement in Saudi Arabia, it seems to be in opposition to that regime. Outside of the Arab world, the Iranian revolutionary regime and the Talabani regime in Afghanistan clearly derive from politically successful fundamentalist movements. Their relevance to the present argument would require a rather extensive analysis to explicate. In my preliminary judgement, however, the conclusion of such an analysis would be that the Iranian revolution was only briefly seen by Arabs as an example that might be exported to the Arab world, and for a number of reasons has not had any deep influence in shaping fundamentalist thought and policy there; while the Talabani example has been without such influence.

Part II
The Iron Curtain rising

4   From internationalism to nationalism?

Poland 1944–96

Jerzy Tomaszewski

During the 1970s and 1980s an observer of the Polish political scene could see a xenophobic wave that was developing more or less in tandem with the decay of the Communist system of power. Similar changes occurred in other countries of east and central Europe, sometimes with tragic consequences. It was concluded by some that the end of the Communist system had made possible the revival of nationalist chauvinism which had effectively been suppressed by the totalitarian regimes. However, a more detailed analysis of events and trends since 1944 suggests a much more complex picture. My intention here is to re-examine basic facts concerning the changing attitudes of the Polish ruling party (or, more exactly, the factions inside it) towards national minorities. I will try to answer the questions: to what extent did the Communist system suppress (or try to suppress) ethnic conflicts and eliminate negative stereotypes of 'aliens'? And was the collapse of Communism the main reason for the outburst of national hatred?

The Communists and national traditions

It is true that the Communists who dominated the so-called people's democratic countries after the Second World War proclaimed internationalism and condemned nationalism – or, more correctly, chauvinism[1] – in their ideology, programs and propaganda. At the same time, they tried to gain the confidence of the major nations of each country by playing on patriotic feelings and the traditions of the majority including the traditions of national struggle for independence and/or unification. It was a task of reconciling the national tradition with internationalist ideology and current political needs. There were, in fact, significant differences between the individual states and parties. In Poland, it was possible to recollect an old motto of Polish fighters for national independence. 'For your and our freedom' (*Za waszą i naszą wolność*), and to proclaim that solidarity with oppressed peoples was a significant part of the national tradition. The party propaganda stressed that Karl Marx had approved of the Polish uprisings.

It proved far more difficult and sometimes impossible to integrate the national traditions of certain other countries in the new political pantheon and to exploit them for propaganda purposes. Czech and Slovak Communists had ideological difficulties with Karl Marx's derogative opinions about their nations and his condemnation of national movements (notably in 1848) among small Slavic nations. The changing attitudes of Bulgarian Communists on the so-called Macedonian question was another good example.[2] There were indications that after the September 1944 coup some Bulgarian Communist leaders were ready to accept the integration of the Pirin region with the Macedonian Republic (at that time a member of federal Yugoslavia). In 1948, after the Soviet–Yugoslav conflict, their attitude changed and even the very existence of the Macedonian nation was denied. Contemporary Bulgarian historians have condemned this old Communist standpoint as national treason (Ангелов 1997a, 1997b). Another case was Romania, where the patriotic tradition of the fight for national unity proved to be a rather troublesome matter for the Communists because of the post-war incorporation of Moldavia into the USSR.

In Poland, where the Communists under the name of the Polish Workers Party (PWP *Polska Partia Robotnicza*) (after 1948 Polish United Workers Party, PUWP, *Polska Zjednoczona Partia Robotnicza*) had relatively limited political influence, national traditions were emphasized particularly strongly, though selectively. The first and most important question was the fight against Germans, who were presented as a centuries-old enemy of the Polish nation (sometimes journalists even wrote about 'the German race' thereby adopting – if unintentionally – the Nazi vocabulary). This was in accordance with popular feelings after the tragic experience of war and occupation. It also corresponded with the political legacy of the National Democratic Party (*narodowa demokracja*), the traditional protagonist of chauvinism. On the other hand, it was better to forget or to downgrade the tradition of uprisings against Russia. These were defined as struggles against tsarism that had been fought shoulder to shoulder with the Russian revolutionaries who later created the Soviet Union. The even more awkward Polish–Soviet war 1919–21 was explained as the result of Polish imperialism.

The situation for the Bulgarian Communists was more convenient. They could stress the role of Russia in the liberation of their country from Turkish despotism (*osmanskoto igo*) in the nineteenth century. Sofia is one of only two capitals in eastern Europe where the monument to Tsar Alexander II still remains standing (the other is in Helsinki), and is regarded as a memorial to Bulgarian–Russian friendship. Streets in Bulgarian towns were named after Russian commanders and politicians whose role in Russian history was often deprecated in the Soviet Union.

Ideology and politics

A result of the implementation of the nationalist ideology in its radical variety – and at the same time as the Soviet policy – was the expulsion of the non-Polish population after 1945. The expulsion of Germans – approved in Potsdam in the summer of 1945 by the three Great Powers – was probably inevitable after five years of Nazi occupation and also bearing in mind the attitudes of many German citizens of the pre-war Polish Republic, as well as the atrocities committed during the war by the German administration, *Wehrmacht*, and individual citizens in the name of the German nation.[3] A similar decision was taken in other countries and today Czech intellectuals are debating the reasons, consequences and political and moral status of the expulsion (*odsun*) of Germans from the Czechoslovak Republic.[4] The cases of Belaruses, Lithuanians and Ukrainians were different as their national leaders were accused of collaboration with the Nazi regime. This issue was about the Polish–Soviet relationship and the governments of both countries signed agreements providing voluntary exchange of population. In reality, Belaruses, Lithuanians and Ukrainians who lived in Poland did not want to leave their native villages and towns. It was necessary to exert force – more or less officially – before they departed 'voluntarily' to the relevant Soviet republics. Many of them were deported afterwards to the eastern regions of the Soviet Union. One can observe a striking coincidence: the anti-government Polish conspiracy tried to compel the local, non-Polish peasants (notably Belaruses[5]) to escape to the USSR, while the Communist-dominated administration – with the noteworthy exception of individual activists who did not subordinate their convictions to the needs of Soviet policy – also supported the exodus. The pressure was felt particularly by the Ukrainians.[6] A significant number of them did not yield, however, and remained in Poland.

The Ukrainians who did not emigrate were later expelled to the Polish western and northern provinces. The authorities hoped (in conformity with the Soviet policy) that the Ukrainians who were dispersed among the Polish peasants would assimilate. In 1946, the Greek rites of the Catholic Church, which were adhered to by the Ukrainians, were formally abolished. The bishops in the USSR announced their voluntary union with the Orthodox Church, while the Greek Catholic bishops in Poland were arrested by the Soviet authorities.

The Jews were in a different situation, as their fate during the period of Nazi rule made any anti-Jewish policy impossible. Prior to 1939, the Communists (as well as the other left-wing political parties) had defended them against radical nationalists. Be that as it may, the majority of Jews emigrated before 1950. There was, however, a certain ambivalence in Polish attitudes towards the Jewish population. The participation of several people of Jewish origin in the government and administration established under Soviet auspices[7] seemed to validate an old anti-Semitic stereotype, according to which Communism was created and introduced by Jews (and people serving Jewish interests), expressed in the term *Judeocommune (żydoko-muna)*. Armed groups (remnants of anti-German groupings faithful to the Polish government-in-exile) fighting against the Communists murdered members of the PWP, as well as Jews considered to be responsible for and the embodiment of Soviet domination (Kersten 1992: 76–89).

It would be difficult today to know if such anti-Jewish sentiment really was so widespread and deeply rooted in Polish society. We can at least note that many people were convinced of its existence and this was probably the reason for the vacillating attitude of the Catholic clergy after the infamous pogrom in Kielce in the summer of 1946 when a mob, convinced that a Jew had tried to commit a 'ritual murder', murdered forty-two Jews (Wrona 1991).[8] The Catholic authorities were probably afraid that open condemnation of the crime and 'blood libel' could be interpreted as political support for the Communists.

The PWP (later PUWP) underscored with apparent success that the reborn Polish Republic was a country of only one Polish nation, without minorities which undermined the internal stability of the inter-war Poland, according to a view inherited from the pre-war radical nationalists.[9] It was, therefore, not surprising that schools for national language groups were forbidden (in the case of the Germans and Ukrainians), or closed after a short period of existence (in the case of Belaruses), or were reluctantly tolerated at first and then closed after several years (in case of the Jews). The party and government opposed the nationalism of the national minorities (including Zionism, after a short period of apparent tolerance in accordance with the initial Soviet policy towards Israel), encouraged national feelings among Poles, and tried to promote internationalism and friendship with the Soviet Union, the so-called socialist countries, and colonial nations which fought against imperialist (that is Western) powers.

Politicians and, with a few exceptions, scholars were not interested in the situation of Romanies (*Polska Roma*). This nation suffered heavy losses during the German occupation as Romanies were considered to be subhuman and were murdered in camps. A separate Romany sector existed in Auschwitz.

After 1949 the Polish authorities tried to integrate the Romanies into the Socialist system and subject them to the control of the administration, but with very limited success (Ficowski 1989: 47–50). The socio-economic changes in Poland negatively influenced the situation of nomadic Romany groups. Other Romanies, mainly artisans settled in villages, were often unable to pursue their traditional professions. Old biases against the Romanies – found in many nations in Europe – remained unchanged, but the repressive system of power prevented open assaults on them (Bartosz 1994: 48). On the other hand, nothing was done to change popular superstitions and prejudices. There are even reasons to believe that the unsuccessful efforts to force the nomads to accept jobs in factories and to resettle them in modern housing or to transform them into farmers (as was tried in Czechoslovakia), reinforced the negative image of Romanies as swindlers and lazy, petty criminals who were unfit for normal life in a socialist society.

The ambivalent propaganda

The political propaganda used was a peculiar mixture of traditional chauvinism with socialist internationalism, both useful instruments for current political needs and both more or less in line with the policy of the USSR. A characteristic case was the reception by politicians and official journals of Soviet propaganda concerning the tricentennial anniversary of the 'reunification' (*vossoedineniye*[10]) of Ukraine with Russia, which, in fact was an indirect negation of the independent existence of the Ukrainian nation. In Poland this kind of propaganda was denounced by many people but only in private.

There remained significant differences between individual countries. In Bulgaria, Romania and even more so in Hungary, propaganda and state education tried to belittle or even condemn national traditions and to exaggerate the 'progressive' significance of the alliance with Russia (after 1917 – the USSR). This last point was accepted relatively easily in Bulgaria as the Bulgarians achieved their national independence thanks to the Russian–Turkish wars.[11] The wartime alliance of Bulgaria, Romania and Hungary with Nazi Germany may explain the critical attitudes of Communists towards the national tradition. The political propaganda in Czechoslovakia exploited the traditional influence of panslavism, paradoxically an ideology which had been promoted in the past by conservative politicians who were opponents of any kind of socialism. After 1950, it included a significant component of anti-Semitism (under the disguise of 'fight against Zionism', following the example of the USSR). In addition to stressing the tradition of friendship between Polish and Russian revolutionary activists, historians in Poland wrote of the democratic traditions of the Polish struggle for national independence and often stressed the significance of the struggle against German imperialism (*Drang nach Osten*), which was identified with the German Federal Republic. The Polish victory (with the help of Lithuanian, Ruthenian and Czech forces) over the Teutonic Order near Grunwald (in German tradition – near Tannenberg) in 1410 was another convenient symbol.

The propaganda and education prepared fertile ground for the instrumental use of chauvinism in the inner-party conflicts. In 1956 (covertly) and 1968 (openly), certain factions of the PUWP exploited anti-Semitism as a weapon against their rivals. These factions were helped by the 'licensed' Catholic association 'Pax' which had its roots in the extreme nationalist and totalitarian groups active before 1945. After 1989, this association renamed itself 'Civitas Christiana'. Today they are strident

anti-Communists who often assail the people from the former illegal democratic opposition.

The death of Stalin in 1953, the reversal of many of his orders, and
the political changes after the Twentieth Congress of the Communist Party
of the Soviet Union in 1956, strengthened the more liberal strands in the
policy of the PUWP and raised hopes for the future. At the same time,
these changes facilitated the open manifestation of chauvinism, especially
in Lower Silesia, where in the second half of 1956 anonymous, threatening letters were sent to private individuals and in some places, especially
in Dzierżoniów and Wałbrzych, anti-Semitic demonstrations and even
assaults occurred (Bełdzikowski 1994: 10, 23). The Jews were accused of
having taken part in the establishment of Communist power. Some people,
including a group of politicians from the top echelons of the PUWP,
suggested that responsibility for abuses of power and crimes committed
by the security agencies lay almost exclusively with Jewish officials and
that after Stalin's death Jews conspired to weaken the Socialist system in
Poland by introducing 'cosmopolitanism' and slandering the patriotic traditions of the Poles. For some of the accusers, it was a quest for a scapegoat
which could be blamed for their own crimes. The propounders of anti-
Semitic views were supported by the Soviet politicians.

According to an anonymous report about a meeting of regional party
leaders:

> 'Soviet comrades' at the meeting had explained to the Polish side that
> power should be in the hands of provincial Party secretaries, who are
> 'real Poles and patriots' and not weaklings like members of the govern-
> ment who are not only influenced by Jews and cosmopolitans but are
> themselves Jews. Mazurov and Baranov argued that to save Poland
> and Socialism, all Jews must first be removed from all important polit-
> ical and administrative positions, the press and radio.
>
> (Anonymous 1971: 19)

A possible indirect confirmation of Soviet influence in supporting anti-
Semitic trends was the appearance of anti-Semitic opinions in the armed
forces which were not challenged by all high ranking officers, although
quite a few condemned declarations of that type (Rudawski 1996: 210–13).
In 1956, however, there were people inside the Central Committee of the
PUWP who tried to introduce a more reasonable policy towards the
national minorities. Anti-Jewish declarations and assaults were condemned
by intellectuals, the mass media, and a majority of politicians.

From internationalism to anti-Semitism

After 1953, the PUWP helped to develop education in the languages of
the national minorities and supported the development of their cultures

'national in shape and socialist in essence'. It was possible for them to organize national cultural associations and to publish journals in their own languages but under PUWP supervision. When in 1956 the leadership of PUWP was taken over by Władysław Gomułka and his friends, the Central Committee organized a special office whose task it was to fight chauvinism and discrimination against the national minorities. In 1957, the Central Committee wrote a letter to Party members which read:

> Once again we forcefully stress the internationalist nature of our Party. There is and can be no place in it for people who cultivate nationalist, chauvinist and racist views. We cannot tolerate people who try to contaminate Party ranks with the poison of nationalism and anti-Semitism. We must have special penalties against comrades who hold posts in the party or state offices. . . . Recognising the principle of equal national rights, the Party struggles for a complete observation of constitutional rights, which guarantee every citizen the right to work and to hold all state, social and Party posts in accordance with his professional and moral-political qualifications.
>
> (Sław 1958: 32–3)

The situation deteriorated slowly with the 'restoration of order'[12] from 1957 onwards. The reinforcement of the authoritarian system of government was followed by the elimination of people who were accused of working for the liberalization and democratization of the state, as well as those of Jewish origin. The activists of the national minorities were often placed under surveillance by the secret police.[13] On the other hand, some possibilities still existed for scholars to study the history of national minorities in Poland even if their efforts were limited by censorship which tried to prevent any opinion that might prove an irritant for Soviet politicians. In spite of these difficulties, it was possible to publish articles and books presenting the history and culture of the national minorities in Poland, and even to mention their distinguished leaders, people who in the USSR were 'non-persons'. These writings, which were printed not only in Polish but in the minority languages, influenced readers in neighbouring Soviet republics as well.[14] It was a paradox that a kind of rehabilitation of the national pasts of Belarus, Lithuania, and Ukraine was to some extent possible in Poland where there had been a sad record of discrimination against national minorities prior to 1939.

It should be stressed that the Roman Catholics – with the notable exception of the growing number of intellectuals – more often than not lent their support to the chauvinist attitudes. The Church was under strong political pressure and had to defend its influence on the Polish society. This may be seen a reason for stressing the Roman Catholic traditions which were usually equated with patriotism and opposition to all 'alien' influences. This strengthened ethnic conflicts and gave them a religious inflection. It is true that, in spite of the Soviet-inspired elimination of the Greek Catholic (Ukrainian) parishes, some Polish bishops (however reluctantly) helped to maintain the Greek rite in a few parishes with Ukrainian populations. However, Ukrainian priests encountered impediments in practical life.[15] The Polish parish priests discriminated against children and their parents who spoke Ukrainian and who declared their adherence to the Greek rite. They also tried to disrupt the regular introduction of Greek Catholic prayers and ceremonies. Even the attitude of the Primate of Poland, cardinal Rev. Stefan Wyszyński, was ambiguous to say the least, although this might have been due to pressure and demands from the secret police.[16]

Another sad case were the ethnic conflicts in the villages on the Polish–Slovak border where parish priests tried to ban prayers and singing in the Slovak language in church. The parishioners appealed in vain to the bishop and eventually asked the provincial committee of the PUWP for help.

A notable exception was 'The message of Polish bishops to their German brothers in Christ's pastoral office' (*Orędzie biskupów polskich do ich niemieckich Braci w Chrystusowym urzędzie pasterskim*) of 18 November 1965. The document was an attempt to initiate a Polish–German dialogue in order to overcome traditional antagonisms. It became the object of sharp criticism for the PUWP press. It was, however, a significant step forward with regard to the situation of Germans living in Poland (Madajczyk 1994).

The internal fight for power in the PUWP developed anew in the second half of the 1960s. One of the groups involved gathered around General Mieczysław Moczar. He was a former commander of a Communist partisan group during the Second World War and the post-war head of security organs in Łódź which were responsible for the persecution of members of the non-Communist underground. From 1964, he was also the Minister of Interior and in charge of the police. In his ministry Moczar nominated a specialist for Jewish affairs (a man who later tried to pass himself off as an historian and was even nominated a professor) who drew up a list of persons of Jewish origin. However, the Jews had been dismissed from the army as early as 1962 (in June 1962 General Wojciech Jaruzelski was appointed deputy minister of the national defence). Here, too, Soviet influence played a significant part (Eisler 1991: 48–51).

The Six Days War of 1967 became a pretext for an open offensive by chauvinist forces. Following the Soviet example, Poland severed its diplomatic ties with Israel. However, the sympathies of a considerable part of Polish society were with Israel ('"our" Jews defeated "their" Arabs'; 'their' being the forces supported by the Soviet Union). An anti-Jewish campaign operating under the slogan of a struggle against Zionism developed. The term 'Zionists' denoted in fact Jews and people who were descended from Jewish forebears even when they were not aware of the fact. The faction which tried to assume leadership of the PUWP and seize dictatorial power in Poland, claimed that Jews were a subversive force inside the party, and that they had introduced revisionism[17] and Jewish nationalism. A convenient coincidence was a wave of student protests against the ideological campaign. The ensuing persecutions affected primarily students and intellectuals. Many people, but especially those with Jewish names, were arrested. Andrzej Werblan, who was at that time chief of the PUWP's Department of Science and Education, asked:

> Why is there a relatively large number of persons of Jewish origin among certain groups of the intelligentsia in our country, in certain domains of scientific research, chiefly the social sciences, as well among those holding responsible posts in certain central institutions . . .? Why do we observe particular susceptibility to revisionism and the growth of Jewish nationalism in general and Zionism in particular in the attitude of certain Jewish milieus or amongst those of Jewish descent?

He then performed an 'analysis' and drew the conclusion which justified anti-Jewish purges: 'No society wishes to tolerate the excessive participation of a national minority in the power elite and particularly in the organs of national defence, security, propaganda and foreign affairs' (Werblan 1968: 66, 69). The chauvinist campaign was supported by a substantial part of the Polish press (among them a popular daily *Życie Warszawy*, the lawyers' association weekly *Prawo i Życie*, the atheist association journal *Argumenty*, and a journal for young readers *Walka Młodych*) that had been taken over by the followers of Moczar, as well as the demonstratively Catholic 'Pax' Association, even if the Church hierarchy had denounced the latter. Before 1939, its leader Bolesław Piasecki was known as a charismatic activist in an extreme nationalist faction of the national democratic movement and a political writer professing a totalitarian ideology. This campaign was full of personal slander. Because of censorship, it was impossible to answer accusations or to explain the truth in the press. An infamous case was an assault by 'unknown culprits' on the well-known writer, composer and Catholic journalist, Stefan Kisielewski, a member of parliament, who nicknamed the political system in Poland 'the dictatorship of dark men' (*dyktatura ciemniaków*).

The Catholic hierarchy openly condemned the persecution of students and intellectuals and the restrictions on the freedom of information. But there was no such clear and direct condemnation of the anti-Semitic campaign, and the pastoral letter of bishops issued on 3 May outlined only in general terms their attitude towards Jews.[18] There were, however, some parish priests who joined the attacks against Jews.

The events in Poland ran parallel to quite different changes initiated in Czechoslovakia where an influential faction of the Communist Party tried to develop a democratic variant of the Socialist system. No wonder that there was writing on the walls in Warsaw declaring: 'All Poland awaits

its own Dubček' (*Cała Polska czeka na swego Dubczeka*). The widespread enthusiasm for the Prague Spring raised additional anxiety among the leaders
of the PUWP. They considered, and rightly so, the popular feeling to be
a threat to the existing system (cf. Garlicki and Paczkowski 1995) and a
result of revisionist influences on young people and intellectuals. This fear
was exploited by the totalitarian faction of the PUPW.

It would be interesting to investigate the individual attitudes of people
engaged in discrimination against minorities and particularly the promotion of anti-Semitism. One could name persons who had no personal biases
against Jews and did not believe in anti-Jewish stereotypes and slander. A
good example was Kazimierz Kąkol, chief editor of the weekly *Prawo i
Życie*. People like him probably exploited this kind of propaganda because
they considered it to be a useful instrument in political intrigues. However,
several other politicians – including members of the PUWP – strongly
believed in the reality of international Jewish plots against Poland and
Socialism. There were also other members in the top echelons of the
PUWP who joined – though reluctantly and belatedly – the apparently
victorious chauvinist trend. But there were also rare cases of Communist
politicians who protested against anti-Semitism and resigned from their
posts, without having been able to avert the danger of a strange alliance
of Communism and Fascism. In the latter group there was Edward Ochab,
the president of the State Council (a post more or less equivalent to the
President of the State) and Adam Rapacki, Minister of Foreign Affairs.

It is true that the faction which promulgated anti-Zionist propaganda
and tried to suppress any opposition with police force did not succeed and
could not gain full power. One assumes that their attempt, however timid,
to exploit anti-Soviet attitudes in Polish society raised suspicions in Moscow.
Moczar lost his ministerial post in July 1968 and several months later
became a member of the State Council. Formally this was a promotion,
but in reality was a reduction in his real power. At the same time, social
and economic tensions in Poland intensified and shortly after 'March 1968'
the revolt of workers in December 1970 overturned the unpopular political
leadership. However, this neither changed the system of government nor
the structures of power. Perhaps the most significant change was the general
disbelief in the ideological arguments of the PUWP and the growing conviction that things could not remain as they had been before, along with a
belief in the strength of the working class.

The politicians who gained the influential posts after 1970 openly
rejected chauvinism and proclaimed internationalism (which, as before,
was understood to mean friendship with the Soviet Union). At the same
time, however, they forged the slogan of 'national unity' and the national
(ethnic) uniformity of the citizens of the Polish People's Republic and
secretly discriminated against the national minorities. Belarus and Ukrainian intellectuals in Poland after 1968 complained that they suffered because
of limited opportunities to print their books and journals in their native

languages and received less financial help for their cultural activities, and some national cultural institutions were even lost.

The events of 1968 (referred to as the 'March events') had a profound impact on the political life of Poland. The Communist politicians' struggles for power officially introduced chauvinism, and particularly anti-Semitism, into the ideology of an influential faction of the PUWP. This faction strove for a more rigid dictatorial system (there were even opinions expressed that it was a kind of 'red Nazism'), and tried with some success to find allies among the followers of extreme nationalist right-wing movements in Poland which were traditionally anti-Communist but promoted totalitarian views. The 'licensed' Catholic politicians of 'Pax' tried to legitimate this mixture of chauvinism, totalitarianism, xenophobia and remnants of traditional Marxism with a superficial layer of traditional religious slogans. They could freely use their own daily *Słowo Powszechne* (which gained a well-deserved notoriety in 1968) and other journals, whereas the democratic Catholic intellectuals suffered more or less open discrimination. The circulation of a distinguished Catholic weekly *Tygodnik Powszechny* and similar journals was restricted by the authorities on the grounds of a lack of paper.

The chauvinism promoted by some PUWP politicians had only a limited impact on the intellectuals. Only a few individuals of minor importance openly joined. The anti-Semitic campaign became an opportunity for third-rate scholars to oust their distinguished colleagues and to take over their posts. This not only affected the social sciences[19] though in this field the persecutions were probably the most devastating. Polish economic sciences were particularly hard hit and many known and distinguished scholars lost their jobs and often emigrated.[20] A *casus pascudeus* (hideous case) among historians was an attack on a book by Janusz Żarnowski (1973) who was accused of subordinating facts to his views 'against the obvious historical truth' by underestimating 'the Jewish hatred of Poles' in inter-war Poland and by neglecting the class roots of the ethnic conflicts (Borkowski 1974).[21] This article, comprised of anti-Semitic stereotypes, provoked protests among serious historians, but it was impossible to publish rejoinders. The author was only allowed to answer after a long delay (Żarnowski 1977). Another article was allowed in a Jewish journal after having to delete any allusion to the book or the attack (Tomaszewski 1975). More reasonable historians, including those close to the Moczar faction, preferred to avoid direct engagements with these writings.

The opposition and minorities

After a brief period of economic prosperity, the end of 1970s was marked by growing difficulties, social tensions, and a new wave of protests. The political opposition joined forces with the spontaneous outbursts of social unrest and the weakened administration could not prevent these developments. The opposition and particularly the intellectuals started to print clandestine publications called 'the second circulation', as opposed to the first official and censured circulation. This kind of activity developed to a much greater extent after December 1981 under martial law. It should be stressed that intellectuals from the national minorities played their part in this movement.

The radical nationalists counterattacked through journals published under the auspices of local extremist factions of the PUWP, which promoted chauvinist propaganda directed against Ukrainians and Jews (Śliwa 1997: 135–6). The most widely known of these was the weekly *Rzeczywistość* founded in 1981 in Warsaw. The secret services exploited chauvinism, and especially anti-Semitism in the fight against the democratic opposition, and even spread illegal writings containing anti-Semitic propaganda. They were popularly nicknamed 'the third circulation'. This kind of propaganda, which tried to present the democratic opposition and changes in the Catholic Church as a 'Jewish conspiracy', convinced naïve believers even among the rank and file clergy. It is also true that these attempts to exploit old stereotypes and chauvinism were on the margins of the PUWP and government. It was an unofficial (or at least semi-official) action which was looked on with embarrassment by the more civilized politicians. The official dogma was that the PUWP – in accordance with the entire tradition of the Communist and socialist movement – was against any chauvinism and defended the equality of people irrespective of their ethnic affiliation and language. There were, however, surprising inconsistencies in the official position. The infamous daily issued by the Ministry of the National Defence, *Żołnierz Wolności*, published slanderous assaults including anti-Semitic comments on distinguished opposition figures. But at the same time Minister Jaruzelski expressed quite different views. One can only speculate on the reasons and wonder if the Minister had any influence on his own official journal.

The majority in the democratic opposition was variously engaged in defending minority rights and fighting against the 'official' chauvinism. There can be no doubt, however, that the anti-Communist forces were divided and that in some cases these groups or individuals shared only one conviction, namely that the existing political system had to be changed if not destroyed. Among opponents of the system were the followers of the traditional, radical nationalist camp. It was a paradox that there were people in the PUWP who sincerely believed that the opposition was inspired by an 'international Jewish conspiracy', while at the same time certain opponents of the PUWP considered the party to be a creature of the same plot (Moczulski 1978–9; Krzepkowski 1985. See Śliwa 1997: 134–5).

The officially sponsored chauvinism, and especially the anti-Semitic attacks, actually discredited itself to some extent in the eyes of many people. Young people in particular, who had rarely ever met a Jew, tried to find information about Jewish culture, Jewish life, and the situation of Jews in the past. The same thing applied to the other national minorities. The politicians and journalists who had inspired the wave of chauvinism achieved the opposite results to those they had intended.

What changed after 1989?

The revolution of 1980 and the political transformations initiated in 1989 after the transitory period of 'the martial law' changed the situation. Previously suppressed opinion emerged and gave the impression that chauvinist ideology had earlier been suppressed by the Communists. This was, however, only partially true. We have already seen that chauvinism existed inside the ruling PUWP and among its allies, and that it was a characteristic feature of several journals and some books published with the approval of the censor after 1968. It was also present among the political and ideological adversaries of Communism.

The main difference was that after 1989 there were no formal limits to presenting these views. Most authors who expressed their xenophobic opinions used more primitive and radical language and almost all of them condemned (often very sharply) Communism irrespective of their previous political affiliation. It was not a transition from internationalism to nationalism but from a kind of PUWP-sponsored chauvinism to a peculiar alliance of the old dogmatic 'internationalists' with the anti-Communist radical nationalists. It is necessary to stress, however, that this did not eliminate the influence of anti-Semitism among the activists of the PUWP. A significant fact was that in 1988 no official document opposing anti-Semitism appeared and only two semi-official comments were published. In March of that year *Trybuna Ludu* (an official PUWP daily) printed an ambiguous article signed by two obscure journalists and *Nowe Drogi* (a PUWP ideological tribune) published an article written by an historian, who unfortunately had not had access to the necessary documents (Kozik 1988). There were, however, strong pressures inside the party to issue an official declaration condemning the wave of anti-Semitism as early as 1968.[22]

A new and important factor was the rapid political disintegration of the anti-Communist opposition which had previously been united in the fight to establish a democratic system in Poland. The emerging political parties represented different views on current issues, the politicians who were previously friends now became rivals. Additional factors were the local social and political conflicts which in several cases were connected with religious and ethnic differences. An interesting case was the situation in Białystok region where a significant Belarus population lives. Local social conflicts between the original town dwellers and young immigrant villagers, ethnic and religious differences or rivalries, and memories of the mysterious political crimes committed in 1944 and 1945 influenced the political behaviour of people.

A similar and even more incendiary mixture developed in Przemyœl region which was the former homeland of the Ukrainians expelled to the western or northern regions of Poland who had slowly and with difficulty returned to their native country. The conflicts exploded over the attempts to erect memorials to Ukrainians killed in battle against the Poles, and to build churches. The most peculiar controversy concerned the church in Przemyśl. The building, a former Greek Catholic cathedral, had been handed over to the Roman Catholic order after 1945, but in 1996 was destined to be the official seat of the head of the Greek Catholic Church in Poland. Even the authority of Pope John Paul II, who visited the city, could not influence the Polish and Roman Catholic opponents of this plan. The local enemies of the Ukrainians prevailed. The monks destroyed the old wooden dome which they considered to be a symbol of the Greek rite. In actual fact it was a replica of the dome of St Peter's church in Rome and was considered to be a historical monument protected by law (Wilczak 1996).

Many local conflicts seemed to be of little significance, but there were signs of the persistence of traditional stereotypes and other more important problems. The Polish–Ukrainian conflicts were linked to different under-standings of history, and different attitudes towards the Ukrainian national movement in the twentieth century. Opinions about the actions of the Ukrainian Insurgent Army during the Second World War, the radical, nationalist terror against the Polish population of Western Ukraine, and the mass expulsion of Ukrainians living in Poland after 1944, are still matters of dispute and the reason for conflict (Stasiński 1997). It may be that there are external influences sustaining these mutual recriminations and contro-versies as it is known that the former Soviet Union was deeply interested in presenting the Ukrainian national tradition in the worst possible light.

After 1989, the Polish opposition (and notably the trade union, Solidar-ity) cooperated with the Roman Catholic clergy which provoked incredulity and fear among the Orthodox or Greek Catholic population (Belaruses and Ukrainians), often with good cause as the local Polish Roman Catholic parish priests were not blameless. These feelings were reflected in the elec-toral campaigns and in the results: the minority population often voted against the non-Communist candidates.

Local conflicts were also observed at the other end of Poland in Silesia. However, they seem not to have been as dangerous as the ones mentioned above. Perhaps one of the reasons is the relative religious uniformity of the local population and the influence of the Bishop in Opole, Rev. Alfons Nossol, Professor of the Opole University and a man with great personal authority, who had approved the use of German language in the churches of his diocese in 1989. It is necessary to add, however, that several other bishops disapproved of his attitude (Urban 1994: 195–8).

All of these conflicts, which are rooted to some extent in traditional stereotypes and prejudices, also have contemporary political significance.

The democratic changes allowed antagonism against Romanies to surface in public life. There was a tragic case when the people in the small towns of Konin (September 1981) and Mława (June 1991) rioted against a few Romany families living there. Other cases have been reported and seem to be even more frequent in other countries like Czechoslovakia and Romania (see Bartosz 1994). Investigations indicate that the Romanies are the object of the most virulent ethnic prejudice.

Contemporary Poland and the Jews

A characteristic feature of the Polish political scene today is the presence of chauvinist publications which are circulated without any difficulty. As a rule, they are of a rather primitive standard[23] and enjoy only a limited circulation, but they contain sharp attacks against alleged Jewish[24] or other alien influences including in Poland. These books and journals often spread false information and slander which is prohibited by law and should therefore be prosecuted by the state attorney. I have not heard of this ever happening, however. On the contrary, there are cases where the state attorney when informed about the publications declined to intervene (Tomaszewski 1996: 18; Tomaszewski 1997: 16).

An analysis of the authors (when their identities are not hidden behind pen names) indicates that there are three main groups. One group represents the dinosaurs of the traditional extreme nationalist groups who claim allegiance to the radical national democratic tradition.[25] The second consists of the former PUWP active members or the people who collaborated with the party, notably former (and perhaps even current) members of the 'Civitas Christiana' (the former 'Pax') association, the Democratic Party etc., who rapidly changed their loyalties in the new political situation, declared their opposition to Communists and tried to 'rehabilitate' themselves in the eyes of the people by declaring their ultra-nationalist views.[26] Similar trends were evident in other post-Communist countries. In the third group are young adherents of miscellaneous groups, sometimes simple fighting squads operating under the auspices of a small party or association. They are, as a rule, useful instruments in the hands of activists who make up for a lack of followers with extreme actions of dubious legality.

Influential politicians who enjoy general respect and who pretend not to see or hear the chauvinist allusions or declarations among followers and activists are a much more serious threat. This was the case with the former president Lech Wałęsa. He created a Council which had to express opinions and give advice in matters pertaining to Jews. On an official visit to Jerusalem, Wałęsa apologised for anti-Semitism in Poland. But he also made ambiguous remarks in speeches and interviews, notably during the election campaign. When his friend, Rev. Henryk Jankowski, expressed openly anti-Semitic views in a sermon, Wałęsa 'did not hear' anything and declined to comment. It is true that the local bishop admonished Rev. Jankowski and forbade him from taking part in political activity in the church, but the priest did not change his behaviour for a long time and another admonition was necessary. Another case is that of the contemporary leaders of the alliance called Electoral Movement 'Solidarity' (*Akcja Wyborcza 'Solidarność'*) who avoid openly criticising chauvinist statements made by local leaders. The same tolerant attitude towards chauvinism (including anti-Semitism) is characteristic of other politicians (Olszewski 1997).

A concern for the future is the existence of groups of young people who are attracted by the radical nationalist slogans. Some of them are on the edge of criminality and are used as fighting squads by peripheral groups. More surprising is the participation of individual students in the radical nationalist movement (Podgórska 1997).

It would, however, be a mistake to overestimate the strength of political chauvinism in mainstream politics. It is a feature of the Polish political scene that hardly any people with serious ambitions declare themselves to be nationalists (*nacjonalista*). Politicians dissociate themselves from any chauvinism (at least in words) and argue that they are only defending Polish national interests. In contemporary Poland it is shameful to be an anti-Semite. Serious politicians try to present themselves as people without any ethnic biases or superstitions. For example, some years ago the leader of a small but vociferous political party, who was known for his anti-Semitic *feuilletons* published in a Warsaw weekly in 1968, established a council to deal with minority problems and approached people who were known for their anti-xenophobic views.

To some extent the attitude towards Jews can be considered a kind of litmus paper of the intellectual atmosphere in Poland, including changes in favour of the national minorities (in spite of the often quoted chauvinist declarations of minor politicians in the press). The Ministry of Culture and Art was and is an important source of financial support for the cultural activities of the national minorities in Poland. Thanks to this help, the associations representing the national minorities are able to publish several journals and books in their national and the Polish languages. The Ministry of Education undertook – however reluctantly and under strong pressure from outside – to develop teaching in national languages in primary schools, and to a limited extent provided schools with curricula in these languages.[27]

A significant factor, whose impact will be seen in the future, are projects meant to popularize knowledge of national minorities. These even extend to the curricula of some universities. An institution – the Inter-Departmental Research Centre on Jewish History and Culture (*Międzywydziałowy Zakład Historii i Kultury Żydów w Polsce*) – was established in 1986 at the Jagiellonian University in Cracow. In 1990, the Mordechai Anielewicz Centre for the Study and Teaching of the History and Culture of the Jews in Poland (*Centrum Badania i Nauczania Dziejów i Kultury Żydów w Polsce im. M. Anielewicza*) at Warsaw University was organized with the financial help of a businessman from Tel Aviv, Dr Jack Fliderbaum. The Jewish Historical Institute (*Żydowski Instytut Historyczny*) in Warsaw organized seminars for teachers of history and published literature, and initiatives have also been taken by the Chairs of Ukrainian Language and Belarus Language at Warsaw University. These are only some examples of university initiatives. Independent national institutions have also been established. In Warsaw, there is The Ukrainian Archives (*Archiwum Ukraińskie*), a centre for the study and publication of literature on the history of Ukrainian and Polish languages. In Białystok the Belarus Historical Society (*Białoruskie Towarzystwo Historyczne*) publishes a journal in Polish and books in the Belarus and Polish languages. In Oœwiêcim, at the end of 1996, a Centre for Records and Studies of Romany Culture and History in Poland (*Ośrodek Dokumentacji i Badań Dziejów oraz Kultury Romów w Polsce*) was established.

The most significant progress has been made in the research and teaching of Jewish history and culture. Since 1990, competitions for the best MA and PhD theses about the history and culture of Jews have been organized with the help of the Polish–Israeli Friendship Society (*Towarzystwo Przyjaźni Polsko-Izraelskiej*) and the Jewish associations. Three competitions of this kind have taken place so far and several of the authors who have won have made their mark as professional scholars. The 'Shalom' Foundation and the Jewish Social and Cultural Association (*Towarzystwo Społeczno-Kulturalne Żydów w Polsce*) began to organize similar competitions in 1993 for secondary school students, which has attracted growing interest.

An important and relatively new factor is the changes among the Roman Catholic clergy and the lay Catholic intellectuals. The traditional chauvinist and especially anti-Jewish attitudes are disappearing as the Catholic authorities (including the Pope) condemn ethnic and religious hatred, and promote tolerant attitudes and an ecumenical dialogue. The declarations on the relations between Christianity and Judaism made by John Paul II, the Polish-born Pope, and himself a witness of the Holocaust, have been of crucial significance for Polish–Jewish relations. The Pope's statements inspired changes among the Polish clergy. This made it possible to issue a pastoral letter which was read out in almost all churches on 20 January 1991, which contains not only a condemnation of anti-Semitism, but also the following: 'We express ... earnest regret about all the acts of anti-Semitism which took place at any time and were performed by any person on Polish soil' (*Kościół* 1995: 43–4).

An important contribution to the propagation of these views was made by the Academy of Catholic Theology (*Akademia Teologii Katolickiej*) in Warsaw which has organized conferences and symposia on Christian–Jewish relations and has published books on this issue. In 1994, the Academy established the Institute for Catholic–Judaic Dialogue (*Instytut Dialogu Katolicko-Judaistycznego*). The official standpoint of the Church

authorities presented above has found its way into textbooks and recommendations for religious instruction in schools. The author of a critical
analysis of the current situation concluded:

> It is clear that a lot has been done in the past five years in this field,
> even though today's situation will not satisfy everyone. One wishes
> that more time be spent on the Jewish–Christian question and that it
> receives more attention.
>
> (Królikowski 1993: 32)

It is true that the traditional fundamentalist and chauvinist views have not
vanished immediately. They have, however, lost their credibility and religious sanction. There are even works published by priests with academic
titles which call into question, if indirectly, the views expressed *ex cathedra*
by John Paul II (Poradowski 1993). These are extreme cases. More often
one meets the traditional stereotypes, though less blatant, although there
are some priests and Catholic institutions which distribute anti-Semitic
writing. Be this as it may, the chauvinist and particularly anti-Semitic attitudes now openly contradict the official standpoint of the Catholic Church.

I do not have enough information even to try to sketch the changes
that have taken place inside the Christian churches in other countries.
According to some sources, the Primate of the Czech Republic, archbishop
Miloslav Vlk (himself an historian), is acting in accordance with the guidelines of John Paul II. At the same time, however, a textbook was published
in Prague about the history of the Catholic Church – with the approval
of the relevant state authorities – which included the blood libel (Mráček
1995: 90).[28] An indirect confirmation, perhaps, that the Czech Catholic
Church is no less divided than the Polish.

A legacy of the Communist system

The opinion that xenophobia previously suppressed by Communism was
released by the shift towards democracy in Poland and other eastern and
central European countries cannot be maintained. In reality, the Communist system – contrary to Communist ideology – encouraged chauvinism
in selected areas of political life and exploited it as a convenient political
weapon. There was in addition the official propaganda of the so-called
proletarian internationalism. The result was a mixture of dogmatic Communism and radical chauvinism expressed by marginal political groups.
These attitudes coexisted alongside the diminishing influence of traditional
chauvinist views among the anti-Communist opposition but sometimes also
alongside centuries-old superstitions.

On the other hand, there was and is a much more influential trend
towards better understanding of the national and religious minorities. The
attitudes prevailing in Polish society were probably based on traditional

views, comprised of various superstitions, old stereotypes and suspicion of 'aliens', i.e. the national minorities. Opinion polls indicate that these attitudes are now slowly changing and that popular views are becoming more welcomng towards national minorities (except for Romanies). But there are significant exceptions when local conflicts are coloured by ethnic or religious differences.

It would be more correct therefore to say that in Poland – and other countries of central and eastern Europe – there was in the past a period of hypocritical internationalist ideology mixed with xenophobia which was often exploited in political intrigues, alongside official opposition to chauvinism, when it was considered as presenting a danger for the ruling party. More often than not this policy helped to maintain old stereotypes and superstitions in the general consciousness, making reasoned debate on the subject impossible. We have now entered a new period in which open discussion of the many and contradictory views on minorities, traditions, ethnic and national interests and interethnic relations is possible. The task of scholars, teachers and the media is to promote understanding of the history and culture of the minorities involved.

Notes

1 The English term 'nationalism' comprises several notions which are expressed in Polish (and in some other languages) with different words. The Polish term *nacjonalizm* should be translated into English as 'chauvinism' or 'radical nationalism'. At the same time, it would be risky to translate English 'nationalism' as Polish *nacjonalizm* or Czech *nacionalismus* without taking into consideration all the circumstances in which the term was applied.

2 An interesting, however biased, source is a collection of Bulgarian contradictory statements (Чашуле 1970).

3 Cf. Kobylińska *et al.* (1992) on the tradition of Polish–German relations.

4 The polemical views are presented in a collection of essays (Černy *et al.* 1990).

5 The recollections of people who managed to resist this pressure were published in 1996–7 in the monthly *Čzasopis*.

6 The expulsion is well documented in a contemporary edition prepared by the young Ukrainian historians, *Polish citizens* (Misiło 1996).

7 There was even one authentic Zionist leader among the high-ranking officials, Emil Sommerstein, prior to 1946 the head of the War Reparations Office, who was, however, deprived of any real political influence. He emigrated to the USA.

8 The author quotes *in extenso* documents which do not necessarily confirm his opinions exonerating the primate. Cf. Scharf (1996: 81, 252).

9 This was repeated in the summer of 1981 by Albin Siwak, a worker and member of the Political Bureau of the Central Committee of the PUWP from 1981–6, whose political declarations were most often written by the people who preferred to remain unknown.

10 The Polish language does not contain the exact equivalent of this term and the Polish press could have avoided absurd terminology and used the more appropriate word 'unification' (*zjednoczenie*) instead.

11 Many years later a distinguished Bulgarian historian (and Communist politician) remarked in a private conversation that the Communists achieved an almost impossible feat: a general dislike of Russians among the Bulgarians.

12 This ironic term – *obnovení poøádk* – was used in 1979 by the Czech scholar Milan Šimeèka who described the situation in his country after 1968.

13 I had personal experience of this surveillance. A security officer wanted to know if I was of Belarus origin after I had published an article on Belarus history. He probably wanted to check the register of Belarus activists.

14 For an example, see Tomaszewski (1992).

15 An important source are memoirs and documents: Дзюбина (1995).

16 This is the explanation offered by Rev. S. Dziubyna (Дзюбина). See: Dziubina (1997).

17 The word 'revisionism' in the political language of that time denoted a deviation from 'the only right ideology' towards liberal and democratic interpretations of Marxism. It may be interesting to note that in 1938 the followers of a totalitarian trend in the Polish ruling camp considered that the Jews were a destructive factor in the Polish Republic because they leaned towards a democratic system of government. (The relevant document was printed in *Teki Archiwalne*, new series, vol. 1 (23), Warsaw 1996).

18 The document was published by Raina (1994: 270–2). His comments on page 268, however, distort the meaning of the document. For an attempt at a scholarly analysis, see Eisler (1991: 325–8).

19 An example of this was the fate of Prof. Józef Hurwic, the distinguished specialist in chemistry and Dean of the Department of Chemistry of the Warsaw Technical Institute, who was deprived of his posts, and – under heavy pressure – decided to emigrate. Cf. Hurwic (1996: 129–45).

20 Among the distinguished economists who were deprived of the right to teach students were Prof. Michał Kalecki, Professor of the Central School of Planning and Statistics (Szkola Główna Planowania i Statystyki, now Szko3a G3ówna Handlowa) who enjoyed an international reputation. The Rector of this school at that time was Prof. Wieslaw Sadowski.

21 'Przeglad Humanistyczny' which published the article fell in disrepute in 1968. Later a kind of political appreciation was published, more balanced and deprived of the anti-Semitic bias: Stasiak 1975.

22 The Rector of the Jagiellonian University, Prof. Józef Gierowski, who paid a visit in January 1988 to the Hebrew University in Jerusalem, was authorised by one politician to inform his hosts that such a declaration was pending.

23 There was even a book published in which the author whom the editor claimed was an 'an outstanding Polish philosopher of history' declared his conviction that the infamous blood libel was a proven fact (Koneczny 1995: 341).

24 E.g. 'Ojczyzna','Najjasniejszej Rzeczypospolitej', 'Szczerbiec'. Cf. Grabowska (1996). The author quotes strange books and journals, and indicates that the Catholic institutions are engaged in the distribution of these prints.

25 Staszewski (1996) quotes views of this kind, including a unique and absurd case that denied the existence of the Holocaust.

26 This was the case with the daily 'Slowo – Dziennik Katolicki' (formerly 'Slowo Powszechne') which lost many readers. In April 1997, the daily changed owner and chief editor, but this did not help and it closed. Its successor is another daily 'Nasz Dziennik' which openly resuscitated a radical nationalist message. The daily, which often stresses its fidelity to the Catholic faith, did not publish the famous Vatican document on the Holocaust of March 16, 1998, but only printed a short notice.

27 Not all the ministers of education have been engaged in these initiatives. Most of the credit goes to professors Henryk Samsonowicz, his deputies: Anna Radziwill and Andrzej Janowski, and to Jerzy Wiatr.

28 This book aroused the indignation of many people, cf. 'Lidové noviny' 24 and 30 III 1995;'Respekt' 10 IV 1995; 'Pecko. Víkendová príloha Práce' 29 IV 1995.

5 Nationalism, internationalism and property in the post-Cold War era*

Katherine Verdery

The fall of Communist Party states in Eastern Europe and the former Soviet Union during 1989–91 – signaling, in popular parlance, the end of the Cold War – is part of a broader change in world political and economic processes. A sign of the change is that 'nationalist' and 'internationalist' political positions and rhetoric have come to be combined in unexpected ways. Alongside this have arisen other kinds of communitarian activity, among them an increased public presence for fundamentalist religious groupings worldwide, and considerable debate in several European and North American countries around the pluralizing notions of diversity and multiculturalism.

In this chapter I explore the relations among internationalist and nationalist political positions in post-Cold War Romania. I attempt to tie them to one of the most significant transformations of post-Communism: the reorganization of property relations. I argue that the idioms of nationalism and internationalism are anchored in struggles over forms of property and in competing strategies for surviving the transitional period of the 1990s. I begin by reflecting on the title of our volume.

What does the post-Cold War era mean?

To begin, I offer a highly schematic overview of what I think the end of the Cold War 'means', and I briefly link this with the property theme to be discussed more fully below. I start with the assumption that over the past two decades, there have been fundamental changes in the global economy, as capitalist firms have adopted new practices in order to recover from the recession that began in the early 1970s. I will not enter into the alternative explanations for this change (see, e.g., Harvey 1989; Offe 1985) nor discuss the emergent forms themselves in any detail. Rather, I emphasize how the changing global economy relates to the collapse of the Soviet empire.

As I have suggested elsewhere (Verdery 1996: 30–7), among the strategies by which Western firms and banks coped with the recession of the 1970s was to export capital and credits, enabling recipient countries to 'modernize' by purchasing Western technology.[1] Countries of the Soviet bloc were especially attractive customers for this policy, since Western lenders saw them as more likely to repay loans than were other, Third World economies (Bunce 1985: 35–6). At the same time, these countries were eager to borrow, for Communist Party leaders had realized that structural reform of their systems would undermine the Party's monopoly on power; instead, they saw it as preferable to try to solve their economic difficulties by borrowing from abroad to modernize production (cf. Bunce 1985: 34–44).

This proved, however, a fatal calculation. From the early days of the blockade of the Soviet Union, reinforced by the lowering of the 'Iron Curtain', the Communist bloc had survived in a larger capitalist world by creating a tight boundary around itself. This boundary, evident throughout the Cold War, clearly distinguished 'inside' from 'outside' and retarded any processes (trade, flows of labor and communication, etc.) that might cut across it. The decision to increase borrowing from Western countries, however – the substance of the 'thaw' we know as *détente* – made a serious breach in the system's boundary. From this point on, it would prove increasingly difficult to delimit 'inside' from 'outside'. *Apparatchiks* involved in the trade interface with Western corporations, for instance, found they could no longer treat foreign trade as simply an external site to be plundered (cf. Staniszkis 1991), and leaders could no longer give one speech for foreign consumption and another for a domestic audience, expecting the compartmentalization to hold. Through debt relations, Western lenders gained unprecedented leverage over internal politics, as was evident from the Polish crisis in 1980.

What began as a relationship of mutual convenience in the 1970s ended in the collapse of socialist societies in 1989–91; they proved unable to cope with the breach in their boundary under changed global conditions (see Verdery 1996: 33–4). Three aspects of the new global order are relevant to explaining the end of the Cold War: (1) the rise of 'flexible specialization'; (2) a large-scale process of 'enclosing the commons'; and (3) an altered and diminished role for states. First, the rise of flexible specialization brought production and distribution techniques that put the socialist political economies at an even greater disadvantage in international trade than they had already had in competing with the products of the West's 'Fordist' mass production (ibid.). That is, the new techniques (such as just-in-time inventory, small batch production, increased attention to consumption and the refinement of niche marketing, extensive use of computers to reorganize production spatially, and coordination of the economy by finance capital) ran directly counter to the production methods of socialist firms (hoarding of materials, mass production, an emphasis on producer over consumer goods and a general neglect of consumption, low computerization, and the attempt to exclude external finance capital). The discrepancies between socialist production and flexible specialization made the former largely uncompetitive in world markets; this impeded the plans of socialist countries to pay off their international debts with export earnings. The result was an internal crisis in the centrally planned economies, integral to their collapse in 1989.

A second characteristic of the emerging global economy is what some lawyers refer to as a worldwide process of 'enclosing the commons'.[2] Numerous sites that used to be seen as repositories of collective goods and values are now up for 'privatization', in a variety of forms. These include, most obviously, state-funded enterprises being made into private companies (as in Britain, France, and the US, in addition to formerly socialist countries), along with increased struggles over property rights. The struggles occur in domains as varied as surrogate-parent arrangements, biotechnological exploitation of body parts, patenting of crop varieties, disputes about intellectual property and copyright, and claims concerning 'ownership' of cultural property or the physical remains of dead ancestors. In all these, ownership claims are being lodged concerning things that were not seen as subject to such claims before. I believe this kind of 'enclosure' is the appropriate context in which to understand the insistence of international financial agents (such as the IMF and World Bank) upon privatizing property in the formerly socialist bloc. (Their insistence was joined, of course, with pressures toward privatization internal to each country as well.) Thus, the end of the Cold War meant unfencing the once-protected collective property of the socialist period and exposing it to exclusive individual ownership claims.

Privatization is intimately tied with a third major process in the contemporary world: the 'downsizing' and reconfigured role of states. Welfare states everywhere are being cut back, and activities once sustained from the public purse are being turned over to 'the private sector'. One might see this process as the consequence of the rise of finance capital to a dominant role in economic coordination (Harvey 1989), and financial agents' concomitant unwillingness to see large fiscal resources lying locked up in state welfare and bureaucratic management (instead of passing through private circuits more likely to generate profit). For both firms and states in the post-Cold War era of flexible accumulation, 'lean and mean' is the watchword. This poses special problems for the states of socialism, which were among the fattest and most protective states in the world and therefore become candidates for transformation. International pressure to privatize socialist economies[3] is central to that process, since it was through managing state property that Communist Parties secured the revenues to support their welfare expenditures and their bureaucracies. Dismantling state property thus deprives former party-states of revenues usable for public purposes and pushes their political economies more fully into line with the lean-mean standards being set elsewhere.

With this brief summary, I emphasize that the 'post-Cold War era' of our title – as well as the 'nationalism and internationalism' with which we are to link it, as I will show – reflects global economic changes and the politics those entail. The 'internationalism' of European integration, NATO expansion, and the 'common European home' is as much a path to facilitating capital flows as it is a program or doctrine (perhaps the more common understanding of internationalism, as discussed in the volume's Introduction). In my view, it is impossible to understand contemporary nationalism and internationalism without bearing this in mind. For the former Soviet bloc, the end of the Cold War is part of an era in which the entire inventory of socialist state property has become vulnerable to takeover, the world's last remaining institutionalized labor movements are being swept away, and a massive apparatus of bureaucrats skilled at living off the state is being forced to fend at least partly for itself. Do these post-1989 realities have anything to do with nationalism and internationalism, and with whether those are weakening or growing stronger?

Nationalism and internationalism: some Romanian examples

In order to think further about this question, I should clarify how I understand the terms nationalism and internationalism; as our editors' Introduction shows, the terms have many definitions. Rather than seeing them as doctrines, I treat them as idioms utilized in political struggles. The struggles often, in the contemporary world of postsocialism, concern what relation national leaders should establish with larger capital flows. 'Nationalism', in this view, names a political idiom that defends localized strategies toward national prospering; it gives the 'nation' pride of place and is suspicious of initiatives from abroad, which it often sees as purposely undermining the nation's interests. 'Internationalism', on the other hand, labels an idiom that also celebrates national values but sees the condition of the nation's prosperity to be its wider linkages (for instance, a 'return to Europe' will best enable the nation to flourish).

In this light, it makes less sense to ask whether 'nationalism is growing' than whether – and why – the political appeals that invoke the national idiom seem more prevalent or more successful than before, and how they connect with internationalist idioms. To identify the idioms employed may not be the end of the line, analytically speaking, for they may refer to other, unnamed processes as well, which it is our task to discern. The following example using events in Romanian politics of the 1990s will clarify my meaning.

In the wake of the Romanian 'revolution' (which most Romanians now call the 'events') of December 1989, the government passed into the control not of a dissident opposition, as in the Czech Republic, Hungary, and Poland, but of second-tier Party *apparatchiks*, who gradually pushed aside the dissidents with whom they had at first seized power. Former Communist bureaucrat Ion Iliescu became president of a party presently (2000) named the Party of Romanian Social Democracy (I will refer to them as the Socialist Democrats).[4] It soon became clear that this party's policies owed much to those of its Communist predecessor, and that this was not necessarily a drawback: the continued popularity of socialist welfare measures (howsoever diminished) brought Iliescu's party a second electoral victory, in 1992. Its main opponent was an oppositional umbrella grouping, the Democratic Convention (the 'Convention'), which had no unified policy orientation but tended toward neo-liberalism.

Although Iliescu's government talked much about reform, it accomplished relatively little of that; particularly in the area of privatizing state companies, it made almost no progress at all. An apparently puzzling feature of this regime was its close alliance with not only other socialist parties but also several Romanian nationalist groups; this gave Iliescu's government a decidedly populist and nationalist tone that one might think peculiar for remnant socialists. As against the Democratic Convention, which entered the 1992 electoral campaign with the slogan of a 'return to Europe', the Socialist Democrats' chief campaign promise was a nationalist 'we won't sell our country to the foreigners'. One might easily see here a contest between 'internationalist' and 'nationalist' political platforms, the latter claiming to serve both economic and political independence while accusing the former of subservience to foreigners.

I prefer a different interpretation. 'Nationalism' was the stance of all those politicians who wanted to protect a form of autarkic national economy in which numerous *apparatchiks* would continue for as long as possible to do what they were already skilled at: make their living by milking the state and retaining a centralized economy to facilitate this, while excluding foreign competitors from the game. (In one celebrated scandal, the Intercontinental Hotel was 'privatized' by selling it to two Romanian businessmen who had bid only *half* the amount offered by the foreign Marriott Hotel chain.) The 'internationalism' of the Socialist Democrats' political opponents, by contrast, sought to define the 'national interest' internationally, through integrating Romania into European economic and military structures. This policy would have the effect of undermining their socialist-democrat competitors, by bringing in 'foreign capital' to dismantle the socialist welfare state and centrally planned economy on which the former socialist *apparatchiks* lived. In other words, the initial political dominance of the former Communist Party apparatus, which used a nationalist rhetoric, compelled the Democratic Convention into using an internationalist one, while pursuing a policy of international alliances that would undercut their opponents.

Both the Convention and the socialist-democrat leaders, then, aimed to gain and consolidate power. The kinds of temporary alliances they were prepared to strike, and the language in which they cloaked their ambitions, *looked* more different ('nationalist' vs. 'internationalist') than I believe they were. Each represented a group strategy for political dominance, not a doctrine or a program.

This interpretation seems to be borne out by the fortunes of the two political groupings on the eve of the November 1996 elections. As the Convention rose in opinion polls and the Socialist Democrats declined, amid a profusion of corruption scandals, nearly all their political allies jumped the socialist-democrat ship to sign on with their erstwhile political enemies in the Convention. The victorious Convention government proceeded with haste to cement its international connections by implementing World Bank- and IMF-promoted privatization programs, whose effects would include seriously diminishing the power of the state. Those programs would thus destroy the principal job base once monopolized by socialist-democrat *apparatchiks* and prevent their return as such. Meanwhile, the contacts of Convention members with international organizations before 1996 gave them an edge in newly emerging forms of livelihood, as employees of and participants in the world of 'projects' that foreign assistance entails (see Sampson 1996). The new jobs included staffing numerous NGOs, serving as consultants for World Bank projects, becoming intermediaries for foreign firms, and so on. These jobs demand skills of language and self-presentation that older Party *apparatchiks* tended to lack but that the 'internationalist' opposition had made a point of acquiring.[5]

During 1997, the Convention government launched an intensive campaign for first-round entry into NATO. Although this may seem an unequivocally internationalist policy, it had as well the decidedly nationalist aim of securing NATO protection against future Russian expansionism. To achieve NATO entry the Convention government took enormous political risks, conceding to a number of demands by Romania's Hungarian minority in order to obtain a treaty with Hungary and also signing a treaty with Ukraine that soft-pedaled Romanian claims to some territory in that country. Both policies (required for NATO entry) brought loud criticism from the socialist-democrat nationalists. Convention leaders were probably gambling that if the campaign for membership were successful, it would give them sufficient political capital to weather both their opponents' accusations of treachery and also the effects of the austerity policies the Convention had also instituted. The gamble failed, and the Convention shortly thereafter disintegrated into several squabbling factions.

Significantly, the campaign for NATO membership was framed as a matter of *patriotism*. During the winter of 1997, for example, electronic mail signed by Convention President Emil Constantinescu urged Romanians abroad – especially those in the US – to exert pressure on their home governments in Romania's favor, as their patriotic duty. The request even asked that all such patriots send copies of their interventions to President Constantinescu.[6] We see from this that the Convention was not arguing for internationalism *as opposed to* nationalism but rather for the international *as the condition of* national prospering. One might make the same point from the opposite direction by showing how the nationalistic Socialist Democrats could use a language of internationalism to preserve their control of public resources. In a conversation with the socialist-democrat functionary who had drafted the legislation for returning land to its former owners, I learned that he had written the law according to 'European standards', specifically those of France. The period in French history that he took as his model, however, was the 1950s, and the functionary said nothing about either the notable *étatisme* of French policy at the time or the fact that one-fifth of Romania's arable land was to remain state property, managed by former *apparatchiks*.[7]

I am arguing, then, that in post-Cold War Romania, 'nationalism' and 'internationalism' are not opposing doctrines exclusively attached to different parties. Both serve rather as idioms, employed in fields of power by competing elites to marshall allies in various internal and external arenas. There is nothing specifically post-Cold War about this behavior: it has been central to Romanian politics for hundreds of years (see Verdery 1991: Chapter 1). What *is* specific to this period, however, is the way in which the competing parties and their rhetorics are connected with property and with post-Cold War privatization.

Romanians strategize into the post-Communist era

The collapse of Communist Party rule ushered in new political processes, of which the most often cited are democratization, privatization, and the creation of markets. Although these proceeded somewhat more fitfully in Romania than in other Eastern European countries, it was clear to the old/new political elite that the previous system and their position in it could no longer be reproduced by the old mechanisms. The ensuing period was one in which different groups strategized different adaptations to a new and constantly changing situation. Central elements of this situation were shifting definitions of what counted as 'capital' and 'property'. For the Iliescu faction of the former Communist Party, their prior position had rested on the exercise of skills in managing a certain type of property – socialist property – and on the accumulation of political rather than monetary capital. Their strategy now was (1) to preserve a large component of socialist property, formulating privatization policies so complex that exclusive individual ownership would emerge but slowly and using their access to state property as a cushion; and (2) to move toward mixed property forms – what David Stark (1996) calls 'recombinant property': combinations of collective and private property rights.

While many of them became rich in this way, they were able to do so initially by using their *political* positions – to acquire kickbacks and inside access to the wealth of both old and new firms, for example. Not all in the former Communist Party leadership followed the same path. Since the members of that Party and their networks of connections had mostly survived the revolution, however, they could always resort to strategies resting on their control of political capital.[8] This kind of strategy tended to accord with tactical use of a nationalist rhetoric, for the reason given above: as long as the state and ownership structures of the Communist period were not substantially modified by 'foreign' influence and programs of privatization, political capital and exploiting public resources would remain viable paths to a prosperous future for individuals with access to them. Placing stringent constraints on the movement of outside capital into the Romanian economy would also allow time for emerging 'entre-pratchiks' to learn the ropes in a milieu favorable to their success.

Members of the former dissident opposition rarely had that kind of political capital at hand to maintain or improve their social status, but they might use their control over capital of a different sort – moral capital, based on their opposition to the Communists and necessarily politicized by Western attention to them (Verdery 1996: Chapter 5). As representatives of Romania's conscience and bearers of its 'universal' intellectual values, these people were especially likely to become involved in Western-based NGOs and local 'civil-society' organizations (minorities' councils, grassroots political organizations, ecology movements, feminist groups, rural development initiatives, and so on). This sort of activity did not require access to a specific form of property or political position; it was most common among those who effectively had nothing but intellectual or moral capital assets. Persons who followed this route could do so from either nationalist or internationalist positions, addressing different alliances and constituencies. For instance, a writer could claim eminence as a defender of specifically national values, or as one who integrates those values into international circuits. The Soros Foundation has been a prime employer of people who prefer the internationalist route to fructifying their special form of capital.

Still other ways of strategizing oneself into the new order required having or gaining access to private property: obtaining land and implements to go into commercial farming for oneself; using one's car as a taxi to build up a private taxi company; setting up sidewalk kiosks (thus privatizing public space) to sell goods bought in Turkey or Greece and then expanding into larger-scale trading; using one's personal apartment to set up sewing machines for a line of unusual 'designer' clothes; opening a consulting firm to collaborate with US scholarly research projects, etc. People who followed this path generally had little political capital to exploit and thus employed their skills as agronomists, chauffeurs, petty traders, seamstresses, or sociologists in order to accumulate wealth, which they could keep because of new legal protections for private ownership. Again, such persons might avail themselves of both/either nationalist and/or internationalist rhetorics and alliances, but their success depended on modifying the socialist property regime.

From these examples we can see that expanded private ownership enfranchised some new actors in the political economy while posing something of a threat to others. The latter tended to take more 'nationalist' political positions, at least some of the former taking more 'internationalist' ones. The rhetorics thus had to do with pursuing upward mobility or retaining one's hold on privilege. They acquired efficacy, however, as mediated by property relations of different kinds: state, recombinant, private. Actors involved in these strategies might appear to be individuals, but I think they are more often collectivities: political parties; various kinds of corporations (limited liability companies perhaps consisting of only one or two people, large joint-stock companies, etc.); networks and cliques including those I have elsewhere called 'unruly coalitions' (Verdery 1996: 193–202), which might be shadows of the previous Communist Party organization; ongoing forms of state property (state farms, public utilities, state-run firms) with their managing directors. To the extent that these collectivities attain clear, formalized 'identities', it is in part through establishing property relations through which they come to be defined as actors *qua* owners.[9]

To carry this discussion forward, I will define what I mean by property and how I see its relationship to 'identity'. My way of doing so distinguishes my approach substantially from those for whom 'national identities' are an unproblematic aspect of 'nationalism'. This discussion will enable me to nuance my earlier view of nationalism and internationalism as political idioms.

Property and identity

Property has many definitions. It has been treated as a relation to 'things', as a relation *between persons* with respect to things, and as abstract bundles of rights and powers. In a fascinating paper, Thomas Grey (1980) points out that each such definition reflects the organization of different social systems. In feudal societies property was indeed a function of relations among persons and the rights and obligations attached to them – true also of the property relations many anthropologists find in pre-capitalist economies (see, e.g., Gluckman 1965; Malinowski 1935). With the emergence of bourgeois societies the emphasis went to property as rights in 'things', drawing attention away from the social relations implicated with them. In late twentieth-century capitalism, the emphasis has come to be placed more on the rights than on the things, as non-thing-like abstractions (intellectual property, trademarks, techniques, futures, junk bonds) become ever more important sources of income. These different meanings and operations of property can of course coexist in a single time – copyright was a major subject of property dispute, for example, in early bourgeois societies (see, e.g., Hesse 1991).

Given how each definition of property – as relations, things, and bundles of rights – refers to property at a specific time and place, I prefer to use a more general one.[10] I see 'property' as a label for ways of organizing access to social values among recognized social actors. This process simultaneously defines (1) the values (profits, power, fame, clients, sanctity, etc.) and the resources for realizing them (land, financial wealth, political capital, feasting, exchange practices, sacred knowledge);[11] (2) the social actors whose access is organized; and (3) the means through which access is regulated (rights to land, relations of obligation, exchange relations producing renown, recognition of charisma, etc.). Access may be organized through a notion of 'rights', through powers not necessarily seen as rightful, or through other means. Establishing access to values, i.e., a property regime, is tied up with questions we might call moral – questions as to what is right, or proper (such as 'rights' to 'property'[12]). A property regime entails determining *who* (what kind of actor) *should* have what kind of access (through what sorts of relations) to what sets of values and how these 'shoulds' are to be enforced.

Because access can be organized only *for someone*, property regimes necessarily define the kind(s) of social actor that *count* as 'someone': individual human beings, clans or other kinship groupings, corporations, the Communist Party, the 'people-as-one', nations, and so on. To organize access for the various kinds of recognized actors means to establish among them various relations (of debt, exchange, obligation, contract, accountability) and practices (with respect to use, exclusion of others, enjoyment, and alienation). The unitary identity of social actors is produced in part through their being posited as occupying a unitary relation or set of relations to the value(s) in question.[13] That is, a 'clan' *becomes* a real entity in part because all clanspeople are thought to be identically related to some value – a sacred spot, a clan territory, secret knowledge. Part of any given property regime, then, is a set of recognized social actors with distinctive 'identities'; what kinds of actors these are will vary from case to case. In one case, actors known as *households*, *lineages*, *aristocrats*, and *the king* may be the actors most fully recognized in organizing access to values, while in another case recognition goes to *individuals*, *corporations*, and *the state*.

'Property' as I have defined it thus entails privileging certain kinds of relations, and certain kinds of social actors, over others. To analyse a property regime is to specify the kinds that are privileged and the means of privileging them. It is also to look for alternative definitions of value and to ask how one of these comes to dominate the others (become hegemonic), even if not completely, and how it comes to be challenged by alternative values and organizations of access. That is the process now occurring in the formerly socialist world, and I believe the angle of vision it promotes can help us think more deeply about nationalism and internationalism in the post-Cold War era, from the East European perspective. In the following section I outline the property regime of socialist systems, employing the terms I have set out here. I limit myself to the legal, i.e., official, property organization.

Socialist property and its restructuring

Among the central values to which socialism's property regime organized access were production for production's sake (as opposed to, say, production for profit), accumulations of political power (as opposed to, say, of monied wealth), promoting social welfare (as opposed to, say, ideas about individual accountability), and rational bureaucratic management (as opposed to, say, individual initiative). Socialism privileged certain kinds of relations (vertical redistribution over horizontal market exchange, clientelism and patronage over contractual obligation, competition among bureaucratic segments rather than among enterprises). Additionally, it privileged certain kinds of social actors: 'persons', small-scale collectivities ('cooperatives', contracting units, usually households, within these), and also larger ones within the national society ('the Party', 'the state', 'the people-as-one') and supranational ones as well ('international socialism'). Some of these actors were explicitly linked to the four kinds of property recognized in socialist law: social (or state), cooperative, private, and personal property (see Kornai 1992). It protected the former pair more extensively than the latter. I will illustrate how some of these social actors (persons, cooperatives, the state, the Party, and the people-as-one) were constituted specifically through property relations.

'Persons' or individuals were recognized as actors through holding a full bundle of property rights (use, exclusion of others, enjoyment, and alienation), but only with respect to a very small set of material objects known as 'personal property'. This included cars, clothing, houses (for those who did not live in state housing), furniture, and other personal effects (pictures, books, dishes, and so on).[14] The 'person' was the point at which these two sets of rights and objects intersected. A second kind of actor, 'cooperatives', became so by their members' unitary relation to property of a different kind: the pooled resources – land, implements, labor, knowledge – of all persons who had contributed these values to that specific collective's operation.[15] A person who had not contributed to any of these values was not part of that cooperative (though she/he might be part of other cooperatives). People's remuneration for work in a cooperative was a function solely of their labor, not of what they had initially donated to it. Through their leaders, cooperatives had rights of management and use with respect to all cooperative property. Their rights of enjoyment were constrained, however, by state claims to part of their product; state demands (technically 'illegal') relating to the Five-Year Plan infringed upon cooperatives' rights to exclusive managerial control, and they enjoyed only partial rights of alienation.

Cooperative property was not to be confused with the social (or state) property that constituted larger social actors. Among these were the 'state', defined by its full bundle of ownership rights – including alienation – over all means of production not managed in cooperatives (though socialist states tended *de facto* to usurp control rights over those as well). It exercised these rights as the executive organ of the 'people-as-one', the entire society, defined by its collective title to the entire national 'patrimony' (the full set of values) created by all the society's working people (e.g., all Romanians, all Hungarians, all 'Yugoslavs'). The 'Party' as a unitary entity was constituted by its *managerial* rights over social property. These three entities (state, 'people-as-one', and Party) were all constituted with reference to social property, then, but through different and overlapping relations to it.[16]

This outlines the property regime being assaulted by current programs of privatization. Let us place against it the alternative envisioned by external actors such as Western economists, the IMF, and Western banks. That alternative dismantles the cooperative entities in favor of 'corporations' and 'individuals'. It deconstitutes the state and Party as owners and managers of 'social property' by disaggregating and allocating that property to corporate or individual owners. The state is reconstituted in a lesser role, as guarantor of the property rights now lodged with lower-level social actors. By seeking to remove the restrictions on foreign access to the once-collective values of socialism, the alternative further attenuates the entity 'the people-as-one', loosing 'aliens' into its midst. The new property regime will privilege values of efficiency and the accumulation of profits over those of equity and accumulating means of production. It will emphasize principles of liability and strong accountability, locating these among lower-level social actors (individuals, firms), in place of the emphasis on assets and weak accountability characteristic of, and located in, the party-state as manager of social property. The relations most important to it will be legally enforceable contractual relations among clearly bounded social actors – persons, corporations – focusing on debt, rights to revenue, and horizontal exchange in place of the relations privileged under socialism (such as vertical redistribution, clientelism, and an emphasis on credits over debts).

In brief, the privatizing and commons-enclosing aspect of the post-Cold War era entails a radical restructuring as to which social values will become central, which kinds of social actors will be recognized as deserving access to them, and which kinds of relations will be privileged in organizing that access. What does all this have to do with nationalism and internationalism? It is precisely in terms of nationalism and internationalism that many of these issues are being fought out.

I have argued above that property regimes, in organizing access to values, help to create certain kinds of social actors as real, effecting their unity by according them access to values in a unitary way and thereby shaping their identities. If this is so, then crucial to the fate of identities is the regime of circulation thought appropriate for the values that focus the identities in question – clan identities, corporate ones, national ones, etc. Should values be thrown into circulation or will that compromise the identities they help to ground? Annette Weiner, in her provocative book *Inalienable Possessions* (1992), addresses precisely this issue. Examining exchange systems in the Pacific, she observes that much of the extravagant giving of objects – such as the kula valuables made famous by Malinowski or the native American potlatch of the Pacific Northwest – must be seen against the objects that are *never* given away and that are viewed as icons of the group's identity. When is circulation of values permissible, she asks; which values may circulate and which may not, reaffirming the group's identity (reaffirming its very existence) precisely by being kept out of circulation? One might broaden the question: how are some kinds of social actors constituted by putting objects *into* circulation while others are constituted by keeping objects inalienable? Thus, one might say that individual Trobriand participants in the kula are rendered social actors by putting valuables *into* circulation, thus collecting renown, while Trobriand kinship (lineage, clan) groupings are constituted by their chiefs' *withholding* from circulation the most valuable of the kula objects, for as long as possible.

With this in mind, we may take nationalism and internationalism as labels for alternative political positions on the questions of which social actors should be recognized and how the values that 'identify' them should circulate. The positions form not a binary pair but points on a continuum; let us arbitrarily label two points toward the continuum's two ends 'nationalism' and 'internationalism' and associate these with the two political groupings I described above, Romania's Socialist Democrats and Democratic Convention. One dimension on which they differ markedly is on how extended will be the circuits along which 'Romanian values' should travel, and what values should be permitted to travel them. I will discuss this for the following values: agricultural land, non-agricultural assets, and the boundaries around the nation's territory (its 'property').

Although the Socialist Democrats' rhetoric while they were in office frequently conformed to the rhetoric of international actors, their political practice consistently sought to restrict circulation of values, confining circulation not merely to the national borders but (under cover of this) to smaller groupings of former *apparatchiks*. In 1991, the socialist-democrat-dominated parliament passed a land law that permitted recreating individual private property in land, but the manner of implementing the law clearly aimed to reconstitute and to empower collective actors in agriculture at the expense of individual ones, and to preserve dispersion of rights rather than their bundling (cf. Heller 1998). World Bank and USAID personnel found their attempts to assist with land restitution impeded at every turn.[17] The socialist-democrat government strove to keep state farms from being privatized at all.

As for non-agricultural state firms, the Socialist Democrats made their privatization even more difficult, leading many foreigners and local would-be businessmen to renounce plans for creating new forms of enterprise.

The government placed strict limits on foreign participation in joint stock companies; anecdotal evidence suggests that networks of socialist-democrat *entrepratchiks* strove to prevent 'outsiders' (i.e., *other* Romanian citizens) from gaining a toehold in the process of transforming state assets, thereby monopolizing future possibilities for themselves and their cronies. In foreign policy, the Iliescu government was noteworthy for its tendency to expand the national space by (1) refusing to negotiate over territory disputed with Ukraine; (2) supporting the idea of reunification with Romanian nationalists in the neighboring Republic of Moldova ('Bessarabia');[18] and (3) resisting Hungary's support of the Hungarian minority in Transylvania. Thus, the Socialist Democrats' 'nationalism' consisted of invoking 'national values' in the process of their own consolidation as a new class, while placing friction against the circulation of any values they deemed important for their enrichment.

With its victory in November 1996, by contrast, the new Democratic Convention government took immediate steps to release agricultural land from the restraints the Socialist Democrats had placed on its circulation. The Convention-dominated parliament moved to privatize state farms by breaking them up and returning the land to its original owners (something the Socialist Democrats had resisted doing). Moreover, the Convention legalized land sales to foreigners and permitted people living abroad to claim return of their property (both prohibited by the Socialist Democrats). It loosened regulations for foreigners wanting to participate in other aspects of the Romanian economy and launched a campaign to privatize state companies whose break-up the Socialist Democrats had hindered. In other words, it began releasing the circulation of Romanian values into supranational circuits, and in its treatment of Romanian 'properties' it privileged the identities of individual and corporate owners rather than of 'the nation' or 'the state'. It proved much more willing than the Socialist Democrats to compromise on how large and how firmly bounded the national territory should be (through border-fixing treaties with Ukraine and Hungary). Whereas the Socialist Democrats had put most of their energy into obstructing the circulation of values, defining these as 'Romanian' even while struggling to monopolize them within unruly coalitions of *entrepratchiks*, the Convention gave itself over to promoting circulation, in hopes of enhancing the nation's prosperity, as well as their own, and reducing that of their opponents.

Thus, the relation among nationalism, internationalism, and property in post-Cold War Romanian politics of the 1990s looked something like this: an idiom of 'nationalism' was connected with large frogs surviving and growing fat in small and stagnant ponds where 'Romanian property values' were immobile; an idiom of 'internationalism', by contrast, was tied with tiny frogs struggling to survive and grow as 'Romanian property values' are swept along in huge global streams. It would be misleading, however, to see these as enduring programs tied to specific political groups.

Not long before their election, some in the Convention had been promoting a nationalist plan for uniting Romania with Bessarabia and expelling from their alliance the political party of Romania's Hungarians. The nationalist and internationalist idioms were situational, and although each political formation might tend to use one idiom, both were readily available to both formations.

We might define both nationalism and internationalism in the way Brubaker defines the former: as 'a complex web of political stances, cultural idioms, organizational networks, and transborder social relations' (Rogers Brubaker 1996: 145). These stances, idioms, and networks take on special meanings in post-Communist states because the thorough-going modification of socialist property regimes potentially creates new social actors, new definitions of value, new organizations of access to them, and new positionings of all of these in global circuits. In this moment of transformation social groups struggle to influence the sorts of property regime that will at length emerge, and they do so by mobilizing strategies that we might label nationalist or internationalist. But these are not cast in stone. To see either of these as a doctrine or principle would be to rigidify unacceptably the processes of maneuver through which emergent social actors strategize their exit from the socialist world.

Acknowledgements

My thanks to Ashraf Ghani (once again) for helpful conversation about this chapter, and to participants in my two graduate seminars on property rights (1996 and 1997) for furthering my ideas of what property is.

Notes

1 This was facilitated by the vast sums of petrodollars deposited in US banks after 1973.
2 Thanks to Michael Heller of University of Michigan Law School, for this observation.
3 There are internal reasons for shrugging off welfare functions also, including the states' inability to afford the cost of all those social services and the symbolic value for 'new' governments wanting to prove their anti-Communist character to Western lenders and their own publics.
4 This party's label has changed several times, usually to mark yet another schism within it. It began as the National Salvation Front, then became the Democratic National Salvation Front, then the Party of Romanian Social Democracy. The party is different from the Social Democratic Party of Romania (comparable to Social Democrats in Germany), hence I refer to them as the Socialist Democrats.
5 In the interests of clarity I am considerably oversimplifying here. The Convention was markedly more 'internationalist' once it gained power than it was at an earlier phase, when it was competing with the Socialist Democrats to define *national* values, with much less reference to international circuits (see Verdery 1996: Chapter 5). Moreover, there is no guarantee that the Convention will remain consistently internationalist: it is all very well to undermine the former

resource base of one's opponents (political positions for *apparatchiks*) to prevent
their return, but as Convention members themselves become accustomed to
holding such positions, they may find themselves becoming more hesitant about
full-scale privatization. Even so, however, I argue that people associated with
the Convention were more likely to have already exploited other possibilities
(such as NGO work) that made them less fully dependent on bureaucratic positions than were their opponents.

6 Thanks to Mihai Pop for passing this email message on to me.

7 Thanks to Ashraf Ghani for the point about France. As for ongoing state control
of land, the land restitution law of 1991 returned to former owners the land
held in *collective* farms but not that in *state* farms (about 21 per cent of all arable
land). See Verdery (1996: 134 n. 2) for further clarification.

8 Many members of the former Securitate, for instance, opened fancy shops and
boutiques and proceeded to behave like 'entrepreneurs', but they were able to
do so only because their political connections gave them access to choice retail
locations.

9 Such actors also include nation–states or subnational regions in the interstate
system, with their territories as their property, exclusively owned and guaranteed through international contracts.

10 I cannot claim universal validity for this definition, whose specificity to the
present moment may in time become clear; I claim only that this definition is
not the same as others whose link with specific social orders is clear already. I
am assuming here that it makes sense to talk about 'property' for a variety of
social orders, from 'primitive' to 'civilized' (cf. Lowie 1928; Hallowell 1955),
though this point is arguable.

11 I do not presume that the values are 'scarce', which may be a notion more
useful in thinking about capitalist property relations than about other kinds.

12 For an illuminating discussion of how notions of 'property' emerged from the
moral universe of questions of 'propriety' in the work of so pivotal a thinker as
John Locke, see McClure (1996) (also Rose 1994: Chapter 3).

13 For an ingenious illustration of this point, see Myers (1989).

14 'Personal' and 'private' property were not the same thing. The former were the
kinds of objects I have mentioned. The latter referred specifically to means of
production, particularly land. The different socialist countries differed considerably in the extent of this – private landownership in Poland amounted to
about 79 per cent of all land, whereas in Romania it was about 5 per cent.

15 'Cooperatives' referred to two main kinds of social entity: what were known as
'collective farms' (as opposed to state farms) and tradesmen's cooperatives –
small workshops of shoe-makers, seamstresses, cabinet-builders, and so on, as
opposed to the socialist shoe, textile, or furniture factories.

16 Other social actors constituted by specific property relations include 'socialist
firms', with specific funds of resources exclusively managed by each.

17 I have this opinion from officials entrusted with that task in the above-named
organizations.

18 The present Republic of Moldova was at various times part of the Romanian
principality of Moldavia or of the Romanian Kingdom; Romanians usually refer
to it as Bessarabia. The country's very shape is quite different with Bessarabia
in it – as it appeared in weather maps on the PDSR-controlled television.

6 The little nation

Minorities and majorities in the context of shifting geographies

Seteney Shami

> Following the tradition of classical Russian literature, which revealed the value of the inner life of the so-called little man, I have attempted to reveal, to the best of my abilities, the significance of the epic existence of the little nation.
>
> (Fazil Iskandar 1983)

Introduction: latter-day nationalism

The nation–state today is embattled simultaneously from above and from below. From above, transnational linkages and solidarities make national boundaries increasingly permeable and supranational organizations, corporations and movements increasingly mobilize far-flung populations. From below, discourses of statism are appropriated by subordinated peoples who thus turn the tables on their oppressors. Identities that were denied in the era of modernism have found both the means of communication and the means of destruction to inscribe themselves on the world map and to threaten the territorial integrity of many contemporary states.

To many commentators on the emerging shape of the world, the two arms of the pincers squeezing the state represent contradictory tendencies. Supranational linkages are seen as working toward greater inclusiveness, cosmopolitanism and globalization, whereas ethnonationalism works towards particularism, insularity and localization. Yet, the increasing complexity of a world that can no longer be seen in terms of bipolar geopolitical blocs, should alert us to resist dichotomies and explore the interpenetrated and overlapping arenas of contemporary de- and reterritorialization. The global and the local are interpenetrated realities, and transnationalism and ethnonationalism are intertwined solidarities, sentiments and practices (see Shami 1998). To see global/local processes and trans/ethno-nations in terms of schismogenesis, as categories that progressively divide populations in time and space, is to miss the way that they not only inform one another but actively construct one another. For example, minority peoples previously encapsulated within nation–states are becoming self-conscious diasporic transnational communities. This reinforces, and simultaneously casts into question, the minority/diaspora's sense of co-ethnicity as well as their place in the national imagination. These positionalities are fraught with ambiguities which are important to recognize rather than to polarize.

In order to transcend interpretations of political identities and movements as either impulses of atavistic primordialism or as promises of post-nationality, it may be particularly helpful to explore the contours of the emerging (so-called) 'world community' from the viewpoint of hitherto 'unrepresented' peoples. These 'new' peoples, whose histories were long subordinated to the dominant narratives of others that denied them peoplehood, statehood and nationhood, embrace the opportunities presented by globalization in particular and illuminating ways. Politically pursuing the creation of ministates, they create alternative international organizations such as the UNPO (the Unrepresented Nations and Peoples Organization founded in 1991 and based in The Hague). Exploiting their own economic marginalities, they create alternative trade routes for the circulation of goods, currencies and military hardware. While the attention of analysts is focused on transnational companies, futures trading and global capital in global cities, there also exists an underbelly of this world economy, an informal global network of exchange, reciprocity and trade that escapes national constraints and borders as successfully as the most powerful multinational.

The ambiguous status of the contemporary nation–state may be articulated most clearly in political discourses and confrontations but it is, of course, also being produced economically. Economic production and transactions are increasingly carried out on a global scale and in circumvention of state and interstate control. Transnational corporations appropriate national managerial and working classes and structural adjustment cripples the ability of the state to control production, consumption and welfare. Even development aid from the center to the periphery, once seen as the tool of state-building *par excellence*, is increasingly transmitted directly from international bodies to the local level. While the stated aim remains that of 'spreading democracy', this is to be achieved not by developing state mechanisms but by strengthening civil society and ensuring human rights. Through this, state structures and practices are transformed and the relationships between the state and its citizenry grow increasingly complex.

Within these unfolding contexts, I would like to reflect on the relationships between majorities and minorities, as concepts and as practices, mainly through the example of one diasporic community, the Circassians, and to a lesser extent, the Chechens. Changing sentiments of loyalty, politics and identity provide the backbone of my discussion but the question of state boundaries and economies are equally central to how transnationalism is experienced and how globalization is practiced. The interpenetrations of ethnonationalism and transnationalism in the Circassian

case (Shami 1995, 1998) highlight the fragmented nature of ethnic identity, the disjunctures caused by encounters with the homeland and its
inhabitants, and the multiplex motivations of the people who forge the
pathways of their 'ethnoscape' (Appadurai 1996a: 33). In this chapter,
the focus is on the ramifications of these encounters and changes for
minority/majority relations within national settings. The fact that these
national settings and imagined communities are themselves peripheral and
contested in the world lends these ethnic relations and dynamics particular poignancy and contingency.

Majorities and minorities: the Caucasian experience

The Circassians and the Chechens trace their descent from the indigenous peoples of the north Caucasus. Pushed out by the Tsarist Russian
expansion into the Caucasus, and encouraged by the Ottoman Empire,
large numbers of Circassians, possibly up to 1.5 million, left for the
Ottoman domains (cf. Berkok 1958; Karpat 1972, 1990). Mass migration
for the Circassians peaked in 1864 (Karpat 1985) and somewhat later for
the Chechens. The immigrants were settled by the state as agricultural
communities in various parts of the Empire, first in the Balkans and later
in Anatolia and the Syrian Province. Today, they form communities of
different sizes and characteristics in some Balkan countries and in Turkey,
Syria, Jordan and Palestine/Israel. Secondary migrations to Germany,
Holland (mainly as labour migrants from Turkey) and the United States
(New Jersey and Orange County, California) created new communities
from the 1970s onwards. In the Russian Federation, the Circassians live
primarily in the three newly formed republics, previously autonomous
regions, of Kabardino-Balkaria, Karachaevo-Cherkessia and Adygeia, as
well as in some villages and towns within the republic of Ossetia and
others linked to the administrative districts of Krasnodar and Sochi. The
Chechens have their own republic of Chechnya. These divisions represent Soviet policies such that the Circassians having failed to qualify as a
'nation' instead became the titular nationality in one republic and two
autonomous regions. The three 'nationalities' that were formed, Cherkess,
Adygei and Kabardian, were minorities within their republics and today
constitute only between 10 and 48 per cent of the inhabitants of each
republic (Teague 1994).

Circassians and Chechens are Muslim except for Circassians in the
Ossetian Republic who comprise four Christian villages and one town.
Other north Caucasian groups such as Daghestanians, Ossetians, Abkhasians and Ubykh also formed part of the nineteenth-century migrations and
are found in the same countries of the Middle East. Convergence between
different groups took place in the places of settlement. Intermarriage
between the various groups outside the Caucasus also blurs distinctions

between them while reinforcing their common identity *vis-à-vis* the 'majority'.

Although these identities were constructed in constant reference to a space, a 'homeland' in the north Caucasus, this space was devoid of geographical detail, or territoriality. Cut off from the Caucasus by 130 years of history and boundary construction, Circassians of the Middle East were only dimly aware of the Circassians in the Caucasus and the trickle of emigrants who came after 1917 and after World War II gave accounts of forced Russification. In contrast, for many Circassians today, the sociopolitical relationships and cultural representations linking the multiple locales and the homeland with one another constitute a field of transnational intersections. Political, economic and kinship links are being forged between the various communities and places. Some families and individuals have migrated back especially from Turkey and Syria. Large numbers of Circassians have visited at least once and many go back every summer for extended stays. Some import–export businesses have been formed and scholars and politicians go back and forth. For a significant part of the first Chechen–Russian war, President Dudayev's foreign minister was a Chechen from Jordan.

The north Caucasus, a series of small peoples, republics and states that remain after the break-up of the Soviet Union within the Russian federation, the 'ethnic fringe' of Russia, poses some of the greatest challenges to the consolidation of Russian nationalism in the post-Soviet era. At the same time, the 'homelands' that the Caucasus presents to its diasporic descendants is a fragmented and contested terrain. Circassians and Chechens within the Caucasus are scattered, divided by borders, interspersed with other ethnic groups and have experienced successive displacements and exile and endured the complex politics of Soviet 'nationalities question'. Difficulties of transportation, visas, border crossings, residence permits and living conditions quickly dispel any romantic notions of an in-gathering from the diaspora.

There are three images of the Caucasus that are being constructed through scholarship and media:

1 The first image is that this region is a zone of ethnonationalism, of 'eruptions of long-repressed primordial national consciousness' (Suny 1995: 3), of violence, primitivism and revenge.
2 Related to the first image is the one that this region represents a boundary between Islam and Christendom, the northern rim of Islam's 'bloody borders' in Huntington's (1993: 35) stark phrase.
3 An outcome of these first two images is the common conclusion that this region is insular, isolated and unable to enter the 'world community' and engage in peaceful commerce and partake of economic prosperity and global accumulation (Goldenberg 1994).

The Caucasus appears therefore to represent the dark side of nationalism, the antithesis of internationalism and the failure of globalization. Ethnography, however, deconstructs these images through descriptions of encounters between groups, collective negotiations of identity, individual narratives and life stories, and radical transformations of the 'local' and 'the everyday'. None of the ethnographic moments presented in this chapter, in and of themselves, are coherent or systematic or present clear alternative routes to post-nationality and cosmopolitanism. Yet taken together, the sometimes tragic, sometimes pragmatic, trajectories that are described highlight the inchoate nature of identity and life on the periphery, on the one hand, and the open-endedness of the choices that may lie ahead on the other.

As self-conscious transnational diasporas are produced, minorities belonging to the same ethnic group are linked with one another in a variety of ways. This has several effects: within the ethnoscape itself, encounters with one another show up the profound disjunctures in ethnicity and lead to reconstructions of history and identity. Within each national setting, however, the diaspora itself becomes a resource that is used by minority peoples to renegotiate or to reaffirm their location within the national setting and their place within the imagined nation. In this way transnational identities simultaneously challenge and reinforce national boundaries and the hegemony of the majority.

The journeys to the homeland have dislodged boundaries that had been constructed over a century of community building in the countries of the diaspora. By casting into question the central components of Circassian identity, the relations between minority and majority also begin to be questioned and long-standing premises concerning the struggles for maintaining difference begin to crumble. The question for the minority becomes, where is home? And in defending one's identity against 'the other' or the 'majority', where is the home front?

The Caucasus: the home front?

My first trip to the Caucasus in 1992 was as part of a tourist group organized by an enterprising Jordanian travel agency. The group comprised 76 people, half Circassians traveling for the first time to the Caucasus and half Jordanian Arabs attracted by the cheap price of the tour. For 600 dollars, all inclusive for two weeks, the advertisement promised first class hotels and excursions in 'the most beautiful land in the world'. Unfortunately, the vision of the homeland and of tourist heaven both began to fall apart from the moment of the arrival at the airport of Mineralnye Vody near the city of Nalchik, the capital of Kabardino–Balkaria. The porters were on strike and the immigration officials were nowhere to be found. Things got worse. The hotel was a disaster, an uninspiring monumental structure with broken down bathrooms and balconies filled with pigeon droppings. Dinner was unpalatable and the portions meager. A wailing broke out in the disappointed group of tourists and the home-coming Circassians knew that they were in for a difficult two weeks.

Over the next days, schedules were confused, day trips were cancelled or changed without notice, the food grew even worse and it was discovered there was little to do in this provincial backwater city. During the excursions, the group broke up into two buses: one with the Circassians maintaining a stiff upper lip, while the 'Arab bus' resounded with vociferous complaining interspersed with good-humored singing and joking. The Arabs teased the Circassians, 'Is this the beautiful heaven that you mourn so much? It is so backward!! You are lucky that you came to Jordan.' The Circassians whispered among themselves, 'We must not say a thing, or it will be bad for us in Jordan. They are just jealous. Have they ever seen such beautiful scenery, do they have such greenery in their country?'

In addition to touring, the Circassians in the group were busy locating relatives.[1] The lobby of the hotel filled up every day with local Circassians and others from countries such as Jordan and Syria who had migrated or who were visiting. I accompanied a couple as their newly found relatives took us on a two day visit to the village of 'origin'. We returned well-fed and carrying supplies for our trip onward to Maikop, the capital of the Adygeia republic.

Meanwhile, a request was brewing in the Arab bus – they did not want to go to Maikop, but straight to Sochi, the well-known resort on the Black Sea, preferably by plane. The Arabs said, 'There is nothing except relatives in Nalchik and Maikop, we want to go to Sochi.' The Circassians said, 'They are jealous because they have no relatives here and they see how our relatives are happy to see us and take us to their homes and give us good food to eat.'

Eventually, tensions calmed down and the trip continued to Maikop as planned. In comparison to the other two cities, the amenities in Sochi were good and the seaside spectacular. The trip ended as it began, however, as on the return flight the air circulation system on the airplane broke down and alternately blasted cold and hot air. The weary group returned thankfully to Amman and immediately succumbed to bronchitis and laryngitis.

This experience of the homeland for the Circassians was quite different than others I witnessed later. It was made doubly alien by the tour group format and by having to maintain a common front *vis-à-vis* the 'Arabs', who became transformed in this context from fellow-Jordanians to 'the other'. It is important to emphasize that Circassians in Jordan enjoy high social status and a strong political presence. When framed in terms of ethnicity, 'Circassians' and 'Arabs' are perceived as opposing categories, but there are numerous categories that cross-cut this opposition and the Circassian sense of 'Jordanianess' is one of their prominent features.

Furthermore, Circassians from Jordan themselves often vigorously denounce the 'backwardness' of the Caucasus and extol the virtues of their life-style in Jordan. But in front of the 'majority' of the state where they are a minority, it was important that their original 'homeland' should be superior or at least equal to, Jordan, which in turn became the metonym for Arab heritage and culture. Unable to make the argument of 'more modernity' or 'more culture' the Circassians on the tour resorted to a different indisputable 'truth,' the physical beauty of the place, the *natural* and hence enduring superiority of the Caucasus.

Jordan: the home front?

James Clifford argues that 'Diasporic language appears to be replacing, or at least supplementing, minority discourse' (1994: 311). Circassians in different locations balance their diasporic and minority discourses in various ways. Nowhere, however, does this mean that the politics of identity and the jockeying for positions within nation–states is growing any less important as a result of the increasing involvement with transnational ethnicity. Rather, the 'objective' existence of the diaspora, becomes yet one more resource that minorities may utilize in lobbying for their various and heterogeneous claims.

In Jordan, Circassians and Chechens today form largely middle-class urban communities with favorable representation in government bureaucracy, parliament and the military. Circassians and Chechens originate from neighboring regions in the north Caucasus and share a great many cultural similarities, although the languages are different and mutually unintelligible. The two communities in Jordan have always perceived themselves as clearly distinct from each other, while the difference is not obvious to many other Jordanians. The Circassians form a larger, wealthier community while the Chechens number much less but pride themselves on being more tightly knit and organized under a unified leadership.[2] Intermarriage between the two communities tends to be rare, while intermarriage with Jordanian Arabs is quite widespread. With the beginning of parliamentary life in Jordan, the two communities have had two seats jointly allotted to them in the lower house of parliament. This has recently been increased to three seats with the expansion of electoral circles and the numbers of parliamentary seats. The distribution of these seats between Circassians and Chechens has always been a bone of contention between the two communities and traditionally one Chechen and one Circassian have tended to occupy these seats, now increased to one Chechen and two Circassians.[3]

The links and relationships that have been forming with the Caucasus have had important and transformative effects on the conceptions of identity and narratives of history in the two communities. Moreover, political events taking place in the Caucasus have also had their impact in Jordan.

The Abkhasian–Georgian war (1992–3) and the Chechen–Russian wars (1994–7 and 1999–2000) were powerful protracted events that affected the two communities in interesting ways.[4] First, they served to mobilize the communities in Jordan. Ethnic organizations worked diligently to collect aid for victims in the Caucasus and organized lectures, solidarity meetings, press conferences and demonstrations in front of the Russian Embassy. These activities also helped bring the Circassians and Chechen communities closer to each other. Second, the leaderships of both communities called upon support from the King of Jordan to facilitate the transport of medical and food aid to the Abkhasian war zone. The King supplied two airplanes and received two Caucasian horses as thanks in return. These gestures reasserted the often-times reiterated 'traditional' bonds of trust and reciprocity between the Circassians and Chechens and the royal family. Third, parliament representatives from both communities used these events and activities to increase their popularity in their own and in each other's communities. They also used them to build bridges with the Islamic movements and parties with whom the Circassians particularly had not previously allied themselves. Since the conflict over Chechnya took on a representation of a religious war, it became an issue over which the parties could agree and develop a common platform.

Overall, the events in the Caucasus, which were the outcome of a politics 'local' to the Caucasus and resulting from the break-up of the Soviet Union, had important reverberations in Jordan. They helped revitalize the role of the ethnic associations and community leaders. Many non-Circassians, and especially the younger generation, who until then were uninformed about, and oblivious to, the history of the Caucasus and the origins of the Circassians and Chechens, began to see this history and area as the embattled frontiers of Islam. The wars in the Caucasus also served as an outlet for some young Circassian and Chechen men who, marginalized by suffering from the high level of unemployment and severe economic recession in Jordan, volunteered to go to the battlefront and become martyrs for Caucasian independence.

These various developments in Jordan were not without internal contradictions. Official government support and sympathy were much stronger during the Abkhasian conflict when Russia was clearly on the side of the Abkhasians than during the Chechen conflict. The latter even caused a small but significant diplomatic crisis as Russia accused Jordan of sending 'mercenaries' to Chechnya. The support of the Islamists for the Chechen community increasingly took the tone of blaming the government for not supporting their loyal citizens at the time of adversity and as a proof of the regime's lack of adherence to Islamic principles. Within the communities, the Chechen leadership was sharply divided on the policies of Dudayev, Maskhadev and Basaev. Circassian parliamentarians seized the opportunity to show that they were more responsive to the Chechens than their own leaders. The protracted duration of the Chechen–Russian wars led many Circassians to see the Chechen position as impractical intransigence. One Circassian drew historical parallels as he said,

> These Chechens have really proved that they are crazy. It is their fault that we are in this country at all. In the nineteenth century they also did not know when to give up and just live with the Russians. They kept fighting till they got us all kicked out of the Caucasus.[5]

The course of the second Chechen–Russian war, however, and Russian military violence against civilians has united Circassians and Chechens in Jordan.

Inchoate nationalism

Nationalist discourses are clearly an important constituent of diasporic communities. Historical images circulate within ethnoscapes but are refracted differentially in different locations. For one Circassian in Jordan, the current Chechen conflict explains his identity and position as a 'diasporian'. Elsewhere, including in the Caucasus and in Russia, the same historical period of the Russian–Caucasian wars (*c.*1760–1864) is interpreted in various ways. These range from seeing the present as a continuation of historical struggles for independence, to proof that the Caucasus had been part of Russia for more than a hundred years, to testaments that the Russian military had not yet learnt that 'When a Shah is a fool, he attacks Daghestan.'[6] In addition to revolving representations, transnational ethnoscapes may also be marked by the simultaneity of political action. Chechnya declares its independence from Russia and, in Jordan, Chechens and Circassians come together to demand their right as loyal citizens of Jordan to come to the aid of their homeland in distress. Chechen fighters take hostages in Daghestan (January 1996), and Chechen and Circassian diasporians in Turkey hijack a ferry boat in Trabzon on the Black Sea and threaten to blow it up in the Bosphorus. Moscow and Amman, Trabzon and Grozny: improbable places are linked through people forging 'roots *and* routes' (Clifford 1994: 308 emphasis in the original).

Nationalism notwithstanding, the 'homeland' and its characteristics are important to construct not only as narratives of identity and history for internal consumption within the ethnic group. They are also necessary for maintaining a certain image and position of the minority within the majority. A homeland that is a *state*, is not only important for self-definition or as aspirations for self-determination, but is also a way of rooting oneself in the diaspora. A diaspora population that cannot claim a state of origin, at least in the past, is simply a scattering. A land of origin, no matter how beautiful, is simply a topography of incomplete meanings.

The long history of the Circassians as tribal peoples on the peripheries of empires, although heroic, is not enough of a past to ensure a place on

the world map. A Circassian in Jordan once commented, rather uncon-
vincingly that: 'Every people has had a state at some time, ours was
Mameluke Egypt.'[7] Not to possess a homeland of equal standing as the
majority is to truly be cast out in the world of nation–states, to be orphaned
in 'the family of nations' (Malkki 1992: 33). To journey to the homeland,
therefore, only to find oneself a minority there as well is particularly exas-
perating for the Circassians.

Encounters between the Circassians of the diaspora and those of the
Caucasus throw into sharp relief the variety of identities that have developed over time and raise uncertainties about the future. Whatever
fronts are maintained in the face of the 'other', among themselves
Circassians argue over who has more *khabza*,[8] who is more Circassian,
who is more civilized and modern, what the future should look like and
where one can be truly Circassian. The north Caucasus, as the 'ethnic
fringe' of Russia presents a dubious location for the rooting of the future
nation. The nationalism that can be produced in these marginal lands is
rife with contradictions.

As mentioned, the Circassians in the Caucasus constitute minorities in
the republics where they are the titular nationality. Contacts between the
inhabitants of these three republics were at a minimum throughout the
Soviet years and divergences marked the evolution of language and identity. Disjunctures were created and maintained by a politics of philology.
For example, the three 'nations' were regarded as speaking different
'languages' and separate Cyrillic-based alphabets were devised for each
one. Today many Kabardians state that they are not Adygei and when
speaking Russian or English will refer to their language as Kabardian as
opposed to Adygeian. When actually speaking this language, however, they
will refer to it as *Adygebze* (the tongue of the Adyge) and to their traditions
as *Adygekhabze* (the customs of the Adyge).

Other markers of identity also exhibit interesting ambiguities. In Soviet
times, the various republics and 'nations' all had their folklore dance
troupes and every local village and town had youth dance groups
that served as a recruiting site of the official troupes. The Caucasians
(especially the Kabardians and the Georgians) were notably successful in
winning all-Union contests and representing the Soviet Union abroad.
Folklore was thus elaborated and celebrated and research was conducted
into dance forms, as well as into local customs that could be symbolically
performed through dance. Yet Circassians in the Caucasus today argue
that this was not a celebration of identity or a perpetuation of tradition
because the performers in these groups were not necessarily Circassians.
The majority, in fact, were not, but could be Russians, Armenians or any
individual chosen on the basis of skill rather than ethnicity.

The importance of several centuries of Russian settler colonialism also
cannot be discounted in understanding the fragmented nature of Circassian

identity in the Caucasus. If 25 million Russians are found outside the borders of the Russian federation, in the republics of the 'near abroad' (Banuazizi and Weiner 1994: 16), then within the Russian federation, their presence is even more significant. The characteristics of the Russian presence in these republics have been described as creating 'bifurcated societies' (Banuazizi and Weiner 1994: 78). Indeed, there are significant arenas where Russians and Circassians and other groups seem to lead parallel lives, such as in the domestic sphere and in rural life. The inter-penetrations, however, are as significant as the fractures, as is clear in the arena of politics, administration and work.

In spite of the successive fragmentation of Circassian identity, whether in the diaspora or in the Caucasus, attempts are being made to construct common grounds. Organizations such as The World Circassian Association (est. 1990) and The International Circassian Academy of Sciences (est. 1993) bring together a variety of Circassians from around the world in annual meetings. Differences in language and dialect, as well as in percep-tions of political strategy cast strains on the proceedings of these meetings. The dominance of Russian as a *lingua franca* is also a problem for the Circassians of the diaspora. One Circassian from Jordan noted ironically: 'When they discuss, they do so in Russian; when they argue, they do so in Circassian.'

In the opening ceremonies of these meetings, in the music and dance festivals that accompany them, commonalities are easier to find and emotions flow more harmoniously. The folklore groups, now composed entirely of Circassians, perform not only their own justly famous dances and songs but others that they have researched by traveling to diaspora communities. Speeches call for all Circassians to come closer together, so that 'their heartbeats may become as one'. Families who have migrated back from Turkey, the US and Syria climb onto the stage to be wildly applauded and all join in a song that goes: 'O Circassians around the world / Hear me around the world / Lift up your head O Caucasus / We have no right to be lost.'

The symbols that unite the Circassians on these occasions, however, can only be described as inchoate. The new flag of the Adygeia Republic has been adopted by the World Circassian Association as the 'official' Circassian flag. It shows three crossed arrows within an arc formed by twelve stars on a green background. The flag is mentioned in historical sources as having been the banner under which Circassians of the Black Sea coast rallied against the Russians in the early nineteenth century (Berkok 1958). Nowadays, however, as it is raised on a pole by political leaders or brought on stage by triumphant dancers, the Circassian flag is always accompanied by the flag of the Russian Federation. Circassians wonder among themselves about the flag: what do the arrows mean? War, because they are arrows? Or peace, because they are bound together?

Or hunting, because they are only three? And the stars, whom do they represent? Why are there twelve of them? These queries are intertwined with more poignant questions about common origins and historical relations between the different groups: Are the Circassians descendants of the Scythians? Are the Adyge and Abkhaz distant cousins or separate peoples? Whose language or dialect is purer? Was traditional social hierarchy a source of injustice, or a division of labor? And so on ...

It does not appear that these kinds of questions, so important for fashioning a national imagination, are being resolved or subjected to a hegemonic discourse. An exhibition on Circassian archaeology and folklore organized in conjunction with a meeting of the World Circassian Association in 1993 embodied these ambiguities in its very title. The entrance of the museum proclaimed in big yellow letters against a red background: 'If you are a Circassian ...' The completion of the if/then clause is left open to interpretation. Nothing in the exhibition itself pointed directly to the answer. On the surface, the phrase seems to leave open the possibility that there is a choice – that one may choose or not choose to be a Circassian. However, other meanings are contained within it. This expression, in its incomplete form, is often said to children when they misbehave. It therefore carries with it the authoritative, didactic weight of countless ancestors placing the responsibility for perpetuating a culture and a people onto the younger generation. It leaves unspoken, however, the ways in which this perpetuity is to be achieved. If you are a Circassian ... then you will understand.

Globalization in the periphery

Diasporas need a homeland and preferably a homeland that is a state, was a state or will be a state. While the imagination is limitless, the possibilities of creating a state by peoples whose very legitimacy as a people is not recognized domestically and internationally are severely limited. The fact that the homeland is being produced by people who are simultaneously involved in multiple settings and polities means that rather than the construction of a bounded entity or territory, there is the construction of an interpenetrated and fragmented terrain or field of action. The result is an inchoate nationalism that seemingly cannot get beyond a protean and fluid understanding of itself.

What kind of nationalism is it that can emerge in peripheral areas by marginalized peoples? Furthermore, what kind of nationalism can be fashioned in an era of globalization? The nationalist impulses described above are occurring in a very different context than postcolonial movements of the past. Yet recent publications exploring various aspects of the internal politics and the geopolitical implications of the break-up of the Soviet Union tend to use past models of state and nation-building and argue that the Central Asian and Caucasian republics 'fit this model of successor states to empires' (Banuazizi and Weiner 1994: 5–6). The discussions focus on nationalist elites, the role of neighbouring countries, the possible emergence of new regional blocs through pan-Turkism, pan-Iranianism and Islamic fundamentalism, and the role of the great powers in providing regional stability.

Many of these studies also continue to use the labels and categories of analysis constructed by the Soviet state in their analysis of nationalism and ethnic violence. Little attention is paid to the micro-politics of the construction of identity in the Soviet period, in spite of an initial extensive literature on 'the question of the nationalities' (see Szporluk 1994). The focus tends to be on the nationalities that were embodied in the republics of the Union (for example, Azerbeijan, Armenia, Georgia, etc.), generally ignoring the varied peoples within them as well as those within 'Russia' such as the peoples of the north Caucasus (Olcott 1995; Suny 1995). The impact of Soviet practices of deportation, collectivization, the creation of enclaves and the severance of people and territory also tends to be overlooked (IOM *et al.* 1996).

Disregarding the historical construction of identity and the sites of its production means that the 'black box of primordialism' (Appadurai 1996a: 139) remains unpacked in the post-Soviet space. Dually trapped in the language of modernization theories and Soviet studies, many scenarios of the post-Soviet space disregard the weight of history. Glossed over are the differences between Russian colonialism and West European colonialism and the differences between the Soviet state and premodern empires. Also ignored are contemporary forces of transnationalism and globalization.

Ethnicity and nationalism, even in the forms described above, are not the only sentiments, practices and activities linking the peoples of the Caucasus with other parts of the world. The regions of the post-Soviet space are more than ethnoscapes and there are sentiments other than nationalism that mobilize people in these peripheral places, Islam for example. However even political Islam which appears as though it is focusing the passions and energies of diverse peoples into organized channels of violence and struggle, is experienced by individuals as a set of contradictions.

Omar and Hayrettin: martyrs of some sort?

In the Caucasus, the in-coming residents from the diaspora include large numbers of young men. Many come as students and drift into working in the various import–export businesses that are mushrooming and into the politics of inchoate nationalism. The brief narratives of two young men, one from Turkey and the other from Jordan, show some of the common threads that draw them to the Caucasus but also show the differences of experience that translate into the politics of the Caucasian borderlands.

Hayrettin began telling me about his journey from Turkey to the Caucasus by saying that he was about to recount a 'destan', an epic. He saw his arrival in the Caucasus as a culmination of a series of important decisions and convictions. In the Caucasus, however, his epic had disintegrated into a rather lonely and prosaic life. Born in a village in Central Anatolia, Hayrettin had ended up a worker in a textile factory. His life mainly acquired meaning through what he called 'dernekcilik' or association-ism. He was a talented member of the folklore dance troupe in the local Circassian association, and for him this was not just an evening activity but his whole life. Ever since the possibility of the return to the Caucasus opened up, he kept trying to save money to go. He had heard about the Caucasus all his life from his maternal grandfather. His grandfather would say, 'Don't ask me about the Independence War (of Turkey). That was not our war, ours was against the Russians in the Caucasus.' Hayrettin thought hard about why the Circassians had left the Caucasus. At first, he believed the argument that it was for religion, because they were Muslims and wanted to live in Muslim lands. But later he became convinced that it had been a Russian-Ottoman conspiracy. Because of this, and the complicity of Circassian leaders, many had fallen off the overcrowded ships into the Black Sea. So many Circassians drowned in the sea that Circassians until today do not eat fish that had eaten the bodies of their ancestors.

His first opportunity to visit the Caucasus was through the participation of his dance troupe in one of the festivals of the World Circassian Association. He looked for his relatives and they took him to their village. It was Ramadan, they were fasting, and he was not. They prepared food and drink for celebrating with him and when he told them that they could not drink alcohol and fast they asked him what he was so upset about, given that he was not even fasting?

His parents were against his coming to the Caucasus but he saved 2,000 dollars and came by boat from Trabzon to Sochi with two friends, one an Ossetian, the other a Chechen. They took the train to Nalchik where they met two Circassian students from Syria who helped them when they first arrived. The three friends stayed together in a sanatorium in Nalchik and made some money by selling foreign cigarettes and exchanging dollars on the black market. The other two then went on to their own 'republics' and Hayrettin moved in with some students and enrolled in the university for language classes. He worked at odd jobs.

Hayrettin's epic was sidetracked into a long description of his disillusion with his relatives in the Caucasus, that they did not get along with one another, that some were not interested in meeting him, that although others invited him to come over but they never bothered to come and visit him or see how he was living. So many other things shocked him when he first came. The alcoholism, the drunken noises from the hotels, not being able to go out at night because it was not safe. And yet the natural beauty of the place captivated him, it is a heaven on earth. He began to get to know the dance troupe in Nalchik and as he got closer to them and listened to their ideas, he began to see that not all people here were the same. The artists and dancers were working for the people, fighting for the people. He said, 'I began to understand that I would not be alone here.'

When Hayrettin was telling his story in 1993, the Abkhasian–Georgian war was at its peak. A few months later, he went to Abkhasia and was no longer heard from.

Omar came to the Caucasus from Jordan in 1993 at the age of 23.[9] After high school and a stint of working on the railway, Omar went to fight in Afghanistan. He had read in the magazines that came to Jordan about how the Muslims were being killed there, women and children. He took a plane and went to Peshawar, all by himself, and then joined an organization funded by Saudi Arabia. He spent six months being trained on tanks, automatic weapons and mines and how to forge passports. He stayed for a year and a half but then left because he gradually became disillusioned with the organization which he had joined. On the way back to Jordan, Omar passed through Saudi Arabia and decided that he wanted to study *Shari'a*. He wanted to study in Medina where there are *shaykhs* who teach the real religion. He liked Medina very much but as an Arab he had to wait a year to be accepted into the school. He thought that as a Russian he would be accepted immediately to study *Shari'a*.

Here he was in the Caucasus for six months and he still didn't have the passport. He discovered that there was no way to get the passport except by getting married. He first went to Maikop and found a woman to marry but then the arrangements fell through. He didn't quite trust her either and was suspicious of her continuous male visitors. He came to Nalchik and found another woman. She was 37 years old and a lawyer and had an adopted son Hajmurat.[10] But so far it was not clear when they would get married. In describing his situation in the Caucasus, Omar was despairing. He said that he had lost everything here. He had one drink and then it was all over. He managed to hold out for four months, but then he surrendered to temptation. But he said that he still prayed. If he forsook that as well then he would no longer be a Muslim. He left saying that he had to go pick up Hajmurat from kindergarten.

Three and a half years later (January 1997), I had a chance encounter with a friend of Omar's in a music shop in Amman. He had come in with three Circassian musicians from the Kabardinka folklore group of Nalchik who were performing in Amman and wanted to buy recorders. He said, 'Do you remember that day we met in Nalchik there was that young man with glasses? He was martyred in Chechnya. Well, I guess he was martyred . . . we have to say he was martyred. You know he used to drink and pray, drink and prostrate himself.'[11]

What do lives like Hayrettin's and Omar's tell us about nationalism and internationalism? Their energies are spent in restless movements between various countries and border zones, prey to contingencies, earnest whims and random strategies. Omar stumbles across Islam on a railway track in Jordan and travels to Afghanistan to fight for Islam, women and children. The route to the passport that he needs in order to seek true Islam goes through his ethnic identity. As a Circassian, he can transform himself from an Arab to a Russian for the purposes of acquiring Islam. The Caucasus for him is not a homeland, it is just a stopover, a transit way station. En route to Islam via the Caucasus, he is overcome by the place, its women and children. He has one drink and 'loses everything'. Finally in Chechnya, he loses his life for the cause of Chechnian Islamic nationalism, though he is neither a Chechen nor a nationalist and perhaps no longer really a Muslim.

Hayrettin, on the other hand, comes seeking his homeland, but fails to find his family. Just as in Turkey, his only community is the dance troupe. Having lost a sense of purpose, he, like Omar, drifts and ends up dropping out of sight in Abkhazia.

The Chechnyan wars would seem the perfect example of Islamic militancy intertwined with virulent ethnonationalism. Omar's life and death would seem the perfect contradiction. For Omar, states are not the issue. If anything, states and their politics are the obstacles to achieving knowledge and faith. Nationality is simply a passport. Marriage is simply a tactic. The aim is to circumvent the restrictions imposed by states. At the same time, deprived of structures and leaders that help him to maintain his faith and his morals, Omar finds himself lost along the way. His last stop is Chechnya.

It may seem odd to emphasize the globalization of the Caucasus through a discussion of Islam. To many, Islam is no better than ethnonationalism in being an atavistic, primordial sentiment that is opposed to democracy, inclusiveness and internationalism. Central Asia and the Caucasus regions are now being assimilated into the Islamic world and the Middle East (as well as into the Third World) through the 'imaginative geography' of scholarship (Said 1978: 49). Thus the region is not only represented as characterized by ethnic violence, but also as the northern 'fault line' between Islamic and Christian civilizations and as one of the 'bloody borders' of Islam (Huntington 1993: 39, 35).

Remaking Central Asia and the Caucasus as 'the ex-Soviet Middle East' (Hooson 1994: 139) not only reverts several decades of a more sensitive and historically informed scholarship on Islam, it also reduces the lives of the people involved into 'a type' (Said 1978: 230ff.). Historically, Islam has been a trans-state, trans-societal phenomenon reproduced, in its diversity, though a circulation of goods, ideas and people.[12] It continues to be so in the Caucasus today and, in this way, Islam reflects and participates in the making of a transnational world. Islam in these regions is neither monolithic nor homogeneous (Gross 1992; Fuller 1994). Encounters between dislocated peoples and experiences across boundaries engender new interpretations of Islamic identity and faith and well as new types of relationships between Moslems. However, Islam may be the last thing on some people's minds as they traverse borders.

Lena and Sveta: economics über alles

Economics that have escaped the boundaries of the state and new ways of exchanging and consuming are actually mobilizing larger numbers of peoples than either nationalism or fundamentalism. While nationalism, fundamentalism and commercialism are not mutually exclusive, yet the ways in which resources are flowing and profits are being made may tell us more about change at both the local and global level and about the production of modernity than the focus on boundary construction.

Lena and Sveta, two sisters from Kabardino–Balkaria, are among the hundreds of thousands of people, mostly women, involved in 'suitcase trading' between the ex-Soviet Union and neighboring countries, an impressive development which has been dubbed in the Turkish and Arabic media as 'the Natasha phenomenon'. I met Lena in Istanbul airport in 1993. A Circassian female friend from Jordan and I had been waiting for six hours to board the charter flight to Mineralnye Vody. Beside ourselves and three or four others, the passengers, the majority of them women, were coming back from a 'shopping tour' to Istanbul. At the time, Lena was 24 years old and had been coming to Istanbul every two weeks for the past seven months. She was financed in this enterprise by her older sister, Sveta, who had first started coming one year before but then got tired and started sending Lena instead. Lena used to work in a factory until she got married three years earlier and had a baby. Her husband works as a driver at a hospital and frequently has night duty. Now that she is travelling regularly to Istanbul, Lena leaves their baby son with her mother-in-law when she goes on her trips.

Lena is attractive with blue eyes, dark skin, two twinkling gold teeth on each side of her mouth and a money bag tight around her slim waist. She was with a group of four other Circassian women. She said that the shopping tour included about 70 people, about 20 of whom were Circassian. The others were Russians, Chechen, Nagoy, Kushha. The women sat in small clusters, clearly of the same ethnic group, and did not interact with others except briefly. Lena said, 'with your *tlepkh* [people/nation] you at least know that you will not be thrown out if you try to sit'. We told Lena that we were going to attend the meeting of the World Circassian Association in Maikop. She had not heard of the association or the meeting and did not show much interest.

Lena said that one of the women in her group, Rima, was their 'mother' because she had been coming to Istanbul the longest. She spends more time in Istanbul than in her own home. She takes care of them and makes sure that they do not forget anything in the hotel. Lena said that they all came for shopping and trade, no-one was a tourist, except for Rima's son, Artur, who came along this time just for fun. Lena said 'he is our spoiled son'. Artur was about 20 years old, dark, lanky, unshaven, wearing a California T-shirt and black pants. As he lounged around, Lena and the others occasionally hugged him and gave him bits of sausages and rolls that they brought out from their bags.

They used to come for four-day trips but now the planes were only once weekly and they had to stay a whole week which was too long. As part of the trip they were now taken for three days to a seaside town whose name she did not know. There were nice chalets, the sea was clean and a Turk fell in love with a young woman in their group, thereafter called 'super-mademoiselle', and bought them all a lot of beer and Fanta.

Lena said that the trip including the passport fees costs 400 dollars and the profit she makes on the goods she buys is about 400 dollars. It takes about two weeks to sell what she buys in one week. 'We don't make much profit,' she said, 'the work and tiredness is hardly worth it.' She described how she smuggles dollars hidden in the heels of her slippers as they are only allowed to take out limited amounts. This time she also smuggled out some grams of gold. As for selling the goods she buys, she and her sister go to the open-air market in Nalchik from midnight to be sure to get a good place where a lot of people pass. The market, she says, is like the *hajj* [pilgrimage to Mecca] with people going round and round.

As we checked in, I put one of Lena's bags with mine saving her from paying overweight penalties. Some groups of three or four women appeared to have a leader who checked their luggage for them and recorded what each one owed. The 'suitcases' were either huge soft carryalls, or home-made out of strong plastic garbage bags wrapped around the goods and firmly taped with masking tape. Each woman checked in several bags and in addition carried at least two onto the plane itself.

When the time came to board the plane a great deal of pushing ensued. Lena looked out for my friend and me, telling us where to stand and where to go. As the wave of women with their huge bags made for the stairs to the plane, she looked around good-humoredly and said, 'Now you should take a photograph!' Later, however, as she struggled to place her bags on the plane she said in a whisper, 'I hate these Russians, I could kill them, they are so pushy.'

On the plane, she said that each person had two seats so that they could place their things. The chairs fold up and the bags are put beneath them. Some women sit on their bags, others hold them on their laps. There is no attempt to fasten seat-belts and the plane begins to take off while people are still settling in. The stewardess comes by slap-dashedly handing out drinks. Lena said, 'Ask for Fanta, it is the best.'

As the plane took off, Lena whispered to herself at some length. When asked, she said that she did not know how to pray but that she pleads with God. She asked us if we knew how to read the Koran and when we said yes, she asked, 'What is in it that it was forbidden for us to read?' We struggled to explain and she lost interest. She said that her son's name was Islam, was it a name from the Koran? We tried to explain.

At Mineralnye Vody airport, Lena was met by her sister, Sveta, her husband and her brother-in-law. Lena was worried because her passport had been confiscated as she passed through immigration. Sveta said, 'Don't worry, my hands are dripping with dollars, I will get it back.' It turned out that Lena's passport had expired before the trip but Sveta had bribed an official to let Lena pass on her departure.

It was 2 a.m. by then and my friend and I had nowhere to go, so Lena invited us to spend the night at her home. Home for Lena was in a hostel for hospital workers and consisted of one room and a shared kitchen and bathroom with three other families. Her husband went back to the hospital and she and Sveta unpacked the bags. Checking the purchases against a list, Sveta praised Lena's shopping abilities. The bags were filled with clothes, mostly three-quarter-length leather jackets. They cost 90 dollars and they would sell them for 100. Lena also had bought herself some clothes and brought her son and Sveta's two sons shorts and clogs and small leather jackets.

Over supper/breakfast of chicken, tomatoes and chocolate biscuits, Sveta talked about her trading activities. She said that people went to Turkey, Syria, the Emirates, China, Germany and Poland. The best goods are cigarettes (Marlboros) and electronic equipment. She asked us if cigarettes would sell well in Jordan. Sveta sends Lena to Turkey, a brother goes to China, she herself goes to Poland. She and a group were going to go to Germany to buy cars but they were still waiting for their visas. They had sent their passports to Moscow for the visas but one of the group turned out to be a narcotics smuggler so the visa was refused for all of them. Visas for Turkey and some countries could be obtained locally but for European countries they had to go to Moscow. It takes a long time because everybody in Russia is sending their passports and you have to wait for your turn.

With the money she is making she is going to buy two houses, one for each son (aged 4 and 6). She has enough money to buy three houses. When she first got married, she did not understand anything. They built a house and some of her effort went into that house but her mother-in-law decided to have it registered in the name of Sveta's husband. She should have had it in her name, specially since many people here get divorced. Her village is 100 kilometers from Nalchik but she comes and goes, sometimes twice a day, for her shopping trips. We commented that in Jordan, Circassians believe that they do not make good merchants. Sveta replied, 'Given our conditions now, one cannot be generous anymore. I cannot give my brother a leather jacket for a hundred dollars because I have to sell it.'

After a few hours of sleep, we got up and Lena and Sveta urged us to eat a breakfast of chicken, macaroni and raspberry compote. Sveta said that Turks are not hospitable. When some Circassians there invited her they only gave her tea and small things. They also serve the tea in tiny glasses. She kept waiting and waiting for the food and it never came. They told her that in Turkey people only live till 50. She said to them, 'With food like this I am not surprised.' As a result of what she said, when her sister went to visit them, they gave her many things to eat. It is easy to be hospitable in Turkey, you can go out of the house and buy what you need if guests come. Here sometimes you cannot find anything for your guest and it is very embarrassing. Turkey is dirty, their skin gets dried up there. And it is very strange that they buy [drinking] water. Here the best water comes out of the ground and the air is clean.

Having made contact with the friends with whom we were going to stay, we left Lena and Sveta promising to visit them in the market the next Saturday and to go with them to their village the following week.

In its heyday the volume of trade between shopping tourists and Turkish entrepreneurs was estimated to be between 5,000 million to 8,000 million dollars annually (Yenal 1998). As early as in 1992, three million suitcase traders visited Turkey in one year (Goldenberg 1994). This transnational economy and globalized market are developing without the help of corporate structures and in the near absence of state control over the movement of goods and money. While ethnicity plays a part in this trade, it is not the determining or only factor. Language is no barrier as buyers and sellers bargain digitally by flashing different totals on their calculators at each other. Still a remarkable number of shopkeepers in the Laleli district of Istanbul speak Russian and the shops and hotels abound in signs written in Russian.[13]

This segment of an emergent global informal economy existed alongside official Turkish policy towards the Caucasus and Central Asian states which aims to 'end their isolation from the West and to facilitate economic recovery and political stability' (Sayari 1994: 182). Since these countries are not politically stable, however, official economic policies have not been as successful as was hoped. After perceptively describing the intricacies of politics and economics in the Caucasus, a journalist concludes that these regions cannot yet be integrated into the world community. This is due to an 'unyielding nationalism' which means that '[T]here is no energy left for the debates about economic reform that have been taking place in Russia and other, more stable, republics' (Goldenberg 1994: 214). This conclusion is surely accurate in terms of official interstate relations in the world community. However, *people* from these regions are daily transforming local, regional and global economies in ways that are not subject to national or international regulation. Political instability also does not seem to have been a deterrent to the numerous Chechen women waiting at Nalchik airport to go on a shopping tour to Istanbul at the height of the first war in 1995.

In the north Caucasus, even the charter flights to various parts of the world are organized by fly-by-night companies. In Istanbul and Aleppo tickets are sold out of shabby shops and shady travel agencies in back streets. At Nalchik airport one bargains over the price of the airfare with women entrepreneurs who wander around clutching bunches of tickets. A ticket does not ensure a seat on the flight but just the right to join the crowd that pushes through the airport waiting room and up the gangway to the plane. Mobility is the order of the day and people live their lives with maximum flexibility. In 1995 as I worried in Nalchik airport about getting on a flight to Istanbul from where I was connecting to a flight to Stockholm, I was cheerfully advised by a helpful woman to go to Mineralnye Vody airport (90 km away) and take the afternoon flight to Moscow, from where I would surely find a flight to Stockholm at some point.

Almost every woman and many of the men I met in the north Caucasus were engaged in some way or another with the trade in commodities and consumer goods. Doctors at the sanatoriums, historians at the state academy, directors of rural kindergartens and housewives were all busy buying and selling. A complex of sentiments and perceptions surround this new economy and its implications. As Sveta explained, generosity and the gift are giving way to trading and exchange. Conspicuous consumption is changing social relations and mistrust is increased due to the 'paralegal' nature of these activities. The women who travel as 'suitcase traders' are perceived by many as engaging in a shameful activity. Popular opinion in Turkey and elsewhere links this trading and mobility with prostitution. Rumors abound about decent Turkish men in Black Sea provincial towns abandoning their wives for a glamorous Natasha.

In the Caucasus, husbands and fathers who allow women to engage in suitcase trading are sometimes described as emasculated. A young man complained that young girls were no longer polite but 'want to drink cognac and use bad words'. The changes in the domestic sphere, however, go beyond the perceptions of gender. While the small margins of profit and the limited nature of the goods involved may make this trading seem 'petty', the impact on the domestic economy is potent. The huge and fancy villas that are being built, especially in the rural villages of origin, are owned by women. Family relations and roles are turned upside down. Artur, the tall 20-year old accompanying his mother to Istanbul, was being treated as a child by women barely a few years older than himself. While a successful woman entrepreneur showed me the house that she was building for herself and her married son, the son quietly and sulkily went on spackling the walls with gold-dust paint. Later he talked at length about how much better it had been under Communism, economically and politically. The Soviet Union had been first in technology and economy and scared the whole world. Communism had protected the small nationalities. Now the economy has collapsed and the 'Russian ideology' is to get the small nations to fight one another.

Sveta, on the other hand, does not look back. She speaks with great confidence about the dollars 'dripping from her hands' and her ability to navigate in the local bureaucracy and global economy. She is also confident of the superiority of her culture, its hospitality and generosity, and of her country, its air and water. She does not appear troubled by a 'loss' of identity or the meanings that should be attached to arrows and stars on a flag. The changes that Sveta will forge may go far beyond what the organizers of the exhibition 'if you are a Circassian . . .' imagined as constituency the rest of the sentence.[12]

Conclusion: modernity unbound

The break-up of the Soviet Union has meant, among other things, that '[I]n December 1991, Soviet citizenship ceased to exist leaving 287 million people in need of a new identity' (IOM *et al.* 1996: 17). There is no doubt that nationalism is an important force in the current post-Soviet space where there are '164 ethnoterritorial disputes and claims' (ibid.: 3). However, nationalism is not the only mobilizing sentiment or practice and it, in itself, embodies the local and the global in interesting ways. The selective disappearance or permeability of borders has had many results, from allowing new ethnoscapes to be formed to the re-emergence of trade routes that had been sundered by a century of industrial capitalism and half a century of modern state building. The 'Islamic world' has also been reconfigured, opening the way for new interpretations of identity and faith. Finally, modernity is no longer exported in orderly channels from a world center to peripheries. It may even be produced by enterprising women transporting cheap commodities wrapped in garbage bags on decrepit airplanes.

Modernity has been suddenly unbound from the frame of the nation–state, with which it used to (notionally, that is) form a seamless unity that was furthermore exportable from the center to the periphery. As Appadurai puts it, modernity is 'at large' (1996a). This means that its production, politically and economically, has been hijacked from the purview of elites, many of whom have resorted to a nostalgia of the pre-modern in the form of heritage politics or even to a sort of imperial cosmopolitanism. The masses, on the other hand, appear to have embraced modernism with a vengeance, the results of which we are yet to behold.

In addition to many other things, globalization involves the syncretic assimilation of commodities, signs and information in different ways in different locales. The north Caucasus may be a peripheral area in the 'world community', but it is one where many histories and economies are intertwined. One small people, the Circassians, call on Russian, Ottoman, Arab, Islamic, Mameluke and local history in order to reconstitute themselves within the swirling forces of transnationalism and globalization. From a small airport in Nalchik, airplanes take off for Peking, Aleppo, Dubai and Istanbul carrying women who are rooted in their local reality but are transforming the global economy.

Is this cosmopolitanism? Is this globalization? Ulf Hannerz (1996) rightly points out that not all forms of mobility and not all interconnections are forces of globalization. He says 'in a stricter sense, cosmopolitanism would entail a greater involvement with a plurality of contrasting cultures to some degree on their own terms.' (1996: 103). Sveta and her sisters are hardly concerned with contrasting cultures except in the most basic terms. Is it paradoxical that the involvement with a plurality of cultures should be more within the purview of the so-called 'ethnonationalists' or 'Islamic militants' rather than of the traders in consumer goods? Or is it another indication that 'modernity is decisively at large, irregularly self-conscious, and unevenly experienced' (Appadurai 1996a: 3)? In this uneven, irregular spread of modernity, where can one locate the local in a particular locality?

On the surface, the provincial towns and pastoral villages of the north Caucasus seem like a backwater, just isolated places, 'full of relatives' and little else. Tourism, perhaps the fastest transformer of idyllic nature, has not yet been able to catch a foothold. The small scale excitement generated by a meeting of the World Circassian Association or a demonstration in support of Abkhasia, hardly compares with the rallies and high pitched excitement of events in the Middle East for example. Although there is satellite television in every house, it is difficult to find a fax machine or to place an international call. It would appear that nowhere could be more local and, if anything, the demise of the Soviet Union is making the north Caucasus even more local.

Yet is it? Hannerz's discussion of the local (1996: 26ff.) opens up the following questions when applied to this particular context: What is 'everyday life' for Sveta, Lena and thousands others who spend most of their time in airports and airplanes? What 'long-term relationships' are there for Omar who arrives in Nalchik and Chechnya from Jordan via Afghanistan or for Hayrettin who is disillusioned by his relatives and drifts between the republics of the North Caucasus? Can one find a 'source of continuity' in a performance of the Kabardinka folklore group playing 'Blissound' Italian recorders purchased from the Circassian owner of a music shop in Amman and performing an Abkhasian dance as they observed it danced in a village in Turkey? What is 'repetitive, redundant' for a little boy called Hajmurat, picked up at kindergarten by his new Jordanian 'father' who then gets killed in Chechnya? What 'face-to-face' encounters lead to Caucasian horses being sent to the King of Jordan in gratitude for support to the Abkhasians? Finally, what are the 'shared understandings' in the open-air markets where people go round and round, like the *hajj*, and purchase goods made in China, Turkey and Poland?

Rather than features of a homogeneous 'local', these connections and transactions could be seen as forms of what Appadurai has termed 'vernacular globalization' (1996a: 10). It appears that modernity is no longer modular. Paraphrasing the Maikop museum we could say 'if modern . . .'. Ethnography shows us the myriad ways in which the phrase could be completed.

Notes

1 Relatives are usually identified through common family names or through the village of origin, if the memory of the latter was retained. The genealogy is generally constructed through a presumed (male) sibling relationship in the generation of the emigration thus creating a sort of global partilineality.
2 The size of these communities is unknown since censuses do not identify people by ethnic origin. Impressionistic sources put the Circassions at around 30,000 and the Chechens at 5,000.
3 In the latest parliamentary elections in 1997, Circassians won all three seats and for the first time Chechens do not have their own representative.
4 At the time of writing this chapter, the Chechenyan capital Grozny and major towns had come under Russian military control. However, there are continuing clashes and the war cannot be said to be over.
5 The reference here is to Imam Shamil (of the Daghestan region rather than Chechnya) who fought Tsarist Russia from 1785–1859. The Chechens rallied to Shamil's call for a holy war more than the Circassians who mostly did not and fought their own battles. Some Circassian regions made peace treaties with the Russians earlier but others continued fighting until 1864.
6 Persian adage quoted in Blanch (1960: 60).
7 The Mameluke slave sultanates of thirteenth to sixteenth century Egypt included several Circassian dynasties.
8 A complex term in Circassian encompassing the meanings of custom, tradition, way of life and essence.
9 For a fuller narrative of Omar's journey see Shami (1998).
10 Haji Murat is the name of a Caucasian hero in Tolstoy's (1896) novel with the same title. Haji means one who has undertaken the pilgrimage to Mecca. Here the title and the name were collapsed into one name for the little boy.
11 In Arabic: 'yiṣrab wa yisjid, yiṣrab wa yisjid'. Literally: drinks and prostrates, drinks and prostrates.
12 For a discussion of Islam and transnationalism see Shami (1996). For a discussion of the reinvention of Orientalism in Central Asia and the Caucasus see Shami (1999).
13 It should be noted that since this article was first written, the volume of suitcase traders to Turkey has fallen dramatically and the Laleli district is reportedly 'dead'. In Turkey some say that Greece has become the favored destination over Turkey because of cheaper prices. It might rather be a reflection of the drastic devaluation of the ruble. This does not invalidate the point about globalization but rather proves it, showing these women's mobility and sensitivity to markets.

Part III

Attachments and arrangements

7 The grounds of the nation–state

Identity, violence and territory[1]

Arjun Appadurai

Love of the nation

Nationalism today is both under pressure and under suspicion. The forces of globalization create the pressure. Worries about the global spread of xenophobic violence fuel the suspicion. Yet nationalism has frequently been a source of high normative hopes, of popular struggles for freedom and of reliable contexts for the provision of justice and security for many human beings. This positive face of nationalism is still with us in, for example, the optimism of Mandela's South Africa. This dual biography of nationalism raises a large interpretive question. Has there been some set of inexorable developments which dooms nationalism to be repressive, xenophobic and anti-liberal, or is there still a place for the nation as a way of organizing new ways of imagining civility, justice and security? Since much of this chapter is a critique of what I call *predatory* nationalism, I will return to the question of what might be called *emancipatory* nationalism in the conclusion.

Nationalism involves, sometimes implicitly and sometimes blatantly, an order of commitment to a social abstraction which is historically unique. In plainer terms, nationalism involves the willingness to kill – or to die – for the good of a plainly artificial collective form. There are, of course, a few stock explanations of this fact. One is that the nation somehow takes on the affective pull of prior sacred orders. But since it simultaneously subverts these very orders in other regards, simple transfer of affect is not a good explanation. A second explanation is what might be called the balloon theory, in which the we – the sentiments of some prior ethnic group are seen to be simply inflated and dressed up in national clothing. This solution simply shifts the problem and has the additional drawback of leading to various discredited primordialist accounts of nationalism. A third explanation is reflectionist and functionalist and usually involves some theory of inequality (Marxist or otherwise) with some version of 'scape-goat' theory to account for nationalism as a displaced affect which is really about something else. This theory suffers from the same defects as the balloon theory and has the additional problem of explaining intense affect in the idioms of structural resentment. The fourth explanation simply sees nationalism as an effect of state propaganda exercises in the modern era. In addition to being circular, this account relies on actually believing that you can fool all of the people all of the time. There are subtler accounts of the historical paths through which the modern sense of peoplehood is produced, but they usually add little that does not depend on some version of the four ideas I have outlined. Even the richest recent works to explore the affective dimensions of nationalism (Anderson 1991; Balibar 1991) do not give us much that is new on the peculiar power of nationalism – as a social abstraction – to mobilize strong affect.

Love of the nation, it is evident, is no mere figure of speech. Parades bring people to their feet. National anthems produce lumps in the throat and flags induce tears in the eye. Insults to national honor can greatly assist internal mobilization and violations of national sovereignty can create irate mobs. Sacrifice, passion, anger, hate are all part of the symphony of affects in which love – here love of the nation – is the orchestrating force. So regularly has love of the nation been invoked by nationalists through every medium of communication that we have ceased to pay attention to its peculiarities.

Can this peculiar affective mode be illuminated by examining the principle of territorial sovereignty? Yes, if we recognize that love of the nation is both a peculiar form of love and also the love of a peculiar kind of object. Consider first what sort of love it is. It is neither erotic nor agapic love (to invoke the classic distinction): it is both. It is erotic in the sense that it involves the sensation of connection, possession and pleasure. It is agapic in the sense that it is communal, 'selfless' and even abstract. It is this peculiar sort of love to which we give the name 'patriotism'. The history of patriotism (and matriatism) as a sentiment is yet to be written, but when it is written it will solve some part of the puzzle of what may be described as *full attachment*. By full attachment I mean that *surplus of affect* which exceeds civic commitment, attribution of legitimacy to a state, or even what Habermas has called 'constitutional patriotism'.[2]

Full attachment

We need to distinguish between three dimensions of the politics and history of the modern nation–state: the problem of legitimation, which essentially pertains to some durable form of consent to a state or regime; the problem of integration, which is essentially a problem of logistics, power and proce-dure; and the problem of what I call 'full attachment', by which I mean just that mysterious surplus of attachment which, in Habermas' words, appeals more strongly, for modern citizens, 'to their hearts and minds than the ideas of popular sovereignty and human rights' (Habermas 1998).

The distinction between full attachment and legitimation requires partic-ular care. Legitimation is in fact tied up with issues of consent, compliance and the procedural recognition of the modern state by its citizens. Full attachment (or patriotism or loyalty, in more common terms) involves something more than the imputation of legitimacy to a sovereign state by its citizens. Its surplus of affect (which is also the justification for using the concept of 'full attachment' rather than the easily available ideas of patriotism, loyalty or, simply, nationalism) is more libidinal than procedural. Though modern states find confirmation of their legitimacy in various forms of mobilization and conscription, there is nevertheless something here which exceeds the problem of legitimation.

The question of why large groups of individuals united by some sort of republican commitment to a modern legal-political order should experience an order of attachment to each other and to the state-defined territory with which they identify which allows them to kill and die in its name is an unsolved puzzle. It is even more puzzling when we consider that these individuals often have prior local or sub-national attachments that have to be explicitly erased by national propaganda in order for nationalism in its strong form to exist. No theory of folk identity, however plausible, can account for the affective side of nationalism, since it is only through the vehicle of the nation–state that such theories come to be at all successful. Likewise, as I observed earlier, it will not do to assume or imply that the nation–state simply continues to exploit the transcendent, religious, sacral mystique of just those orders which it has, in other respects, served violently to repudiate.

In short, the largeness, historical diversity and abstractness of the social relations encompassed (and valorized) by the modern nation–state make it difficult to understand the willingness of modern citizens to kill and to die for it. Thus the passionate excess that is expressed in full attachment is especially puzzling in view of the extent to which modern political orders require a virtually transcendental commitment to rules, procedures and impersonal structures of authority.

The puzzle of full attachment is impervious to three widespread and influential interpretive moves. Benedict Anderson's important thesis about print-capitalism and the spread of nationalism from the Americas to Europe and then to the colonies (and the many subsequent extensions of this argument), does not offer any decisive breakthrough on this question, although it sheds important new light on the links between racism, imperialism and cults of death (Anderson 1991). An offshoot of Anderson's general theory, which links nation to narration, is also interesting and suggestive but only shifts the explanation of full attachment to the domain of mass mediation and narrativity. The third view, so widespread that it is hard to find an original author for it, is that modern nation–states produce this surplus of affect by various kinds of rituals and symbols (flags, holidays, commemorations, exhibitions, cemeteries, stamps, cenotaphs and the like). The trouble with this latter approach to 'full attachment' is that it assumes, wrongly, that rituals stoked by calculation can mechanically produce durable collective effervescence. This alchemical view of ritual – which is frequently underwritten by an equally unspecified sense that any sort of national propaganda simply works by definition – finds little sustenance in any close analysis of actual ritual processes. The idea that modern nation–states borrow the mystique of some form of primordial folk identity to complement the force of democratic legitimation provided by the voluntary association of free and equal citizens is not entirely wrong. But it obscures what may be a more disturbing mechanism by which the modern nation–state secures what I have called full attachment, apart from any claims to legitimacy. Full attachment, rather than coming from an authentic prior sense of shared community (whether based on language, history, soil or some other primordium), might actually be produced by various forms of violence instigated, perhaps even required, by the modern nation–state.

Many other theorists of nationalism would agree that the modern nation–state is able to mobilize, conscript and deploy its citizens in warfare (or preparation for it) because it already has some prior (and plausible) claim to full attachment. But a more parsimonious explanation would be that the modern nation–state *requires* various forms of violent mobilization in order to 'produce the people' (in Balibar's terms) and, in Foucault's terms, to deploy the techniques of modern governmentality (census, mapping, sanitation, surveillance, incarceration). Put more simply: violence (internal violence associated with ethnic cleansing; more capillary techniques of surveillance and schooling; or external violence associated with expansion, empire and colonialism) produces full attachment, rather than the reverse. To explore this argument and to understand what looks like an intimate link between nationalism, full attachment and violence, I turn to a discussion of what may be called 'predatory identities'.

Predatory identities

We know that most modern nations achieve their sense of their cultural homogeneity in the face of remarkable and known diversities and fierce micro-attachments that have to be erased, marginalized or transformed. Few modern nations emerge seamlessly out of previous ethnicities. Whether it is peasants being turned into Frenchmen, Scots being turned into Britons, Hindus into Indians, for some nations to be imagined, others have to be deemed 'unimaginable'. Majorities do not exist until they are counted, mapped and mobilized. And minorities do not exist until there are majorities. As several recent theorists have noted, national memory requires large amounts of forgetting, notably the forgetting of prior nodes of identification, previous enmities, more intimate attachments. How are these miracles accomplished, even if they command consent sway only for a decades? At least in part through the mobilization of predatory identities.

By predatory identities I mean large-scale group identities that seem to require – as a rigid requirement of their mobilization and force – the restriction, degradation or outright elimination of other identities, usually numerically, culturally and constitutionally 'minor' ones. Predatory identities operate in a zero-sum ethos where affiliates of one identity, their growth and welfare are constructed to be culturally compromised, politically incomplete or spatially insulted by the presence of other, 'victim' identities. Such 'victim' identities also emerge mysteriously and contingently and are not always predictable in advance: thus, while it may have been easy to predict that 'ethnic' Chinese in Malaysia or Muslims in India are obvious candidates as objects of predation, it would have been less easy to predict that Sikhs in India or Muslims in Bosnia would have emerged as 'victim' categories.

Let us begin with the issue of number and scale. I have elsewhere suggested some reasons why the politics of the 'new ethnicities' involved with the public violence in the last few decades are partly artifacts of their numerical largeness (Appadurai 1996a: Chapter 7). We are dealing frequently with 'imagined communities' that number in the tens of thousands and, frequently, in the millions. From this numerical fact about the context of 'predatory' identities, there follow several implications. First, the relations within these groups are only partly face-to-face. Their intimacies are abstract, produced by various mediated experiences of mobilization, narration and communication. Second, these mediated experiences draw on, disseminate and re-present day-to-day relations which anchor these numerical abstractions in narratives of intimacy, which are then re-articulated as instantiations of threats to an abstract set of claims and rights which are projected in the idiom of honor, integrity and purity.

Large-scale and abstract identities turn predatory in part by annexing attributes, images and experiences that are intense, immediate and concrete. In this way, what are often mere *terms*, designating large populations covering diverse territories, become *names*, indexing forms of attachment that are highly charged, honor-bearing and sensitive to insult.

The standing modern model (and primary source) for the mobilization of large groups as if they were small-scale, intimate identities is that of the nation. Nationalism – the positive affect which nations seek to produce and nurture – is the primary and ideal form of the mobilization of large groups through techniques of *identification*. Modern nations, as it has been widely pointed out, somehow succeed in a mysteriously contradictory exercise: they simultaneously supplant prior sacral orders in the name of something secular and forward-looking, while preserving, in a host of symbolic and ritual claims and techniques, the sacral legitimacies of earlier forms of large-scale identification. It is this fact that has tempted a number of observers to turn to primordialist explanations of contemporary ethnic violence. In such theories, older religious wars have simply reappeared under new guises. In such cases as Northern Ireland, Sri Lanka, Bosnia and India, where large-scale 'religious' identities were a crucial part of premodern civil society, such explanations are especially tempting. They are wrong, for reasons I have substantially addressed elsewhere (Appadurai 1996a). Briefly, they cannot account for the fact that large-scale violence in the premodern history of these identities was relatively rare; that the stakes attached to these identities were dramatically different from those that obtain under modern states (whether liberal-democratic or totalitarian); and that the absence of mass media in these contexts made the entire process of 'imagining' shared life worlds part of a quite different logic of affiliation and identification.

There are variable historical roads from the ethnic roots of modern nationalism to the construction of large-scale predatory identities, in places like Indonesia, Rwanda and Pakistan, and I cannot discuss them all here. What they have in common is the need of *modern* states, however much they may aspire to work as rational-legal-bureaucratic orders (in the Weberian sense), based on the voluntary association of free and equal citizens, to construct and nurture some sort of discourse of the Volk, whether linguistic, sanguinary, territorial or organic-historical. From the United States to Papua New Guinea, some plausible answer has had to be supplied to answer the question: what magic halo distinguishes *this* group of modern citizens from the next one? Pressures to cleanse internally and expand imperially are frequently exercises in supplying answers to this question.

Put even more simply, the endemic need for nation–states to mobilize citizenries on the grounds of sacral attachments to the nation-form, which always justify calls to military service, if nothing else, invariably opens the door to recasting these attachments in majoritarian forms, as grounds for some groups to turn predatory and claim the space of the nation and/or the apparatus of the state itself. This is the link between predatory identities and predatory nationalisms.

Predatory nationalisms find their most fertile contexts where ethnicist criteria of being and belonging become primarily tied to the procedures, rewards and spoils of the state apparatus, whether it is electoral, totalitarian or authoritarian-populist. In other words, predatory identities thrive where their successes can have (or promise to have) material gains of a large sort from the coffers of the state. Here we are back with the contradiction between the modern nation–state as a legal-bureaucratic association and as a organic expression of folkness, acutely observed by Arendt in *The Origins of Totalitarianism* (1967). But this very general contradiction, while it may provide the broadest causal frame for explaining the rise and form of predatory identities, can only serve to explain specific forms and contexts of predatory nationalism when it is linked to particular cases and spaces.

Space and violence

The central problem with current discussions of space is, as with the understanding of violence, that the nature of the leap between macro and micro discussions seems daunting. On the one hand, there is a growing body of work, lying at the boundaries of political geography, international relations, and urban studies, which is re-examining the links between territorial sovereignty, political integrity and security, in relation to contemporary nation–states (Agnew and Corbridge 1995). Some of this work focuses on new regional formations and breakaway nationalisms, other work focuses on the comparative study of territorial disputes (Lustick 1993), yet other work focuses on the role of mega-cities in fostering non-national zones for transnational economies of labor and production (Sassen 1991). Much of this work, directly or indirectly, recognizes that the territorial integrity of nation–states is not always viable in an era of globalization and that the various forms of 'realism' characteristic of an earlier period in the discipline of international relations, require serious modification (Connolly 1991; Shapiro 1994). The principal implication of much of this work for the study proposed here is that we have to be prepared to understand a world in which human migration, mass mediation and porous state-boundaries have created new disjunctures between soil and territory, between citizen and resident, between national space and the space of daily security and sustenance (Appadurai 1996a; Yeager 1996).

While political scientists and students of international relations have been re-examining the links between territory, state boundaries and interstate relations, more culturally oriented theorists have been increasingly preoccupied with the problematics of 'imagined' communities, invented 'traditions' and circulating vocabularies of nationalism (Anderson 1991; Chatterjee 1986). This has led to an understandable focus on major sites of national spectacle and commemoration and, in general, to the sacred spaces of national identity and ethnoreligious solidarity. What I will do is explore the puzzle of full attachment by looking more closely at the issue of territoriality. There is much to be said for the vital role of territory – more specifically of territorial sovereignty – in distinguishing the modern nation–state from prior and parallel forms of collective social life and governance. Everything else that is invoked as vital to the nation–state – both by its theorists and by its ideologues – is a principle of attachment that the nation–state shares with other sociopolitical forms. Blood, race, language, history, 'culture' – all have pre-national expressions and non-national applications. They can be used to justify, extend or inculcate love of the nation but they are not distinctive of the national form. Without some idea of territorial sovereignty the modern nation–state loses all coherence.

Naturally, the idea of territorial sovereignty in Western political history does not descend *ab nihilo* in the sixteenth or seventeenth century. Like other major socio-legal ideas, it has a complex genealogy with roots that go back to Roman ideas of royal dominion. But one does not have to be a specialist in the history of Western law to recognize that the *modern* idea of territorial sovereignty is new in several striking ways, notably the following: it vests dominion not in the person of a king but in the abstraction called the 'state', which is in turn conceived as an instrument of popular rule; it requires boundaries, meaning specific lines of demarcation between adjacent states, rather than frontiers, which are zones of transition between polities; it decisively severs the link between land as *property* (typically the property of the king) and land as the space of popular sovereignty as such.

One consequence of this new sense of spatiality is that space and number begin to be linked, and majorities (associated the techniques of the census, taxation and conscription) become claimants to the voice of popular sovereignty. Predatory nationalisms thus appear to grow and thrive in situations where the relationship between state policies, ethnic majorities and minorities, and borders appears to create an accelerating cycle of ethnic exits, national paranoias and ethnic cleansings which lead to further exits. The African subcontinent is particularly rich in this pattern of ethnocidal identities, notably in the increasingly complex ethnic politics which appear to link Zaire, Rwanda, Burundi and Tanzania. The transformation of 'Hutu' and 'Tutsi' into mutual predators, in different spatial and national settings, combines several features of the genealogy of predatory identities: colonial census policies which create fixed, large-scale, exclusive categories where there were previously shifting categories of identification; postcolonial policies pursued by corrupt states seeking civic legitimation through ethnic terror; and refugee flows which these unstable polities are in no position to sequester from their internal politics.

In the formation of some modern predatory nationalisms, imagined threats to 'religious' identity are vital, so the question of how religion is imbricated in the production of religious identities cannot be avoided. Here the example of the growth of Hindutva, the ideological marker of a virulent form of right-wing Hindu nationalism which has emerged in India in the last decade, is especially instructive. Much splendid work has been done on what is called 'communalism' in the last decade in India (Chatterjee 1993; Das 1995; Ludden 1996; Pandey 1993; van der Veer 1994). Furthermore, because of the well-studied colonial, precolonial and postcolonial dynamics of the present phenomenon of 'Hindutva', we are uniquely situated, with the many movements that fall under the rubric of 'Hindutva', to examine the genealogy of a predatory identity and to test the relevance of 'religion' to such a genealogy.

One interesting conclusion to be drawn from this literature about predatory Hindutva has not yet been closely observed. It is the possibility that predatory Hindutva is the outcome of the growing and unavoidable tension between the workings of secularism as a constitutionally mandated feature of the legal-bureaucratic state in postcolonial India (which withholds political legitimacy from Hindus, or Hinduism) and the continuing (and even growing) call for attachment to the nation ('India'). This tension is a built-in inducement to the mobilization of majoritarian, organicist, nativist leanings best provided by militant Hinduism. Thus, quasi-legitimized by the power of nationalist rhetoric in postcolonial India and simultaneously de-legitimated by India's unofficial commitment to democratic secularism in the distributive policies of the state, Hinduism becomes Hindutva (a predatory form of nationalism) in an effort to explode this contradiction by erasing the gap between 'Hindu' and 'Indian' and by capturing, to the extent possible, the apparatus of the state through a mixture of parliamentary and extra-legal techniques, including the periodic unleashing of ethnic violence against non-Hindus, usually Muslims.

There are, of course other factors special to the Indian case: the long-term cultural articulation of Hindu and Muslim identities; the pervasive linkage of religious and caste groups to vote-banks in Indian politics; the continuing tensions of Partition which guarantee a constant fear about Indian Muslims as potential traitors, a fifth column for Pakistan, the peculiar tension between civil and personal law, the growth of the distance between wealthy middle classes and a truly disenfranchised rural and urban underclass, the struggle over positive discrimination in favor of 'backward' castes and the like. But the structuring motivation, perhaps also of the widest general application, is the simultaneous de-legitimation and tacit relegitimation of 'Hindu' as a category of political affiliation. But to examine how these virulent forms of religious identification take spatial-territorial expression, we need to look closer to the ground, at ethnic violence in cities like Bombay.

Bombay, a city with a population in 1998 over 10 million and clearly likely to become one of the mega-cities of the twenty-first century, has had a well-deserved reputation for ethnic tolerance, commercial drive and openness to migrants from the rest of India. Yet the growth of the Shiva Sena (a Bombay-based right-wing ethnochauvinist party) to a major power in the city, the state and the country have been part of a growing politics of intolerance to non-speakers of Marathi, the majority language of the state of which Bombay is the capital. In the latter part of the 1980s, there was a convergence between the growth of Hindu nationalist parties at the level of national politics and the ethnic chauvinist politics of 'regional' parties such as the Shiva Sena. The heating up of anti-Muslim politics throughout this period culminated in the planned destruction of a major place of Muslim worship, the Babri Masjid in the provincial town of Ayodhya in Uttar Pradesh, in December 1992. In the wake of this major act of violence against India's Muslims, preceded and followed by a steady effort to marginalize and terrorize Muslims throughout India, there were massive outbreaks of violence against Muslims in Bombay, as well as a major bomb explosion, widely attributed to international Islamic terrorists (much as with the New York World Trade Building bombing). All this took place in the period from December 1992 to March 1993.

There is a considerable body of material which has been published on the Bombay riots.[3] This material contains enough descriptions and testimony to provide a detailed picture of specific incidents, actors and locations. What emerges is a complex picture of organized crime, police collusion, political bungling, lumpen involvement and economic and spatial stress. Also, what emerges clearly is the direct effort of the Shiva Sena (in speeches and editorials in its party newspaper) to link the ethnic geography of Bombay to the national geography of Muslims and to Pakistan as the enemy.

A crucial link between micro-episodes of extreme violence and national politics was a ritual innovation by the Shiva Sena – the *maha-arati* (rough gloss: great offering) – a type of public religious performance with no prior mandate, which was specifically and widely deployed to monopolize, sacralize and aggressively colonize streets in key neighborhoods, with an eye to intimidating Muslims in the public sphere. It is through such performances – among a host of other organizational and discursive practices – that the Shiva Sena succeeded in turning Bombay into a living simulacrum of a sacred 'Hindu' public space rather than a poly-ethnic, commercial, secular urban world.

Bombay, like many mega-cities of the world of the late twentieth century, is characterized by the following: the gap between rich and poor; the spatial fortifications that divide the residences of the rich from the living spaces of the poor; the high incidence of 'informal' sources of livelihood for the poor; the dramatic intercutting of civic, sacred and commercial spaces; the dramatic force of transnational currency, images and arms; the growth of private militias. In these circumstances the line between international and civil wars tends to become blurred as does the line between the territorial boundaries of the nation–state and the demand for 'pure' spaces of day-to-day ethnic habitation. Predatory identities thrive (especially in their capacity to draw the energies of street thugs, neighborhood bosses, local mafia and petty criminals) when issues of endangered ethnonational identity are successfully 'downloaded' into the crowded, necessarily mixed spaces of everyday work and life.

It is in part such 'downloading' that accounts for the success with which nations subordinate, erase or eradicate prior attachments. But what actually happens in places like Bombay and Karachi, Sarajevo and Hebron, Djakarta and Los Angeles, and in countries as different as Cambodia, Rwanda, Yugoslavia and Indonesia in the last few decades seems to elude our analyses. We know that episodes of large-scale violence in the name of ethnicity have some common features in these and other settings that we know from the national headlines. We also know that other factors – the power of the state, the health of the economy, the sudden arrival of new immigrants, fear of new forms of marketization, paranoias about democratic government, work to make these settings in other ways very different. But the black box remains largely black: we do not know what, in a characterization I used elsewhere, turns 'cool' identities into 'hot' ones. Seeing how national space is inscribed into particular places, especially large societies gives us some understanding of this transformation.

It is not difficult to see that the politics of national (and transnational) space has 'imploded' (Appadurai 1996a) into specific localities and in particular into certain major cities, such as Los Angeles, Beirut, Sarajevo, Bombay and into smaller satellite cities. The sense of sacredness, integrity, sovereignty and security previously associated with national spaces, sites and monuments has, in some cases, imploded (or folded, or became scaled down) into cities, neighborhoods, buildings and sometimes even specific streets and houses. It is in such cities that, most frequently, policies of ethnic displacement, slum-habitations, illegal housing markets, informal commercial uses of public space, pressure on civic resources and organized crime interweave to link work, property, residence and leisure.

Spatial practices (in the sense of de Certeau 1984) in big cities subject to the pressures of migration, global resource-flows, and heavy media saturation, are always delicate efforts to balance formal and informal economies, police and criminal elements, disparate castes and classes, dissonant public practices of religion and ethnicity, and high-intensity displays of political, religious and ethnic muscle. It is in the intersection between such heavily fraught urban ecologies and national and transnational battles over religious identities and claims that the worst episodes of inter-ethnic violence can break out.[4]

The link between large numbers, urban fragilities and state-sponsored categories of identification and affiliation creates a special climate of uncertainty in which extreme bodily violence can thrive. I have recently suggested that such violence can be viewed as a distorted form of vivisection, in which the body of the ethnic enemy can be violated in the most extreme ways, as a method of resolving such uncertainty (Appadurai 1998a). Such intimate violence is frequently tied up with images of secrecy, masks and betrayal, all of which carry the underlying sense that bodies simultaneously reveal and conceal ethnic identities. This duality produces forms of violence which are both sudden and extreme. Such violence, typically described in the idiom of the 'riot', invariably intensifies the sacralization and nationalization of streets, houses, neighborhoods and other aspects of the spaces of ordinary life. The most powerful document of such reinscription of everyday space is to be found in Northern Ireland in the last few decades (Feldman 1991).

It is in such events of extreme collective violence that we can see the spiraling loop which produces predatory nationalisms out of the materials of relatively benign ethnic oppositions and differences. The historical processes which exemplify these spirals surely vary in many ways but they all testify to the causal inversion that I proposed earlier: certain forms of violence produce nationalism rather than the reverse. Once in motion, the cycle of violence incorporates both dimensions and, in theoretical hindsight, nationalism itself has been seen more often as the cause than as the effect of collective violence. However, this complex causal cycle requires much fuller historical investigation than the present context allows.

Conclusion: globalization and governance

It remains now to ask whether all nationalism is doomed at some point to turn into predatory nationalism because of the generality of the logic that links space, territory and full attachment. I think not, but my optimism requires a rethinking of the conceptual and normative architecture of the modern nation–state. It appears to me that the recent efflorescence of nationalisms (as well as the intensity of their self-assertion) is intimately connected to the very processes that have eroded the capabilities of many states to monopolize loyalty. Here I take recourse to a particular understanding of the current crisis of the *system* of nation–states (not this or that particular nation–state) as a problem of globalization, an argument I have begun to develop in some earlier work (Appadurai 1996a, 1996b) and return to in this concluding section.

As supranational processes steadily erode the sovereignty of nation–states, some sort of transformation in global systems of governance will be required. Given the insecure basis of many national sovereignties, traditional international legal and economic arrangements are unlikely to be effective in this regard. If so, what means for providing positive, voluntary and peaceful forms of supranational consocation can we imagine? In the absence of such forms, we will enter an unpredictable and unregulated form of supranational politics, dominated by the unfettered play of large-scale global organizations unattached to specific sociomoral communities. Where are we to find some sort of moral counterpoint to the unfettered play of global capital and some form of large-scale attachment to ground the building of morally and socially meaningful lifeworlds in which politics, of some positive sort, can continue? Can we find peaceful forms of supranational politics which might provide the sort of glue that nationalism provided for the nation–state in an earlier era, but minus its built-in violence and artifice? This is the key question of supranational politics in the era of globalization, and I can hardly deal with its many ethical and institutional implications here.

What I can suggest is a line of thinking which departs more radically from the existing conceptual architecture of the modern nation-form. The current crisis of sovereignty besets not just individual nation–states but the very system of nation–states, yet the vast majority of solutions to this crisis assumes the eternal and self-evident logic of the nation–state as the central form of articulation for modern politics. Contrarian thinking, which stresses the radical potential of organizations like the World Trade Organization, of global environmental and feminist movements, of treaties to regulate nuclear proliferation and spread the values of human rights, still takes the conceptual framework of the system of nation–states as largely non-negotiable. This mode of thinking continues to see meaningful forms of translocal political association as non-overlapping, formally equal, spatially bounded envelopes containing coherent clusters of citizens, cultural loyalties, resources, and legal-political procedures for the provision of justice and the monopoly of violence.

However, as I have argued at greater length elsewhere, we may need to abandon precisely the idea that space, cultural identity and distributive politics need to be contained in formally equal, spatially distinct and isomorphic envelopes, the design which undergirds the architecture of the modern state. Indeed, I have tried to show that it is this very isomorphism which frequently leads to extreme violence. In the modern system of nation–states, international governance normatively relies on a single and homogenous set of units – nation–states – which inspire and negotiate all forms of supra-local political interaction. But the world in which we live is formed of forms of consociation, identification, interaction and aspiration which regularly cross national boundaries. Refugees, global laborers, scientists, technicians, soldiers, entrepreneurs, and many other social categories of persons constitute large blocks of meaningful association that do not depend on the isomorphism of citizenship with cultural identity, of work with kinship, of territory with soil, or of residence with national identification. It is these delinkages which might best capture what is distinctive about *this* era of globalization.

These kinds of delinkage are clearly threats to the architecture of national sovereignty which we owe to the Treaty of Westphalia. But might they also be sources for thinking of new forms of full attachment which are peaceful, politically productive sources of well-being and for designing effective mechanisms for the distribution of security and dignity to large populations? Is it possible to think, in the first instance normatively, of a world in which the logic of citizenship and the logic of full attachment (what, in a problematic way, is produced in classical nationalism) do not require a single common political container, the nation–state?

Put another way, can we think of a global politics which admits of a heterogeneity of *overlapping* forms of governance and attachment (some national, some statist, and others neither), rather than one which requires a homogeneous set of interacting units? This sort of heterogeneity, which might involve negotiations between many kinds of large-scale political organizations, raises a host of practical problems about rights, wrongs and peaceful large-scale governmentality. But the prior problem is conceptual and normative: are we prepared to think of a world in which the procedural virtues of the modern legal-bureaucratic state and the moral and cultural needs of human groups for all sorts of attachments, including what I have called full attachment, are not played out in isomorphic, mutually exclusive, spatial-political envelopes?

If such a thought experiment can be constructed, then we may be freed from what seems to be an inexorable logic which leads from modern states to predatory nationalisms, a line of development whose analysis has dominated this chapter. If benign (or emancipatory) nationalism is to become both real and widespread, it will rest on a different architecture for the relationship between space, governance, and identification. A full discussion of that architecture must recognize its utopian qualities. Without some such fundamental architectural revision, love of the nation must become an obsolete sentiment, or worse, a mere alibi for deadlier kinds of affect. Of course, it might be argued that the new forms of consociation and attachment that emerge are not really nations at all. In that case, in pursuing the potential of these new forms, we have nothing to lose but our terms.

Notes

1   This chapter was first presented as a paper at the Nobel Symposium on 'Nationalism and Internationalism in the Post-Cold War Era' held in Stockholm from September 7–10 1997. I have benefited considerably from the reactions of others present on that occasion and from the encouragement of the editors of this volume. Work on this version was partly facilitated by a Fellowship from the Open Society Institute (New York).
2   The reader may wish to consult a recent debate surrounding Habermas' ideas about the future of sovereignty and citizenship in *Public Culture* (1998), which includes an essay by this author (Appadurai 1998b).
3   For a good overview of this literature, see the essays by Sharma, Heuze, and Lele in Patel and Thorner (1995), and Masselos (1994). A vivid journalistic picture of the 1992–93 riots can be found in Padgaonkar (1993).
4   This highly compressed picture of Bombay in the late 1980s and early 1990s will be considerably expanded in a forthcoming book on ethnic violence in the era of globalization being researched by the author of this chapter.

8 From Khartoum to Quebec

Internationalism and nationalism within the multi-community state[1]

Kalevi J. Holsti

Humanity is constantly struggling with two contradictory processes. One of these tends to promote unification, while the other aims at maintaining or re-establishing diversification.

(Claude Lévi-Strauss 1976: 361)

The French anthropologist Claude Lévi-Strauss made this observation at a time when the forces of integration and fragmentation were not so conspicuously present in the international system. Liberal internationalism, which by the 1920s had become a common expectation if not a very accurate description of international relations, was the set of tenets and hypotheses about historical development that emphasized growing international collaboration and perhaps ultimate integration, or unification in Lévi-Strauss' idiom. That vision has not died through World War II and the Cold War. Today, metaphors such as 'spaceship earth', the 'global village', 'shrinking planet', and 'globalization' express the same optimistic ideas as those enunciated as early as the late eighteenth century by Jeremy Bentham, and increasingly frequently by British liberals throughout the nineteenth century. The idea is relatively simple: increased contacts between individuals and political communities – usually formatted as states – will lead to increased empathy, understanding, international collaboration, and perhaps to formal political amalgamation or integration (cf. Goldmann 1994: chapter 1). On the face of it, nationalism should be antithetical to internationalism, since it emphasizes distinctness and promotes separation rather than integration. In a particularly virulent form, it has also promoted the idea of national superiority, domination, and even supremacy. It is for this reason that most English-language textbooks of international relations in the 1920s and 1930s, and even through the Cold War, characterized nationalism as a source of conflict rather than of international understanding and collaboration. Lévi-Strauss' observation challenges the common liberal assumption of an historical and inexorable movement toward international integration. Fragmentation, represented by various modes of nationalism, is as much a force in the world today as is integration.

Yet, there is a different current of thinking about nationalism that has seen it not only as compatible with internationalism, but as actually promoting it. In the mid-nineteenth century, for example, Mazzini worked for the unification of Italy using the argument that a unified people brought into the framework of a single state would enhance the possibilities for international cooperation. Woodrow Wilson planned and advocated the post-World War I order on the idea that reciprocity-based international cooperation can take place only between democracies, and that peoples residing in states based on natural communities of culture, language, and religion would provide a secure foundation for peace in Europe. Wilson was not alone in this hypothesis. It had become a fundamental belief of all those who championed the concept of national self-determination. A revindicated nationalism would put an end to the agitation and conflicts that had raged in the multinational empires of Europe prior to the Great War. This same hypothesis was extended to cover the colonial territories after World War II. Once liberated from the colonial yoke, the newly-independent countries would help fashion what was to become the first truly global international order. Nationalism, in brief, made internationalism and thus peace possible.

Most analysts since 1989 have returned to the thesis that nationalism and internationalism are not only simultaneous processes in the contemporary world, but also incompatible. Post-Cold War studies of the 'New World Order' (or Disorder) have emphasized that with the waning of superpower ideological competition, long suppressed nationalism was re-appearing (cf. Brown 1993). Events in Yugoslavia and other former socialist states provided the empirical fodder for these proclamations. As for the Third World, observers have written of the 'coming anarchy' (Kaplan 1994), the 'tale of two worlds' (Goldgeier and McFaul 1992), 'zones of turmoil' (Singer and Wildavsky 1993), '*le nouveau moyen âge*' (Minc 1993), and 'the clash of civilizations' (Huntington 1993). All seem to be saying the same thing, though in somewhat different terms: the end of the Cold War has brought forth an era characterized most notably by rampant nationalism, political fragmentation, humanitarian emergencies, and civilizational conflicts. The West, according to these observers, is the arena of true internationalism, where the Kantian Pacific Union of democracies has made war between states increasingly unlikely if not unthinkable. This is the region where nineteenth-century liberal internationalism has finally triumphed and become institutionalized, where liberalism's optimism has become vindicated after years of fighting the two great totalitarianisms, fascism first, and communism later. There are few today who argue that such claims can be made about other areas of the world. The West, the assertion maintains, has overcome the main negative aspects of nationalism and embraced the tenets and practices of liberal internationalism.

The rest of the world is still grappling with major forces of fragmentation ranging from tribalism to nationalism, mostly without success. Lévi-Strauss' contradictory processes seem to be in full swing today.

Testing liberal internationalism: between states

Let us review briefly the main propositions of liberal-internationalist thought. The standard liberal internationalist argument is summarized in what we might term the 'Bentham hypothesis'. Free trade and communication between peoples will not only enhance prosperity, but will also promote cooperation, empathy, and friendship among peoples. These in turn will ultimately reduce conflicts bred of nationalism and chauvinism (cf. Richardson 1997: 16). For Cobden, Mill, and in the thinking of Lord Palmerston, trade is the greatest engine of peace.

> It is that the exchange of commodities may be accompanied by the extension and diffusion of knowledge – by the interchange of mutual benefit engendering mutual kind feelings . . . It is that commerce may freely go forth, leading civilization with one hand, and peace with the other.
>
> (Bourne 1970: 255)

This idea has become a staple of contemporary liberal thought. Echoing his predecessor as Britain's Prime Minister, John Major (1992) declared in 1992 that 'trade is a peacemaker – one of the most powerful and persuasive'. Similar themes have been expressed dozens of times by political leaders from almost all major countries and a high proportion of lesser powers.

The 1975 Helsinki Agreements and the 1991 Charter of Paris, as well as the principles underlying the European Union, institutionalize the main tenets of liberal internationalist thought. They state that if you want peace between countries you must have the following:

- democratic practices within states;
- free flow of goods, people, and ideas between societies;
- strict observation of human and minority rights;
- private markets and freedom to trade.

To the extent that relations between states in western Europe conform to these norms and requirements – and they do largely – the internationalist position is sustained. Perhaps in Western Europe we are beginning to see the end of international politics as that term has been used conventionally. We see instead something more akin to politics within a federal state. Cultural, language, and religious differences persist, but do not express themselves in the practices or ideas of domination, subordination, and military threats. Politics within Europe and North America are certainly more 'national' than the relations between ethnic/cultural groups in Rwanda or in post-Cold War Yugoslavia. In the latter there is a 'state of war' between groups within states.

Testing liberal internationalism: within the state

Within many regions of the contemporary world, the main political problem is not relations between states but relations between communities within states (Holsti 1996: Chapter 1). Since most states are made up of numerous communities distinguished by language, religion, ethnicity, and some combination of them, current problems of peace and war revolve around 'sub-nationalism'. This is not the nationalism of the *state*, as the problem was usually understood throughout most of this century, but the nationalism of groups within states. If the main tenets of liberal internationalism can be demonstrated in relations between states and individuals, is there any reason to believe that they should not operate similarly between distinct communities within the state?

Most wars since 1945 have been internal rather than between states. The ratio of intra- to inter-state wars (excluding anti-colonial wars) is about seven to one, and most wars between states or major armed interventions began as domestic armed conflicts (Holsti, 1996: Chapter 2).[2] The relations between communities, and between communities and governments in many states are actually microcosms of the inter-national in the sense that they involve relations between nations (defined as distinct groups) even though they conduct those relations within the context of a state. If we can see groups that coexist reasonably peacefully within the context of states, then we might expect similar results in relations between states. The reverse is that if communities *within* states cannot coexist peacefully, we should not expect our Bentham hypothesis to hold in relations *between* states.

Looking at the record since 1945, we can easily come to pessimistic conclusions. The predictions and expectations of liberal internationalism have not been borne out in many areas of the world. The list of secession wars, civil wars, and politicides directed against specific groups or analogues of nations within the state is lengthy. There have been at least sixty secessionist movements since 1945 involving some level of violence; thirty of them persist today (Heraclides 1997: 500–3). From Khartoum to Quebec, from Zagreb to Zanzibar (1964), and from Bosnia to some in Belgium, members of distinct communities announce loudly to their fellow citizens: 'we do not want to live with you'. Collaboration, mutual understanding, empathy, and continued integration obviously are not the values in play in internal wars and violent secessionist movements.

It is a problem that is actually or potentially relevant to all multicommunity states. It transcends dichotomies such as rich–poor, developed–

underdeveloped, Western–non-Western, and the like. Impoverished Sudan has been racked by civil war since the early 1980s. The Parti Québecois began its long march to separation from wealthy Canada about the same time. A comparatively old state, Spain, has weathered Basque separatism for a generation, while a relatively new state, Yugoslavia, finally fell to pieces in three brutal, interconnected wars. The record of carnage, violence against one's fellow citizens, and humanitarian disasters since 1945 would seem to support Jean Jacques Rousseau's pessimistic challenge to the Bentham hypothesis: trade and other forms of contact and interaction between states and peoples increase, rather than decrease, conflict. The record of relations between groups within states in the contemporary international system poses a serious challenge to liberal internationalists who have always assumed that more transactions and interactions between distinct social groups have peace-building and possibly integrative consequences.

Framing the problem

Internationalism is ultimately a theory or hypothesis that identifies the mechanisms through which the conflict-promoting consequences of social difference can be transcended to create normally peaceful relations between groups. Contrary to Realist arguments about the consequences of anarchy – fear, threat, conflict, and war – the liberal view offers the possibility of anarchy *and* peace. It tells us the necessary and sufficient conditions for distinct peoples and communities to live in peace with each other, even when they are separated juridically, politically, and culturally. Liberalism starts with optimistic assumptions about human nature and the results of human aggregation. Left to their own devices, people are naturally sympathetic and empathetic. Bentham, in contrast to Rousseau's pessimism, posited a natural harmony between societies, a harmony that was disrupted only by the actions of despotic governments (cf. Hinsley 1963: 83–7). Realists see peace as an exceptional condition in international relations. Liberal internationalists see war as the anomaly. It has been portrayed in the liberal literature as a disease, as a mistake, as a deviation, as a pathology associated with despotisms of various kinds, indeed, as anything but normal. The abnormality is usually explained in terms of nationalism, decision-making errors, lack of understanding, misperceptions, despotism, and militarism. But these are all the problems of *elites*, as Bentham and Wilson suggested, not of people at the grass roots.

The solutions flowing from such diagnoses are usually found in the realm of democratization, such as allowing more popular control over foreign policy and rendering the official relations between states more transparent (e.g., Wilson's criticisms of 'secret diplomacy'). These liberal diagnoses and prescriptions all derive from the view that 'ordinary' people can be trusted to live and conduct their mutual relations in peace if not in total harmony. The same themes emerge from current metaphors such as the 'global village'. The more people listen to each other, communicate, and trade, the better their relations. Foreign aid, cultural exchange programs, and international tourism are all founded on such tenets. If they are valid, then they should apply equally to relations between communities within states as to relations between states.

What, exactly, is the contemporary problem of relations between communities within states? Why have we seen so many politicides (Rummell 1994), internal wars, secessionist movements, and other phenomena that suggest the strong pull of localism, parochialism, exclusiveness, and intolerance? Why is ethnic cleansing – invented long before the Bosnian Serbs practiced it in the 1990s – such an odious yet seemingly common response to societies that have been reasonably integrated for long periods of time? We can turn to political philosophers to look for answers, but strangely they do not prove very helpful.

Theories of the political community

Hobbes (1651/1962) solved the problem of communities within states by ignoring them. His state of nature was populated not by groups, associations, classes, or other affiliations, but by a *multitude*. By some sleight of hand, this multitude becomes a political community whose members contract with the Leviathan to establish law and order in a 'Common-Wealth'. The contract remains, however, between individuals and the Leviathan, which becomes the sole legitimation of the collectivity. Hobbes does not problematize the community either in the state of nature or in the 'Common-Wealth'. The 'multitude' do not seem to have defining borders. They do not have any indication of identity; and there are no bonds of fraternity or even special bases of enmity between their members. Yet, somehow they make a contract that leads to a country that is distinct from others. The multitude somehow become a political community, but one without any significant distinctions among its members. There are apparently no communities within the community.

French philosophers such as Montesquieu and Rousseau had a great deal to say about societies or 'peoples'. But they framed the problem primarily as an issue of relations between the sovereign and the people. Montesquieu, for example, extolled the virtues of public associations and social groups lying between individuals and the state as 'weeds and . . . little pebbles that be scattered along the shore; so monarchs whose power seems unbounded, are restrained by the smallest obstacles' (quoted in Bereciartu 1994: 20). These are important, but the bigger question of 'what is the political community?' is left unanswered. Montesquieu and other philosophers of the era assumed that the larger political community is simply the sum of the royal subjects living in a bounded realm whose territorial limits were formed through centuries of wars, marriages, and alliances. For Rousseau, the imperatives of forming a *national* consciousness and *national* citizenship are crucial for transcending mediaeval social constructs, but he did not raise the issue of exactly who is a citizen. Thus, issues that so preoccupy so many countries in the 1990s did not loom significantly in the seventeenth- and eighteenth-century mind, which was comfortable with the historical definition of states. The first solution to the problem of political community, then, is simply to ignore it. The critical question in early modern political philosophy was not the relations between communities within the state, but between individuals and the state. The problem was governance and the bases of legitimacy, not the nature of the governed. A state is a permanent entity that has been established and legitimized through long historical development. But this is not the condition of most contemporary states.

The second solution is to define the state in terms of its constituent peoples or, preferably, people. Nineteenth-century Romantics and their contemporary heirs cannot solve the problem in this way, however, because states are relatively permanent entities while 'peoples' are variable. Even when Herder and Fichte were writing, there were very few pure 'peoples' cohabiting a single geographic space. Population migrations over the millennia made the idea of a 'pure' people a myth which could find empirical validation only in a few remote islands or precivilization regions. A second difficulty is that the idea of 'natural communities' based on language, culture, religion, ethnicity or some combination of them is by definition exclusionary. Those who do not share the attributes are outsiders, to be dealt with through special means such as minority status, geographic separation, exclusion, expulsion, or murder. Any measure that provides special status can always be changed. No official minority can ever feel secure, knowing that what has been granted can always be taken away. There can be no genuine equality between groups that have different legal statuses within states.

If all political communities were based solely or primarily on the physical and cultural attributes of their populations, then the history of the world would have been very different. At the time of the French Revolution, less than one-half of the population spoke French. The dialects of Italy were so diverse as to make mutual comprehensibility between 'Italians' impossible at the time of Italian unification. Indeed, most of the states of Europe did not achieve full language integration until the late nineteenth and early twentieth centuries. Would it have been possible to order the map of Europe according to population migrations and the language-learning skills of millions of people? How can we deal rationally with constantly shifting 'identities' in the context of a political community that must have some permanence if it is to exist as more than a paper idea? Herder, Fichte, and Hegel did not solve the problem of political community. But by proposing to fit variables – populations and 'identities' – into a constant – states – they set the stage for many of the miseries of the

contemporary world. They provided a rationale for political fragmentation that is a serious challenge to the idea that groups within states can
live in harmony.

Attempts to base states on 'natural communities' were made in 1919,
with mixed results. They worked reasonably well in the case of Finland,
Estonia, Latvia, and (until 1938), in Czechoslovakia. Elsewhere, solving
the problem of multinational empires by carving them up according to
their 'natural' populations led to the European wars of the 1920s and
1930s, to the massive exchange of populations between Greece and Turkey
in 1922–3, and to the Sudeten crisis that was a forerunner of World War
II. If we can criticize Hobbes and his eighteenth-century successors for
ignoring the problem of political community, we can judge Herder, Fichte
and their successors equally harshly for coming up with a solution to the
problem of political community that failed to acknowledge the necessary
distinction between states and nations, and for promoting the idea that
the only legitimate foundation for a state is a distinct population. Perhaps
in the 1830s, such solutions might have made some sense in some
quarters of Europe. By 1919, it proved mostly catastrophic. And, in the
postcolonial and post-socialist states, it is an impossibility. To carve up
Africa according to language/ethnic frontiers (if we could locate them)
would result in more than three thousand 'states'. Central Asia would
pose only a slightly less impressive challenge. Tajikistan is not made up
of constituent nations that have some organic coherence. It is, rather,
more like an 'ethnic soup'. To carve up India into its constituent 'natural'
communities would prove impossible. What would one do with a Gujarati-
speaking, Parsee resident of Bombay? Where does she belong? A Sikh
'Kalistan' solves no problems of inter-communal relations, unless the large
Hindu and Muslim populations of the Punjab were ethnically cleansed.
The only 'permanent' solution to the 'natural' country idea is either moving
populations or moving frontiers. Neither is a solution that can be implemented peacefully and neither is really permanent.

The third solution to the problem of political community lies in Roman
antiquity and the Italian city states of the Renaissance. It was resurrected
during the French Revolution. The solution is deceptively simple: the political community is to be comprised of *citizens*.

The concept of citizen helps to solve a number of issues surrounding
political communities and political community. First, as seen in France
when it was first incorporated into the revolutionary ethos, it broke down
the clear distinction between the monarch–nobility alliance on the one
hand, and the king's subjects on the other. The *citoyen* symbolized the new
freedom of the individual from his or her subordinate status of bondage
under the rubric of *sujet*. To the extent that all people above a certain age
are citizens, they are also legally equal and equally free. Second, the
concept of citizenship in the late eighteenth century helped to heal the
wounds of religious strife. The political community, badly suffering from

the conflicts of the sixteenth and seventeenth centuries, would now develop bonds of shared citizenship (Wells 1995: xviii). This is fraternity. Third, common citizenship could also create a new identity and focus for loyalty, competing with the numerous localisms that prevailed in eighteenth-century France. Citizenship was important for creating common bonds to replace or supplement ties based on language, locality, religion, or ethnicity. The fragmentary consequences of France's polyglot and localized populations was well recognized at the time of the Revolution. Lazare Carnot reported to the French National Assembly in 1793 that '[i]f . . . society had a right to proclaim its will and secede from the major unit . . . every district, every town, every village, every farmstead could declare itself independent' (quoted in Østerud 1997b: 170). Fourth, the concept of citizenship in its French guise provided status and the bases of civic pride. Citizenship is in a sense *earned*. It is something one gets, or becomes, and not something one simply inherits through birth. One *qualifies* for citizenship, while other identities are simply passed down (in later generations, of course, citizenship is earned solely by birth within the country and upon reaching maturity). Thus, there is the feeling of belonging to a distinct political community. Overall, then, the use of the term citizen 'embodied a claim and a rejection: the claim to equality before the law, the rejection was that of a God-given authority' (Bernier 1989: 232). Finally, the concept of citizenship implies equality. At the social level, the substitution of *citoyen* for *monsieur* and other caste titles provided a new basis for tearing down birth-based privilege. At the legal level, it clearly meant that there was only one law for all citizens regardless of attributes, inheritance, failures or successes. And, at the political level, it meant – as the *Declaration of the Rights of Man and Citizens* proclaimed – that all equally share in the right to participate in the political life of the community. In brief, the concept of citizenship was the foundation of the slogan of popular sovereignty, 'liberty, equality, fraternity'. Citizenship provides a foundation for achieving and maintaining each of these values, and thus provides a secure and *permanent* foundation for a political community.

Although the French were soon to dilute the equality component of citizenship by establishing 'active' and 'passive' categories (the latter including children, women, servants, and those without financial means), these political maneuvers were concessions to class interests rather than to religious, ethnic, or language distinctions. As a tool for nationalizing policies, citizenship is a powerful means of diluting social identities in favor of membership in a wider society (Shotter 1993: 116).

The concept of citizenship trumps the problem of changing identities that is endemic to all communities and population groups. Citizenship is a constant. This may be its most important attribute as far as the stability of political communities is concerned. Identities, in contrast, come and go. Europeans in the seventeenth century identified themselves primarily by a combination of region, language, and religion. By the end of the twentieth century they employ any number of variables: age, region, gender, ethnicity, language, sexual orientation, religion, and the like. In the twenty-first century they might well be based on other criteria. Take a hypothetical, though realistic, example. At the turn of the twentieth century, as we know from ethnographic studies (cf. Connor 1990), migrants to the United States from eastern Europe and Russia identified themselves primarily in terms of the town or region rather than the country from which they originated. So, our hypothetical European might change over the generations like this: in 1900, he identifies himself primarily as an Orthodox Sarajevan. Thirty years later, his daughter might identify herself primarily as a Yugoslav, but with strong attachments to Bosnia. In 1993, her son would proclaim loudly that he was a Serb and would have no truck with Bosnian neighbours, whether Muslim or Croat. Yugoslavia was just a bad experience, although he rooted for the Yugoslav basketball team in the 1988 Olympics just as loudly as his Muslim neighbours. Perhaps this man's great-granddaughter will define herself primarily as a European who happens to come from a place called Bosnia.

The example is of course biased in the sense that statehood in the Bosnian region has never been stable during the twentieth century – precisely because political leaders have sought to mold the state around nations. In contrast, France, Denmark, Sweden, and Portugal can look back to a history of statehood that spans at least one-half millennium. Within states of reasonable duration, the concept of citizenship takes care of the problem of shifting identities. One is legally, and equally so, a citizen of France, Denmark, Sweden, or Portugal regardless of one's identity of the year. And once a citizen, one has equal rights, duties, and responsibilities regardless of other attributes.

Yet, for all the social and political benefits of equal citizenship, it does not resolve the seemingly human propensity or need to make social distinctions that lead to effective inequality. It also fails to address the problem that civic patriotism might not be a sufficient substitute for the emotional and other comforts that derive from clannishness and 'identity' politics. We must not forget that France was one of the first 'nationalizing' (Rogers Brubaker 1996: 5) states that in the sixteenth century launched a major project to destroy most vestiges of localism. Major steps along the way were the introduction of conscription and the citizenship concept during the revolution, and Napoleon's creation of 83 *départements* to replace the historical administrative regions of France. France's wars were a major filip for creating a sense of *national* emergency. Another was to institute an education system where French became the only language of instruction. Other languages in France were left to die. Movements advocating secession from France were made illegal. Historically there have been strong motivations for the state to 'nationalize' its population, to assimilate smaller communities into the majority, and to promote civic rather than ethnic or language nationalism (cf. Rogers Brubaker 1996). But what the French could do throughout several centuries prior to the Great War is much more difficult today, particularly when the social 'distance' between, say, Bretons and Parisians are much closer than the distance between Muslims and Christians or animists in contemporary Sudan. 'Nationalization' projects in the twentieth century, particularly since 1945, have met substantial resistance, and have often been accompanied by violence. In many instances, they have failed.

States have thus devised a number of arrangements that acknowledge the need for distinctions within the rubric of equal citizenship. They devolve or share power between the state and group levels: federations (both symmetrical and asymmetrical), autonomous regions, confederations, treaties guaranteeing minority rights, reservations, tribal lands, and the like. The ubiquity of such arrangements suggests that common citizenship does not fully solve the problem of how distinct communities can success-fully relate to each other within the context of a single state. Clearly, the internationalist hypothesis that increased communication, trade, and exchanges result in mutual empathy, understanding, and ultimately, inte-gration, has not been the case in many states. We have all of these devolution and special status arrangements precisely because some com-munities feel discriminated against, fear the actions of the 'national' government or a social majority, or seek security behind administrative and territorial borders. Indeed, the idea of the civic state bringing together diverse populations appears to be under assault almost everywhere in the world. The idea that different communities can live in harmony seems increasingly in question. And if that is the case, must we then also expect the worsening of relations between states?

The coming crisis of the civic state?

The constitutions of most modern states indicate that a very significant majority are civic, where rights are guaranteed equally for all. Yet, the roster of armed violence within them suggests that constitutional guaran-tees are not sufficient to maintain peace between individuals and groups within many states. Western images of rampant ethnic animosities within countries are also created and sustained by scholarly and media observers and analysts. I repeat previous examples. A highly respected American international lawyer speaks of 'ancient hatreds' pervading ex-Yugoslavia (Gotlieb 1995: 28). Samuel Huntington (1993), Robert Kaplan (1994), Max Singer and Aaron Wildavsky (1992), Alain Minc (1993) and many others have employed terms such as the 'coming clash of civilizations', the 'coming anarchy', and 'zones of turmoil', '*zones grises*', and '*le nouveau moyen âge*' to warn us against new threats and new sources of armed conflict within the post-Cold War world. In this literature, Yugoslavia, Somalia, Rwanda, Tajikistan and Liberia are supposedly prototypes of what we can take to be 'normal' problems in the Third World and the post-socialist states.

These are important examples. But they also distort the overall picture. We cannot deny the significance of the Rwandas of the world, but we must resist temptations to see them as typical or the beginning of a trend that supposedly has emerged with the end of the Cold War. Is the civic state really under siege?

The first point to emphasize is that armed conflicts involving different communities within states did not begin with the end of the Cold War. Most of the current internal wars began, in fact, long before 1989 or 1991. Myanmar has had armed conflict since independence, becoming acute after the military takeover of 1962. The Eritrean armed struggle for independence began in 1961 and ended successfully thirty years later. The armed insurrection of the southern Sudanese began in the late 1960s, was followed by a peace, and then resumed in 1983. The civil war in Sri Lanka dates to 1983, although the problems of the two communities there long antedate the beginning of armed hostilities. Indeed, 113 internal wars out of a total of 126 (to 1995) began *before* 1989 (figures in Holsti 1996: Chapter 2 and Appendix 1). These data do not suggest that the end of the Cold War 'unleashed' a new wave of nationalism, or that suddenly 'ancient animosities' emerged because the great powers had terminated their long ideological–strategic rivalry. Western analysts all of a sudden discovered 'ethnic wars', many of which were not primarily about ethnicity, and most of which had been going on long before 1989. The intellectual myopia caused by the Cold War is the basis of these perceptions. Academics and media analysts, as well as peace groups, were so mesmerized by East–West relations that they ignored or were blind to what was going on in the rest of the world. A nuclear war, which was the least probable military event, certainly after 1961, was the great fear. But no lives were lost on account of nuclear weapons, while millions perished through armed conflicts and politicides within the new and some not-so-new countries.

The second point is that internal wars have not been confined to the Third World and the post-socialist states. The Irish problem continues, as does the intermittent 'war' by the Basques. Many Corsicans do not feel that French citizenship reflects their interests and 'identity', while about one-half of the francophones in Quebec wish to secede from Canada, although not by violent means. Czechoslovakia, a fictional civic state created in 1919, broke apart peacefully, but if we think of Yugoslavia as a European area, the three wars there remind us powerfully that liberal tenets about the effects of interactions, communication, and trade do not always hold, even within long-unified states.

The third point is that many of the armed conflicts and internal wars since 1945, though having ethnic dimensions, are not usually about 'ancient hatreds', 'identities', or national revindication. They involve many other matters that have to do specifically with leadership, politics, and political agendas rather than with relations between individuals and communities. There is certainly no 'ancient hatred' between francophone and anglophone québecois. We have seen many figures that show the social and family integration that united 'identities' in ex-Yugoslavia. Intermarriage between members of distinct communities comprised about one-quarter of all marriages. Demographic maps of Bosnia show conclusively that most of the republic's districts were significantly multinational and significantly peaceful until 1992. Only 11 of 111 districts had a majority population group of 90 per cent or more. The remainder were truly bi- or trinational (Woodward 1995: fig. 8–1).

Where were the 'ancient hatreds' that supposedly animated these integrated peoples to practise ethnic cleansing, mass murder, and rape of friends and neighbours? Were these the *normal* sensitivities that lay lurking for generations until the end of the Cold War and the collapse of Yugoslav authoritarian rule? In fact, they were not, at least not for the most part. Political leadership, fear, and 'tipping events' (see below) created situations where a 'kill or be killed' psychology took over. Ethnic nationalism had little to do with it. Slavenka Drakulic (1993: 50–2) provides a good description of how ordinary people of different communities live peacefully most of the time and how nationalism is manufactured for political purposes:

> Along with millions of other Croats, I was pinned to the wall of nationhood – not only by outside pressure from Serbia and the Federal [Yugoslav] Army but by national homogenization within Croatia itself. That is what the war is doing to us, reducing us to one dimension: the Nation. The trouble with this nationhood, however, is that whereas before, I was defined by my education, my job, my ideas, my character – and, yes, my nationality too – now I feel stripped of all that. I am nobody because I am not a person any more. I am one of 4.5 million Croats ... One doesn't have to succumb voluntarily to this ideology of the nation – one is sucked into it. So right now, in the new state of Croatia, no one is allowed not to be a Croat.

This lament was repeated by hundreds of thousands of Bosnians who during the war refused to identify themselves primarily as Muslims, Croats, or Serbs, and who wanted to maintain or restore the pre-war multi-community political order. Similar or even greater numbers in Rwanda refused to accept the government's attempt to classify peoples as Hutus or Tutsis and ignored or resisted the mass mobilization that preceded the ethnocide of 1994. There is much evidence, in brief, that contrary to much of the post-Cold War literature, there are few primordial hatreds in the world. Most of the peoples and communities who live in multi-community states get along most of the time. This is the norm. Communal and interethnic violent conflicts are by any standard *unusual* events.[3] They have identifiable etiologies, among which 'ancient hatreds' are not prominent. To repeat: it requires political leadership and mobilization to create what so many have termed chaos and anarchy; it requires mobilization to challenge the Bentham hypothesis.

That these tragedies should be seen as exceptional rather than typical is underlined by the numbers of states in which multiple communities coexist peacefully within the context of various devolution devices, and/or in which a sense of civic nationalism transcending particular 'identities' flourishes. Finland was one of the first post-1919 countries to demonstrate how it is possible to transform a restive minority (the Swedish-Finns) into Finns who happen to speak Swedish as their native tongue. Malaysia, once an arena of considerable ethnic tension, has become a virtual civic state where loyalties now transcend ethnic, language, or religious communities. The same pattern prevails in most Caribbean countries, in Fiji, in Thailand, and in a significant number of multi-communal African states. Indeed, there are so many examples of successful multi-community states, that the main liberal internationalist tenets may not be fundamentally challenged by the events of ex-Yugoslavia, Rwanda, and many others since 1945. And most important, the old Bentham liberal idea that left to their own devices, peoples can live in peace, while it is governments (or political leaders) that mess up things, is also supported. As we will see below, most of the internal wars and other forms of violent conflict since 1945 have been instigated not by spontaneous communal conflicts, but rather by specific acts of government or other political leaders who stand to gain from playing ethnic cards and nationalist mobilization.[4] There are many problems within multi-community states, but the data do not support the argument that ancient hatreds between communities within these states are either the typical or the primary source of the problem.

Within and between states: essential differences?

The reader may object that it is inappropriate to test the main hypotheses or tenets of liberal internationalism in a domestic context. One obvious difference is that within most states governments maintain law and order and effectively *prevent* inter-communal violence. There is no analogy in relations between states. The peaceful coexistence of communities within states may be explained not by mutual understanding, empathy, and the respect that comes from natural intercourse but by the deterrent capacity of governments. One could argue, for example, that without a strong army and police in India, the country would have collapsed years ago in frenzies of inter-communal strife and killing. The state is not just a passive, disinterested Leviathan. It rules from the 'awe' it possesses over the 'multitudes' and also, as the famous drawing of Leviathan indicates, by wielding the sword. The Leviathan is created precisely because without it, life in the state of nature would be indeed short, nasty, and brutish. The Leviathan is a mighty deterrent.

But this view of governance is incorrect on two counts. First, Hobbes's concept of the state of nature is inadequate on both psychological and sociological grounds. Many have attacked Hobbes on this issue, so there is no need to repeat this here. The second objection is based on empirical observation of multicultural societies in both the historical and modern contexts. We have no comparative empirical studies on the question, but most people, most of the time, appear to coexist peacefully in multicultural societies. They do so through a variety of formal and informal arrangements, pragmatically developed over long periods among people who understand that for ordinary commerce and lives to work, coexistence is the only low-cost alternative. The Moors resided in Spain for centuries, in part separate, but later taking part in the social and even political life of Castile and Andalusia. Muslims and Hindus, as well as many other groups, coexisted in India long before British colonization. Melanesians and South Asians have lived largely separately, but in reasonable peace in Fiji since the nineteenth century. The list of examples is almost endless. In this regard, the Bentham hypothesis is generally correct: left to their own devices, peoples can learn to live in peace if not complete harmony with each other.[5]

The record since 1945 is quite clear: it is not distinct communities that, without a state deterrent, would war incessantly against each other. *Rather, it is the state itself which has been the instigator of most ethnically-related conflicts.* Political philosophers have not confronted this problem. None has promoted the vision of the state as a tormentor of its own citizens. Nothing in Hobbes's concept of the state could serve as a prototype or justification for Hitler's treatment of German Jews, Communists, homosexuals, or Roma. Marx would have denounced Stalin's Gulag, the deportation of millions of minority members into the far reaches of the Soviet Union, or his deliberate starvation of millions of Ukrainians during the 1930s. If one were to interview members of the many minorities and peoples 'at risk' today, they would claim that the main threat to their security and to the means of livelihood emanates less from their neighbours than it does from the state (cf. Gurr 1996). For it is the state, through its government officials, that mobilizes most pogroms, ethnic cleansing measures, expulsions, and ethnocides. So-called 'ethnic wars' are not usually spontaneous uprisings of long-suppressed hatred. They are instigated by political leaders, often acting in the name of the state. Consider the main ethnocides and politicides of the twentieth century. The annihilation of Armenians by Turks during the Great War; Stalin's centrally directed and organized massacres, purges, and organized hunger in the Ukraine; Hitler's Holocaust; the Indonesian military's destruction of about half a million Communists and other 'suspects' in 1965; Idi Amin's approximately 300,000 victims, at first mostly members of rival tribes, but later including anyone suspected of disloyalty; the millions killed during Mao Tse-tung's 'Great Leap Forward' and 'Great Proletarian Cultural Revolution;' Pol

Pot's annihilation of about 10 per cent of the Kampuchean population; and many others. The most recent example, of course, was the 1994 massacre of up to half a million Hutus and moderate Tutsis by well-organized Hutu militias. Earlier massacres in Rwanda (1962) and Burundi (1972) were similarly organized. These did not represent the spontaneous outbreak of 'primordial hatreds', but the carefully planned, deliberate destruction of designated populations for political reasons.[6] None of this conforms to Hobbes's image of the deterrent state – nor to any other conception of the state by a recognized political philosopher.

This is not to deny that in some circumstances non-organized inter-communal violence has erupted. The partition of India in 1947 was accompanied by millions of deaths, most of which occurred without central leadership. In 1984, after the assassination of Indira Gandhi by one of her Sikh bodyguards, pogroms by Hindus against Sikhs in various locales of India occurred. Some of the deaths in Indonesia in 1965 were basically the settling of private scores by Indonesians against the Chinese minority and even among themselves. Pogroms against Biafrans (not identified by the populations in question as a distinct nationality) in northern Nigeria in the autumn of 1965 were instrumental in leading to the Biafran secession war. Other cases could be cited. But they tend to be fairly rare events compared to the centrally organized massacres, politicides, and ethnocides of the late twentieth century. To repeat: it is the state rather than 'primordial hatreds' that is the source of most internal conflicts and 'ethnic wars'. To understand why this is the case, we need to review briefly the historical origins of multi-community states. After this excursion, we can return to the contemporary situation to see how well the Bentham hypothesis holds.

The birth of multi-community states

In the European contexts, states were formed over a long period. Hobbes's multitude was perhaps an apt description in the sense that with some notable exceptions such as the Scandinavian countries and Portugal, the populations that made up the principalities, kingdoms, and other political units of early modern Europe were not cohesive in 'natural' terms. The United Kingdom, created in 1707, was a combination of Scots, Welsh, Irish, and English, all distinct 'peoples'. At the time of the French Revolution, less than one-half of France's population could speak French. Breton, langue d'Oc, Italian, Spanish, and innumerable regional dialects made communication difficult. In 1790 the French National Assembly was forced to translate its decrees into all the languages or dialects spoken throughout the country (Bereciartu 1994: 14). Almost one century later, when Italy was unified, less than 3 per cent of the population of the peninsula spoke a mutually comprehensible tongue, leading a politician of the era to declare that 'We have created Italy, now we must create Italians'

(*The Economist*, 22 Dec. 1990: 43). The observation reflects and presages the immense 'nationalizing' (Rogers Brubaker 1996: Chapter 1) projects that most European states undertook over the centuries to create homogenous, loyal populations out of the heterogeneous societies that had made up the royal realms. The means ranged from promotion of a single vernacular, through publicly-financed national education policies, to the construction and manipulation of national symbols, and to expulsions of those who refused to assimilate (e.g., the Moors in Andalusia).

The old states of Europe had the luxury of time. Many began the great 'nationalizing' project by the sixteenth century and had more or less completed it successfully by the dawn of the twentieth century. A few states based on a predominant natural community were founded in the aftermath of the Great War. These included Poland – actually a resurrection – Finland, and the Baltic republics. Where population distributions were too messy to create single-community states, fictions were created. These included the Soviet Union, Czechoslovakia, and Yugoslavia. A variety of 'nationalizing' projects (including massive population transfers in the Soviet Union) competed with localizing enterprises such as federalism, but all ultimately failed to sustain these fictions once central authority collapsed or eroded. The first two broke up more or less peacefully (in the case of the Soviet Union, to everyone's surprise); the latter ended at the cost of three grisly wars. Seventy years of experimentation and nationalizing policies had failed to create a political community based on solidarity between diverse peoples.

Colonies were not created to become states. That is a fundamental difference between most post-1945 states and their European predecessors. Most colonies were fictions from the very beginning. They were colored designations placed on maps created by Europeans for European purposes. One of the most important innovations of the European map was the lineal frontier, a concept that did not exist in most non-European societies. Thus, a bureaucrat in London could look at the map and note that all the red-colored areas were under British jurisdiction, while all the blue areas were under French jurisdiction. The same bureaucrats in Europe's capitals had also attached names to these spaces, names that had no meaning or history in the areas concerned. Togo, Nigeria, Cameroon, Sierra Leone, Ivory Coast, and the like do not refer to spaces that had such names prior to European colonization. These designations, created in London, St Petersburg, Paris, and elsewhere arbitrarily bifurcated 'natural communities', joined others that had never cohabited areas previously, and in general created a whole series of artificial polities. In Africa, all of this was formalized at the Berlin Conference (1884–5), to which not a single African was invited. As for the island colonies, formerly homogenous populations were rendered heterogeneous by the import, first, of slaves, and later of indentured labor. Fiji, the Caribbean islands, Hawaii, and Guyana are examples. As for the settler colonies, the indigenous populations were either massacred (Argentina, Tasmania), placed into reservations (United States, Canada), or assimilated.

Robert Kaplan (1996: 70–1) describes nicely the founding story of one colony, Togo. It is not atypical.

> I had come by airplane from Freetown to Lomé, capital of Togo, a country that may be less fact than fiction. Togo . . . illustrates [West Africa's] geographical quandary: Population belts in West Africa are horizontal, and human habitation densities increase as one travels away south from the Sahara and toward the tropical abundance of the Atlantic littoral. But the borders erected by European colonialists were vertical, and therefore at cross-purposes with demography and topography. For example, the Ewe people . . . are divided between Togo and Ghana. In addition, Togo has been bedevilled by tensions between its southern peoples and the Voltaic peoples of the north. . . . Togo, rather than an organic outgrowth of geography and ethnicity, was a result of late-nineteenth century German greed. . . . In 1884, the Germans landed a ship here and staked out a claim. This was the basis for the national identity of Togo.

This story is repeated throughout Africa, Central Asia, the Middle East, and elsewhere. The geographic spaces concocted as colonies did not coincide with the social, demographic, and commercial spaces of the populations that inhabited the areas. Thus, most post-1945 states began under double jeopardy. They contained multiple communities created during the colonial enterprise, but they had no history of united statehood other than the mostly short-lived colonial apparatuses that had been imposed on them from the outside. Colonial populations were never 'subjects' of European crowns in the same way that Bretons, Scots, or Alsatians were. Yet, upon achieving independence either through peaceful or violent decolonization, these diverse peoples had to become citizens of countries that began as creations of European bureaucrats' imaginations. The leaders of 'national (*sic*) liberation' simply adopted the colonial territorial designations as the foundations for their new states. Precolonial political forms were never considered seriously, and alternative projects such as African Unity – a single African state – never got far beyond the realm of rhetoric.

The artificial nature of the colonies was revealed shortly after – and in some cases, even before – independence. India was partitioned at the cost of millions of lives. Wars pitting distinct communities resisting the nationalizing projects of the majority Burmese began shortly after independence, and picked up velocity quickly after the 1962 military *coup d'état*, when the new leaders canceled all pretenses of autonomy for minorities. The Biafran war of secession erupted only a few years after Nigerian independence. Similar wars began in Eritrea (another fiction, the Eritrean–Ethiopian federation having been cobbled together under United Nations auspices), Sudan, Sri Lanka, Chad, and elsewhere. Just like the Italians of 1860, the leaders of the new states had to create 'nations'. They did this through a variety of means, mostly entailing centralization, the imposition of languages, the expropriation of lands and territories, and the violent suppression of all forms of dissent and decentralizing sentiment. The old tensions between the demands of 'nationalization' and the desires of autonomy have been no less a feature of post-1945 states than of European states. The difference is that the post-1945 states began with almost no assets in terms of common loyalties, identity, and history.

How to cobble together diverse peoples into something resembling a 'normal' country? Most rulers of post-1945 states had very weak bases of legitimacy. The heroes of the wars of national liberation had their warrior status, but that was not a particularly solid foundation for ruling diverse populations after independence. Few warriors sought to legitimize their rule through elections. Many proclaimed themselves presidents- or emperors-for-life, and their performances as economic managers ranged from mediocre to disastrous. Some, like the Marcos in the Philippines, the Samozas in Nicaragua, Mobutu Sese Seko in Zaire, Saddam Hussein in Iraq, and Nicolae Ceausescu, became major 'kleptocrats' who, with their cronies, plundered the wealth of their countries. Clientelism, corruption, and patrimonialism provided the glue that kept some of the post-1945 states together. Others were kept together by fickle tyrannies featuring rule based on coercion, terror, and murder.

For others, there was the 'ethnic card' to play. One of the findings of my work on seventeen humanitarian emergencies (Holsti 1997) is that in fifteen of the cases, systematic policies of exclusion by governments, practiced against identifiable communities within the state preceded the warring and killing. Exclusion included both access to political power or official positions and withholding or unequally applying government services. The forms of exclusion ranged from informal apartheid-like policies, through fraudulent elections or disenfranchisement of distinct community members, to harassment, expulsions (New Win's expulsion of the Indian population in Burma in 1962; Idi Amin's expulsion of Asians from Uganda in 1972), and death squads, and, finally to ethnocide as in eastern Pakistan in 1970–1, Rwanda in 1962 and 1994, and Burundi in 1972.[7]

In the most extreme cases the policies were preceded by a 'tipping event' (Hardin 1995) that ignited ethnic mobilization and ultimately, organized violence directed against a community. In 1991, the new Croatian state declared its Serb population to be a minority, and immediately began dismissing ethnic Serbs from government positions, thereby fueling the fear that underlay the Serbs armed resistance in the Krajina. In Bosnia, the April 1992 plebiscite approving the declaration of Bosnian independence from Yugoslavia immediately rendered the Serbs into a minority, and thus helped launch the war. In April 1994, it was the death of Rwanda's president in an air crash – attributed to Tutsis – that was the signal to unleash the Hutu militias against the Tutsis. Other tipping events included assassination of a political leader, minor armed uprisings, guerrilla incursions, and the like.

There is also strong evidence that communal warfare is associated with the breakdown of political authority. Again, it is not primordial hatreds, but fear that can rupture normal relations between peoples. Michael Ignatieff (1993: 18) nicely captures the situation as it developed in ex-Yugoslavia:

> No one in these [Yugoslav] villages could be sure who would protect them. If they were Serbs and someone attacked them and they went to the Croatian police, would the Croats protect them? If they were Croats, in a Serbian village, could they be protected against a night-time attack from a Serbian paramilitary team, usually led by a former policeman? This is how ethnic cleansing began to acquire its logic. If you can't trust your neighbours, drive them out. If you can't live among them, live only among your own. This alone appeared to offer people security. This alone gave respite from the fear which leaped from house to house.

In ten of the seventeen cases it was the government that began the violence, and not the distinct community. And in none of the cases did the humanitarian emergency result from spontaneous inter-communal warfare. The patterns in all seventeen cases were similar. In a risk rather than a cause–effect analysis, I found that some kinds of states are much more likely to endure or suffer a humanitarian emergency than others. The states with the highest risk share the following attributes: (1) the state is new (e.g., post-1945); (2) the polity is made up of several distinct communities, with no significant majority; (3) the government systematically excludes one or more distinct communities from government office and government largesse; and (4) a minority rules over a majority (cf. Ahmed 1996: 25, 70). Tipping events turn what historians call a 'powder keg' into armed conflict. What we have here is a pathology of state development, rather than primordial hatreds between communities. The state in most cases is the organizer and instigator of armed conflicts that may or may not have an ethnic dimension to them. But the pathological condition is not universal and not even very common either in the Third World or elsewhere.

Political scientists are no less immune to the lure of conflict, crisis, and mayhem than are the media. The volume of research on state failures, ethnocides, politicides, and internal wars vastly outweighs the research on *successful* post-1945 states. But to test the Bentham hypothesis, we have to look at the successes as well as the failures. My rough estimate is that the former significantly outnumber the latter, and hence there is considerable evidence to support the liberal internationalist hypothesis. For every Rwanda, there is a Mauritius or Malaysia. For every Burundi there is a Barbados and Benin. For every Sudan there is a Surinam or Seychelles.[8] Contrary to Western analysts who, at the end of the Cold War, predicted an era of 'anarchy', 'chaos', '*nouveau moyen âge*' and 'turmoil' in the Third World, the great untold story is one of some amazing successes. Left on their own, as Bentham believed, most people most of the time will coexist, and as commercial, educational, and communications networks develop between them, they find various ways to harmonize their interests sufficiently so that they can live together without fear. There is no authoritative explanation in the literature on ethnicity why differences of ethnicity, language, or culture necessarily provide more grist for social conflict than differences of class, political persuasion, or gender.

From Khartoum to Quebec: harbingers?

Yet, there is little room for complacency. The Bentham hypothesis cannot lead to predictions of certainty. In an age of 'identity politics', when the forces of globalism homogenize cultures and undermine diversity, the appeal to distinctness based on attributes rather than interests is great. The tension between nationalizing or globalizing policies, representing conformity and homogeneity, and localism representing diversity, continues today as much as it was a feature of French politics in the late eighteenth century. There are no certain recipes for creating genuine civic states encompassing several distinct communities. The Sudan was from its beginning a high risk case. There was nothing in Sudan's history to suggest that it could ever become a reasonably integrated political community. A colonial fiction – though with some historical content in the ancient form of Nubia – it was conquered first by the Egyptians (1820–2) to be transformed into a secure entrepôt for the slave trade, and subsequently by the British (1898). Upon achieving independence in 1955, it immediately succumbed to tribal, sectarian, and ethnic violence. This was terminated by the 1972 Addis Ababa agreements by which the country was politically and administratively decentralized. During the next decade, however, the Nimeiry government began to renege on many of the 1972 decentralization provisions, culminating in the 1983 imposition of *Sharia* law upon the entire territory. The highly lopsided pre-1972 political order, which favoured the Muslim and northern peoples compared to the highly diverse Christian and animist ethnic stew of the south, began to re-emerge not only in the constitutional domain, but also in development policies and exploitation of resources. Nimeiry's policies were a classical case of a 'nationalizing' enterprise designed to establish the permanent hegemony of one population group or category over others. The government confiscated lands owned by non-Muslim pastoralists, excluded non-Muslims from political office and access to government programs, and organized a major war against those who resisted (cf. Lee 1997; Rothchild 1997: Chapter 8). Its program for assimilation has been a disaster. Under present and foreseeable circumstances, there can never be a civic state encompassing the several communities because one cultural group, which holds all official political power within the state, wishes to impose alien religious and legal systems upon others. One simply cannot create a single political community out of such diversity, at least not if it is sought by compulsion and coercion.

On the surface, Quebec represents an entirely different situation. A distinct people long antedating English Canada, Quebec joined the Canadian federation in 1867. Canada is a model civic state. Its population is made up of dozens of major ethnic and aboriginal groups who participate in the politics of the country at local, provincial, and national levels. Legal and political equality are guaranteed in the Charter of Rights and in the constitution. Federal and provincial governments spend hundreds of millions of dollars to support programs of bilingualism and multiculturalism. Indeed, Canada (along with India) is one of the few countries in the world where taxpayers support groups in their programs and policies to remain distinct. There is no 'nationalizing' project. Quite the contrary, the slogan that politicians use – in complete contrast to Sudan – is 'unity through diversity'. Diversity is a source of national strength, not weakness.

Quebec is no exception. The provincial representation in Ottawa is extensive. The last three prime ministers of Canada have all come from Quebec. Legislators from Quebec make up about 25 per cent of the House of Commons, which is proportionate to the Quebec population in Canada. There are dozens of cabinet ministers, supreme court justices, ambassadors, and top civil servants, all from Quebec. Quebec receives more revenues from the federal government than it raises for Ottawa in taxes. Francophone québecois do not despise or hate anglophones, whether within Quebec or elsewhere in Canada. Indeed, many of them identify themselves as Canadians first and québecois second. In brief, there is no exclusion, no 'primordial hatreds', no discrimination in terms of government largesse, and no fundamental threat to the language or culture. So, what is the problem?

It is a problem on many different levels. Partly it is a question of status. Quebec was a founding 'nation' of Canada, one of two 'peoples' who in 1867 created the country through confederation. In contrast, today it is seen by most anglophone Canadians as just one of ten provinces. Many resist the idea that Quebec should have a status that is distinct from that of the other nine provinces. So, here are two clashing visions of a country: the first, a confederation of two founding *peoples* (social), the other a federation of ten equal *provinces* (territorial). There is no apparent way to transcend or compromise these competing visions.

At the political level, there are constant debates about policy. Many québecois believe that provincial policy priorities cannot be achieved within the context of a federal system in which many powers reside at the center. Despite considerable devolution of power towards the provinces over the past decade, many québecois are convinced that on truly important issues, including language and culture, federal priorities stand in the way of provincial aspirations. Quebec constitutes a distinct political community that cannot develop itself sufficiently within the federal system. After decades of constitutional wrangling, little has changed and frustrations remain. Therefore, sovereignty – secession – is the only solution.

The situation is of course more complicated, but our purpose here is not to try to solve the problem of Quebec. It is to indicate, rather, that even in the most civic of states, where political and legal equality are the rule rather than the exception, where there is a high degree of interaction, mutual sympathy, and even common identity, and where there is equal access to government and government largesse, some will want to separate. The Bentham hypothesis, in these cases, is not supported. The result of high interaction patterns is not integration, but the search for distinctiveness and separation; not solidarity but more distance.

Yet, the obvious conclusion from both the Sudan and Quebec cases may turn out to be more complicated than it appears at first sight. For neither Sudan nor Quebec represents in fact a case of conflict and secession that necessarily leads to the creation of an ethnic state. If we are to believe the arguments of both the Africans in Sudan and many – though by no means all – francophones in Quebec, the purpose of separation is not to build a state based on some hypothesized 'natural' community, but to create instead a *different kind of civic state*. The war in the Sudan is primarily a war of resistance, not of secession. Its purpose is not to create some sort of 'black' Sudan, but rather to force the government in Khartoum to abide by its own constitution, that is, to sustain a civic state in which all citizens have equal rights and in which no group tries to impose its culture, language, and/or religion upon others. The spokespersons of the Sudan Peoples' Liberation Movement claim their purpose is to create a 'democratic, united, socialist Sudan' (Lesch 1994; Rothchild 1997: 236–8). The war, then, is one over the nature of the state, not whether one segment of its population will withdraw to create its own ethnically confined state. Many Muslims, on one hand, want a state incorporating a political community based on faith , not ethnicity, language, or culture. The Africans and nomads, on the other, want a civic state based on a community of citizens that transcends ethnic, language, and religious differences.

Similarly, the aspiration of most (there are important exceptions) separatist québecois is not to create an ethnically-based state, but a state comprised of the total and highly diverse population of the territory called Quebec. It incorporates the francophone language core, to be sure, but also includes one-fifth of the population made up of anglophones, indigenous 'first nations' and literally dozens of allophone groups which have English or French as their second (and third) language. An independent

Quebec would guarantee equal rights for all, including the right of the anglophones to have their children educated in English.

Sudan and Quebec, then, do not represent clear cases of fragmentation based on ethnicity, 'ethnic conflict' or a 'coming anarchy'. They are, rather, examples of different ideas about the nature of political community, but with some separatists in both countries actually opting for the civic conception of the state. In most of these cases – though less so in Quebec – separatists have good reason to want their own state. It is for reasons of equity, protection, and security more than identity. Separation is primarily, though not exclusively, a response to perceived and actual threats to individuals and groups. Though I have no statistics on the matter, my general impression is that the vast majority of people living in multi-community states would vastly prefer to remain residents of civic states, provided that they could share equally in both access to politics and to government programs. There are, of course, separatist movements that have other aspirations. A few, such as the nationalist elites of Croatia, the Srpska Republic, the LTTE in Sri Lanka, and possibly the Turks in Cyprus, want to create a separate state because they are convinced that they do not want or cannot live in harmony with other communities. Most population groups most of the time aspire and wish to live together, but only if it can be done on terms of equality, security, and dignity. Regimes that seek to undermine these values will likely face the consequences which include, *in extremis*, wars of separation and secession.

Conclusion

The debate between Bentham, Rousseau, and Herder continues and has not been resolved. There will always be tensions between nationalism and internationalism, not only between states, but within states. Liberal internationalism, or what I have called the Bentham hypothesis, has prevailed in Switzerland, Finland, Singapore, Malaysia, most Caribbean countries, and many others. It has been championed in the secular federal republic of India – the world's most diverse country – but it is always under strain either from those who want to found political communities on racial, ethnic, or religious bases, or from weak and insecure regimes that play the ethnic card to sustain themselves in power. It is also being politically tested in Canada, Belgium, and in other civic states, not for reasons of fear but more for equity or status.

The tension between internationalism (integration) and nationalism (diversity) cannot ultimately be resolved. The two forces have never been fully reconciled except at the expense of one over the other, usually by force of arms. Various formulas for special status of distinct communities within the state may help sustain diversity and different 'identities'. They may even provide the emotional glue for some individuals who require something more than a civic identity. But such special designations may

also have the consequence of destroying civic loyalty and thus make fraternity with other communities within the state more, not less, difficult. Special
status accentuates differences rather than accentuating the similarities that
are required in the concept of citizenship. Just like sovereignty emphasizes
a distinctness that many people believe attenuates international solidarity,
so might juridical designations such as 'minority', special status, distinct
society, or autonomy promote a form of diversity that dilutes civic unity.

The norms of the current international system are not supportive of
more political fragmentation. Civic states encompassing more than a single
community are the norm, not the exception in the world. The United
Nations, and state practice, have constantly reiterated the theme that the
principle of national self-determination does not apply to 'peoples' or
'nations' except in highly circumscribed conditions (e.g., where a distinct
community faces ethnocide). Self-determination was used as a principle or
justification for dismantling the Ottoman, Russian, Austro-Hungarian, and
German empires at the end of World War I, and again to provide ideological support for the great de-colonization venture. For obvious reasons,
however, most post-1945 countries insist that de-colonization was the ultimate act of self-determination, and that groups within the post-colonial
state cannot justify secession with that doctrine. Practice has followed
preaching. Secessionist movements have received little aid outside of their
diasporas (cf. Heraclides 1990). Perhaps the ultimate symbol of the pervasive strength of the norm of civic statehood was India's peacekeeping
intervention into Sri Lanka, where its forces ended up fighting for the
unity of the state *against* co-ethnic Tamils. Despite innumerable attempts
sponsored by the United Nations no one is willing to accept formal partition of Cyprus – an obvious long-range solution to the problem – for the
reason that it would create another precedent for legitimizing ethnically-
based states. Similarly, the Dayton Accords point to the eventual
reunification of Bosnia, albeit under a highly decentralized federation of
states based on ethnicity. Armed ethnically-based secession has succeeded
only a few times since 1945: in Pakistan (1971), Eritrea (1991), Croatia
(1991), and Bosnia (1992). Major peaceful secessions have included
Singapore and Slovakia, as well as the break-up of the Soviet Union. None
was greeted with international enthusiasm, for each represented yet another
victory for the political community based on ethnicity, language, religion,
or some combination of them. Each was, in some way or another, a refu-
tation of the Bentham hypothesis. Each demonstrated the pull of localism,
and in some extreme cases such as Croatia, the profoundly intolerant
message to co-citizens: 'if you are not one of us, we don't want you in
our state. The only tolerable basis for a political community is similarity,
not diversity.'

The Bentham hypothesis has been confirmed most notably in post-1945
Europe. Trade, travel, technology, the common experience of war, and
other factors have extended broad and deep social bonds, have helped

forge broad ideological consensus on liberal principles and practices, and have reduced the likelihood of interstate war almost to zero. Civic-style nationalism has replaced chauvinism. Similar developments have taken place in large areas of the western hemisphere, a point that is underlined by the fact that there has been no interstate war in South America since 1941. But contrary to Fukuyama's (1989) argument, liberal norms between and within states have not yet become universal. There is a crisis of state-hood and governance within many countries, particularly those featuring weak frameworks of legitimacy, and governance characterized by fraud, extortion, clientelism, coercion, and occasional politicides and ethnocides (Holsti 1996, 1997). Too many governments remain a menace to their peoples. In most of these areas, it is not primordial ethnic hatreds that lie at the root of the problem, but governments and sub-national leaders which play the ethnic and religious cards to further their own agendas. If Bentham was essentially right about relations between peoples, regrettably Rousseau was also right about governments: a large number of governments are arbitrary and coercive. Many are corrupt, use the state as a vehicle for personal enrichment and the establishment of virtual dynasties, and systematically exclude certain communities from the political process and from enjoying access to government services. Laws are used to favor some groups against others (cf. Canovan 1996: 74). In such circumstances, how can communities identify with the state? If the state is the predominant threat to inter-communal coexistence, then certain groups cannot and will not extend loyalty to it no matter how well people of different attributes get along at the grassroots level. And, as we have seen in the case of Quebec, even liberal states may not always succeed either. Bentham's hypothesis has not and probably will never become a universal norm. The attractions of clannishness, of distinct identity, of difference, and of diversity will always challenge the uniformities and integration implied in the liberal internationalist ethos. Internationalism and exclusive forms of nationalism remain in tension, but when we look at Europe and at many post-1945 states, Bentham's observations and expectations seem to be emerging increasingly as the normal rather than the exceptional.

Notes

1   I am grateful to Lisa Bournelis for research assistance.
2   I use a standard definition of war as organized armed violence involving a minimum of 1,000 casualties annually. At least one of the parties must constitute an armed force.
3   In a recent study, Fearon and Laitin (1996) provide significant data on the very low levels of interethnic violence in the former Soviet republics and in Africa. In the latter region, in fact, there were only twenty incidents of interethnic armed violence in all countries for all years between independence and 1979. In contrast, there were fifty-two civil wars (some of which may have had ethnic components). They conclude that from about 1960 to 1979, 'communal violence, though horrifying, was extremely rare in Africa' (p. 717).

4   The massacres in Rwanda had spontaneous aspects to them, but the Hutu-led militias had organized and planned the ethnocide long before the event occurred. A pogrom of Sinhalese against Tamils occurred in Colombo in July 1983 after a Tamil attack on a Sri Lankan military unit. There are several other examples of spontaneous communal violence, including India in 1984 (see below), but the vast majority of deaths within states since 1945 have occurred as a result of government policies, 'politicides', civil wars, or secession struggles (cf. Rummel 1994).

5   Fearon and Laitin (1996) present an extended discussion and analysis of the mechanisms – including 'in-group policing' – that help ethnic communities maintain peaceful relations. They also examine the conditions that help lead to conflict spirals.

6   For a careful analysis of the combination of spontaneous and organized sources of the Rwandan genocide, see de Swan (1997).

7   The actual forms of discrimination amount to at least two dozen. For a list, see Heraclides (1997: 495–6).

8   For one of the few studies that compares the political processes that lead to communal conflict compared to countries where communities coexist peacefully, see Horowitz (no date).

9 To be a European citizen

Eros and civilization[1]

J. H. H. Weiler

Prologue

One of the most engaging doors to the study of the Talmud is the trac-
tate *Pirke Avot* – the Lessons of the Fathers. It is in Hebrew rather than
Aramaic; it is aphoristic rather than exegetic; its normative appeal is to
Ethics rather than to Law. Like beauty, its banality or profundity is in the
eyes of the beholder.

Among its most celebrated intellectual heroes is Hillel – Old Hillel. He
is most famous for three things. First, he took the impossible imperative
in Leviticus 19:18 Love thy Neighbor as thyself – and recast it as the
much more doable 'Do not do unto others what you would not have them
do unto you'. There is an exquisite irony because in his own lifestyle he
abided by the original Leviticus edict and not by his own more pragmatic
recast. His life was a living ode to tolerance and in the evolution of legal
normativity the House of Hillel stands for the indispensability of equity in
the hands of the custodians of Nomos. Finally he is the author of the
following memorable aphorism which can become a metaphor for Citizenship and for the principal themes of this chapter: 'If not I, asked Hillel,
who shall be for me? But if I am only for myself – what am I worth?'
Here we have captured two of the most fundamental questions of social
organization which citizenship and its closely associated concept of nationality seek to address: Who are we and How are we to live together?

More raw and basic you do not get. His aphorism captures, too, the
inherent tension and symbiosis encapsulated in citizenship and nationality.
The tension between identity and normativity, between the eros of the 'I'
(individual or collective) and the civilizatory constraints of the social. But
also the symbiosis: How we choose to live together will define who we
are.

In this chapter I shall deal, artificial as it may be, with the first of these
two issues – the who are we bit and examine citizenship as identity in the
European context.

European citizenship: dilemmas and contradictions

The challenging tensions between national consciousness and multicultural sensibility take place not only within the classical state but also at the transnational level of which the European Union is one of the most developed. A focal point is the recent discussion concerning European Citizenship. The 1992 Treaty of European Union (The Maastricht Treaty) introduced the concept. Its citizenship clause provided: 'Citizenship of the Union is hereby established. Every person holding the nationality of a Member State shall be a citizen of the Union.' The recent 1997 Amsterdam Treaty modified the Maastricht Citizenship Clause by adding the phrase '[c]itizenship of the Union shall complement and not replace national citizenship'. This is a trite, banal phrase. But it reflects a profound anxiety and offers a literary device with which to address, analytically and normatively, some of the deepest dilemmas in constructing the ends and means of transnational integration within the framework of the European Union. One way of describing this chapter is to say that in it I want to explore the anxiety and offer a normative interpretation of this provision, not what the provision means, but what it ought to mean.

But there is more to European citizenship (and to this chapter). The ever-growing discussion on the politics of European citizenship has an exquisite Janus-like quality. For many the concept is considered one of the least successful aspects of Maastricht, trivial and empty, and hence irrelevant. From this perspective, those who believe in it are engaged in wishful thinking and those who fear it suffer from paranoid delusion. On this view, the recent modification was another unnecessary and empty gesture placating dreamers and loonies. For others, European citizenship is an important symbol with far-reaching potential and dangers. The story of European integration is, after all, replete with ideas and policies which, at inception, seemed trivial and empty, but which later attained a life of their own. From this perspective the Powers-that-be made a Pascal-like wager. Empty and irrelevant maybe. But why take risks?

The two views are not altogether contradictory and I wish to track and explain elements of both. I have no interest in making predictions about the future of the concept and its attendant policies. But to the extent that ideas and symbols shape attitudes and, maybe even policy options, the discourse of European citizenship is important not only to the theory of European integration but also to its praxis. In this chapter I build on work I have done in this field since 1995 though, in one fundamental respect – the articulation of the relationship between Member State nationality and Community citizenship – I have modified my earlier position significantly.

With inimitable acerbity, Perry Anderson begins his essay 'Under the Sign of the Interim' as follows:

172 J. H. H. Weiler

> Mathematically, the European Union today represents the largest
> single unit in the world economy. It has a nominal GNP of about
> $6 trillion compared with $5 trillion for the US and $3 trillion for
> Japan. Its total population, now over 360 million, approaches that of
> the United States and Japan combined. Yet in political terms such
> magnitudes continue to be virtual reality. Beside Washington or Tokyo,
> Brussels remains a cipher. The Union is no equivalent to either the
> United States or Japan, since it is not a sovereign state. But what kind
> of formation is it? Most Europeans themselves are at a loss for an
> answer. The Union remains a more or less unfathomable mystery to
> all but a handful of those who, to their bemusement, have recently
> become its citizens. It is well-nigh entirely arcane to ordinary voters;
> a film of mist covers it even in the mirror of scholars.
>
> (Anderson 1997)

And bemused they should be. It was Maastricht which bestowed the august
title of 'European Citizen' on Member State nationals. Even the handful
for whom the Union is, perhaps, less than an unfathomable mystery, would
have to admit to some perplexity at this new innovation. Citizens of the
Union were to enjoy the rights conferred by the TEU and be subject to
the duties imposed thereby. But the Citizenship chapter itself seemed to
bestow precious few rights, hardly any that were new, and some explicitly directed at all residents and not confined to citizens. Even if we were
to take the entire gamut of rights (duties are usually forgotten in most
accounts of European citizenship) granted under the Treaties to European
citizens, we would be struck by the poverty of provisions normally considered as political and associated with citizenship. Thus, we find (unrealized)
promises of true free movement and residence throughout the European
Union situated uncomfortably with relatively trivial guarantees of political
participation in local and European Parliament elections for those
Community citizens taking advantage of those very partial freedoms. And
whereas the discipline of a European Common Marketplace in which
goods would circulate freely was long understood (even if resisted in practice) as necessitating a European Common External Tariff towards the
rest of the world, the same logic – internal free movement and residence
requiring a Common European 'membership' policy – has been rejected.
European Citizenship emphatically does not mean what it has come to
mean in all federal States: a 'communatirization' of the actual grant of
citizenship or even an harmonization of Member State conditions for such
grant. The exclusive gate-keepers remain the Member States.

The question of 'added value' cannot but be raised: With very few
exceptions, the rights (and duties) associated with European citizenship
predated Maastricht. In the past they attached to nationals of the Member
States. Given the way this saga has evolved, what if anything, we may

ask, has been gained by adding a new concept, citizenship, to a pre-existing package of rights and duties rather than, as one may (or might) have expected adding new rights and duties to a concept? And the 'What?' leads to a rather big 'Why?' If the powers-that-be had, as is evident, no intention of substantially enlarging those rights and duties already attaching to nationals of their respective Member States; if they had no intention of making in relation to humans that critical move that was made in relation to goods, why do anything at all?

There are even deeper dilemmas than this political riddle. Citizenship and nationality are more than an element in the mechanics of political organization. We live in an era – perhaps the entire century – obsessed with questions of individual and collective identity. The treatment of the celebrated 'other', the other in our selves, in our midst, and the other clamoring at our doors or shores is an issue extremely high on the public agenda in most European societies.

Interestingly, as we slouched towards a new *fin-de-siècle*, after close to fifty years of European integration, the captivating idea of nation and people retained a surprising amount of their astonishing allure and grip on our collective psyches. And I do not only refer to the new found nationalisms in the 'Alt-Neu' Europe of the East. Is the European debate in Great Britain really moved by economic differences on the desirability of EMU or, instead, by political differences concerning, identity and control of national destiny? Was the debate over Maastricht in France (which split the electorate straight down the middle) or Denmark (that voted against) not about the same thing? And is it mere teasing to suggest that *fin-de-siècle* Vienna – *première* edition *circa* 1900 – boasted a far more cosmopolitan *Geist* than its current miserable shadow 100 years later?

The fault lines of this debate are usually not about differences in the self-understanding of the nation and the state. Typically in these debates many of the integrationists proclaim, usually in good faith, to be deeply concerned with, and committed to, national identity and national welfare and all the rest. They simply argue that the European Union will enhance these goals and values rather than threaten them.

Despite this attachment, the vocabulary of citizenship – nationality – peoplehood, the classical concepts from the armory of statecraft and political theory which address these issues, the only ones we have, seem to provoke complicated reactions. The words – nation, people, citizenry – often strike us as cynical when uttered by our political masters, as in 'The British people do not want . . .', pernicious when employed by the far Right of Le Pen or Haider, and embarrassing when discussed in good society other than to denounce them. Who will admit to being a nationalist – the very word is pejorative? And in an environment which worships at the alter of multiculturalism, who will own up to a thick concept of peoplehood or even citizenship? And if one does own up, it is only to imagine a society of 'others'. (How greedy and cruel of some – usually comfortably positioned – to rob the real 'others' of their 'otherness' by claiming that we are all 'others'.)

This ambivalence may explain why the introduction in the Treaty of Maastricht of a European Citizenship has struck so many not simply as bemusing but as problematic. At one level and to some it symbolized yet another bold encroachment on the national by its worst antagonist, the supranational. At a deeper level it seemed to be tinkering with one of the very foundations of European integration.

If, indeed, the traditional, classical vocabulary of citizenship is the vocabulary of the state, the nation and peoplehood, its very introduction into the discourse of European integration is problematic for it conflicts with one of Europe's articles of faith, encapsulated for decades in the preamble to the Treaty of Rome. Mystery, mist and mirrors notwithstanding, one thing has always seemed clear: That the Community and Union were about 'lay[ing] the foundations of an ever closer union among the peoples of Europe'. Not the creation of one people, but the union of many. In that Europe was always different from all federal states which, whether in the USA, Germany, Australia and elsewhere, whilst purporting to preserve all manner of diversity, real and imaginary, always insisted on the existence of a single people at the federal level. The introduction of citizenship understood in its classical vocabulary could mean, then, a change in the very Telos of European integration from a union among the peoples of Europe to a people of Europe. With the change of the Telos would commence – some would hope, others fear – a process which would eventually result in people thinking of themselves of European in the same way they think of themselves today as French or Italian. Citizens of Europe would become not only formally, but in their consciousness, European citizens.

The introduction of European citizenship to the discourse of European integration could, however, mean not that the Telos of European integration has changed, but that our understanding of national membership has changed, is changing, or ought to change – possibilities that have been discussed widely at the national and European level, most recently in a comprehensive work by the British scholar Jo Shaw (1997). It would be changing because of a change in our understanding of the state and the nation as well as a change in our self-understanding and our understanding of the self. If citizenship classically postulates a sovereign state, is it not anachronistic to introduce it in an age in which, as MacCormick (1995a) has shown so lucidly, sovereignty itself has become fragmented, and states constitutionally cannot even pretend to have control over their most classical functions: Provision of material welfare and personal and collective security?

Think, too, of the linguistic trio – identity, identical, identify. Surely no self is identical to another. It is trite to recall that identity, in an age where for long choice has replaced fate as the foundation for self-understanding is, to a large extent, a political and social construct which privileges one (or one set) of characteristics over all other, calls on the self to identify with that, and is then posited as identity. It is equally trite to recall that the modern self has considerable problems with the move from identical to identity to identify. I may be German, or Italian or French. But is that my identity? What about being male or female? Or a Stones lover or Beatles lover (Verdi or Mozart, if you wish)? As the referents of identity grow, would it not be more accurate, in relation to the self today, to talk of my differentity?

This construct should not be confused with multiculturalism, in some way it is its opposite. Whether in the USA or Hungary the labeling of people as black, or White male, or Jew etc. as a basis for group political entitlement is the celebration of a bureaucratically sanctioned polity of 'multicultural' groups composed of monoculturally identified individuals – the antithesis of individual differentity.

Constructing, then, a new concept of citizenship around the fragmented sovereignty of the porous state and the fractured self of the individuals who comprise those 'states' – citizenship as a hallmark of differentity – could have been and could still be a fitting project for Union architects. That would be the major challenge to the conceptualization of European citizenship. Especially, since accepting and celebrating the differentity of individuals offers a new lease of life to the nation – nationality becoming a legitimate rather than oppressive bond among the individuals comprising the nation.

Such an architecture will have to explore both the shape of the construct and the technologies to sustain it. In the remainder of this chapter I will explore some of the available approaches and will offer my own variant too.

The affective crisis of European citizenship

As we shall see, the introduction of European citizenship brought about a deep sense of malaise and public disaffection with the European construct which threatened to undermine its political legitimacy. Understanding this disaffection is an important background to the subsequent unfolding saga of constitutional engineering.

The expression of the disaffection was manifest in the reaction to the Treaty of European Union – a public reaction which ranged from the hostile through the bewildered to the indifferent. The discontent was not with the Treaty itself – it was with the condition of Europe itself. What accounts for this attitude? For this change in fortune towards the idea of European integration?

There is, first, what one could term the paradox of success. In its foundational period, the European construct was perceived as part of a moral imperative in dealing with the heritage of World War II. Governments and states may have been happily pursuing their national interest but the European construct could be cloaked with a noble mantle of a new-found idealism. Rendering war as neither possible or thinkable and restoring economic prosperity in a framework of transnational social solidarity were key elements of that idealism. But once achieved, once you remove the moral imperative and its politics as usual with the frustrating twist that in Europe you cannot throw the scoundrels out at election time. So you try and throw the whole construct out.

Arguably, public attitudes go even deeper than that. We come here to a more sobering consideration in this regard, whereby the European Union may be seen not simply as having suffered a loss of its earlier spiritual values, but as an actual source of social *ressentiment*. Here are the highlights of what surely deserves much more than this superficial summary. In his pre-choleric days, Ernst Nolte wrote a fascinating study on the origins of fascism in its various European modes. Consider, chillingly, the turn to fascism in Italy, France and Germany at the beginning of the twentieth century. In his profound comparative analysis of the cultural–political roots of the phenomenon, the common source was identified as a reaction to some of the manifestations of modernity.

At a pragmatic level, the principal manifestations of modernity were the increased bureaucratization of life, public and private; the depersonalization of the market (through mass consumerism, brand names and the like) and the commodification of values; the 'abstractism' of social life, especially through competitive structures of mobility; rapid urbanization and the centralization of power.

At an epistemological level modernity was premised on, and experienced in, an attempt to group the world into intelligible concepts which had to be understood through reason and science – abstract and universal categories. On this reading, fascism was a response to, and an exploitation of, the angst generated by these practical and cognitive challenges. So far this is a fairly well-known story.

Eerily, at the end of the twentieth century, the European Union can be seen as replicating, in reality or in the subjective perception of individuals and societies, some of these very same features: it has come to symbolize, unjustly perhaps, the epitome of bureaucratization and, likewise, the epitome of centralization. One of its most visible policies, the Common Agriculture Policy, has had historically the purpose of 'rationalizing' farm holdings which, in effect, meant urbanization. The Single Market, with its emphasis on competitiveness and transnational movement of goods, can be perceived as a latter day thrust at increased commodification of values (consider how the logic of the Community forces a topic such as abortion to be treated as a 'service') and depersonalization of, this time round, the entire national market. Not only have local products come under pressure, even national products have lost their distinctiveness.

The very transnationalism of the Community, which earlier on was celebrated as a reinvention of Enlightenment idealism, is just that: universal,
rational, transcendent, and wholly modernist.

To this sustained and never resolved angst of modernity we have new,
fin de siècle added phenomena as illuminated brilliantly by Brian Fitzgerald
(1996). To capture these phenomena we can resort to what José Ortega
y Gasset (1996) called *creencias* – the certainties of life which needed no
proof – both in the physical and social world: water falls downward, there
is a difference between machines and humans, higher forms of life differentiate by gender, etc. To the sustained challenge of modernity is added
a profound shattering of the most fundamental *creencias* – deeper still, a
shattering of the ability to believe in anything. It is worth tracing some of
the manifestations of this process.

There is first, or was, for a sustained period in the twentieth century,
the assault of the reductive social sciences. Not only are things not what
they seem to be, but their reality always has a cynical malevolence. Public
life and its codes mask power and exploitation; private life with its codes
masks domination. By an inevitable logic this assault turned on itself,
whereby the illumination brought by these insights was not a vehicle for
liberation but in itself for manipulation. The epistemic challenge of post-
modernism deepens the shattering. For, in the old, modernist perspectives,
there was at least a truth to be explored, vindicated – even if that truth
was one of power, exploitation and domination. One can find distasteful
the post-modernist self-centered, ironic, sneering posturing. But, without
adjudicating the philosophical validity of its epistemic claim, there is no
doubt that the notion that all observations are relative to the perception
of the observer, that what we have are just competing narratives, has
moved from being a philosophic position to a social reality. It is part of
political discourse: multiculturalism is premised on it as are the breakdown
of authority (political, scientific, social) and the ascendant culture of extreme
individualism and subjectivity. Indeed, objectivity itself is considered a
constraint on freedom – a strange freedom, to be sure, empty of content.
Finally, the shattering of so many *creencias* (of the notion of *creencia* itself)
has found a powerful manifestation in the public forum. It is dominated
by television which distrusts and, by its pandering, non-judgmental trans-
mission or cheap moralization, itself undermines *creencias*. This occurs in
a vertical forum in which each viewer is isolated and addressed alone,
unable to hear and join the objections of other viewers. To the angst of
modernity is added the end-of-century fragmentation of information, and
the disappearance of coherent world view, belief in belief and belief in
the ability to know let alone control.

There are many social responses to these phenomena. One of them
has been a turn, by many, to any force which seems to offer 'meaning'.
Almost paradoxically, but perhaps not, the continued pull of the nation–
state, and the success in many societies of extreme forms of nationalism

(measured not only in votes and members but in the ability of those extreme forms to shift the center of the public debate) are, in part of course, due to the fact that the nation and state are such powerful vehicles in responding to the existential craving for meaning and purpose which modernity and post-modernity seem to deny. The nation and state, with their organizing myths of fate and destiny, provide a captivating and reassuring answer to many.

Here too the failure of Europe is colossal. Just as Europe fuels the angst of modernity it also feeds the angst of post-modernity: giant and fragmented at the same time, built as much on image as on substance, it is incomprehensible and challenges increasingly the *creencias* of national daily life. This is not to suggest that Europe is about to see a return to fascism, nor most certainly should this analysis, if it has any merit, give joy to *fin-de-siècle* chauvinists, whose wares today are as odious as they were at the start of the century. But it does suggest a profound change in its positioning in public life: Not, as in its founding period, as a response to a crisis of confidence, but fifty years later as one of the causes of that crisis.

In the realm of the symbolic, citizenship should reflect the ethos of the polity. If European citizenship should serve as an icon of identification, if this is what Europe has become – what is one identifying with? On this reading the collective enterprise of constructing or redefining a European citizenship is part and parcel of constructing and redefining a European ethos. How disappointing to observe the response of the powers-that-be.

To be a European citizen: the official bread and circus vision

There is a legend about the genesis of Article 8 according to which the issue of citizenship was far from the mind of the drafters of the TEU until the very last minutes when one Prime Minister (Felipe Gonzalez according to this legend), unhappy with the non-EMU parts of the Treaty, and conscious of the brewing legitimacy crisis in the European street, suggested that something be done about citizenship. A skeptical Intergovernmental Conference (IGC) quickly cobbled the Citizenship 'Chapter' in response. It is, of course, a legend. IGCs do not happen in that way as pointed out in O'Leary's (1996) admirable new book. But it could be true to judge from the content of Article 8.

As already mentioned, as is commonplace, the treatment of European citizenship both in the TEU itself and, subsequently, by the institutions and the Member States of the Union, is an embarrassment. The seriousness of this notion – after all the cornerstone of our democratic polities – and its fundamental importance to the self-understanding and legitimacy of the Union are only matched by its trivialization at the hands of the powers-that-be. One has to believe that the high contracting parties understood the fundamental nature of citizenship in redefining the nature of the Union – and it is this understanding, rather than misunderstanding which lead them to the desultory Article 8 and its aftermath. Which returns us to the 'Why' question. Why, indeed, open Pandora's box at all?

The recently concluded IGC offers us two clear clues. In the Commission's input to the Reflection Group we find the first: In the eyes of the Commission the two key values which make Union citizenship most worthy and, thus, worth developing to the full are: (a) that citizenship reinforces and renders more tangible the individual's sentiment of belonging to the Union; and (b) that citizenship confers on the individual citizen rights which tie him to the Union. It is endearing and telling that the Commission describes the relationship between Union and citizens using the terminology of ownership, and that it is the citizen which belongs to the Union. When the Irish Presidency put out its mid-term report on the IGC, this Freudian *glissade* was corrected. It is Europe which belongs to citizens, we were assured this time in the very opening statement of the Document. And this was followed by '[t]he Treaties establishing the Union should address their most direct concerns'. These were then listed as respect for fundamental rights, full employment, etc. This approach is followed through in the new Amsterdam Treaty. There is, on my reading, only a semantic difference in these two official statements which is echoed in similar statements from Council and even Parliament.

What is the political culture and ethos which explain a concept of citizenship which, for example, speaks of duties but lists none? Which speaks of the rights of citizens but not of empowering them politically? Which, in a dispiriting kind of Euro NewSpeak denies to all and sundry the nation-building aspect of European citizenship while, at the same time, appeals to a national understandings of citizenship expecting it to provide emotional and psychological attachments which are typical of those very constructs which are denied?

Is it the discourse of civic responsibility and consequent political attachment at all? Or is it not closer to a market culture and the ethos of consumerism? Is it an unacceptable caricature to think of this discourse as giving expression to an ethos according to which the Union has become a product for which the managers, alarmed by customer dissatisfaction, are engaged in brand development. Citizenship and the 'rights' associated with it are meant to give the product a new image (since it adds very little in substance) and make the product ever more attractive to its consumers, to reestablish their attachment to their favourite brand. The Union may belong to its citizens but no more, say, than a multinational corporation belongs to its shareholders. The introduction of citizenship on this reading is little more than a decision of the Board voting for an increased dividend as a way of placating restless shareholders.

A word should be said about fundamental human rights and European citizenship. I myself will be arguing that human rights have an important place in the construction of a meaningful concept of European citizenship.

But all too frequently in this discourse even human rights are commodified and represent just another goodie with which to placate a disaffected consumer of European integration. A first typical feature of most official discourse is the conflation of citizenship with (human) rights. This has become so natural that it seems both right and inevitable. I consider this conflation as part of the problem. If the problem is defined as alienation and disaffection towards the European construct by individuals and the medicine is European citizenship, an essential ingredient of this medicine becomes human rights, more rights, better rights, all in the hope of bringing the citizens closer to the Union (Ladeur 1997). Even if there is some truth to that, the picture is, at a minimum far more complex in the current European context.

I think rights do have that effect in transformative situations from, say, tyranny to emancipation. But that has long ceased to be the West European condition. Somewhat polemically let me make three points to illustrate that the nexus rights closeness is not nearly as simple as the IGC literature suggests.

Reflect on the following. Take, say, an Austrian or Italian national. Their human rights are protected by their constitution and by their constitutional court. As an additional safety net they are protected by the European Convention on Human Rights and the Strasbourg organs. In the Community, they receive judicial protection from the ECJ using as its source the same Convention and the constitutional traditions common to the Member States. Many of the proposed European rights are similar to those which our citizen already enjoys in his or her national space. Even if we imagine that there is a lacuna of protection in the Community space, that would surely justify closing that lacuna – but why would anyone imagine in a culture of rights saturation, not rights deprivation, that this would make the citizen any closer to the Community? Make no mistake: I do think the European human rights patrimony, national and transnational, has contributed to a sense of shared identity. But I think one has reached the point of diminishing returns. Simply adding new rights to the list, or adding lists of new rights, has little effect. Rights are taken for granted; if you managed to penetrate the general indifference towards the European construct by waving some new catalog or by broadcasting imminent accession to the ECHR, the likely reaction would be to wonder why those new rights or accession were not there in the first place.

For the most part rights set 'walls of liberty' around the individual against the exercise of power by public authority. The rights culture, which I share, tends to think of this as positive. But at least in part, at least psychologically, it might have the opposite effect to making the individual closer to 'his' or 'her' Union. After all, every time you clamor for more rights, which in this context are typically opposable against Community authorities, you are claiming that those rights are needed, in other words that the Union or Community pose a threat. You might be crying 'Wolf' to score some political point, or you may be right. Either way, if you are signaling to the individual that he or she need the rights since they are threatened, it is not exactly the stuff which will make them closer to their Union or Community (Smith 1992).

Finally, there is very little discussion of the divisive nature of rights, their 'disintegration effect'. Deciding on rights is often deciding on some of the deepest values of society. Even though we blithely talk about the common constitutional traditions, there are sharp differences within that common tradition. Some of the rights highest on the Christmas list of, say, the European Parliament, noble and justified as they may be, could if adopted for the Community be celebrated by the political culture in some Member States and regarded with suspicion and worse in other Member States. Remembering the Grogan v. SPUC abortion saga, which the ECJ inelegantly but perhaps wisely ducked, will drive home this point.

Mine is not an anti-market view, the importance of which to European prosperity is acknowledged. But it is a view which is concerned with the degradation of the political process, of image trumping substance, of deliberative governance being replaced by a commodification of the political process, of consumer replacing the citizen, of a Saatchi & Saatchi European citizenship. To conceptualize European citizenship around needs, even needs as important as employment and rights is an end-of-millennium version of bread and circus politics.

Towards the reconstruction of a European ethos

Do we need a European citizenship at all? The importance of European citizenship is a lot more than a device for placating an alienated populace. It goes to the very foundations of political legitimacy. The European Union enjoys powers unparalleled by any other transnational entity. It is not a State but in its powers it is pretty close. It has, *inter alia*, the capacity to do the following:

- to enact norms which create rights and obligations both for its Member States and their nationals, norms which are often directly effective and which are constitutionally supreme;
- to take decisions with major impact on the social and economic orientation of public life within the Member States and within Europe as a whole, considerably enhanced with Economic and Monetary Union;
- to engage the Community and, consequently the Member States by international agreements with third countries and international organizations;
- to spend significant amounts of public funds.

Europe has exercised these capacities to a very considerable degree. Whence the authority to do all this and what is the nature of a polity which has these powers?

One place to look for the answer would be international law. Let us discard this as artificial and formalistic. International law can neither explain nor legitimate the reality of Community life. If not that, then what?

In Western, liberal democracies public authority requires legitimation through one principal source: the citizens of the polity. The deepest, most clearly engraved hallmark of citizenship in our democracies is that in citizens vests the power, by majority, to create binding norms, to shape the socioeconomic direction of the polity, in fact, all those powers and capacities which, I suggested, the Union now has. More realistically, in citizens vests the power to enable and habilitate representative institutions which will exercise governance on behalf of, and for, the citizens.

Under our constitutional understanding of the Treaty – was that not what was achieved? I know that some believe this. Individuals as subjects? Lawyers recite dutifully that the Community constitutes a new legal order for the benefit of which the states have limited their sovereign rights, albeit within limited fields, and the subjects of which comprise not only Member States but also their nationals.

But note: individuals are subjects only in the effect of the law, which is very important to bringing cases before court. In this sense alone it is a new legal order. But you could create rights and afford judicial remedies to slaves. The ability to go to court to enjoy a right bestowed on you by pleasure of others does not emancipate you. It does not make you a citizen. Long before women or Jews were made citizens they enjoyed direct effect. Citizenship is not only about the politics of public authority. It is also about the social reality of peoplehood and the identity of the polity.

Citizens constitute the demos of the polity – citizenship is frequently, though not necessarily, conflated with nationality. This, then, is the other, collective side, of the citizenship coin. Demos provides another way of expressing the link between citizenship and democracy. Democracy does not exist in a vacuum. It is premised on the existence of a polity with members – the demos – by whom and for whom democratic discourse with its many variants takes place. The authority and legitimacy of a majority to compel a minority exist only within political boundaries defined by a demos. Simply put, if there is no demos, there can be no democracy.

But this, in turn, raises the other big dilemma of citizenship: who are to be the citizens of the European polity? How are we to define the relationships among them? A demos, a people cannot, after all, be a bunch of strangers. Are we not back then to the changed Telos, to nation building and all that? How should we understand and define the peoplehood of the European demos if we insist that the task remains the ever closer union among the peoples of Europe?

Are we then faced with a crucial choice: reject European citizenship and content yourself to living in a polity which may provide you with bread and circus a-plenty but which lacks the core of individual political dignity and public legitimation? Adopt European citizenship and fundamentally change the very Telos of European integration from its unique concept of Community to, frankly, a more banal notion of nation building? This is an unappealing choice.

In offering a resolution I want to bring together three elements: I first want to re-articulate my understanding of the special nature – and identity! – of the European polity as encapsulated in the term supranationalism. It is the central concept for understanding the ethos of Europe, a key in the understanding of citizenship. Mine, as will appear, is a politically conservative view since it insists not simply on the inevitability of the nation–state but on its virtues. I will then restate the move of decoupling nationality from citizenship, a key idea which Closa (1992), O'Leary (1984), Ingram (1995) and others have helped explore in the context of European integration. Finally, I shall recouple them but in a specific European geometry. This geometry reflects – as citizenship should – the unique supranational values of the polity.

In trying to explain the ways in which the Community is, or has become, supranational, most discussion over the years has tended, interestingly, to focus on its relation to the 'state' rather than the 'nation'. This conflation of nation/state is not always helpful. Supranationalism relates in specific and discreet ways to nationhood and to statehood. To see the relationship between supranationalism, nationhood and statehood, I propose to focus in turn on nationhood and statehood and try and explore their promise and their dangers. First, then, nationhood. I have culled here, without doing any justice to the originals from some of the old and new masters Herder and Mazzini, Berlin, Arendt (1967) and Gellner (1983), A. D. Smith (1992) and Tamir (1993).

It seems to me that, at least in its nineteenth century liberal conception, two deep human values are said to find expression in nationhood: belongingness and originality. (It should immediately be stated that nationhood is not the only social form in which these values may find expression.) Belongingness is inherent in nationhood, nationhood is a form of belonging. Nationhood is not an instrument to obtain belongingness, it is it. What are the values embedded in belonging, in national belonging, beyond the widely shared view that belonging is pleasant, is good? We can readily understand a certain basic appeal to our human species which is, arguably, inherently social: the appeal that family and tribe have, too. Part of the appeal is, simply, the provision of a framework for social interaction. But surely one has to go beyond that: after all, much looser social constructs than nationhood, let alone tribe and family, could provide that framework. Belonging means, of course, more than that. It means a place, a social home.

The belonging of nationhood is both like and unlike the bonds of blood in family and tribe, and in both this likeness and unlikeness we may find a clue to some of its underlying values.

It is like the 'bonds of blood' in family and tribe in that those who are of the nation have their place, are accepted, belong, independently of their achievements – by just being – and herein lies the powerful appeal (and terrible danger) of belonging of this type – it is a shield against existential aloneness. The power of this belongingness may be understood by the drama and awesomeness of its opposites: isolation, seclusion, excommunication.

But nationhood transcends the family and tribe, and maybe here lurks an even more tantalizing value: nationhood not only offers a place to the familyless, to the tribeless, but in transcending family and tribe it calls for loyalty – the largest coin in the realm of national feeling – towards others which go beyond the immediate 'natural' (blood) or self-interested social unit.

And, indeed, belongingness of this type is a two-way street. It is not only a passive value: to be accepted. It is also active: to accept. Loyalty is one of those virtues which, if not abused, benefits both those on the giving and receiving ends.

Ironically, the artificial belonging of nationality, once it sheds its ethnic and culturally repressive baggage, has an altogether more poignant meaning in the age of multiculturalism. Precisely in an epoch in which individuals and groups develop myriad identity referents and in which a culture of rights and entitlement invites social dislocation, its artificiality gives it its bridging potential.

This is the place to acknowledge, too, the virtues of autochthony – the nexus to place and land, the much maligned soil. Blood and soil have, of course, horrific associations which need no exploring here. But not only must we acknowledge the hold which the spatial has in conditioning perception, sensibility and, hence, identity. One must also realize the appeal and virtue of autochthony as an antidote to the fragmentation of the postmodern condition.

The other core value of nationhood, in some ways also an instrument for national demarcation, is the claim about originality. On this reading, the Tower of Babel was not a sin against God but a sin against human potentiality; and the dispersal that came in its aftermath, not punishment, but divine blessing. In shorthand, the nation, with its endlessly rich specificities, coexisting alongside other nations, is, in this view, the vehicle for realizing human potentialities in original ways, ways which humanity as a whole would be the poorer for not cultivating.

It is here that one may turn from the nation to the modern state. It is worth remembering at the outset that national existence and even national vibrancy do not in and of themselves require statehood, though statehood can offer the nation advantages, both intrinsic as well as advantages resulting from the current organization of international life which gives such huge benefits to statehood.

I would argue that in the modern notion of the European organic–national nation–state, the state is to be seen principally as an instrument, the organizational framework within which the nation is to realize its potentialities. It is within the statal framework that governance, with its most important functions of securing welfare and security, is situated. The well-being and integrity of the state must, thus, be secured so that these functions may be attained. That is not a meager value in itself. But to the extent that the state may claim, say, a loyalty which is more than pragmatic, it is because it is at the service of the nation with its values of belongingness and originality. (This conceptualization underscores, perhaps exaggerates, the difference with the American, truly radical, alternative liberal project of the non-ethnonational polity, and of a state, the Republic, the organization of which, and the norms of citizenship behavior within, were central to its value system.)

It is evident, however, that in the European project, boundaries become a very central feature of the nation–state.

There are, obviously, boundaries in the legal–geographical sense of separating one nation–state from another. But there are also internal, cognitive boundaries by which society (the nation) and individuals come to think of themselves in the world.

At a societal level, nationhood involves the drawing of boundaries by which the nation will be defined and separated from others. The categories of boundary-drawing are myriad: linguistic, ethnic, geographic, religious, etc. The drawing of the boundaries is exactly that: a constitutive act, which decides that certain boundaries are meaningful both for the sense of belonging and for the original contribution of the nation. This constitutive element is particularly apparent at the moment of 'nation building' when histories are rewritten, languages revived, etc. Of course, with time, the boundaries, especially the non-geographical ones, write themselves on collective and individual consciousness with such intensity that they appear as natural – consider the virtual interchangeability of the word international with universal and global. It is hard not to think, in the social sphere, of the world as a whole without the category of nation (as in international). Finally, at an individual level, belonging implies a boundary: you belong because others do not.

As evident as the notion of boundaries is to the nation–state enterprise, so is the high potential for abuse of boundaries. The abuse may take place in relation to the three principal boundaries: the external boundary of the State, the boundary between nation and state and the internal consciousness boundary of those making up the nation.

The most egregious form of abuse of the external boundary of the state would be physical or other forms of aggression towards other states. The abuse of the boundary between nation and state is most egregious when the state comes to be seen not as instrumental for individuals and society to realize their potentials but as an end in itself. Less egregiously, the state might induce a 'laziness' in the nation – banal statal symbols and instrumentalities becoming a substitute for truly original national expression. This may also have consequences for the sense of belongingness whereby the apparatus of the state becomes a substitute to a meaningful sense of belonging. An allegiance to the state can replace human affinity, empathy, loyalty and sense of shared fate with the people of the state.

There can be, too, an abuse of the internal boundary which defines belongingness. The most typical abuse here is to move from a boundary which defines a sense of belonging to one which induces a sense of superiority and a concomitant sense of condescension or contempt for the other. A sense of collective national identity implies an other. It should not imply an inferior other.

In the attitude to the land, which finds legal expression in the concept of national territory, both the virtues and dangers of nationalism find powerful expression. The national land, the homeland, the fatherland, the motherland, 'belongs' to the nation – and to no one else. Ownership, whether constructed or innate, is one of the most potent modes of attachment. Cultivating the feeling of collective, symbolic, ownership over land is intended not only to enhance a sense of attachment to place and willingness to make sacrifices for it, but is also an important part of social attachment among 'co-owners' and, thus, an important part of the special sense of national 'belongingness'. (Clearly it also mediates the huge disparities in private, 'real' ownership of land.) Land plays, too, an important part in national originality. So much of the culture, highbrow and low, is a reflection of geography and topography and of associated phenomena such as climate. At the same time, the role of territory in the pathologies of nationalism is a living part of the history of the European nation–states and their murderous quarrels which is so well known as to obviate discussion.

A central plank of the project of European integration may be seen, then, as an attempt to control the excesses of the modern nation–state in Europe, especially, but not only, its propensity to violent conflict and the inability of the international system to constrain that propensity. The European Community was to be an antidote to the negative features of the state and statal intercourse and its establishment in 1951 was seen as the beginning of a process that would bring about the elimination of these excesses.

Historically there have always been those two competing visions of European integration. Whilst no one has seriously envisioned a Jacobean-type centralized Europe, it is clear that one vision, to which I have referred as the unity vision, the United States of Europe vision, has really posited as its ideal type, as its aspiration, a statal Europe, albeit of a federal kind. Tomorrow's Europe in this form would indeed constitute the final demise of Member State nationalism, replacing or placing the hitherto warring Member States within a political union of federal governance.

It is easy to see some of the faults of this vision: it would be more than ironic if a polity set up as a means to counter the excesses of statism ended up coming round full circle and transforming itself into a (super) state. It would be equally ironic if the ethos which rejected the boundary abuse of the nation–state, gave birth to a polity with the same potential for abuse. The problem with this unity vision is that its very realization entails its negation.

The alternative vision, the one that historically has prevailed, is the supranational vision, the community vision. At one level aspirations here are both modest compared to the Union model and reactionary: supranationalism, the notion of community rather than unity, is about affirming the values of the liberal nation–state by policing the boundaries against abuse. Another way of saying this would be that supranationalism aspires to keep the values of the nation–state pure and uncorrupted by the abuses I described above. But it is still a conservative modernist vision since it does not reject boundaries: it guards them but it also guards against them.

At another level the supranational community project is far more ambitious than the unity one and far more radical. It is more ambitious since, unlike the unity project which simply wishes to redraw the actual political boundaries of the polity within the existing nation–state conceptual framework, albeit federal, the supranational project seeks to redefine the very notion of boundaries of the state, between the nation and state, and within the nation itself. It is more radical since, as I shall seek to show, it involves more complex demands and greater constraints on the actors.

How, then, does supranationalism, expressed in the community project of European integration, affect the excesses of the nation–state, the abuse of boundaries discussed above? At the pure statal level, supranationalism replaces the 'liberal' premise of international society with a community one. The classical model of international law is a replication at the international level of a liberal theory of the state. The state is implicitly treated as the analogue, on the international level, to the individual within a domestic situation. In this conception, international legal notions such as self-determination, sovereignty, independence, and consent have their obvious analogy in theories of the individual within the state. In the supranational vision, the community as a transnational regime will not simply be a neutral arena in which states will seek to pursue the national interest and maximize their benefits but will create a tension between the state and the Community of states. Crucially, the community idea is not meant to eliminate the national state but to create a regime which seeks to tame the national interest with a new discipline. The challenge is to control at the societal level the uncontrolled reflexes of national interest in the international sphere.

Turning to the boundary between nation and state, supranationalism is meant to prevent abuses here, too. The supranational project recognizes that at an inter-group level nationalism is an expression of cultural (political and/or other) specificity underscoring differentiation, the uniqueness of a group as positioned *vis-à-vis* other groups, calling for respect and justifying the maintenance of inter-group boundaries. At an intra-group level nationalism is an expression of cultural (political and/or other) specificity underscoring commonality, the 'sharedness' of the group *vis-à-vis* itself, calling for loyalty and justifying elimination of intra-group boundaries.

But, crucially, nationality is not the thing itself – it is its expression, an artifact. It is a highly stylized artifact, with an entire apparatus of norms and habits; above all it is not a spontaneous expression of that which it signifies but a code of what it is meant to give expression to, frequently even translated into legal constructs. Nationality is inextricably linked to citizenship, citizenship not simply as the code for group identity, but also as a package of legal rights and duties, and of social attitudes.

Supranationalism does not seek to negate as such the interplay of differentiation and commonality, of inclusion and exclusion and their potential value. But it is a challenge to the codified expressions in nationality. Since, in the supranational construct with its free movement provisions, which do not allow exclusion through statal means of other national cultural influences and with its strict prohibition on nationality/citizenship based discrimination, national differentiation cannot rest so easily on the artificial boundaries provided by the state. At the intergroup level then it pushes for cultural differences to express themselves in their authentic, spontaneous form, rather than the codified statal legal forms. At the intragroup level it attempts to strip the false consciousness which nationalism may create instead of belongingness derived from a non-formal sense of sharedness. This, perhaps, is the first Kantian strand in this conceptualization of supranationalism. Kantian moral philosophy grounds moral obligation on the ability of humans not simply to follow ethical norms, but, as rational creatures, to determine for themselves the laws of their own acting and to act out of internal choice according to these norms. Supranationalism on our view favours national culture when, indeed, it is authentic, internalized, a true part of identity.

There is another – Enlightenment–Kantian idea in this discourse. Supranationalism at the societal and individual, rather than the statal level, embodies an ideal which diminishes the importance of the statal aspects of nationality – probably the most powerful contemporary expression of groupness – as the principal referent for transnational human intercourse. That is the value side of non-discrimination on grounds of nationality, of free movement provisions and the like. Hermann Cohen (1995), the great neo-Kantian, in his *Religion der Vernunft aus den Quellen des Judentums*, tries to explain the meaning of the Mosaic law, which calls for non-oppression of the stranger. In his vision, the alien is to be protected, not because he was a member of one's family, clan religious community or people, but because he was a human being. In the alien, therefore, man discovered the idea of humanity.

We see through this exquisite exegesis that in the curtailment of the totalistic claim of the nation–state and the reduction of nationality as the principle referent for human intercourse, the Community ideal of supranationalism is evocative of, and resonates with, Enlightenment ideas, with the privileging of the individual, with a different aspect of liberalism which has as its progeny today in liberal notions of human rights. In this respect the Community ideal is heir to Enlightenment liberalism. Supranationalism assumes a new, additional meaning which refers not to the relations among nations but to the ability of the individual to rise above his or her national closet.

And yet, at the same moment we understand that these very values, which find their legal and practical expression in, e.g., enhanced mobility, breakdown of local markets, and insertion of universal norms into domestic culture are also part of the deep modern and post-modern anxiety of European belongingness and part of the roots of European angst and alienation. This is, perhaps, the deepest paradox of European citizenship.

Towards a reconstruction of European citizenship: three views of multiple demoi

How does this help us in the construction of European citizenship and demos and the resolution of that crucial choice? It is here that I will try and give normative meaning to the citizenship clause in Maastricht and Amsterdam: 'Citizenship of the Union is hereby established. Every person holding the nationality of a Member State shall be a citizen of the Union [Maastricht].' 'Citizenship of the Union shall complement and not replace national citizenship. [Amsterdam]' As mentioned, the introduction of citizenship to the conceptual world of the Union could be seen as just another step in the drive towards a statal, unity vision of Europe, especially if citizenship is understood as being premised on a statal understanding of nationality. But there is another more tantalizing and radical way of understanding the provision, namely as the very conceptual decoupling of nationality from citizenship and as the conception of a polity the demos of which, its membership, is understood in the first place in civic and political rather than ethnocultural terms. On this view, the Union belongs to, is composed of, citizens who by definition do not share the same nationality. The substance of membership (and thus of the demos) is in a commitment to the shared values of the Union as expressed in its constituent documents, a commitment, *inter alia*, to the duties and rights of a civic society covering discrete areas of public life, a commitment to membership in a polity which privileges exactly the opposites of nationalism – those human features which transcend the differences of organic ethno-culturalism. On this reading, the conceptualization of a European demos should not be based on real or imaginary trans-European cultural affinities or shared histories nor on the construction of a European 'national' myth of the type which constitutes the identity of the organic nation. European citizenship should not be thought of either as intended to create the type of emotional attachments associated with nationality-based citizenship.

The decoupling of nationality and citizenship opens the possibility, instead, of thinking of coexisting multiple demoi. I will present several possibilities of this, which are not necessarily mutually exclusive. One view of multiple demoi may consist in what may be called the 'concentric circles' approach. On this approach one feels simultaneously as belonging to, and being part of, say, Germany and Europe; or, even, Scotland, Britain and Europe. What characterizes this view is that the sense of identity and identification derives from the same sources of human attachment albeit at different levels of intensity. Presumably the most intense (which the nation, and state, always claims to be) would and should trump in normative conflict.

The problem with this view is that invites us to regard European citizenship in the same way that we understand our national citizenship. This was precisely the fallacy of the German Constitutional Court in its Maastricht decision: conceptualizing the European demos in the way that the German demos is conceptualized.

One alternative view of multiple demoi invites individuals to see themselves as belonging simultaneously to two demoi, based, critically, on different subjective factors of identification, in the way someone may regard himself or herself as being German and Catholic. I may be a German national in the in-reaching strong sense of organic-cultural identification and sense of belongingness. I am simultaneously a European citizen in terms of my European transnational affinities to shared values which transcend the ethno-national diversity.

On this view, the Union demos turns away from its antecedents and understanding in the European nation–state. But equally, it should be noted that I am suggesting here something that is different than simple American Republicanism transferred to Europe. The values one is discussing may be seen to have a special European specificity, a specificity I have explored elsewhere but one dimension of which, by simple way of example, could most certainly be that strand of mutual social responsibility embodied in the ethos of the welfare state adopted by all European societies and by all political forces. Human rights as embodied in the European Convention of Human Rights would constitute another strand in this matrix of values as would, say, the ban on discrimination on grounds of nationality and all the rest.

But this view, too, has its problems. In the first place it is not clear how this matrix of values would be qualitatively different from the normal artifacts of constitutional democracy practiced in most European nation–states. After all, all of them are signatories to the European Convention on Human Rights, all of them, to varying degrees share in those 'European values'. Second, a community of value expressed in these terms provides a rather thin, even if laudable, content to the notion of citizenship. And as A.D. Smith (1992) convincingly argues, without resonant fiction of relatedness through memory, and myth and history and/or real kinship, a real sense of membership is hard to come by. It is noticeable that even national polities who supposedly understand themselves as communities of values, such as France or the United States, cannot avoid in their evolution, self-understanding and even self-definition many of the features of communities of fate.

I want to offer a third version of the multiple demoi, one of true variable geometry. It is like the second version in one crucial respect. It too invites individuals to see themselves as belonging simultaneously to two demoi, based, critically, on different subjective factors of identification. And in this version too the invitation is to embrace the national in the in-reaching strong sense of organic-cultural identification and belongingness and to embrace the European in terms of European transnational affinities to shared values which transcend the ethno-national diversity.

But there are two critical differences. One can be German without being Catholic. One can be Catholic without being German. In this model of European citizenship, the concepts of Member State nationality and European citizenship are totally interdependent. One cannot, conceptually and psychologically (let alone legally) be a European citizen without being a Member State national. It is in this respect the mirror of my analysis of supranationalism itself, which, as I was at pains to argue, had no ontological independence but was part and parcel of the national project, in some way its gate keeper.

There is a second critical difference to this model of multiple demoi: its matrix of values is not simply the material commitment to social solidarity, to human rights and other such values which, as I argued, would hardly differentiate it from the modern constitutional, West European liberal state. It has a second important civilizatory dimension. It is the acceptance by its members that in a range of areas of public life, one will accept the legitimacy and authority of decisions adopted by fellow European citizens in the realization that in these areas preference is given to choices made by the outreaching, non organic, demos, rather than by the inreaching one. The Treaties on this reading would have to be seen not only as an agreement among states (a Union of States) but as a 'social contract' among the nationals of those states – ratified in accordance with the constitutional requirements in all Member States – that they will in the areas covered by the Treaty regard themselves as associating as citizens in a broader society. But crucially, this view preserves the boundaries, preserves the Self and preserves the Other. But it attempts to educate the

I to reach to that Other. We can go even further. In this polity, and to this demos, one cardinal value is precisely that there will not be a drive towards, or an acceptance of, an over-arching organic – cultural national identity displacing those of the Member States. Nationals of the Member States are European citizens, not the other way around. Europe is 'not yet' a demos in the organic national–cultural sense and should never become one. The value matrix has, thus, two civilizing strands: material and processual. One that subordinates the individual and the national society to certain values and certain decisional procedures representing a broader range of interests and sensibilities. Of course the two are connected. We are willing to submit aspects of our social ordering to a polity composed of 'others' precisely because we are convinced that in some material sense they share our basic values. It is a construct which is designed to encourage certain virtues of tolerance and humanity.

One should not get carried away with this construct. Note first that the Maastricht formula does not imply a full decoupling: Member States are free to define their own conditions of membership and these may continue to be defined in national terms. But one should not read this construct as embracing an unreconstructed notion of nationalism within each Member State. I have already argued: a nationalism, which seeks to overwhelm the self has been a major source of bigotry and prejudice. A nationalism which acknowledges the multicultural self, can be a positive unifying concept. On this reading European citizenship as a reflection of supranationalism can be regarded as part of the liberal nation project. That, in my view, is the greatest promise of introducing supranational citizenship into a construct the major components of which continue to be states and nations. The national and the supranational encapsulate on this reading two of the most elemental, alluring and frightening social and psychological poles of our cultural heritage. The national is Eros: reaching back to the pre-modern, appealing to the heart with a grasp on our emotions, and evocative of the romantic vision of creative social organization as well as responding to our existential yearning for a meaning located in time and space. The nation, through its myths, provides a past and a future. And it is always a history and a destiny in a place, in a territory, a narrative that is fluid and fixed at the same time. The dangers are self-evident. The supra-national is civilization: Confidently modernist, appealing to the rational within us and to Enlightenment neo-classical humanism, taming that Eros. Importantly, the relationship is circular – for its very modernism and ratio-nalism is what, as I sought to show earlier, is alienating, and would have but an ambivalent appeal if it was to represent alone the content of European identity.

Martin Heidegger is an unwitting ironic metaphor for the difficulty of negotiating between these poles earlier in the twentieth century. His rational, impersonal critique of totalistic rationality and of modernity retain powerful lessons to this day; but equally powerful is the lesson from his fall: an irrational, personal embracing of an irrational, romantic pre-modern nationalism run amok (not to mention a dishonorable failure to acknowledge any personal failing).

For some European citizenship is an icon signifying the hope of transcending state and national society altogether. For others it is no more than a symbol for the demise of the classical European nation–state in the bureaucratic, globalized market. For others still it is the icon of a shrewd, Machiavelli-like scheme of self-preservation of the same statal structure which has dominated Europe for a century and more. Finally it could be regarded as emblematic of that new liberal effort which seeks to retain the Eros of the national its demonic aspects under civilizatory constraints.

Democracy and European integration: to be a good European citizen

The discourse of democracy, too, takes an additional significance in this context. The primary democratic imperative is in bestowing legitimacy on a 'formation' – the Union – which, want it or not, exercises manifold state functions. It was this imperative from which the search for demos and European citizenship emerged. But now we have seen that our construct of European citizenship was also seen as having a particular supranational educational, civilizing function, by submitting certain aspects of our national autonomy to a community which in significant aspects is a community of 'others'. But the civilizing impulse would, surely, be lost if in the Community decisional process, the individual became totally lost, and instead of a deliberative engagement across differences we had bureaucratic subordination.

The question remains then, what, if anything, can be done to operationalize and particularly empower individuals in Europe in their capacity as citizens? This is not the place to rehearse the full litany of the European democratic deficit. But clearly, on any reading, as the Community has grown in size, in scope, in reach and despite a high rhetoric including the very creation of 'European citizenship', there has been a distinct disempowerment of the individual European citizen, the specific gravity of whom continues to decline as the Union grows. The roots of disempowerment are many but three stand out.

First is surely the inability of the Community and Union to develop structures and processes which adequately replicate at the Community level the habits of governmental control, parliamentary accountability and administrative responsibility which are practiced with different modalities in the various Member States. Further, as more and more functions move to Brussels, the democratic balances within the Member States have been disrupted by a strengthening of the ministerial and executive branches of government. The value of each individual in the political process has inevitably declined including the ability to play a meaningful civic role in European governance.

The second root goes even deeper and concerns the ever increasing remoteness, opaqueness, and inaccessibility of European governance. An apocryphal statement usually attributed to Jacques Delors predicts that by the end of the 1990s 80 per cent of social regulation will issue from Brussels. We are on target. The drama lies in the fact that no accountable public authority has a handle on these regulatory processes. Not the European Parliament, not the Commission, not even the governments. The press and other media, a vital estate in our democracies, are equally hampered. Consider that it is even impossible to get from any of the Community institutions an authoritative and mutually agreed statement of the mere number of committees which inhabit that world of Comitology. Once there were those who worried about the supranational features of European integration. It is time to worry about infranationalism – a complex network of middle-level national administrators, Community administrators and an array of private bodies with unequal and unfair access to a process with huge social and economic consequences to everyday life – in matters of public safety, health, and all other dimensions of socioeconomic regulation. Transparency and access to documents are often invoked as a possible remedy to this issue. But if you do not know what is going on, which documents will you ask to see? Neither strengthening the European Parliament nor national Parliaments will do much to address this problem of post-modern governance, which itself is but one manifestation of a general sense of political alienation in most Western democracies.

Another issue relates to the competences of the Union and Community. In one of its most celebrated cases in the early 1960s the European Court of Justice described the Community as a 'new legal order for the benefit of which the States have limited their sovereign rights, albeit in limited fields'. There is a widespread anxiety that these fields are limited no more. Indeed, not long ago a prominent European scholar and judge has written that there 'simply is no nucleus of sovereignty that the Member States can invoke, as such, against the Community'. We should not, thus, be surprised by a continuing sense of alienation from the Union and its Institutions.

What, then, does it mean to be a good citizen in such a polity? And what changes in the structure and process of governance must be contemplated to accommodate such citizenship? It is to these issues that I shall turn in the sequel to this chapter.

Note

1   An earlier version of this chapter appeared in *Journal of European Public Policy*, vol. 4 (1997).

Part IV

Images of world order

10 Nationalism and world order

Stanley Hoffmann

The resurgence of nationalism after the Cold War, in a world in which
states are increasingly interdependent, incapable of providing by themselves the services their citizens expect, and dependent on international
cooperation, gives rise to two kinds of intellectual inquiries. We have seen
a remarkable flourishing of normative works that discuss the ethical implications of nationalism and cosmopolitanism, the claims of multiculturalism,
and the rights and duties of immigrants and refugees vs. the rights and
duties of host countries and their citizens. In my work-in- (slow) progress
on ethics and international relations, I intend to address these issues. This
chapter belongs to the second type of inquiry: the empirical analysis of
this protean phenomenon: nationalism, of the limits and possibilities of
internationalism in a world of leaking, or melting, or shrinking, or diffuse,
and sometimes shared or pooled sovereignty. My purpose is to examine
the extent to which and the conditions under which nationalism is compatible with world order. I will begin by a definition of terms, then digress
through political philosophy, and return to the main themes: is nationalism the enemy of world order? What kind of world order is possible in
a world of nationalisms?

Defining terms

Unlike national consciousness, or patriotism ('sentiment national'), nationalism is an ideology. Patriotism means loyalty to one's nation. Nationalism
is, in my opinion, more than 'a belief held by a group of people that they
ought to constitute a nation or that they are already one' (Haas 1997: 35).
Like other ideologies, it is, first, a reaction to a problem: what is the secular
community which deserves the individuals' highest allegiance and which
will provide them with a common social identity? Second, it provides an
answer, an explanation: we are not merely the members of a nation (whatever the way in which the distinctive characteristics of the nation are
defined); our identity is constituted by our membership in a nation; all
other memberships are partial, or weaker. Third, like all ideologies, nationalism offers a program. At a minimum, it is the promotion and protection

of the nation's integrity and uniqueness. Often, it goes beyond this, and proclaims not only the nation's singularity, but its mission in the world, or its superiority over others.

Nationalism made its appearance at a time when two social phenomena transformed human consciousness and behavior. One was the demise of the monarchic and religious conception of the polity, replaced by an emphasis on the people and its collective will, or on individuals bound to one another by the cement of the nation. The other, emphasized by Ernest Gellner, is the 'delocalization' of the individual in the new economic order of capitalism, the opening or even the destruction of the small and relatively closed communities that had absorbed human lives for centuries (Gellner 1983).

The question remains why these 'delocalized' individuals, these groups that were being told that they were entitled to the mastery of their fates, chose to give their highest allegiance to the nation, and not to the competing claimant, class. Why did the 'imagined community' become the nation (Anderson 1983)? An historical answer emphasizes the fact that in several cases, the state had already established institutions and promoted ideas that created a nation out of a galaxy of ethnic and cultural groups: thus, in the United Kingdom, in France. In other cases, the nation appeared in resistance to foreign aggression or domination: in the Netherlands, in Spain under Napoleon, in Fichte's Germany or Mazzini's Italy, and of course in Poland, Ireland, and the rebellious colonies that became the United States. Despite Marx's conviction, class could not compete. Industrialization and the formation of a proletariat took place within the borders of national states: in Britain, France, Bismarck's Germany, the US, Japan, or of Empires dominated by one nation, such as Russia. The transnational solidarity of class provided symbolic satisfactions to workers embroiled in battles against capitalists and poverty within the confines of the nation–state. But this solidarity, as the tragic history of the Second International demonstrated, never transcended national differences sufficiently, and the workers themselves found in the nation a way of escaping from the constraints and humiliations of their lives as alienated producers. The community of labor was their daily condition. The 'imagined community' they needed was the nation – not only because it transcended class, but because it corresponded to an aspiration to become 'citoyens à part entière' in the nation in which they lived.

Ideologies need mobilized believers who will propagate it and do battle for it. Few ideologies have been so resourceful in their choice of vehicles of propagation. Nationalism has sometimes surged from below, with the help of intellectuals and students, and sometimes – as in Hungary and Japan – from above. It has sometimes been locked in battle with the Church, as in France, and sometimes been carried and supported by the Church, as in Poland. In some instances, it proved to be a powerful instrument of change of the existing class system, as in revolutionary France.

Elsewhere, it contributed to the preservation of the existing class system – as in Britain, or Hungary, or pre-World War I Germany. It often was a force of modernization, as Gellner (1983) and Haas (1997) have chosen to emphasize. But it could also buttress resistance to important elements of modernization, as in the case of Gandhi's nationalism, and in several aspects of Nazi ideology and policies (I am sorry to bring Hitler and Gandhi into the same sentence). It comes in all the forms – four 'revolutionary' and three 'syncretist' – that Haas distinguishes in his elaborate typology (Haas 1997: 46–53). The problem with most of the typologies of nationalism I have seen is that each one refers to only one of nationalism's many dimensions (in Haas' case, it is the attitude toward traditional values; in the famous and overworked distinction between civic and ethnic nationalism, it is the basis of national identity, i.e. the characteristics that differentiate 'nationals' from 'foreigners'). Nationalism, as an ideology, has managed to be compatible with, parasitic on, or destructive of all other ideologies.

Let us turn to the concept of world order. I will annex Hedley Bull's definition (Bull 1997). It is a condition or situation (I would prefer: a construct and a condition) in which the basic requirements of the units that constitute the international system are satisfied: survival, a reasonable degree of security, a low level of inter-unit violence, i.e. a condition of relative stability or moderation. The term also refers to the set of procedures (established both among the major powers and in hierarchical relations) that ensure this condition. They vary, depending on the nature of the units, the number of great powers, the composition of what might be called relevant power (neo-realists tend to focus excessively on military power), and the main ideologies that exist in the system.

World order can be a deliberate goal of states – a policy aimed at producing an international milieu favorable to the material interests and the values of a given actor – or simply the product of policies that are not directly aimed at establishing a certain kind of order. We need also to distinguish between a minimalist conception of it (i.e. the one entailed by Bull's definition), and a maximalist one, which adds to the focus on moderation a focus on fairness, in the relations among the units and even (a supremely maximalist conception!) in the relations between governments and people within the units. Such a definition introduces considerations of justice and humanity into the analysis of world order. Bull himself did so at the end of his lamentably short life.[1]

Political philosophies and nationalism

Among the many reasons why political scientists who study international relations should concern themselves with something as apparently 'non-scientific' as political philosophy, is the fact that many of the philosophical theories, and especially those of the last two centuries, have provided us with images of world order; and they have shown the ways in which several features of the international system (such as its structure) or of the units (such as the domestic political or economic regime) shape, or misshape, world order. Yet one cannot avoid being surprised at how little attention the main doctrines have paid to nationalism. It is as if nationalism, one of the central social phenomena since the French Revolution, and one which has given to the link between the individual and the state a wholly new substance and intensity – thus profoundly affecting the 'game of states' – had been merely tangential or incidental to these philosophies, or inassimilable to them.

For modern realists and neo-realists, basically nationalism does not matter much. In a system of distinct and competing units, be they empires or nation–states or dynastic states or city–states, anarchy (the absence of central power and the frequently violent conflicts that result from it) is a permanent and defining feature. Realists and neo-realists emphasize the rationality of behavior such a feature engenders: the need for each actor to calculate his forces, the interest of prudent actors in establishing and preserving a balance of power so as to moderate the ambitions of trouble-makers, the interest of even an ambitious actor not to behave in such a way as to provoke a coalition of threatened units that could bring it losses instead of gains, etc. It is true that Hans Morgenthau wrote about 'nationalistic universalism', in referring to the twentieth century's totalitarian regimes, but even here nationalism was seen mainly as a rationalization and aggravation of state expansionism. The one Realist who *did* take the force of modern nationalism into account was Max Weber, with his gloomy view of international relations as a contest among national cultures – almost national essences – and as a Darwinian universe in which the bigger ones were bound to swallow the smaller ones (Smith 1986b). This was a view, derived from but far more pessimistic and less 'rational' than Hegel's, which left one with no illusion about the possibility of world order. But the other members of these vast and amorphous schools, German, Swiss, British, American or French, all subscribed, explicitly or implicitly, to the view that in so far as nationalism prevents or distorts a reasonable definition of the national interest – by prodding the state into acting beyond its power, or into building up its power in a way that would backfire – it is to be curbed or excommunicated. Realist nationalists, such as Michel Debré and his great mentor Charles de Gaulle, tried to separate a good and necessary nationalism that gives a sense of identity, cohesion and purpose to the unit in the global 'state of war' (as well as to its citizens in their daily lives), and a wicked nationalism that, in Debré's words, 'was to national feeling what Inquisition had been to faith, a degradation and a disease' (*Une passion pour la France*). The Realist vision of a moderate inter-state order made such a delicate distinction necessary (Hoffmann 1960).[2] For Realists *à la* Kennan or Kissinger – or Lippmann – the intrusion of excess and incompetence into the difficult game of states, resulting from nationalist passions relayed by democratic institutions, breeds only chaos; cool expertise respectful of tradition is needed for world order to be possible in an anarchic world.

Marxism, in essence, tends to deny the significance of nationalism. In international as well as in domestic affairs the relevant actor is class, and nationalism is an ideology that the dominant class uses in order to consolidate its hegemony over the proletariat. The international system is the scene of the dominant elites' rivalries, fueled by uneven economic development. Revolution, when it comes, and whether it begins – in the orthodox version – among the most advanced capitalist countries or – in Lenin's – among more backward ones, will be a world-wide phenomenon. Thus, the nation is either the arbitrary arena in which class conflict is played out, or a basis for the chauvinistic propaganda elites concoct in order to divert the working class from its duty and to delay the revolution. In so far as it was a nefarious nuisance, the range of options for dealing with it went from outright, uncompromising hostility, to the federalist constructions of Otto Bauer. But the fundamental attitude remained one of distaste for an irrational secular faith that took the exploited away from the realities of capitalist exploitation and from the truly significant engines of history: the mode of production and the relations of production. This attitude pervades Eric Hobsbawm's book on nationalism (Hobsbawm 1990).

Liberalism is the philosophy that has most to say on our subject. John Stuart Mill came to national self-determination from his perspective as an advocate of liberal self-government, the former being necessary for the solidity and survival of the latter. Conversely, Mazzini and Michelet, celebrators of a popular nationalism, embraced broadly representative institutions as well. What is clear is that, for post-1776 or 1789 liberals, self-government and self-determination were the two sides of the same coin. One could conceive of a national state in which representative government was pushed aside either in an authoritarian (say, Bismarckian) or in a Jacobin fashion; but this was not a Liberal state. One could also imagine representative institutions for a multinational community. But then, as Mill argued, unless the different national components had consented (in some kind of federal or consociational formula) to these common institutions, one national group was likely, over time, to oppress the others (or else paralysis would prevail).

Liberalism, like Realism, addresses itself to one kind of nationalism only, for two reasons. One is the individualistic basis of Liberalism (economic as well as political). The fundamental actor is the individual, not the group. Among his many rights, the modern individual has a right to a nationality, and to be the (free) citizen of a (free) nation; but the nation is conceived as a community of citizens, bound both to their nation and to its institutions by consent – not by ascriptive features. This, of course, leaves out not only 'ethnic' nationalisms but the 'integral' nationalisms that use Burkean arguments to establish the priority of the nation over the individual. Second, Liberalism offers a vision of a world order based on moderate, democratic, representative nation–states. This was both Kant's ideal of a peace of national 'Republican' regimes, a classic revived by Michael Doyle (1986), and controversially received by skeptics, and Mazzini's vision of harmonious nation–states as a stage toward a finally united mankind. In Kant's and in Bentham's versions, this world order of the satisfied entailed some international regimes, in the form of common norms (Kant) or institutions. In all the versions, the taming of state power by public opinion and by trade across borders would make such a world order possible, by de-fanging, so to speak, the more aggressive potential of nationalism.

As I have suggested elsewhere (Hoffmann 1995a), Liberalism never entirely overcame its original inspiration – which was to emancipate the individual from arbitrary and authoritarian institutions, and to build new ones based on his capacity for reason. The founding fathers of Liberalism – Locke, Montesquieu – wrote before the age of nationalism. In that age, which is still and more than ever ours, Liberalism's problem has been an uneasy relation to reality. It describes only one path to and one form of nationalism (Mazzini lamented that Italy's path turned out not to be the one he had advocated, and Germany switched from the Liberals' fiasco of 1848 to Bismarck's expeditious reliance on force). Liberalism's own conception of the individual and of the nation based on consent was only very selectively applied by liberals: the individual tended to be a white male, and 'inferior' or 'barbaric' peoples were to receive neither self-government nor self-determination soon – Mill and Tocqueville agreed on this. Liberalism *à la* Mill and Woodrow Wilson underestimated the turmoil that so often accompanies self-determination: what is the unit that is 'entitled' to it? What happens to hapless minorities? Unscrambling multi-national omelets – from the Balkans to Québec – has turned out to be a highly frustrating and frequently bloody Sisyphean task. After 1945, granting self-determination to units artificially carved out by the colonizers, in which the intellectuals' nationalism was less a commitment to 'nation-building' than a declaration of war on colonialism, has created big headaches both for the 'liberated' peoples and for world order. Finally, strong national governments have found many ways to keep public opinion national, and to put the free market at the service of national concerns and ambitions.

Thus, of the three main ideologies, one evaded our issue (and this, along with the mismanagement command economies fostered ultimately caused the death of the Communist creed). The other two, whose visions of world order are very different – one centered on states, one on individuals – proved capable of incorporating only a small part of the phenomenon of nationalism: a somewhat castrated nationalism, in the Realist universe, a highly partial sanitized and idealized one in the Liberal world. The challenge nationalism throws to political philosophy has not received an adequate response.

Is nationalism the enemy of world order?

In order to examine this challenge, I will first present the case for the prosecution, and then proceed to a critical examination of it. The case against nationalism has been made often – and rarely better than by Lord Acton. It is the opposite of the Liberal case. It argues that a world in which nationalism is the dominant ideology of states is not 'merely' one of ordinary anarchy, as in the seventeenth or eighteenth centuries. Then, the game of power was a competition of dynastic and mercantilistic interests, a struggle for supremacy among sovereigns. Nationalism, like religion earlier, added a number of poisonous elements to the contest. From the perspective of the unit, nationalism affected both the definition of ends and the available means. It introduced into the preferences of actors such goals as the 'recuperation', through annexation, of nationals living beyond the current borders of the state (Nazi Germany, Milosevic's Serbia) and the propagation abroad of what might be called the 'national formula' – the institutions and values of the actor (the French Revolution and, despite its denegations, the United States after 1945; the Soviet case was one in which the forcible export of a so-called Socialist formula became an instrument of Russian control). The old considerations of honor, glory and reputation were given a new, far more potent and explosive content: tests of will and strength became tests of national merit and virility. Above all, a new set of means was put at the actor's disposal: the mobilization of the population. Social mobilization, which so many theorists of nationalism have presented as a precondition for or a key feature of it (I have some reservations on this point) thus becomes a prelude to national mobilization against a designated enemy. The age of nationalism becomes the age of mass propaganda, universal conscription, general mobilization for the war effort; it turns interstate conflict into the kind of total war that devastated Europe twice in the twentieth century and led to Europe's downfall.

From the perspective of the international system, nationalism crippled one of the main requirements for an effective balance of power: the possibility of flexible alignments. After 1871, there was no chance for Franco-German accommodation, and a factor of permanent hostility was introduced into the rigidifying system. Nationalism also affected the system through contagion. French revolutionary nationalism rudely awakened a dormant German 'national feeling' and gave it a virulent anti-French component; Napoleon kindled nationalism from Spain to Russia. Nationalism provided states with new pretexts for intervening in the affairs of others, in order either to crush or to assist movements of national emancipation; the policies of Russia and of Austria–Hungary in the pre-1914

Balkans, with the help of Serbian nationalism, resulted in World War I. As self-determination gradually became a norm of the system, not only did it qualify the norm of sovereignty as it had been understood before 1789, but it served to undermine sovereignty whenever self-determination affected the integrity of multinational states. It injected a permanent stream of trouble and conflict, either in the form of often bloody secessions (the Ottoman Empire shrank at regular intervals, the Austro-Hungarian one perished in defeat), or in the form of turbulent and bellicose regroupings, successful (Germany, Italy, Poland after 1918) or attempted (Arab post-1945 nationalism, Milosevic's Serbia).

The case for the prosecution thus concludes that a world in which nationalism is both all-pervasive and sanctified is doubly disastrous. First, it is disastrous because of the fundamental contradiction between two constitutive principles or *Grundnormen* of the international system: the principle of inviolable territorial integrity, and that of national self-determination – a conflict that has, in recent years, led to the tragedy of former Yugoslavia. Second, it is calamitous because of the clash, not of civilizations (a very murky concept), but of definitions of what constitutes a nation. Sometimes, this clash remains confined to the domestic arena. Thus, the battle between 'Republican' and integral nationalism in modern France, and the battle between a territorial and secular definition of the Indian nation and a Hindu one, did not spill over into the international scene. But Alsace-Lorraine, Kashmir, Jerusalem, Bosnia, the Falklands, show the international dimension of the ambiguities of national self-determination.

How solid is the prosecutor's case? Its weak point is the underlying assumption of a single and malevolent kind of nationalism. The reality is a blooming confusion and a bewildering complexity. How dangerous nationalism is for world order *may* depend on what brand we are talking about. As always in social science, we need distinctions. Nationalisms can be analysed according to four factors: their origins, their bases, their intellectual formulas, their behavior.

If we examine origins we find that nationalism can be a reaction either to domestic conditions, or to external oppression. The classic cases of the former are Britain and France. Linda Colley has admirably documented the development of a British nationalism of pride, Protestantism and prosperity (Colley 1992). The French case is completely different: French nationalism grew as a reaction against absolutism and a society of orders and particularisms. The central role played by the State in the Old Regime meant that in this battle, the key question was going to be: whose state is it, the King's or the Nation's – and that those who sided with King and Church were expelled from the Nation (cf. Siéyès). Nineteenth-century Russian nationalism also grew in reaction to domestic conditions of political and social oppression, but the nationalists were split between Slavophiles and Westernizers.

Reaction to external oppression, or to conditions experienced as external oppression, is far more frequent. I have already mentioned post-Napoleonic Europe. In the twentieth century, anti-colonial nationalism led to the break-up of colonial Empires, to the victory of Nationalist elites in India, Vietnam, Algeria, Egypt. The collapse of Communism in the Soviet Union led to the emancipation of the Baltic states, of Ukraine and to the astonishing transformation of Soviet officials into nationalist leaders, as in Georgia and in Central Asia. In Yugoslavia, Croat and Slovene nationalisms grew in opposition to what was perceived as Serb exploitation, and Serb nationalism grew in defense of an allegedly global plot against Serbia. Québec's nationalism (like Ireland's) is fueled by perceived 'British' domination.

The first kind of nationalism is less dangerous for world order, although it can be pretty bad at home (British nationalism left little leeway for the Scots and the Welsh, and mistreated Ireland; Jacobin nationalism was both xenophobic and murderous toward *Vendéens* and 'aristocrats'). The second kind spells more trouble for world order – especially when, as in ex-Yugoslavia or in Azerbaidjan and Georgia, minorities are caught in the reshuffling. But such generalizations need to be qualified. On the one hand, in the second group of cases, much depends on how accommodating the 'oppressor' is: see the contrast between Baltic emancipation – relatively peaceful – and Chechnya; or between most of Britain's decolonization, and France's. On the other hand, some of the most interesting cases are those in which nationalism grew out of external as well as domestic conditions. After 1792, French nationalism found a new vigor and turned outward, in reaction to the conservative powers' bumbling aggression. American nationalism, reversing the French pattern, started as a reaction against what was felt as violations by the metropolis, and continued to grow as a celebration of American exceptionalism, a kind of self-congratulation so remarkable that not only was it not acknowledged as a form of nationalism, but it was seen as distinguishing the US from all other nations' nationalism. Contemporary Chinese nationalism developed both in reaction to external humiliations and to domestic degradation. The fact is, that in an international system of competing powers, domestic nationalist revolutions rarely fail to produce external effects, either because states threatened by them intervene (1792, 1918 in Russia, US support of Chiang against Mao, Iraqi attack on Iran . . .) and give thereby a xenophobic twist to the revolution they fight, or because the nationalists, in their drive to modernize their nation, resort to war to test and expand its power (Japan; US expansion to the 'frontier').

If origins tell us little, what about bases, i.e. the fundamental inspiration of the nationalist creed? Are some more dangerous for world order than others? Let us review them. Ethnic nationalism has a particularly bad press, although it is a far from clear and simple notion (ethnic factors 'can be organized and rendered meaningful in various ways, thus become elements of any number of identities') (Greenfeld 1992: 13). But it often deserves its reputation, in part precisely because it is not easy to define an 'ethnie' and conflicts arise out of these discordant definitions (are Croats, Serbs and Bosnians all South Slavs or members of different ethnicities?), in part because the predominance of one ethnic group in a state can create dangers for, and provoke a revolt by other ethnic groups (cf. the Tamils in Sri Lanka, the Hutus in Rwanda, the Ibos in Nigeria), as well as risks of external interventions justified on grounds of ethnic solidarity (Serbia to 'protect' Serbs in Croatia, Armenia in Nagorno – Karabakh). A world in which the borders of ethnic groups would be those of nation–states is both inconceivable, given the confusion about what is an 'ethnie' and the imbrication of ethnic groups, and a recipe for permanent conflict, in so far as the emphasis on this single factor magnifies the differences among peoples and transforms each one into what Erik Erikson called a 'pseudospecies'. When ethnic nationalism turns into a doctrine of racial superiority, the effects abroad can be catastrophic: Hitler's rampages and ravages are unforgettable.

There isn't anything very different to say about religious nationalisms; the combination of religious and secular faiths is highly combustible. The Catholic nationalism in Northern Ireland is fueled by, and in turn reinforces, the Protestant British nationalism of the Unionists. Islamic Fundamentalism, spreading within the borders and in response to the unsolved political and social problems of existing states, is turning into a set of such nationalisms, which find both internal and external enemies easily. The case of Moslem Bosnian nationalism is a curious one: it grew as a reaction to the Serbian view of Bosnians (who were often only nominally Moslem) as a separate ethnic group, among people who, prior to the war of 1992, had seen themselves as part of a multireligious and multicultural Slavic community. The religious component of several apparently secular nationalisms cannot be discounted; we have seen Greek opposition to a Moslem state of Macedonia, and the integral version of French nationalism in its sorry present-day form – Le Pen – shrilly enouncing the 'unassimilability' of Moslems in Christian France. The Hindu version of Indian nationalism is far more exclusive – and specifically anti-Moslem – than the secular, official one.

Cultural nationalism is usually less bellicose, although, as we see in Québec, it can lead to demands not just for special rights aimed at safeguarding a cultural heritage, but for full independence, and to the disregard of the rights of 'lesser' cultural minorities.

What might be called territorial-traditional nationalism is also a milder variety. It is the kind of nationalism whose basis is a common attachment to a given territory and to a history of living together in it; it allows for the coexistence and interpenetration of several cultural groups, ethnies or religions as in Switzerland. This exposes it to severe strains when some of these groups produce their own, separatist nationalism, based on ethnicity, religion or culture, as in the case of the Basques and Catalans in Spain, or the Sikhs in India. But the territorial-traditional foundation tends to allow for institutional compromises.

I have left for the end the case of two universalist nationalisms – nationalisms which claim as their basis a common creed consisting of principles of universal relevance: the United States and France, the two products of early Liberalism, the two melting pots of individual assimilation. Their champions like to present this brand as *ipso facto* good for world order. Reality is a bit less simple. First, the abstract, and (allegedly) universally accessible abstract creed needs to be embodied in specific groups – and repeatedly, the people who act as guardians of the common faith decide that certain alien groups are not fit, for reasons of race, color or religion, to partake of the common creed – the racial divide is still the central one in the US, and Moslem integration in France faces many obstacles. In the French case, the highly assimilationist Jacobin doctrine that fuels the melting pot creates tensions with groups that are reluctant to leave what they deem essential cultural or religious characteristics to the private domain: for instance, Alsatians, Corsicans, Jews of North African origin. While a balance between assimilation and multicultural pluralism has been easier to establish in the US, where the general interest is not seen as superior in essence to particular interests, there are recurrent fears about the divisive effects of multiculturalism, especially when it entails linguistic diversity or different family or work values; the ideology of the common universal creed does not rule out regular witchhunts of 'un-Americans'.

To be sure, what precedes affects internal harmony more than world order. However, second, faith in such a creed brings the temptation of external proselytizing: if our national values are universal why shouldn't the universe benefit from them? The imperialism of free institutions has been a recurrent motif in US foreign policy, just as, after 1792, the French indulged in an imperialism of popular sovereignty, and later – outside of Europe – in an imperialism of the 'civilizing mission'.

I distinguish between the basis of nationalism and its intellectual formula in order to focus on two key institutional issues: the mode of acquisition of nationality, and the philosophy of the governmental system. On the first point: is the nationalism voluntaristic, the acquisition of nationality based on consent, as in Renan's famous formulation (but he also mentioned habituation, traditions, a common experience)? Is nationality imposed on the individual by race, religion, language or culture? Many states try to produce a rather uneasy mix. When the voluntaristic element predominates, nationalism tends to see itself as more peace-loving, more attuned to world order, than when the alternative conception prevails. But as we have just seen, there are many lapses. Either formula can lead to turbulence and conflict, neither guarantees that aliens will be well treated.

Three philosophies of the governmental system can be distinguished. One is Liberal, and usually connected to a voluntaristic conception of nationality. As suggested in the section on political philosophies and nationalism, it is, in principle, less war-prone, at least against other liberal nations. A second philosophy is, like Liberalism, individualistic (government rests on the individuals' consent) and voluntaristic; but it departs from Liberalism in adopting the Rousseauean and Jacobin formula of the general will, which assumes the superiority of that will over particular wills and interests; it is therefore suspicious of multiculturalism and willing to override individual rights if they clash with the common good defined by the general will (France, Québecois nationalism). It is easy to see why this formula could push the balance between passion and reason in the direction of the former, if only by placing common will ahead of deliberation and separation of powers. Finally, there are authoritarian nationalist polities, and they usually are the ascriptive ones; a good liberal has learned to see them, therefore, as doubly dangerous.

What about a fourth factor: the actual behavior of nationalist states? The late French historian Jean-Baptiste Duroselle liked to distinguish inward-looking and outward-looking policies. Many small powers – especially Switzerland – are indeed satisfied with protecting their independence and integrity; but not all: especially not when they also want to protect their kin abroad. And outward-looking policies can be defensive and conservative. What history shows is that the same nation–state can behave in very different ways at different moments.

This long review of nationalist features leads to a conclusion that is different from the prosecutor's but only in degree. Not all nationalisms are evil. On paper, some appear beneficial, in so far as they provide spiritual and material goods for their people. But while some characteristics are more worrisome than others, each feature we examined carries its own load of dangers for world order; and much depends on the circumstances provided by the international system. As we have seen, even peace and world-order-oriented nationalisms can go to war, either defensively or offensively, in certain moments of crisis. And much depends on the degree of homogeneity that exists within the nation's borders: community or cacophony? The one variable we found that appeared less ambiguous than the others: the nature of the political regime, introduces a significant exception into the prosecutor's case – liberal democracies haven't fought each other, are rather reluctant to go to war, and more likely to deal fairly with minorities. But there aren't enough of them, and in the contest with non-liberal enemies, they are perfectly able to overcome their preference for peace, in the name of survival, or of democratic ideology, or of a civilizing mission. Moreover, the process of liberal democratization may be very turbulent at home and abroad. In a word (or so): some nationalisms are evil, and all others can become evil. This, at least, is the lesson of the past. At the end of the 1990s, nationalism, so often pronounced obsolete, is more than ever rampant in the international system, fueling both inter-state and intrastate conflicts. What does this mean for world order?

World order in a world of nationalisms

I will, sketchily, discuss this problem, first in historical perspective, and afterwards with reference to the present international system. Since the American and French Revolutions, nationalism has been both a principle of organization (national self-determination) and a dissolvent of order – even though the continental victors, at the Congress of Vienna, had tried to exorcise both Liberalism and nationalism. World War I resulted both from the national ambitions of some actors, big (Germany) and small (Serbia), and from the fears of dissolution of one multinational Empire (Austria–Hungary). The logic of alliances, enmities, and military time-tables did the rest. The nineteenth-century story could be seen as that of a competition between a 'cosmopolitan liberal nationalism' (the one the Liberal political philosophy proposed, and that countries such as Britain, the US and Republican France tried to approximate), and more particularistic nationalisms, which derailed the former and thwarted the Liberal ideal (quite apart from the fact that it was never extended overseas – or to Ireland).

In the interwar period, cosmopolitan liberal nationalism was on the defensive, besieged by another universalistic cosmopolitan theory (Communism), by the squabbling particularistic nationalisms of many of the new nation–states of the Europe of Versailles and Sèvres, and by the messianic and imperialistic nationalisms of Fascist Italy, Nazi Germany and the military's Japan. In the Cold War era – longer than the interwar period, but shorter than anyone had foreseen – the collapse of the Fascisms resulted in a global collision of two universalisms, a Liberal and a Communist one – behind which two very different nationalisms, an American and a Russian one, pulled the strings, as de Gaulle used to warn. But decolonization sowed the seeds of new, potentially non-liberal, undemocratic nationalisms (Algeria, Vietnam, Pakistan; Cuba could be put into this category). And behind the cosmopolitan façade of Communism, nationalism acted – once more – as a dissolvent, leading to the emancipation of Tito's fragile Yugoslavia (which behaved as a single nation only in its resistance to Moscow), of Red China, and of a Vietnam that didn't want to be anyone's satellite. (Let us not forget Albania.)

At the end of the 1990s, the world system bears some resemblance to the nineteenth-century situation. We have seen a new wave of Liberal democracies, primarily in Europe (but also in Latin America and South Africa). However, it has been accompanied by further nationalist fragmentation: the explosion of the Soviet Union, the divorce between the Czechs and the Slovaks. The liberal democracies are obliged to coexist with a multitude of non-liberal, particularistic nationalisms, from Iraq to Singapore, from Cuba to China. The post-Cold War system's originality lies: (1) in the importance of a global economy that deprives many of the actors of traditional instruments of control (although some like the US remain more 'sovereign' than others), a fact that exacerbates nationalistic reactions of a defensive nature in many countries: we have seen it in France and in Russia, and even in the US (against NAFTA); (2) in a singular configuration of great powers: a unipolar system in some respects, multipolar in others; (3) in the existence of two spheres of conflict, the traditional one of interstate conflicts, such as India–Pakistan, North Korea–South Korea, Iran–Iraq, Israel–the Palestinians (a state in the making), Turkey–Greece, and a huge sphere of intrastate conflicts, some of which result from the clash of competing nationalisms (Yugoslavia, Chechnya, the Kurds vs. the Iraqis and the Turks), while others are the effects of the disintegration of weak, artificial or corrupt states (Zaire, Somalia, Liberia, Rwanda, Cambodia).

This situation creates some formidable problems for world order. In that second sphere of troubles, there is always a risk of aggravation through external intervention. China has muddied the Cambodian waters for a long time, Russia has intervened in Georgia and Tadjikistan, France in African internal conflicts, Turkey in Cyprus. A second issue is the capacity of the *inter*national system to tolerate protracted *intra*-state turbulence, whether it takes the form of bloody wars for either independence or restoration, as in Yugoslavia (or for domination, as in Rwanda), or the form of mistreatment of minorities in new (Croatia, Sudan) or older (Turkey, Iraq) entities. A third issue is the feasibility of the kind of internationalism which represents the maximum achievement of cosmopolitanism so far: a compromise between the cosmopolitan idea that tends towards some form (not necessarily centralized) of world governance, and the existence, and resistance, of multiple actors that cling to their sovereignty either because they are strong (US, China – potentially) or because they feel it slipping. I am referring to the difficulties faced by international and regional organizations in the present system.

As I have suggested elsewhere (Hoffmann 1992), it suffers from a clash, not just between the norms of state sovereignty and national self-determination (already in battling the nineteenth century), but among four universally recognized norms (however different the interpretations of each may be): sovereignty, national self-determination, self-government (democracy), human rights. All four commands are derived from the Liberal scriptures, and it is possible to dream of a world that would respect all four. Alas, as they sing in the *Three Penny Opera*, *nur die Verhältnisse, die sind nicht so*: our circumstances are not the right ones.

Let us move from the purely analytic to the (politically and, I hope, ethically) normative. What is to be done, what is doable in order to contain and to curb the dangers of nationalism? To the problem of external intervention, there are three conceivable approaches. One is simple indifference, due to the absence of collective will and means. Depending on the region, this could lead to an escalation of violence and to a return of forms of colonialism and domination (the scaling down of French military presence in former Black African colonies is welcome news). At the other extreme, one can envisage a collective, and collectively enforced, ban on unilateral interventions – a ban based not on the principle of respect for sovereignty (since these interventions either claim that they are aimed at restoring territorial integrity, or at making self-determination possible), but on the threat to peace and security unilateral interventions constitute. But this remains both unlikely, and also, in some circumstances, inopportune. The third approach is a kind of half-way solution. It would consist either of the collective licensing of a unilateral intervention, putting it under the control and conditions of the Security Council or of a regional organization, or the launching of a collective intervention wherever the conflict threatens peace and security or crushes fundamental human rights, and whenever a unilateral intervention would be likely to make bad matters worse (clearly, a Russian intervention in a conflict that tears apart a former Soviet Republic in the Caucasus or in Central Asia would be less threatening for peace and security than in the Balkans).

This half-way approach brings us directly to the issue of what the international society (a community it isn't) ought to do about internal turmoil, in what I have called the second sphere of conflicts. I have dealt with this issue extensively elsewhere (Hoffmann 1997: 29–51). There is, in this domain, a huge gap between what is likely and what is desirable. What is likely is either collective non-intervention, when the problem appears to be 'safely forgettable (in the Sudan, Sri Lanka, East Timor before 1999, Burma), or, at best, a modicum of humanitarian intervention, as in Rwanda. Non-intervention justifies itself by such varied considerations as a conviction of the futility of coping with civil war (let one side win), the reluctance of major powers to engage forces trained for 'real' wars into peace-making operations, or the difficulty even international policemen have in disarming factions and knocking heads together in faraway countries, etc. This is not very satisfactory, to say the least. My preference goes to a collective reinforcement of two sets of norms. In so far as collective interventions are concerned, I would like to see them undertaken not only when the Security Council determines that international or regional peace and security are threatened but also when fundamental human rights have been violated. And among such violations, I would include not merely genocide but mass killings not covered by the genocide convention (such as those that are aimed at political groups), ethnic cleansing and mass rape. The protection of human rights also requires a return (with improvements) to the safeguarding of minorities, through internationally guaranteed statuses and treaties. It is difficult to see how this admittedly ambitious program of collective interventions could be carried out without an international police force, or at least earmarked national forces at the disposal of the Security Council. In this respect, internationalism is still in infancy.

The first traditional sphere of conflicts – interstate clashes, usually between incompatible nationalists claims – requires a more determined and effective use of equally traditional methods: collective diplomacy to prevent, if possible, and to resolve disputes (in the Palestinian–Israeli case, the monopoly imposed by the US has not brought the benefits Washington expected: the main progress came as a result of Norwegian good offices), as well as collective security against aggression. It remains only too obvious that in the latter case, as well in that of internal conflicts, collective actions are most unlikely to target major powers – a fact that serves, alas, as a legitimizer of the resistance many middle and small powers oppose to collective action.

Finally, concerning the clash of fundamental norms, I have already stated what I deem necessary for the protection of human rights. The respect of both civil and political rights, and of economic and social ones, conceived as rights individuals can legitimately claim, seems to me an obligation that transcends the partly phony debate between so-called Western and so-called Asian conceptions of human rights (there is nothing in Western liberalism that denies the possibility for individuals to form groups that deserve protection, or denigrates the importance of the family; and there is a lot in so-called 'Asian' notions that can be used to muzzle and oppress individuals). Democratic self-government is not a norm that can be enforced from abroad, since democracy is both a set of institutions that need roots in a given society, and a set of practices and *mœurs* that can only be indigenous.[3] But outsiders can certainly encourage or facilitate the establishment of democratic institutions, and we are witnessing the development of new norms, ranging from the requirement of democratic self-government for membership in certain regional organizations (Council of Europe, European Union) to the protection of democracy from coups and the non-recognition of governments established by such coups, in the case of the OAS.

The norm of sovereignty has been turned from an absolute into a conditional norm. It still deserves to cover security from external aggression and interference, and the right of the state to run internal affairs – but only in so far as it respects internationally recognized human rights, and the kind of international obligations that a treaty establishing a global system of criminal justice might, one hopes, establish. This revision of the norm would, if enforced, curb many of the external and internal excesses of nationalism. As for the competing norm of self-determination, this battering ram of nationalism also requires restrictions, dictated both by the pervasive problem of interlocked minorities and by considerations of peace and order. Even if, with Daniel Philpott (1995), one endorses a *prima facie* right to national self-determination, we need new international norms to regulate secessions, so as to make them (1) a last resort; (2) in cases where there are legitimate claims for it (the violation of fundamental rights by the existing state, economic discrimination and exploitation, cultural survival); and (3) resting not on an ascriptive or collective foundation that could lead to continuing or new forms of individual oppression, but on a liberal-individualistic one. Such a revision of the norm of self-determination would, in cases of internal conflicts between competing nationalisms, allow for federal, confederal and minorities-friendly solutions short of full secession.

Nationalism, liberalism, world order

I have few illusions about the likelihood that even the rather non-utopian suggestions presented above will be carried out in the near future. World order remains a fragile construction threatened not only by many forms and implications of nationalism, but also by the temptations to which anarchy always exposes the mightier states, whatever their regime or dominant philosophy, by the divagations and inequities of global capitalism, by the availability of weapons of mass destruction, by the artificiality and weakness of so many non-national states. Above all, the 'national idea' survives, both in old nations and in new ones, as well as in those states that haven't become nations yet, not only because it provides the state with a principle of legitimacy and the people with a source of collective identity and social bonds, but also because no other focus of allegiance transcending the nation–state has yet appeared. States have done their best to prevent this. Some day, nationalist ideologies may fade, because of the glaring deficiencies of the nation–state – but not before a new institutional kit capable of attracting mass loyalty has succeeded in being more than a set of utilitarian and technocratic correctives to these flaws.

If this is so, doesn't the only hope, both for human rights and for world order, remain the liberal vision, especially in its Kantian version, revived by Wilson, empirically corroborated by Doyle? At the core of this ideal, we find the conviction that democratic, representative government tames the bellicose potential of nationalism (through the combination of the citizens' interest in preserving their lives, of rational deliberation and of the separation of powers), and the conviction that liberal self-determination favors harmony rather than conflict – a conviction that inspired Jaurès as well as Mazzini. But much of what I have suggested above tells us that things are not so simple. To recapitulate: even if liberal democracies multiplied, we would be left with a number of major sources of disorder. We would still have all the ambiguities of self-determination and of what constitutes a nation (if the Croats and the Bosnians are entitled to a state of their own, what about the Serbs in Croatia and Bosnia?). We would still find liberal democracies having troubles with minorities that feel oppressed by majority rule – from Canada to India. We would still, in all likelihood, face conflicts between liberal democracy and authoritarian pariahs, conflicts that are often clashes of nationalisms. It would still be possible for a 'peaceful' liberal democracy to undermine another state without war (cf. the US in Chile or Guatemala).

At best, we would achieve two gains: a reduction of violence, and some growth in the *ersatz* of world government that is constituted by two networks, that of public international and regional organizations, that of private transnational associations and regulations. They are not negligible, and they certainly point in a direction spurned by the neo-Realists: progress through the spread of liberal nationalism, the only one compatible, *in principle*, with internationalism. But liberal nationalism can still be an obstacle to the kind of cosmopolitan cooperation world order requires now. It is so because, as Dominique Schnapper argues (and I regretfully agree), institutions of 'a purely civic nature', 'founded on abstract principles' and on an 'intellectual commitment' do not have the 'strength to control passions born from allegiances' to nations (Schnapper 1997: 207–11). In her view, a modern democratic nation, *pace* Habermas, 'cannot be of a purely civic nature', it has to be based on 'the specific values, traditions and institutions that define a political nation'. 'Every organized, democratic society indissolubly carries ethnic elements – cultural, historical, and nationalist – as well as a civic principle'. The 'affective desire of human society' (Elias), the political space for 'choices, arbitrations, obligations, and the desire to exist' (ibid.: 219–20) remain at the national level, despite all the leakages of sovereignty.

The example of the European Union, which she mentions, and which Joseph Weiler discusses in his contribution to this volume, is doubly important in this respect. It shows us how much can be accomplished by liberal democracies, and it shows the limits of cosmopolitanism. On the one hand, the process of European integration since 1950 has almost certainly ruled out war among the Union's members; the recognition of economic interdependence has led not merely to policy coordination but to the creation of a single market of goods, capital and services, to be completed by a single currency and Central Bank. However, we must remember that the enterprise was launched at a time when nationalism had been beaten out of Germany and Italy, and when the two leading 'integrationist' parties of France, the Socialists and the Christian Democrats were more internationalist than nationalist. With the persistence or revival of nationalism in several of the current members of the EU, the quasi-Federal or supranational dream of Jean Monnet seems way beyond achievement.

As integration proceeds, states tend to cling to those leaves of the artichoke of sovereignty that are still in their clutches, and to its heart: diplomacy in the 'strategic-political realm', the domestic configuration of governmental institutions and of politics. Key symbols of national identity, bizarre as they may be, benefit from popular attachment: the Deutsche Mark in Germany, the *force de frappe* in France. It is interesting that resistance to further integration (in the sense of expanded majority rule and a reform of the EU's institutional puzzle) is strongest in a UK whose nationalism is basically liberal-individualistic, attached to the rights of British citizens and to that focus of national loyalty, parliament; and also in France, whose battered nationalism is preserved by the myth of French universalism, and bound up with the concept of an indivisible and untransferable general will. In principle, national identity should be able to exist and persist without nationalism. In reality, when national identity is felt to be threatened – by globalization, by Americanization, by Europeanization – nationalism revives and makes new steps toward internationalism and cosmopolitanism more arduous.

At least, in the European case, we can observe the coexistence of what Weiler calls, imaginatively, the national Eros and the civilization of common European citizenship, largely disembodied though the latter may be. We can hope that over time, at least a modicum of Eros will settle on the common institutions and policies. Europe, so full of doubts about itself – for good reasons – can at least be proud of being ahead of other continents in this regard. Here, partly tamed nationalisms allow for and coexist with an innovative if imperfect new European order. How long will it take for international society to reach this stage – and will it?

Notes

1   See his lectures on Justice at the University of Waterloo.
2   See my analysis of Morgenthau in S. Hoffmann (ed.) (1960).
3   Such roots – fragile and withered – did exist in Germany after 1994, and to a lesser extent in Japan.

11 Why secession is not like divorce

Rainer Bauböck

Introduction

How should boundaries between states be drawn? This may seem a strange question. We live in a world of states with given borders and most governments consider these to be inviolable. Theorists of liberalism and democracy from John Locke to John Rawls have imagined 'states of nature' in which no state exists yet, or 'original positions' in which representatives of citizens reason about principles of justice without knowing their position in society. However, these theorists have not asked how parties in such positions would allocate populations and territories to states. Their concern was with discovering principles for just political rule within given states, not with the act of creating states. There are some good reasons for their reluctance. In the first place, the geographic and ethnographic features of the present state system have emerged from wars and conquests, from coercive population transfers or forced assimilation. This history cannot be undone, even in a thought experiment. Second, even if we could imagine a redesigning of the state system from scratch, we would hardly know how to apply democratic procedures which could guarantee the legitimacy of results. We could call this the 'democratic impossibility theorem' of national self-determination. There are neither objective criteria for political boundaries between populations and territories nor can we rely on democratic plebiscites which always require that the units over which votes will be aggregated are already given.[1] Third, there does not seem to be a pressing need for focusing normative political theory on this question. If existing states could be transformed into perfectly just regimes and if problems of global injustice could be resolved by redistributing resources or by establishing free movement between states, why should then the borders of states be redrawn?

Yet these objections answer to a disingenuous reading of our initial question. We live in a world where conflicts about boundaries between states are endemic. The fact that no plausible theory exists about how to draw state borders from scratch does not imply that there cannot be right or wrong answers to demands for changing a particular border. Once political theory uses the above objections to assert that there is no way of testing the democratic legitimacy of such demands, it is no longer impartial but sides with one of the parties: the incumbents of political power who defend the status quo. There are therefore a number of reasons why this traditional blind spot of liberal theory needs to be filled. The most compelling reason is the fact that disputes over state borders have probably been the most frequent immediate cause of armed conflict in the twentieth century. True, many of these conflicts were triggered by authoritarian regimes and ruthless political leaders who merely used unresolved territorial questions as a pretext for aggression. However, this makes it all the more urgent to come up with democratic formulas how to settle such smoldering conflicts. Second, democracies have not been immune to internal movements challenging their borders, some of which enjoy considerable popular support among dissatisfied minorities. It is enough to list selectively geographical regions like Québec, Northern Ireland, Scotland, the Basque provinces, Corsica, Flanders, South Tyrol, Cyprus, Kashmir or Punjab in order to show the relevance of the challenge for democratic regimes. Third, there is a well-established and powerful ideology which has claimed to provide an answer to this question. This is nationalism. According to Ernest Gellner nationalism is 'a theory of political legitimacy which requires that ethnic boundaries should not cut across political ones' (Gellner 1983: 1).[2] Traditional liberalism has been partly parasitic upon this doctrine and partly opposed to it. But it has not come up with a coherent set of alternative principles how to define the *demos* of a liberal polity and how to settle disputes about its boundaries.

As of today, this critique may already seem somewhat outdated. In the 1990s an impressive new literature on national self-determination and secession has emerged. Some authors attempt to reconcile liberalism with nationalism while others try to show that liberalism provides alternative principles for settling secessionist conflicts. I will argue that these attempts have not been successful so far. We can distinguish three kinds of approaches to our initial question. First, a consequentialist assessment of the effects of secession; second, liberal nationalist attempts to reinterpret the principle of self-determination so that it no longer conflicts with basic liberal premises; and third, rights-based theories focusing on the legitimacy of secessionist claims. What I will try to show is that the divergence of positions within each of these three approaches is greater than the differences between them. Consequentialists may find themselves torn between an act-oriented perspective that tells them to minimize human suffering in each particular conflict and a rule-oriented view that considers the long-term effects of establishing a *right* to secession. Liberal nationalists are more obviously divided into two camps, one of which advocates the formation of homogeneous nation–states while the other one interprets national self-determination as a right to resources for cultural maintenance rather than as an entitlement to form independent states. The strongest contrast is, however, between rights-based approaches which split into choice and grievance theories.[3] Some regard democratic decisions about border changes essentially as a matter of aggregating individual choices, whereas others deny that secession can be justified unless a regime severely violates the individual rights of a group of citizens. If each position in this debate finds its opponents within its own camp, this should tell us something about the limitations of the three approaches.[4]

   The outlines of an alternative argument emerge from examining these oppositions. While a primary right to secession merely based on the desire of a group to govern itself ought to be rejected, one may still accept that threatening with secession may be legitimate if this desire is suppressed by the larger state. This is not a paradoxical position if we can identify solutions which allow for minority self-government without breaking apart the states where they live. A theory of multinational federalism could satisfy this requirement. Two major implications of this view are, first, that secession is not only legitimate when a state discriminates against a regional group of citizens, but also when it violates fair terms of federation and, second, that national minorities ought to respect the unity of federations which grant them fair rights to regional self-government and federal representation.

   The style of my inquiry will be normative and theoretical. I will use specific cases only for illustration and want to refrain from explicit judgements about which side is right or wrong in a political conflict. This reluctance might seem to contradict the practical need for democratic answers to secessionist conflicts which I have just emphasized. Yet my primary purpose in this chapter is the critique of ideas which inform such judgements. I hope it will become clear that this theoretical enterprise does have quite strong implications for the ways how we should assess particular cases. Neither will I address normative dilemmas underlying the most violent national conflicts in the contemporary world. Focusing instead on questions raised by rather benign cases such as Québec may seem like a flight from the harsher realities of nationalist terrorism, civil war or foreign military intervention. However, the target of my critique is deficiencies in currently prevailing liberal and democratic ideas about nations, political communities and cultural diversity. The wealthy and relatively stable liberal democracies of the western world serve as a reference point for this exercise in two different ways: first, by showing that 'national questions' keep haunting even these polities which otherwise can be seen as approaching liberal ideals; second, by demonstrating that the best democratic solutions to these challenges often do not conform to standard liberal or republican premises.

Secession theories: an inconclusive debate?

The consequentialist dilemma: resolving conflicts or preventing their proliferation?

Consequentialism is the idea that all actions and decisions should be morally assessed by their actual or likely consequences. Utilitarianism is a specific variant oriented towards maximizing aggregate utilities or minimizing aggregate harm to individuals affected by an action or decision. There is little doubt that secession may have harmful consequences for many people. An approach which focuses on minimizing harm therefore seems particularly adequate for our discussion.[5]

It is not immediately obvious that this principle would generally tell us to condemn secession. In many real-world cases secession appears as the least costly solution to a protracted conflict. Separation seems defensible as the minor evil if people who are categorized as belonging to different nations generally hate each other, or if their political leaders exploit historical grievances to make them hate each other. Maybe the peaceful break-up of Czechoslovakia prevented an escalation of the conflict? Maybe the early international recognition of Slovenia, Croatia and Bosnia as independent nation–states had not further fuelled the war but had actually helped to forestall a full military mobilization by the Serbian government? Maybe the attempt to impose a federal solution for Bosnia after the war will ultimately fail because further separation is the only way to prevent the conflict from re-escalating? I am not interested in assessing whether any of these arguments are empirically sound. They all involve counterfactual and contestable assumptions about alternative courses of history and thus illustrate the general problem of indeterminacy which haunts purely consequentialist moralities. What is important to understand is that the least-cost argument for secession can only be defended as a strictly contextual one. Once it were generalized it would amount to saying that the nationalist drive towards secession is an unavoidable evil which is somehow inherent in the human condition. While Kant thought that the problem of building a common state should be solvable even for a people of rational devils (Kant 1796/1984: 31), the pessimistic view of nationalism sees societies as populated by irrational devils for whom there is no other solution than to separate them into different states. This ignores the contingency and political agency involved in escalating national conflicts and the many examples of relatively peaceful and stable societies (among them pre-war Bosnia) where people of different ethnicities lived side by side and tended to mix through intermarriage. Moreover, an approach which forecasts the unavoidable break-up of multinational states and merely seeks to limit the social costs of this transformation may have to be rejected on its own consequentialist grounds. When adopted as a general guideline for practical political action it will become a self-fulfilling prophecy. If all external and internal actors behave as if the break-up of a state is inevitable that will surely bring about this very result and will also undermine efforts to contain the proliferation of secessions.

A rule-consequentialist assessment will therefore hardly support the standard nationalist interpretation of self-determination which implies a right of this sort for groups that have a claim to nationhood. While tolerating secession may be the right solution in a particular case this cannot be generalized into a right to secession for all groups in similar cases. Five kinds of negative effects are to be expected from such generalization. First, proclaiming a universal right to national self-determination is fraudulent and raises expectations that cannot be met because of the 'Russian doll phenomenon' (Tamir 1993: 158). No matter how territories are divided into separate states, there will nearly always be smaller groups within each state which can potentially challenge the division in the name of their right to self-determination. Second, a general right to secession may threaten international peace by generating 'domino effects' across international borders or providing a licence for territorial expansion of existing states. When a secessionist group in A is ethnically related to minorities in neighbouring state B, it may jeopardize B's territorial integrity by trying to include parts of B in a newly formed state.[6] When a minority in A is ethnically related to a national majority in B, secession will generally lead to expanding B's territory at the expense of A's. This latter scenario creates an almost irresistible incentive for B to sponsor irredentist movements in A. Secession may spread across international borders by such direct impact but also more indirectly and more widely by imitation of successful examples elsewhere. Third, secession may proliferate internally in large and heterogeneous states by a process of 'cumulative causation' (Myrdal 1957). The break-up of multinational states from the Habsburg monarchy to the Soviet Union and Yugoslavia clearly involved processes by which the most determined secessionist group created conditions under which the option of maintaining unity became less feasible for other groups. In democratic contexts, plebiscitarian procedures for deciding secessionist conflicts may fuel a similar process of dissolution even if a large majority initially does not support it. Imagine a multinational state consisting of three groups, none of which has an absolute majority. Political activists manage to convince a majority within the smallest group to vote for secession. As a result the remainder state would be left with one group forming an absolute majority while regionally concentrated dissenters among the secessionist group would be reduced to a very small minority. This outcome may well convince such dissenters to change their minds and join the new state although they had voted against it and it may decisively bolster a secessionist current among the hitherto loyal second largest minority. Fourth, successfully completed secessions more often than not exacerbate the problem of dissatisfied minorities which they were presumably meant to solve. Newly formed and still weak states have a vital interest in preventing further secessions and regularly resort to political suppression or coercive assimilation of established minorities or of those newly created by the separation. It is true that such policies may contain the proliferation dynamic. However, supporting self-determination with this scenario of stabilization in mind boils down to saying that might makes right. It is plainly inconsistent with the notion of a universal *right* to self-determination to maintain that it can only be enjoyed by those strong enough to grasp political power and to hold on to it. Moreover, the authoritarian temptations for governments in new states formed by secession are themselves a consequence which must weigh heavily against an unfettered right to self-determination. Fifth, such a right will create similar perverse incentives for existing states which want to preserve their unity against potential secessionist challenges by preventing minorities from becoming able to exercise their right. States that would have little to fear from granting special recognition to ethnic and national minorities will then engage in policies of coercive assimilation, geographic dispersal or discriminatory immigration and will resist demands for federal autonomy which otherwise could have largely satisfied the desire for self-government (Buchanan 1997a: 43, 52–5).

Any reasonable consequentialist outlook must try to avoid these effects. It therefore seems imperative that secessionist solutions to national conflicts should be assessed like peace treaties after a war. They must reflect concerns of fairness in order to create a stable new order but they also have to be tailored to a specific conflict in order to end it. And they should neither encourage other minorities to embark on an aggressive secessionist course in the hope of achieving a similar settlement nor scare other governments into suppressing their minorities in order to avoid such an outcome.

The liberal nationalist dilemma: self-determination through independence or autonomy?

The principle of national self-determination is at the core of any attempt to reconcile liberalism and nationalism. This principle raises two questions: who is to enjoy this right and what exactly does it imply? The first question has been answered by various definitions of nationhood. The most famous, although much exaggerated distinction, is between ethnic or civic nations. The former are defined by some presumably objective criterion such as a common descent, language, cultural tradition, or historic territory while the latter are bound together by a common will to form an independent political community and by the historic memory of events like revolutions where this will became manifest. For our question it is quite irrelevant which of these definitions is the prevailing or the correct one. Neither one is compatible with a universal right to self-determination for nations which implies independent statehood. If we define nations 'objectively' by some marker such as language there are many more potential nations which could claim this right than there are potentially independent states (Gellner 1983: 2). And if we define them subjectively by the desire of ruling themselves collectively, we face the additional problem of feedback loops created by self-determination rights. The number of subjective nations may remain quite small as long as every group knows that it is very hard to win independence for a new state but it is potentially without limits if a general right to self-determination were to override the principle of territorial integrity of existing states. A revision of state boundaries that would fully satisfy this interpretation of national self-determination would be self-defeating because it would create states that are so small, so geographically intertwined and so exposed to continuous revisions of their borders that they could no longer be called states.[7]

Nationalist interpretations of self-determination which assume that nations are stable cultural groups sharing certain objective features such as a common territory or a strong subjective sense of belonging and desire for self-government may be able to overcome the problems of discontiguity or instability of territorial borders, but they still create a problem of shrinking size and increasing numbers of states. Some liberal nationalists reply to this objection that there is 'no reason why a city or tiny region cannot be self-determining' (Philpott 1995: 366) and that small states like Andorra, Liechtenstein, or Singapore are doing quite well (Moore 1997: 909). What they forget to mention is that some of these mini-states (like Andorra) even lack formal self-government and that they mostly profit in one way or another from the existence of larger neighbouring states. We cannot infer from the success of a few mini-states in economic and political niches of the present state system that such polities would generally do just as well in a world consisting mainly of states like themselves.

Defenders of a universal principle of self-determination therefore have often limited it to nations which could form sizeable and viable states. Early liberal nationalists like Johann Gottfried Herder or Giuseppe Mazzini could still assume that the many different ethnic and linguistic groups in Europe naturally belonged to a small number of potentially independent nations. After World War I Woodrow Wilson and other advocates of national self-determination already witnessed a rapidly increasing number of would-be nations. The claims to nationhood of smaller and territorially dispersed groups were thus ruled out in the name of preserving a stable international system of states with reasonably secure borders. Instead of breaking down existing states into new units according to the national aspirations of their resident populations, this half-hearted application of the nationalist imperative created new majority nationalisms fighting for 'nationalizing' their state and transborder nationalisms linking minorities to an external homeland (Rogers Brubaker 1996:55–76). In a number of cases the disastrous outcome was a territorial unmixing of peoples so that they would fit into the new nation–states (ibid.: 148–78). The situation of those who found themselves on the wrong side of a border was often bad.

Much worse was that of groups like the Armenians, Roma and Sinti or Jews who had no state to protect them when they were persecuted or to admit them when they were expelled. The end of World War II brought about a new wave of state formation which departed from the principle of national self-determination in a quite different way. National self-determination became limited to single acts of decolonization and produced states whose borders did not coincide with ethnic or linguistic boundaries but simply followed those drawn up by colonial administrations. Concerns about viable size of populations, economic resources and military strength became less relevant, but so did concerns about the cultural homogeneity of new states, too. The very idea of the nation as a single cultural and political unit was grossly inadequate to the patterns of ethnic and cultural diversity in many of the former colonies. However, it became a powerful tool in the hands of postcolonial rulers who used it to legitimate internal oppression or aggression against neighbouring states. The latest wave of state formation which resulted from the breakdown of the multinational Soviet and Yugoslav states illustrates once more the difficulty of containing the chain reactions triggered by claims for national self-determination and the arbitrariness of the criteria which defined the stopping points. A nationalist understanding of self-determination can hardly justify why only the fifteen former Soviet Union republics could claim independence, but not the republics within the Russian Federation, such as Chechnya (Chwaszcza 1998: 474). What these historical records suggest is that neither the radical nor the constrained version of national self-determination are defensible as general principles for deciding conflicts about the boundaries of political communities.

Faced with such objections, contemporary liberal nationalists adopt two different strategies: One retains the interpretation of self-determination as a right to statehood but claims that liberal democracy can rightly and successfully contain the proliferation of such claims; the other one is to understand self-determination as a more modest demand for collective autonomy within given states. The latter argument has been most clearly stated by Yael Tamir (1993), the former has been recently defended by David Miller.[8]

For Miller, national self-determination is not only compatible with, but even required for stable democratic rule. He affirms the need for congruence between nationality and statehood because only the former can unearth resources of solidarity among a democratic citizenry. This part of Miller's theory restates John Stuart Mill's classic argument. Mill regarded nationality as a common sympathy, derived from sharing a common name and history, which feeds a desire for self-government. Without such sympathy government will be experienced as coercive. This is why '[f]ree institutions are next to impossible in a country made up of different nationalities' (Mill 1972: 392). Mill's policy recommendations were straightforward: For their own benefit smaller nationalities should be assimilated while states composed of several nationalities of roughly equal size should split up. He conceded that common subjection under a despotic government may produce a harmony of feelings between different nation-alities. However, 'if the era of aspiration to free government arrives before this fusion has been effected' and 'if the unreconciled nationalities are geographically separate . . . there is not only an obvious propriety, but, if either freedom or concord is cared for, a necessity for breaking the connec-tion altogether' (ibid.: 398).

David Miller defends a principle of nationality along similar lines which focuses 'on the political conditions for securing national identities. The principle tells us to further the cause of national self-determination wher-ever possible' (Miller 1995: 112). 'The drawing of political boundaries should therefore not be seen as a matter of sheer contingency' (ibid.: 188). Miller points out that this approach limits the cases of legitimate seces-sion: '[E]xisting boundaries are put into question only where a *nationality* is currently denied self-determination' (ibid.: 112, original emphasis).[9] Secession is therefore legitimate only in multinational states, and provided that the seceding territory would not form a new multinational state. Miller adds some additional criteria, widely shared among liberals, such as the impact of secession on minorities or the viability of post-secession states, and he advocates only partial self-determination if nationalities are very small, of ambivalent identity or territorially intermingled (ibid.: 113–18). The striking contrast with choice and grievance theories to be discussed below is that the nationality principle would, under the specified condi-tions, not merely *allow* for secession but actually *recommend* or *require* a break-up of multinational states in order to improve the cultural precon-ditions for social solidarity and political freedom.

This seems indefensible to me. Arguments for secession from conse-quences, from choice or from past and present injustices are attractive because they appeal to *intrinsic* values of liberal democracy such as ending oppression, avoiding violent conflict, and providing opportunities for demo-cratic choices. Only illiberal nationalists could claim that the goal of increasing the national homogeneity of states is a good in itself which requires no further justification.[10] Mill and Miller defend such homogeneity as an *instrumental* value, as a condition which is likely to improve the quality of liberal democracy.[11] However, even this argument runs into serious difficulties. First, an instrumental goal should not be allowed to override the more fundamental and intrinsic values. Miller's formula contains no such safeguard. Suppose the German-speaking Alsatians who wanted to stay with France in 1870 had hoped that Paris would grant them the status of a national minority. Would their opting for a multinational France have undermined their case and strengthened the German claims?[12] Second, Miller concedes that in many cases – given his list of criteria probably even in most cases – multinational federal states may be the only possible solution to the problem of how to form stable democracies in a region inhabited by different nationalities. On the one hand, if such states can be viable and decent democracies then national homogeneity surely is not a *necessary* condition for liberal democracy. On the other hand, given the record of authoritarian regimes in fairly homogeneous nation–states, it is obviously not a *sufficient* condition. National homogeneity can therefore be nothing more than a generally favourable background or a first-best solution to the problem. This makes it quite unclear in which sense the principle should serve as a practical guideline. Background conditions cannot always be brought about by political action and attempts to do so are often self-defeating in terms of the goals which they pretend to serve. Even if we conceded that an *existing* sense of common national belonging may strengthen democratic stability and solidaristic attitudes at the level of polities, efforts to *increase* homogeneity by way of assimilation or secession are likely to have the opposite effects. Examining the historical records of how relative homogeneity has been achieved in a small number of Western states we surely do not find many policies which could be recommended for contemporary liberal democracies.

Not all liberal nationalists agree with Mill and Miller. Daniel Philpott asserts that 'any group with a particular identity that desires a separate government is entitled to a *prima facie* right to self-determination' (Philpott 1995: 361) but defends such a long list of very plausible constraints that 'secession . . . truly becomes a last resort; it should be endorsed only when a people would remain exposed to great cruelty if left with a weaker form of self-determination' (ibid.: 382). This comes fairly close to grievance theories of secession to be discussed below. The implication that Philpott fails to draw is that secession can then no longer be regarded as a *prima facie* right whereas the 'weaker forms of self-determination' may well be.[13] On this interpretation, a national minority may have a primary right to self-government rather than to self-determination if the latter implies ultimately a right to opt for independent statehood.

Margalit and Raz (1990) have introduced this important distinction between a right to self-government and a right to self-determination which entitles the group itself to decide where to draw its own political boundaries and whether to become independent.[14] In my interpretation, self-government involves a decisive influence of the group in shaping institutions of government and public policies and in electing their political representatives. In representative democracy self-government presupposes that the group forms a majority in the territory where it is self-governing. Multinational federations may offer a framework to realize this right for all groups which consistently desire it and meet some reasonable qualifications. The right to self-determination, however, cannot possibly be realized for all such groups simultaneously. Margalit and Raz build their theory on an account of the value of 'encompassing groups' which seems to support this idea. While membership in such groups has a strong public dimension, 'its political expression does not require a political organization whose boundaries coincide with those of the group. One may be politically active in a multinational, multicultural polity' (Margalit and Raz 1990: 137). None the less, they believe that

> the importance of the prosperity and self-respect of such groups to the well-being of their members . . . makes it reasonable to let the encompassing group that forms a substantial majority in a territory have the right to determine whether that territory shall form an independent state in order to protect the culture and self-respect of the group.
>
> (ibid.: 141)

I don't think that this conclusion follows from their own account. Given the impossibility to realize this right for all such groups, it would amount to promoting the full value of group membership for some individuals at the expense of denying it to many others.

Among liberal nationalists, Yael Tamir is most consistently opposed to the principle of self-determination as defended by Mill and Miller. She does not entirely abandon the ideal of national homogeneity but regards it as unattainable. '[A]lthough it cannot be ensured that each nation will have its own state, all nations are entitled to a public sphere in which they constitute the majority' (Tamir 1993: 150). The federal approach which I am going to defend has some obvious affinities with this position. Yet there are also some differences. A first objection is merely terminological. In so far as this approach severs the territorial and political linkage between state and nation and is only concerned with the political conditions for the flourishing of cultural groups, I think that it cannot be properly called nationalist. A second one is that it blurs the important distinctions between national and ethnic groups and between territorial and cultural autonomy. Ethnic groups that seek recognition for their particular culture generally do not strive for political self-government. Interpreting their demands in this way can in fact hurt them by providing a pretext for segregation. And while aspirations to national self-government may indeed be satisfied by subdividing the territory of multinational states into autonomous provinces, it is not at all clear that the public sphere of a liberal society can, or should, be subdivided in a similar way. Finally, the image of encompassing cultural groups is misleading for most national as well as ethnic minorities. It underestimates the fragmentation of cultural identities in modern societies and it misidentifies the dominant motives for demanding minority rights. For national minorities political self-government is generally not a means to cultural preservation but the other way round: markers of cultural difference serve as means to stake political claims.[15]

The dilemma of rights-based theories: whose burden of proof?

One need not be a nationalist to be in favour of a general right to secession. The case against entrenching existing borders may also be argued on perfectly liberal grounds. In this section I will consider theories which emphasize individual rights as the basis for political legitimacy. Liberals broadly agree that governments owe equal respect and concern to all their citizens (Dworkin 1976) and that citizens have a basic right to leave their country and expatriate themselves. The disputed question is whether consensual government also depends on a right of citizens to jointly leave a state by seceding from its territory.

On both sides of this debate liberals also share a sceptical attitude towards the principle of national self-determination. What makes them sceptical is the adjective rather than the noun. Many opponents of nationalism try to deconstruct the nation as a meaningful concept. While this is an important step in the argument, it is not sufficient to resolve the dispute. In the first place, deconstruction involves contesting the claims of nationalists that nations are either natural categories of human life or can pride themselves of ancient histories reaching back to early stages of great civilizations. In the modern sense of the word, which links nationhood to claims of political sovereignty, nations have not existed for many more than two hundred years and there is no reason to assume that they will last forever. It is not too difficult to imagine changes in the social, economic and political structure of societies which could lead to a future world without nations. Compared to nations, states are much older and somehow more 'real' as identifiable ensembles of institutions within society and as the basic units of the global political system. Most utopias envisioning a world without states or with a single world-state are rather discredited today. States may lose much of their present sovereignty, but the coexistence of a plurality of identifiable states appears to be an enduring feature of any attractive vision of a future global political system. Second, deconstruction dismisses pretensions that nations are somehow objectively given as the most important and most extensive collectivities of modern societies. For Benedict Anderson nationalism is a particular mode of imagining political communities (1983: 15). For Ernest Gellner '[i]t is nationalism which engenders nations, and not the other way round.' (1983: 55). And Rogers Brubaker urges us 'to treat nation not as a substance but as institutionalized form; not as collectivity but as practical category; not as an entity but as contingent event' (1996: 16).

However, deconstructing the nation in these ways may still be largely irrelevant for normative political theory if we cannot promote alternative ways of imagining political communities in the present world. Some theorists think that the very notion of political community should be abandoned. For them, democracy does not involve or even represent citizens in legislation, but merely gives them the chance to change their rulers peacefully in competitive elections (Schumpeter 1950). It operates basically like a market in which voters maximize their preferences with regard to election results while politicians maximize their chances of winning seats (Downs 1957). These political theories dismiss not only nations, but the very idea of political community as a mere chimera. Normative theories, however, which affirm that democracy is the basic principle of legitimation for political rule, cannot do without a vision of community. What they oppose to nationalism is the idea that democracies are communities of citizenship rather than of nationhood.

Nationalism presupposes that the nation is a cultural and historic community either given prior to the state or shaped by the state. In both cases the borders of nations may be incongruous with existing state borders and the latter should then be readjusted to fit the former. Once we abandon that solution in favour of a democratic conceptions of a community of citizens the borders of states become basically indeterminate. No one has ever seriously proposed that all state borders should generally emerge from democratic decisions. The basic units of population and territory must be taken as already given for any democratic procedure of decision-making which involves aggregating the votes of citizens. This is normally the case in actual conflicts. Borders are not invented from scratch, but the decision is about whether a certain stretch of land should belong to one of two neighbouring states or should itself form a state. Citizens may then decide by plebiscite to which state they want their region to belong.[16] However, even in this situation the prior choice of the territorial units where the votes are cast still largely pre-empts the outcome (Barry 1991: 162; Linz 1993: 366).

Is there a generalizable procedure for resolving this problem which could produce democratic legitimacy for the results of such plebiscites? Harry Beran has suggested such a set of rules. He would allow any secessionist group to determine itself the territory within which it wants the votes to be counted, and to secede if it wins a simple majority, on condition that any other group within the seceding territory may do likewise (Beran 1984: 29–30).[17] Yet this can hardly count as a neutral democratic procedure in which the preferences of all affected individuals have an equal chance to determine the outcome. The suggested rules are clearly not neutral with regard to the alternatives of separation and maintaining unity. The decision is taken solely by the population of a territory which is claimed by the secessionists. People living in the remainder state are not involved. Moreover, if the secessionist party has the right to define the territory where votes will be counted in a first move it will rationally choose the largest area within which it expects to gain a comfortable majority. Even if secessionists miscalculate their support and lose the plebiscite, this does not finally legitimate the unity of the state. Nothing in the logic of Beran's argument would prevent them from trying again

at a later point of time and within a smaller area. Finally, 'the plebiscitarian principle applied to self-determination introduces a zero-sum choice
which does not correspond to the complex social and cultural reality of
many societies' (Linz 1993: 366). The decision to hold a plebiscite polar-
izes the issue and excludes any third alternative between separation and
status quo. Individuals who want to assert dual identities as members of
a national minority and as citizens of a federal state will find their preferences unrepresented in a yes/no vote on separation.

If we want to devise a procedure for deciding border disputes the
outcome of which ought to be equally acceptable to unionists and separatists alike, we have to consider three alternative requirements: a majority
only in the region which wants to separate,[18] an overall majority in the
country as a whole[19] or separate majorities in both parts of the country.
Just as the first rule is biased in favour of breaking the state apart, so the
third rule is biased in favour of the status quo. Neither is the second rule
neutral, because the result would strongly depend on the size of the
separatist group. A small minority would stand poor chances of winning
a national majority. There seems to be no obvious way of subjecting
a change of borders to a democratic test that counts the votes of all
citizens affected, and yields a result which ought to be accepted as binding
by all. The reason for this indeterminacy is that democratic communities
cannot consistently apply the same criteria which establish democratic
legitimacy in elections or referenda to determine their own external boundaries.

This conclusion need not be deplored, rather it could well be seen as
the proper answer to the secessionist potential of nationalism. If all state
borders are arbitrary from a purely democratic point of view, then there
is *prima facie* no good reason to change the existing ones. What is needed
in order to satisfy democratic legitimacy is that all individuals subjected
to the laws of a state should be equal citizens of this state, i.e. enjoy all
the basic rights attached to this status and be equally represented as
members of the political community in its collectively binding decisions.
The legitimacy of borders would then entirely depend on the internal
democratic legitimacy of a regime.[20]

We may call this the liberal republican answer to nationalism. It does
not imply that secession cannot be justified, but it implies that it would
be strongly constrained. In order to understand how this argument works
we need to distinguish between three levels which may be called the ideal,
the semi-ideal and the non-ideal.[21] For ideal theory we imagine a Rawlsian
original position in which existing state borders are not taken into account
and all actors are motivated by concerns of justice. Semi-ideal theory
would assume the same motivation but recognize knowledge about existing
borders and how they have come about. Non-ideal theory addresses the
problem in a realistic context where some, or even most, actors are known
to pursue their interests without concern for demands of justice. At the

level of ideal theory the answer is simply that no democratic solution exists to the problem of drawing borders between states in a hypothetical initial position. At the semi-ideal level people are well aware of the fact that borders have actually been shaped by wars of aggression, annexation, imperial conquest and colonization. *Ex hypothesi*, they and their political representatives will refrain from any further injustice of this sort. They be aware of the fact that there is generally no way of correcting borders that does not generate new injustices. The victims of injustice in the recent past will have claims for compensation but these need not lead to changing state borders or reestablishing formerly independent states. If full justice can be done within the framework of borders as they have emerged from unjust histories, and if any further change is likely to create new injustice, then there is no reason to redraw the political map. Much of the liberal critique of secession seems to be inspired by such considerations. Hope is that in 'nearly just societies' (Rawls 1971) given borders will come to be accepted by citizens because, and in so far as, the state treats them with equal respect and concern. Political integration through democratic citizenship should therefore prevent most border disputes from arising.

Only at a level of non-ideal theory, where we assume that some or most governments continue to act unjustly, can the case for secession be argued for specific circumstances. If a state effectively denies equal citizenship to a minority marked by its religion, language, ethnic origin or phenotype, this group could legitimately break away from its oppressor state and form its own political community or join another state. In a non-ideal world such a group could not be fully reassured that a regime which offers compensation and equal citizenship will not be replaced by a repressive one in the future. However, the changing of borders is still a problematic remedy which should only be resorted to if no more prospects of maintaining a unified democratic polity exist and if secession is not deemed to worsen the situation for other groups in either the new or the parent state. The principle of territorial integrity is thus not only asserted externally for interstate relations but also internally as a constraint on any attempt to secede unless this is seen as the only plausible cure for pervasive injustice towards a group of citizens.[22] Such reasons can be easily accepted in a context of colonialism or of recent annexation. However, in the liberal republican perspective which I have outlined here a principle of restitution might be difficult to defend even in such obvious cases as independence for Algeria or for the Baltic states. In the first place, we would never know where to stop when going back in history to assess historical claims and, secondly, any idea of restitution would have to resort to some prior concept of the nation as a collectivity which had been injured. The alternative justification for secession in such cases is future-oriented: colonization and recent annexations create enduring structures of dependency and general distrust among the formerly subjected populations which fatally undermine the project of integrating the polity through the unifying bond of citizenship.[23]

This argument is still insufficient to defeat choice theories of secession. These can draw the exactly opposite inference from the premise that existing state borders are arbitrary from the moral point of view. If they are, then what wrong is involved in letting groups secede if they so wish, as long as they do not thereby harm those who wish to remain with the existing state? Hillel Steiner claims that 'because the nation's territory is legitimately composed of the real estate of its members, the decision of any of them to resign that membership and, as it were, to take their real estate with them, is a decision which must be respected' (Steiner 1995:17). For Harry Beran democratic legitimacy is based on individual consent which can only be tested by allowing for both individual exit by emigration and collective exit by secession, provided that the latter does not undermine the geographical contiguity and viability of the remaining state and provided that the separating group does not deny a similar right to further secessions from their newly formed state (1984, 1988).[24] In this perspective the pro-secession bias in the procedure suggested by Beran is entirely justified. An equal right for all to choose the boundaries of their state pre-empts any rival claims of states and their populations to the integrity of their territory.

David Gauthier builds a similar defence of secession on the right of each person 'to enter into and continue political association with those with whom she wishes to associate and who wish to associate with her, and to avoid or exit from association with those with whom she wishes not to associate' (1995: 360).[25] However, secession implies the establishment of political authority with exclusive legislation and jurisdiction in a territory. On this condition, free emigration seems to be the only way by means of which every individual may enjoy such a right of political association.[26] It is not so much the requirement of a minimum size but of geographical contiguity which prevents some people from choosing to associate with others to form a territorially sovereign political association. If it is unavoidable that dissenting minorities should be included in the territory of a state which is not their preferred political association then one might at least minimize their numbers. Although the principle then no longer grounds a universal right, it informs us how to choose among feasible sets of borders those which maximize the number of individuals who find themselves in a state which is their preferred one.[27]

Three major problems result from any consistent application of a principle of individual choice to the formation of states. These are the problems of size, contiguity and stability which I have already briefly mentioned above. Liberal nationalists who characterize nations as ascriptive groups sharing a common culture, history, language and relation to a territory may be able to avoid the third and sometimes also the second problem. Choice theorists, however, can circumvent the second problem only by introducing more or less *ad hoc* constraints on secession and they seem genuinely unable to cope with the third one. Geographic discontiguity is a serious problem. There are a few cases where part of the territory of one state lies entirely in another state,[28] but these are only tiny fragments of land and in the present world they clearly represent a more exceptional irregularity than the considerable number of mini-states. If applied consistently, however, aggregated individual choices could create states consisting of a patchwork of various bits and pieces of land in different parts of the world. In areas where they constitute a majority of the population emigrant diasporas could, for example, choose to 'reunite' with their home country by forming an enclave ruled by that country. Allowing for discontiguity would be no big problem if the state were merely an association of individuals. Yet states are also territorial monopolies of legitimate violence and organizations for the provision of public goods from whose consumption no resident in the territory can be excluded. Some theorists think that we are entering an era of deterritorialized *nations* (Basch *et al.* 1994; Appadurai 1996a). But nobody has so far been able to imagine a deterritorialized *state*. Choice theorists are generally aware of this implication of their approach and introduce a requirement of contiguity (Beran 1984: 30, Gauthier 1995: 369; Wellman 1995: 162) which is, however, hard to reconcile with their basic principles. This requirement takes for granted present features of states that are otherwise ignored in their normative principles.

The problem which they have rarely addressed and which must be the most intractable one from their perspective is the requirement for the temporal stability of borders. The preferences of individuals for a state of their choice may change over time and, as shown above, easy secessions will themselves be major causes for reactive shifts of preferences. Choice theorists seem to believe that plebiscites on border revisions ought to be held at the request of any sufficiently large and territorially concentrated group. As we have seen above, Beran's procedure virtually guarantees that any such group will succeed in the end. This would clearly discourage governments to make any long-term investment into developing the material infrastructure, the education and general welfare of the entire population or to enter long-term agreements with other states. With each new secession such common assets would have to be divided and international commitments would have to be renegotiated between newly formed independent states. Allen Buchanan adds a further important reason why easy secession is incompatible with democratic stability:

> A territorially concentrated dissident minority can sometimes use the threat of secession as a bargaining tool to thwart majority rule. Where the majority regards secession by a minority as unacceptable, the threat of secession can function as a minority veto on majority decisions.
>
> (1997b: 302; see also 1991: 98–100)[29]

The stability problem illustrates fundamental differences between individual choices of consumers in markets, collective choices of citizens in democratic elections and the proposed choice of boundaries. In an ideal market, every consumer can 'vote' at any time for any commodity. And the efficiency of competitive markets requires the consumers' ability to change their preferences in reaction to poor quality of commodities or services. In representative democracies citizens cannot cast their votes at any time they choose. But changing individual preferences are still essential for democratic rule. Periodic elections which test such changes help to make rulers accountable and political decisions responsive towards the interests of citizens whom they bind. In contrast, frequent shifts of the citizens' preferences with regard to the borders of the states where they live will undermine the stability of democratic government to the point of breakdown. It is therefore not at all evident that any sufficiently large group that articulates a preference for secession enjoys the right to initiate a plebiscite on border revisions. True, the universal franchise does not justify the act of subjecting minorities to the preferences of a majority.[30] In order to test the consensual character of subjection to collectively binding decisions individuals must indeed be given a right of exit. The freedom to emigrate and to renounce one's citizenship thereafter provides such a test. The individual exercise of this right is only marginally harmful to the political association of those who want to remain,[31] whereas a jointly exercised right to secession disrupts that ongoing association. A right to secession based on individual choice would therefore destroy the very good which individuals are supposed to have a right to choose.

On the one hand, it is difficult to see how democratic governments operating under a constant threat of border changes[32] could possibly perform even those tasks that libertarian theorists generally concede to them, such as the maintenance of internal and external security. On the other hand, it is clear why libertarians who defend a minimal state tend to be more permissive of secession. The more limited the range of public goods provided by a state and the lower the citizens' stakes in their political community, the less harm will be done by a break-up of that state and the easier it will be to divide the common assets. The political passions that secessionist claims raise show that we do not live in a world of minimal states where secession might become a minimal concern. An alternative theory of the political community which better reflects currently prevailing norms sees it as an ongoing cooperative scheme for the production of a large range of public goods. In this view no subpopulation of citizens living in any particular stretch of land within a state enjoys full collective ownership rights over the land they inhabit. The state may rightfully constrain the private use of real estate by defining the state territory as a common asset.[33] Similar arguments apply to most other collective goods which cannot be easily divided in case of secession. What individuals are entitled to in this conception is not just to choose the political association they prefer, but to live in a state that offers a stable guarantee for their rights, is responsive to their interests, and promotes their common good. The alternative choices offered by the options of democratic voice and of individual exit are conducive to bringing states closer to this ideal, whereas easy secession would undermine such efforts.

While the pure choice theory of secession ought to be rejected for these reasons there are several specific applications of choice arguments to particular cases which appear more plausible than the general theory. I will briefly consider three closely related particular defences of a choice perspective: the burden-of-proof argument, the no-fault-divorce analogy and the practical futility of moral judgements on secession.

In real cases such as that of Québec one may adopt two different perspectives. One could deny that the secessionists have a good case by pointing out that Canada is a fairly liberal democracy, that there are many collective assets which cannot be neatly divided between the province and the rest of Canada, and that an independent Québec would immediately trigger claims to further secession and to protection under the federal constitution by the aboriginal first nations in the province. However, we might also ask the converse question whether the rest of Canada has a good case in prohibiting or resisting a secession of Québec. As Will Kymlicka points out, we cannot simply assume 'that the burden of proof lies on those who want to secede rather than on those who want to prevent a group from seceding' (1992: 532).[34] In Canada it seems that even the anti-secessionist forces have implicitly accepted Kymlicka's shift of the burden of proof. From a perspective which condemns any secession that is not caused by serious injustice,[35] it is quite amazing that none of the major political actors at the level of the other provinces or the federal government seems to seriously question that a simple majority in another referendum in the province alone would create a situation in which Canada should no longer resist secession.

Given the objections against a general choice-based presumption in favour of secession rights I would plead for a dualistic and contextualized perspective. Insisting on justification does not put the burden of proof on one side only. Suppose that a secessionist party has no sufficient grievance that would justify dissolving the existing political community and that actual secession would not cause serious new injustice.[36] In this situation our judgement will still be that secessionists are wrong. But that does not imply that unionists would be right in using force to prevent the break-up of the state. If neither the attempt to secede nor forceful resistance against it is warranted by claims of justice, then the case against secession will have to be fought at the level of political argument and this entails that a political decision derived from fair democratic procedures should be accepted by both sides, no matter what the outcome. This is as much as can be said at the level of principle. The question which can only be answered in a specific context is what should count as a fair procedure.

As I have argued above, from a non-nationalist perspective there is no general answer to the questions where to draw the boundaries between the units over which votes will be aggregated and whether a simple majority in the province whose secession is proposed should count as sufficient. However, in a real-world case like Québec, where secession comes as a final challenge after a prolonged struggle for increasing autonomy or for a new division of powers within a federation, many of these questions have normally already been settled beforehand.[37] We cannot conclude from this that the same procedures should be adopted in other instances, nor can we derive a general moral argument for majoritarian choice as a sufficient justification for secession from such a specific case.

Why should we look for justification of secession rather than merely for its permissibility? Choice theories argue that the former amounts to coercively imposing union on parties one of whom is seeking separation. They like to draw the analogy with divorce where liberal laws have shifted from a presumption for maintaining a marriage unless there is a justification for dissolving it towards granting both parties freedom to end the marriage contract without assessing their reasons for doing so.[38] Yet compelling as it may sound, no-fault divorce is an analogy that liberal individualists ought to reject. In contrast with the nationalist view, the populations involved are not like individuals and their unity under a common government is not like a marriage. What divorce has in common with secession is that a decision to end the relation may be harmful to both parties as well as to third persons (such as minor children).[39] These interests have to be taken into account in a fair settlement. However, leaving the choice about ending a marital relation to the individuals concerned is the liberal way of respecting their integrity as persons. According to this view a marriage does not fuse the parties into a new and indivisible collective person. That is why it would be wrong to protect the association by the force of law against the wish of one party to end it. In contrast, even if we regard the two polities that are to be separated in a secession as distinct societies, 'we have to recognize that ordinary intercourse brings political societies into a condition of partial interfusion, to which the ordinary intercourse of individual human beings offers no parallel' (Sidgwick 1897: 247). Comparing secession to divorce therefore means regarding the secessionist group as an individual while treating the total polity as a contractual union between individuals. Yet in the case of secession there is no good reason for making this kind of ontological distinction. What we are faced with in a dispute between unionists and separatists is two competing claims for drawing the boundaries of the political community. The analogy of divorce is only convincing if we adopt the nationalist view which attributes collective personhood to nationalities while denying it to heterogeneous political communities.

A final objection to requiring that secessions be justified rather than merely desired and possible is that judgements reached on moral grounds cannot be made legally binding in the absence of a higher authority accepted by both the existing state and the secessionist group. There seems to be little practical value in a moral position which, for example, would reach the conclusion that the separation of Czechia from Slovakia was wrong. However, this conclusion is premature. In the first place, very few cases are as peaceful as the Czechoslovak separation. Where either secessionists or unionists use force in order to achieve an illegitimate goal, there is a need for an international judicial authority which would at least condemn the guilty party even if enforcement of the decision by intervention from outside may be a thorny issue. Second, in cases where unionists and secessionists refrain from force but cannot reach agreement, an international political authority should offer its good services as a mediator or arbiter. Judges and arbiters have to be provided with standards by which to assess the rival claims. Third, even when a state-wide majority shows a reluctant willingness to accept secession once it gains regional majority support, as in the Canadian case, or when its representatives agree to separation, as in the Czechoslovak case, a moral assessment of claims will still be practically important for the public deliberation which must precede any such decision and which should involve the whole citizenry. The decision whether an existing political union is to be maintained or dissolved is about the basic units of political representation and cannot legitimately be taken by representatives bargaining behind closed doors, where moral arguments have a weaker force than in public settings. I have conceded above that secession which is not sufficiently justified by present grievances should not be forcefully prevented unless it will cause serious injustice. This does not mean, however, that one should refrain from arguing against it, nor that such an argument is merely an academic exercise without political impact.[40]

Why federation should be preferred to secession

My conclusion is that both consequentialist and rights-based considerations weigh heavily in favour of requiring positive justification for secession. Mill's and Miller's objections against multinational diversity and Beran's procedural legitimation of secession through a series of plebiscites do not provide convincing reasons for a right to secession. Secession may then be justified when alternative solutions to a conflict are not available and when grievances of secessionist groups outweigh reasons for preserving the state in question. However, most current liberal grievance theories of secession have two essential flaws. They do not take seriously the most important grievance voiced by national minorities in liberal democracies: the denial or curtailment of their collective self-government within the existing state. And they cannot show why a territorially concentrated minority which manifestly strives for self-government should be bound to maintain the unity the state in which it is present.

Ideas about how to steer clear of this impasse are provided by liberal nationalist theories which defend a right to autonomy rather than to independent statehood. One way to realize this principle is to form multinational federal states.[41] Allen Buchanan seems to promote a similar solution when he argues that a primary right to secession undermines efforts 'to accommodate aspirations for autonomy of groups within the state by exploring the possibilities for various forms of decentralization, including federalism' (1997a: 53). However, both types of theories seem hampered by their basic premises in fully developing a federal response to secession. Liberal nationalists cannot consistently defend the territorial integrity of democratic states against the desire of nations to be sovereign without abandoning the idea that popular sovereignty is grounded in national membership. And individual rights theorists will hardly support the idea of a primary collective right to self-government for national minorities within a federation. They may recommend federal arrangements for prudential reasons in order to accommodate nationalist aspirations and they generally require that post-secession states ought to respect minority rights in their territory. Yet these positions are not easy to reconcile. One cannot consistently deny a right to secession for groups that are unwilling to grant autonomy to minorities in their desired independent state without acknowledging that existing states may forfeit their right to territorial integrity if they refuse similar autonomy to their own national minorities.

A federalist response to secession would have to defend a right to self-government for groups that have consistently raised this demand over several generations. We may call such groups nations or nationalities. The important point is to disconnect their aspirations from a conception of national self-determination which makes such groups bearers of a right to define to their own boundaries and membership and ultimately to declare themselves to be independent states. Democratic multinational federations offer a framework within which the right to self-government can be realized to a large extent. It allows regionally concentrated minorities to decisively shape the public culture of the area where they live and to participate in governing the wider federation of which they are a part. In this approach there are two basic grievances which may still justify the dissolution of multinational federations. One is if the past history of forcible inclusion by annexation or colonization excludes any reasonable expectation that the various communities could form a peacefully united federal polity. The second reason is if federal or provincial authorities do not honour fair terms of federation, for example by severely curtailing regional autonomy or special representation of national minorities in federal institutions. The flip side of this justification for secession is that such groups do not enjoy a right to self-determination or secession as long as the terms of federation are reasonably fair.[42] Specifying such fair terms of federation is a task beyond the scope of this chapter. But it seems to me that this is not only the most promising way out of an impasse in the debate on secession. A federal approach is also attractive because it opens a perspective which rejects the one feature that mainstream liberalism and nationalism have in common: a vision of homogenous membership in an undifferentiated polity. In a multinational federation, individuals are members of their national groups as well as citizens of the federation and the polity is considered as an entity itself composed of several polities.

Acknowledgements

Special thanks to Christine Chwascza, Will Kymlicka and Wayne Norman for useful comments on this chapter.

Notes

1 I will discuss this impossibility at greater length in the section entitled 'The dilemma of rights-based theories'.
2 As Gellner mentions, nationalists mostly speak only on behalf of their own nation while denying similar claims when these are raised by rival groups or states. However, the implicit principle to which nationalists appeal can be stated as a universalist idea (Gellner 1983: 1).
3 Different labels have been suggested for the latter type of theories. Wayne Norman (1998) calls them 'just cause' theories. This seems too wide, because choice theorists could also claim that granting secession to groups who desire self-determination is a matter of justice. Allen Buchanan has called his own approach a grievance theory but has recently suggested the term 'remedial right only theories'. Apart from being somewhat clumsy this seems too narrow, especially if one characterizes these theories as Buchanan does: '[N]o group has a (general) right to secede unless that group suffers what are uncontroversially regarded as injustices and has no reasonable prospect of relief short of secession' (1997a: 44). Buchanan mentions human rights violations and unjust seizure of territory as instances of uncontroversial injustices (ibid.: 37). This account would rule out of court any claims of national minorities that the injustice they suffer is a denial of recognition, of group rights or autonomy. Such claims are bound to be controversial in any domestic context where a group campaigns for them. And the corresponding rights are so specific and contextual that it seems impossible to define an uncontroversial standard in international law for adjudicating all disputes about them. Nevertheless, threatening with secession may well be a justified, or even the only available, response to grievances of this sort.
4 A full theory of secession must cover three different levels: justifications, constraints and procedures. The strongest disagreement among liberal political theorists is on the first and primary question how secession can be justified. They broadly agree on the second question of 'just terms of secession' (Buchanan 1997b) such as guarantees for human and minority rights or the viability of post-secession states. Procedural aspects include the translation of moral into legal rights at the level of national constitutions or international law as well as mechanisms for arbitration between parties in a conflict. Buchanan and Norman have recently presented sketches for an institutional theory of secession which focuses on these issues (Buchanan 1997a, 1997b; Norman 1998). They argue that secession theories should be evaluated by their potential to be translated into law and procedures of conflict solution. In their account, only grievance theories meet this test. While I agree with this conclusion, I think it is still

important to develop justifications for secession which are not too closely tied to existing law and political institutions or to short-term prospects for reforming them. One major reason for this relative independence of moral justification is the sad state of confusion and incoherence in these matters in international law (Moore 1997: 901–2) and even more so in constitutional principles adopted by different liberal democracies.

5 Amitai Etzioni presents a consequentialist argument against a right of secession which instead focuses on the positive target of enhancing democracy. 'We should withhold political and moral support unless the movement faces one of the truly exceptional situations in which self-determination will enhance democracy rather than retard it' (1993: 28). However, what should count as enhancing democracy is clearly more controversial than what should count as harm. Liberal nationalists claim that satisfying aspirations to national self-determination is generally conducive to democracy and choice theorists believe that democracy requires respecting majority preferences for border revisions.

6 The initial refusal by the Greek government to recognize the newly formed republic of Macedonia was rhetorically motivated by concerns about such territorial claims.

7 Choice theories of secession are based on a radically subjectivist interpretation of self-determination which can do without the concept of nationhood.

8 Yael Tamir's position is rather exceptional. Other liberal nationalists such as Avishai Margalit and Joseph Raz (1990) or Margaret Moore (1997) share Miller's preference for drawing borders so as to create maximally homogeneous nation–states and consider alternative solutions such as federalism and minority rights only in cases where national groups are too intermingled to be separated without ethnic cleansing. Daniel Philpott defends a shaky middle ground. He first asserts a *prima facie* right to self-determination that covers both independent statehood and autonomy within federal states (Philpott 1995: 353) but later concludes that secession will be ruled out in most cases and recommends to 'let one hundred federalisms bloom' (ibid.: 364). I want to argue for reversing these priorities, i.e. for a *prima facie* right to federal self-government which implies a conditional right to secession as a last resort only.

9 Miller wants to deny that *ethnic* diversity creates a problem for state boundaries. However, he could be wrong to assume that this conceptual distinction drastically reduces the number of cases to be considered. Miller's list of characteristics of national identities does not distinguish them clearly from ethnic groups (see Miller 1995: 22–5). In my view the most plausible distinction is the aspiration of the former, but not of the latter, to political autonomy or self-government. On both Miller's and my accounts it is irrelevant whether a state officially recognizes a group as a national or ethnic minority. Turkey is therefore a multinational state whose government denies that fact. On a more practical level we can assume that generally only ethnic groups with a sufficient territorial base will be able to develop national aspirations. Size, which is relevant for the capacity to form independent states, may be quite irrelevant for their transformation into national minorities. As Kymlicka points out, the existence of various indigenous minorities or the special status of Puerto Rico and Guam make the US a multinational state (1995: 11). Therefore are there many more multinational states than Miller seems to assume.

10 Jonathan Glover suggests a Kantian imperative for liberal nationalism: 'Always treat nations merely as means and never as ends in themselves' (Glover 1997: 29).

11 This point is also strongly emphasized by Avishai Margalit and Joseph Raz (1990: 137–8, 141).

12 An actual historical case which comes close to this hypothetical alternative was

the referendum held in Southern Carinthia on 10 October 1920 about whether this Austrian region would join the new Kingdom of Serbia, Croatia and Slovenia. The majority of the Slovene population voted for Austria in the expectation that the newly formed republic would guarantee them their rights as a linguistic minority, a hope which was later disappointed.

13 Philpott points out that '[i]t must always be asked, Who suffers the threat or grievance? And the answer to this must always be a group that desires self-government' (1995: 376). However, this argument is entirely consistent with a grievance theory that defends secession only as a *remedial* right. At the same time, the right of groups who qualify for self-government within a federal state can be regarded as a *primary* one whose ultimate justification is the desire for self-government. Of course such a right will also be subject to various constraints. But it is not a right whose generalization would be impossible or disastrous.

14 This contrasts with Yael Tamir's distinction between national self-determination, which she defines as 'the way in which individuals define their personal and national identity' (Tamir 1993: 70) and self-rule which is 'the right of individuals to participate in governing their lives' (ibid.: 69). An individual right to determine oneself to which national, ethnic or religious community one belongs is indeed an essential liberal achievement. However, such individual control over membership does not imply any specific right of the communities or their members. The right to a public sphere for one's culture, which is Tamir's central concern, is, in my view, a genuinely *collective* right which cannot be derived from individual self-determination in her sense of the term.

15 Consider the cases of Québec, Catalonia or Ireland. Québec was a much more 'distinct society' before the Quiet Revolution of the 1960s which thoroughly modernized the province and made it much more similar with Anglophone Canada in terms of everyday culture and ways of life. Nearly all Catalans speak the Spanish language fluently. They would not be deprived of individual opportunities for economic advancement or political participation if Spanish became the only public language in their province. In both Québec and Catalonia the national language has to be preserved because it is the only difference that clearly distinguishes a national polity from the wider state. Were the language border to vanish, geographic mobility would soon undermine the political significance of the provincial borders. An even more obvious case is the Irish one, where religion rather than language serves as a marker of national identities. It is not because they wish to maintain their Catholic tradition that Irish nationalists want to reunite the six counties with the Republic. And the driving motive for Protestant Unionists who want to stay in the UK is not fear for their religious freedom in a united Ireland. What separates them are two different visions of the boundaries of the polity to which their province ought to belong. When dividing lines between different conceptions of membership persist over generations they become marked by some ascriptive characteristic such as language, religion or phenotype. The marker is of course not an arbitrary one but reflects the historical origins of the conflict. However, it would be wrong to interpret nationalism as being mainly about preserving a substantial cultural difference rather than a separate polity.

16 Ernest Renan's well-known definition of the nation as 'a daily plebiscite' is not merely a metaphor but also a practical political guideline for settling disputes about the nation's border: '*Si des doutes s'élèvent sur ses frontières, consultez les populations disputées.*' (Renan 1882: 310).

17 The formation of the Swiss canton Jura seems to be the only historical example where a similar procedure was actually adopted (see Beran 1984; Marko 1995: 500–14). The specificities of the case are, first, that it was about the creation of a new entity rather than the emancipation of an existing one and, second, that

a reiteration of local plebiscites after separation was feasible because it was an internal border change within the federal state. It would have been rather difficult to continue this procedure once sovereign states had already been established.

18 The hurdles for secessionists may be raised by introducing additional criteria such as supermajorities or repeated majorities in a series of plebiscites. The former rule is suggested by Buchanan (1991: 132–5), the latter by Norman (1998). If the probability of winning a simple majority in one run is 50 per cent, the probability of winning majorities in several successive plebiscites must be less than 50 per cent, and so the latter rule also amounts to a supermajority requirement. One may hope that it has an additional cooling down effect, but it may also keep the issue on the agenda and focus attention on the option of secession while detracting from alternative solutions. None of these variations of the first rule takes into account the question of how secession may affect the interests of citizens living outside the province (among them members of ethnic minorities who are seen to belong to the secessionist nation).

19 Lea Brilmayer seems to argue implicitly for this solution: 'In consulting the population of the entire state, one might find that a majority overall wished to remain a single country. What has not been explained is why only the separatists need be consulted' (1991: 185).

20 Jürgen Habermas has recently defended this position: 'Solange nämlich alle Bürger gleiche Rechte genießen und niemand diskriminiert wird, besteht kein normativ überzeugender Grund zur Separierung vom bestehenden Gemeinwesen.' [As long as all citizens enjoy equal rights and nobody is discriminated, there is no convincing normative reason for separating from the existing polity] (Habermas 1996: 171, my translation).

21 See Barry (1992: 279–80) who applies a similar distinction to the problem of free movement of persons between states.

22 As a principle in international relations territorial integrity constrains secession only if it is triggered by external intervention or an irredentist movement supported by another state and if it results in the seceding territory becoming a part of an intervening state. In contrast, secession which is merely endogenous and leads to the establishment of a new independent state would be of less concern to the international community of states. In the twentieth century the principles of national self-determination and of territorial integrity have operated in tandem and the latter has largely replaced the earlier emphasis on viability and minimum size of new states. This explains why during this century the formation of new states through unification and federation has been extremely rare and successful only in cases where there was a prehistory of common nationhood. The general trend is clearly towards increasing numbers and decreasing sizes of new states.

23 Before the war of independence Algeria did not have the status of a colony but was considered a part of France. In the perspective of some French republicans, the justified grievance of Algerians was not so much that their country had been annexed, but rather that they did not enjoy full French citizenship (Audard 1996: 167).

24 See Chwaszcza (1998) for a lucid discussion and critique of these arguments.

25 Pogge (1997: 201–2) defends a very similar argument for choice.

26 According to Gauthier's principle, free emigration would not imply the right to be admitted anywhere else. Because individuals only have the right to associate with those who want to associate with them, states retain full control over immigration and no one's rights are violated if some unfortunate would-be-emigrants do not find any state which will let them in. In contrast, secession is not implicitly constrained by the right of association, but by the general proviso not to improve one's situation by worsening that of others. In a world where Gauthier's

principle were fully applied to states, free movement could be drastically restricted whereas the exit by secession would be rather easy. I suggest that the opposite ranking is desirable and this casts doubts upon the initial premise that we should conceive of states as if they were voluntary associations of the same kind as private clubs (see Bauböck 1994: 160–71).

27 Christopher Wellman defends this interpretation by suggesting that a state whose boundaries are under dispute should 'be carved up so that the secessionist territory would . . . include as many secessionists and as few unionists as possible' (1995, n. 25: 163).

28 For example, Campione d'Italia in Switzerland, the Spanish enclave of Llivia in the French Pyrenees or the Belgian one of Baarle-Nassau in the Netherlands.

29 Multinational federal schemes may still include provisions for minority vetoes, but these ought to be explicit and limited. Both the groups which enjoy them and the kind of laws which may be vetoed should be clearly defined in order to maintain a stable framework for democracy at the federal level.

30 See Wellman (1995: 154).

31 If a large percentage of citizens decide to emigrate at the same time, this could surely be just as disruptive as secession. However, such mass emigration will also serve as an indicator that a regime has become illegitimate because it is not democratic or can no longer provide for its citizens' basic needs. In this case, mass emigration may help to bring about a transformation which establishes a more legitimate regime (as it did during the final months of the German Democratic Republic). In contrast, the wish of a group to secede does not per se indicate that the regime has become illegitimate and should be replaced.

32 Choice theorists often assume that their proposals would produce only transitional instability. For example, Pogge concedes that the backlog of territorial readjustment claims presents a serious short-term problem. 'Once this backlog will have been worked down, however, there may not be much redrawing activity as people will then be content with their political memberships, and most borders will be supported by stable majorities' (1997, n. 17: 218). This underestimates reasons for subsequent changes of borders which result (1) from delayed impacts of successful secessions of one group on other minorities in post-secession states; (2) from shifting demographic balances between groups in mobile societies; (3) from perverse incentives for minorities to abuse a right to secession as a minority veto, which may create a dynamic of originally unintended secessions; and (4) from perverse incentives for majorities to preventively assimilate or disperse minorities which might become capable of secession (Buchanan 1997a: 52), which would create a legitimate grievance of minorities to seek secession.

33   An important role of a people's government, however arbitrary a society's boundaries may appear from a historical point of view, is to be the representative and effective agent of a people as they take responsibility for their territory and the size of their population . . .

(Rawls 1993: 56–7)

Buchanan offers the following quite similar definition:

     Territorial sovereignty is an agency/trusteeship function carried out by the state on behalf of the people as a multigenerational community. It consists of control over borders and the administration of justice, and is not strictly speaking ownership of the land within those borders.

(1991: 13)

The secession of private owners of real estate is therefore not constrained by an overriding property right of the state in the territory, but by a trusteeship which the state exercises on behalf of all citizens seen as a single polity. A group may then be justified in seceding when the state systematically acts towards it in ways which violate the trusteeship that legitimates its authority.

34 See also Beran (1988: 323).

35 I do not wish to make any judgement on whether the Francophone Québecois have sufficient reasons to secede on grounds of justice. From the perspective outlined in the conclusions, this depends on whether terms of federation have been seriously violated. Yet it seems possible to interpret the Québec case as one where the argument from choice is as strong as it can be, simply because reasonable observers disagree on the standards and records of injustice.

36 Few serious observers doubt that an independent Québec would be a liberal democracy based on roughly the same constitutional principles as the Canadian federation – including respect for cultural difference and minority rights (see Carens 1995).

37 What has been settled is the territorial and the majority requirements for a plebiscite on Québec's right to become independent. What remains unsettled, however, is whether northern parts of Québec, which are mainly inhabited by Inuits, then would enjoy a similar right to secede and rejoin the Canadian remainder state. Even in a secession debate as peaceful as the Canadian one, the proliferation logic may unleash a considerable potential for violent conflict.

38 See (Beran 1984: 25), Nielsen (1993: 35), Gauthier (1995: 360, 371), Wellman (1995: 146).

39 According to Donald Horowitz, the divorce analogy suggests 'a neat and clean separation between two antagonists' (1997: 433). However, 'as in domestic divorces, there is nothing neat about it, and there are usually children (smaller groups that are victims of the split)' (ibid.).

40 Allen Buchanan defends the need to work out principles for secession in international law and to empower international authorities to apply them in mediating or adjudicating actual conflicts (1997b: 304). However, he unnecessarily limits his theory to such cases where secession is not consensual, thus conceding too much ground to choice-based approaches. A full theory should be also able to judge non-violent and apparently consensual cases of separation like those of Czechoslovakia. First, as I have just argued, majorities may be simply wrong and we need general principles that guide our judgement of a specific case in order to find out whether separation is to be welcomed or should be objected to. Second, even when majorities on both sides favour the break-up of a state, minorities may be negatively affected (as were the Romanies in Czechia and Slovakia) and their interests should at least be relevant for working out just terms of separation.

41 John Stuart Mill briefly considers federation as a solution *after* separation rather than as an alternative to it: 'There may be cases in which the provinces, after separation, might usefully remain united by a federal tie.' However, he quickly dismisses this possibility by assuming that 'each of them has other neighbours with whom it would prefer to connect itself. (Mill 1972: 398).

42 Wayne Norman (1994) provides an initial outline of a contractarian theory of multinational federalism, Bauböck (2000) discusses this approach and complements the present chapter.

12 Who's afraid of a global state?

Yael Tamir

The aim of this chapter is to analyse the sources of the wide-ranging resentment and dismissal of the idea of a global state. In the process of so doing, one may learn not only about the pros and cons of a world order but also about the nature of political theory as applied to national and international affairs.

Why isn't an idea getting its due place? Answering this question is no easy matter, as one has to prove that the idea in question is worthy of serious considerations and then explain their absence. I will attempt to do both: argue that the idea of a global state deserves theoretical attention and explain the lack of such attention, or worse, the theoretical and political antagonism this idea raises. However, I shall do so in reverse order, starting with an analysis of the resentment to the idea of a global state and then defending it.

Unfortunately, the fate of ideas, like that of individuals, does not necessarily reflect their qualities. No less than in the human sphere, appearances often count more in the ideological sphere than content, and some ideas are rejected simply because others seem much more attractive. Hence, it is not uncommon that some trends of thought draw attention and sympathy despite their faults, while others are rejected regardless of their virtues. It is tempting then to reveal the inner life of the world of ideas and explain the reasons why some ideas are more popular than others. Doing so may allow one to expose hidden agendas, theoretical likes and dislikes, and a whole range of carefully veiled preferences.

This chapter sets to examine the attitudes towards the idea of a global state and explores the reasons for its common dismissal. This analysis is then used as a lever for revealing the agreements and tensions, theoretical presuppositions of liberal political theory and international relations, and the statist commitment they share. The fate of the idea of a global state, it would argue, is determined less by its own qualities than by the attractiveness of the idea it negates – that of the sovereign state. In order to support this claim, it will start by explaining the prominence of this latter idea, try and undermine some of the undue support it receives, and only then turn to count the virtues of the idea of the global state.

The main thesis of this chapter, then, is that the idea of a global state is rejected out of hand mainly because of the political and theoretical prominence of a competing idea – that of the sovereign state. It is clear why politicians would cling to the idea of the sovereign state and strive to retain its prominence. The interesting fact is that the theoretical price of giving it up is as high as the political one.

Forced to abandon the idea of the sovereign state, political theory will lose one of its most useful concepts. It will be left lame, inept to perform some of its most basic tasks. The sovereign state has become the starting point of most of the discussions in political theory. It has been of particular importance to liberal theoreticians as it has provided a conceptual framework that has allowed them to preserve, but not admit, their inherent particularistic – perhaps even nationalistic – tendencies (Tamir 1993: Chapter 6). The existence of the state as a conceptual framework allowed liberals to framed discussions over justice, fairness, and equality within a given, limited entity. Without it, they would have to find ways of either accommodating the demands of moral universalism which grow out of their own normative commitments or justifying their deep-rooted particularism. Opting for the latter will call for a justification of the formation of a plurality of separate political units worthy of autonomy and justified in developing inward looking policies. In short, it will demand a justification of the present structure of world order. This is a task that liberal political theory has never managed to perform adequately.

No more than a state of mind

The claim that liberal political theory fails in its attempt to justify the formation of a world order based on sovereign states may seem surprising, as it often appears as if it has been constantly engaged in confronting the very issue. In order to support it let us examine some of the justifications offered by liberal theorists in favor of a plurality of sovereign states. In order to do so, one must start with a definition of two key concepts: state and sovereignty.

According to Webster's Dictionary, a state is 'a whole people united into one body politic', or to use the Oxford Dictionary version, a state is an 'organized political community with its apparatus of government'. Both definitions are unsatisfactory since the characteristic they delineate is insufficient to define a political organization as a state. A whole people could be united under a local government which falls short of the definition of a state; neighborhoods, local governments, political parties have an apparatus of government. What distinguishes a state from all these political organizations is the fact that it is the sovereign.

A sovereign is a power or authority which comprises the attributes of an ultimate arbiter entitled to make decisions and settle disputes with some degree of finality in a wide range of public domains. In these domains it has 'an unsupervised and irrevocable authority . . . to lay down rules, judge the compliance (of individuals(with these rules, and enforce these rules' (Pogge 1992: 57). To be able to make such decisions, the sovereign must be independent of external powers. For that matter, sovereignty must be exerted over a particular group of individuals inhabiting a well-defined territory. The boundaries, integrity, and continuity of this territory are recognized and respected by the other players on the international scene. Subsequently, only the sovereign itself can surrender its autonomy, or integrity; no other power can legitimately force it to accept such changes.

I adopt this rather crude definition, knowing that no actual sovereign fully accords with it. However, I do not wish to follow here the common objections to the idea of state sovereignty, namely, that no state – not even a superpower – enjoys full autonomy, or that the separation between the different branches of government makes the existence of one locus of authority questionable. For the sake of argument, I assume that an ideal type of absolute sovereignty could be constituted, but over which group and what territory? The inability to provide principles for demarcation, I would argue, is liberal political theory's greatest deficiency which, if acknowledged, should have led it to be more critical of the idea of the plurality of sovereign states and more generous to the idea of a global one.

In the twentieth century, demarcation was justified mostly in nationalist terms. Relaying on John Stuart Mill, Michael Walzer offers a moral account of sovereignty. The justification of sovereignty, he argues, follows from the right to national self-determination, which is the right of a people 'to become free by their own efforts'. Non-intervention is the principle guaranteeing that their success will not be impeded or their failure prevented by the intrusion of an alien power. It has to be stressed, Walzer argues:

> that there is no right to be protected against the consequences of domestic failure, even against bloody repression . . . As with individuals, so with sovereign states: there are things that we cannot do to them, even for their own ostensible good.
>
> (1977: 88–9)

This analogy between individuals and groups is rather problematic, but I do not mean to enter here into a discussion concerning the ontological status of groups and their moral standing as bearers of particular rights. For the sake of argument, I take it as a given that groups exist and rights could be attributed to them. Yet one distinction between groups and individuals seems important: while all individuals are equally entitled to personal autonomy, not all groups qualify as equal bearers of autonomy. One would undoubtedly wish to claim that some special features, of some groups, entitle them to achieve self-determination. But what could these features be?

The adjective 'national' which precedes self-determination suggests that national features define a group as fitting to be a bearer of autonomy.[1] Even if this claim is justified, it does not amount to a defense of sovereignty. The rights individuals have as members of a nation – to speak their own language, follow their traditions, live in accordance with their culture – may demand that they be given cultural, educational, linguistic, and perhaps even religious autonomy, but there is quite a distance between this claim and a claim for the kind of sovereignty characteristic of the modern state. Nationalist arguments may indeed support the rights of national groups to be sovereign with regards to cultural educational issues, but how can national arguments justify sovereignty in either the economic, ecological or strategic spheres?[2]

One may, however, accept the claim that national rights do not amount to a right to sovereignty and yet defend demarcation along national lines for social democratic reasons. Free institutions are next to impossible in a country made up of different nationalities, Mill claimed.

> Among a people, without fellow feelings, especially if they read and speak different languages, the united public opinion, necessary to the working of representative government, cannot exist . . . The same incidents, the same acts, the same system of government affect them in different ways; and each fears more injury to itself from other nationalities, than from the common arbiter, the State.
>
> (Mill 1975: 382)

David Miller defends Mill's thesis. To the extent that we aspire to form a democracy in which all citizens are involved in discussions of public issues, we must foster 'conditions under which citizens can respect one other's good faith in searching for grounds for agreement. Among large aggregates of people, *only* a common nationality can provide a sense of solidarity that makes this possible' (Miller 1995: 98).[3] This seems a rather extreme claim. Nationality may be a very effective way of creating civic solidarity and mutual trust, but it is certainly not the only one. If national homogeneity was a necessary condition for democratic cooperation, then very few states would be able to sustain a democratic regime, and the most vulnerable states of all would be immigrant states composed of an amalgam of ethnic, racial and religious groups. History tells us that such states can develop stable democratic regimes. Moreover, transnational corporations, regional organizations, multicultural political systems and international institutions all prove that cultural barriers can be overcome and trust can be built among individuals of different national backgrounds.

In the 1990s, the wisdom of grounding justifications for sovereignty in national principles has been questioned not only theoretically but also politically.[4] Politics has proven the ideal of a state for each nation to be a pipe dream: The 'Russian doll phenomenon' – i.e. the fact that every 'national territory,' however small, includes members of other nations – disallows territorial division along national lines. Mill himself was forced to acknowledge its influence: there are parts even of Europe, he admitted:

> in which different nationalities are so locally intermingled that it is not practicable for them to be under separate governments . . . and there is no course open to them but to make a virtue of necessity, and reconcile themselves to living together under equal rights and laws.
>
> (1975: 384)

What was evident to Mill when he looked at the Austro-Hungarian Empire is evident to those who nowadays observe the demographic composition of all states, including those who used to see themselves as nationally homogenous: the renewal of national identity and the growing political awareness among members of indigenous nations, and the permanent expansion of communities of immigrant, refugees and guest workers turn all states into multinational entities. They must all then make a virtue of necessity and establish ways of allowing members of different nations to share one political framework. The attempt to use national belonging as a criterion for determining state boundaries thus fails both theoretically and politically. The problem of demarcation remains open. Can it be solved?

Democratic principles cannot be used as guidelines for demarcation, unless a global assembly convenes and reaches a joint decision on the principles of partition. But what might these principles be? Obvious candidates are participation and influence. According to right theories, individuals have a right to participate in the making of decisions affecting their lives. Can these principles serve as guidelines for partition? Not in a world in which circles of influence do not stop at state, or even at continental, boundaries.

It is now clear that governmental decisions to allow the use of chemicals detrimental to the ozone layer, the razing of rain forests, or the pollution of rivers effect the lives of all the inhabitants of the globe. If the Russian government builds hazardous atomic energy plants, the whole of Europe is endangered; if Saddam Hussein accumulates chemical weapons, the whole of the Middle East is threatened; and if, to take a completely different example, the United States government changes its monetary policy, stock markets all over the world rise or fall in response. These are not minor matters and they can influence the lives of individuals much more than decisions taken by their own governments.

Partition could be guided by an attempt to pursue instrumental ends, be they strategic, distributive, or ecological, but could political units established to fulfil such functions be seen as sovereign states? Note that the justification for the establishment of functional units does not derive from the right of any particular group for autonomy, but from the desire to create efficient political systems that will best secure certain individual interests. As efficiency is contingent on a whole range of transient circumstances, a consistent instrumental argument should lead to the conclusion that efficiency-based decisions must be open to permanent revisions. What would be the value of establishing political units adequate to deal with present circumstances only? This is a particularly disturbing question in a rapidly changing world like ours. By definition, then, the integrity of functional political units would be transitory, conditional on decisions taken by a political authority beyond their reach, and, in light of contingent circumstances, that for the most part are beyond their control. In these circumstances, these units could hardly be seen as sovereign.

Moreover, the different instrumental criteria for partition justify the establishment of political units of different scope: national criteria support the establishment of units overlapping the nation, strategic and ecological criteria point to regional units comprising whole continents, distributive criteria may lead to the creation of a global unit, while arguments emphasizing intimacy and active participation would suggest the formation of local, small-scale communities. As none of these criteria are overriding, sovereignty would need to be divided by spheres, and cannot be discussed in holistic terms. Such an analysis justifies the formation of a multi-layered world order but not of a plurality of sovereign states (Pogge 1992).

Even if no principle for partition can be found, a justification for the establishment of sovereign states may be derived from voluntary agreements among individuals. This type of justification seems straightforward: individuals get together and create political units that serve their purposes. The autonomy of these associations derives from the autonomy of the contracting agents. But this line of argument would lead to the improbable conclusion that sovereignty should be granted to any voluntary association that claims it. This would raise severe coordination problems, insecurity, instability and injustice. It was precisely in order to avoid these problems that the idea of state sovereignty emerged in the first place.

One could then claim that only associations which defend human rights, and promote the security and interests of individuals, as well as political stability and continuity may be granted sovereignty. This is the essence of the contractarian approach, in which two major flaws may be detected. The first and most devastating flaw is that contractarian justifications arbitrarily stop at the level of the state. This creates the false impression that these contract theories have justified the formation of a system of separate states. In fact, they have taken this system as given and formulate their arguments within its limits. Let us clarify this claim by examining a well-known example, Hobbes' justification for absolute sovereignty in *The Leviathan*.

According to Hobbes, the need for an absolute sovereign derives from the fact that 'during the time men live without a common Power to keep them all in awe, they are in that condition which is called Warre; and such a warre, as is of every man, against every man' (Hobbes 1949: 64). This situation can be changed only if a power is established 'which hath no other limit but that which is the terminus ultimum of the forces of all citizens together'. But why should this power be a sovereign state? It would be logical to stop at this stage only if the sovereign state established is so strong that no other power can threaten it, or its citizens, but the formation of such a state would lead to the inevitable result that members of all other states would be left unprotected. It would then make sense for members of these states to join the superpower and seek refuge under its protective wings. If all applicants were accepted, a global sovereign entity would be created. Were members of weaker states not allowed to join, they would be left unprotected, suffering from even greater insecurity than in the state of nature. As the right to personal security is universal and the only way to assure that it will be equally distributed is to establish a global sovereign power, Hobbes' justification for the construction of a sovereign entity cannot support the formation of competing sovereign states.[5] Time and space do not allow us to examine other contractarian approaches, but all of them reach the same deadlock: their justifications easily slide into a justification of a global sovereign entity, rather than a plurality of states.

The second flaw of contractarian justifications is that from the need for a sovereign power or a coordinating entity in some particular sphere of public life – such as human rights, personal security, social welfare or ecology – a justification for the establishment of one political entity, sovereign in all major fields, is deduced.[6] In other words, an overlap between justifications concerned with the protection and fostering of different human interests is presupposed, but not proven. It is arbitrarily assumed that the holistic sovereign power that will best serve these interests is neither a local, regional or global institution, but a finite sovereign state.

Let us conclude this section by making a radical claim: none of the justifications for the establishment of independent sovereign states examined here is valid, and yet the inability to justify the formation of sovereign states has not deterred political theorists from making them a corner stone of their theories. This is true even in the present time and age, in which the rapid erosion of the sovereign national state is a well-known political fact.

Long after state boundaries have been transcended by the establishment of regional organizations, multinational corporations, and NGOs, political theorists are still careful not to shatter the sanctity of state sovereignty and integrity. Consequently, multicultural theories currently developed take the core question to be the following: how can state unity be retained despite the growing pressures caused by diversity? Being busy trying to save the state and pasting its pieces back together again, liberal political theorists neglect the more fundamental question: should the unity and autonomy of the sovereign state be retained, or should the state be transcended for some purposes and divided for others?

In those rare cases when this question is raised, theorists tend to clap their hands in despair and defend the state in the name of realism.[7] The existence of states, we are told, is not a matter of justification, but a fact of life. States are here to stay; those who do not accept this are deemed naïve. Let us then examine this objection, because if it is true, the rest of the discussion is meaningless.

What do institutions have to do with it?

From the start, one should remove an accusation commonly raised against supporters of a global state: that of political naïveté. I have no quarrel with the assessment that the ideal of a global state is an unrealistic utopia. My argument, however, does not depend on the feasibility of establishing such a state. It is indeed true that a global state is not about to be established, nor are we likely to see the formation of a just state – a state where resources and opportunities are fairly and equally distributed. Why aren't discussions on issues of justice or equality considered naïve. Why are the difficulties embodied in the construction of just institutions not used to deter theorists from developing theories of justice, while the difficulties embodied in the formation of global institutions are used to trump the idea of a global state? More generally, why do discussions of normative issues within state boundaries bend in the idealistic direction, while discussions concerning normative international matters defer to realistic constraints? In order to answer these questions, we need to examine not only the nature of world order but also the nature of national and international political theory.

The gap between the realistic approach to the international scene and the idealistic approach to internal politics is grounded in a feature of political theory which could be defined as institutional avoidance – i.e. the tendency not to consider the institutional changes implied by normative theories.

It is interesting to note that in neither Nozick's *Anarchy, State and Utopia*, Walzer's *Spheres of Justice*, nor Ackerman's *Social Justice in a Liberal State* does the term 'institution' appear in the index. None of the above authors feels obliged to give the reader an account of how his theory is to be implemented, and although the second part of Rawls' *A Theory of Justice* is entitled 'institutions', no actual institutional reforms are there discussed.[8]

Needless to say, it is a mistake to underestimate the institutional difficulties involved in the implementation of liberal theories of justice, and yet it has become a theoretically productive mistake, as it has allowed normative discussions to dissociate themselves, in the process of sketching moral ideals, from possible hindrances which may prevent their implementation. Institutional avoidance thus leads ironically to a normative radicalism alongside institutional conservatism.

International theory has been pulled in the opposite direction. The poverty of global institutions (and the weakness of existing ones) make it clear that even the most modest normative changes will demand institutional reforms. Skepticism that such reforms can be implemented, and consequently the reluctance to offer them, diminish the willingness to offer innovative normative trends. In the case of international relations, then the high sensitivity to the need for institutional reforms and an acute awareness of the difficulties of bringing them about lead to normative conservatism.

Some may claim that political theory's disregard of actual institutional constraints cannot possibly be an advantage, as it fosters a detached idealistic approach which cannot be implemented. Perhaps, then, our approach to national, rather than international, theory must be reformed. In order to settle this issue, we must ponder a moment on the complicated relations between theory and practice.

Does the inability to realize an ideal in the foreseeable future undermine its importance? Must political theory restrict itself to offering only feasible reforms? To claim that political theory is no more than 'a mere mirror of practical politics, a mere derivation of real social and economic conditions', Ralf Dahrendorf argues, is to sell theory short, 'because there should be the possibility of detachment, of anticipation, of developing images of the future which are not simply a reflection of the present' (1983: 37).

The question, then, is how far should a political ideal distance itself from the present norms and structures? The feasible and the imaginable, John Plamenatz reminds us, 'are limited by the actual' (1967: 23). The term 'actual' here does not mean 'that which is factually true', but 'that which could be imagined'. Practical philosophy, Aristotle taught us, must be limited by the range of imaginable possibilities: 'we do not deliberate about things that we believe cannot, in the nature of things, be otherwise' (Hampshire 1989: 56–7).

We need then to distinguish between those social phenomena 'to which no man-made alternative can usefully be imagined' (ibid.: 56–7) and those which can be altered. This is not a simple distinction to make; slavery, the authority of the monarch, the free-market for industrial products, and the subordination of women were all once seen as parts of the natural order of things and therefore outside the sphere of practical reason. How does a social phenomenon change its status from a natural phenomenon to a social one? Practical reasoning, Stuart Hampshire argues, becomes innovative in human affairs when it demands reasons for accepted social practices and institutions. At first, such demands do not present themselves as intelligible, as the social practice or institution is seen as an uncontrolled phenomenon and consequently the offered explanation and proposed change seem to have no relation to practicality. In this stage, 'the alternative possibilities, perhaps identifiable in retrospect, are not envisaged as real possibilities' (Hampshire 1989: 58)[9] and yet social structures and norms change and what has been unimaginable becomes obvious.

The difficulty is that our imagination is embedded in reality. It is therefore much easier for us to imagine what there is. Moreover, social institutions make great efforts to restrict our imagination, to claim that they are natural, unavoidable, and unchangeable; witness how often the term 'natural' is used in order to grant an idea, or an institution, special protected status: natural law, natural rights, natural borders, etc.[10] Fighting these images is no easy matter.

Nevertheless, neither political theory nor international relations can fall captive to the present. They must be founded on a set of judgments pointing to a contrast between 'the world as it is, or is likely to be, and what would have been better or worse, or what would in the future be better or worse (Hampshire 1989: 15–16). Is then the idea of a global state politically imaginable? I cannot provide a satisfactory answer to this question here, but I would like to look at two arguments raised to support the inconceivable nature of this idea. The first has to do with the supposed Hobbesian nature of international relations, which seems to hinder the possibility of establishing such a state; the second is grounded in the thick pluralism characteristic of the international scene, which seems to hamper the chance of legitimizing such a state by means of the consent of the governed. Let us examine these arguments one by one.

Dancing with wolves

One of the main reasons a global state seems no more than a naive illusion is that the international scene is commonly described in Hobbesian terms. According to this view, the state of nature does not only permit, but may actually require, states 'to pursue the national interest and maximize national power ("to seek power after power") without regard to other considerations' (Cohen 1984: 321). States thus necessarily enter a deadly competition; for each of them the only way to fulfil its duty to its citizens and remove the existential threats imposed on them by other states is to subordinate or exterminate all other political entities. Consequently, the international scene is doomed to remain in a permanent state of war from which there is no peaceful, political escape (ibid.: 24). It is therefore rational for all parties to enter into an arms race that must end in calamity.

Moral dialogue cannot offer a substitute for violence, as in the Hobbesian state of nature in which there is no sovereign the use of moral language is no more than an expression of 'appetites and aversions' which encourages 'disputes, controversies and at last war' (Hobbes ibid.: 216). Attempts to conduct a moral conversation are then, by definition, counterproductive. Sovereign states which possess an internal moral language are, or at least theoretically can be, islands of morality in an ocean of international brutality. State sovereignty should then be defended, even at a high cost.

But the existence of a plurality of sovereign states need not be the only way to assure the durability of a moral – political dialogue. On the contrary, the Hobbesian line of reasoning taken to its logical conclusions implies that the establishment of a global state may very well be an even better solution; it will create a shared global moral language that would allow for an international peaceful dialogue while reducing the likelihood of international conflict and minimizing external threats. The establishment of such a state might then be desirable but, so it is claimed, is a theoretical and practical impossibility.

There are, however, good reasons to reject the Hobbesian description of international relations and its belligerent conclusions. First, Hobbes' assumption that individuals are allowed to take any action necessary for puposes of self-preservation is questioned by many.[11] Second, even if individuals have such a right, it is unclear whether it is transferable to groups. It is far from obvious, Marshall Cohen argues, that 'because individual men have a natural right of self-preservation, states do so as well' (Cohen 1984: 322). This is especially true if this right is derived from the right of individual citizens to self-preservation. A state's failure to defend its ideological influence, its economic advantage, and even its territorial integrity need not endanger the lives of its citizens. The death of a state Cohen rightly claims, may not 'require the loss of a single life. Indeed it may save some' (ibid.: 324).

Third, even if states have a right to self-preservation, this does not imply that they have a duty to behave selfishly. States are not doomed to selfishness. They may very well adopt two kinds of moral ends: self-regarding and other-regarding. The latter may include duties both to the society of states and to foreign human being (Hoffmann 1981: 190). Skeptics may claim that such moral behavior may be permitted but no agent would have an interest in pursuing it, as it might weaken its position and hamper its chances of self-preservation. This might be true in a world in which all agents are of equal power and every political game is a zero-sum game, but in a world in which power is unequally distributed, it may be that some states – especially those that are relatively powerful – can take acts that would benefit others without incurring substantial risks.

This is especially true if the strong parties hold liberal values and endorse a set of liberal commitments; such is the case on the international scene. Hegemony is held by liberal-democratic states which aspire to retain a degree of coherence between their internal and external politics. Michael Doyle's excellent analysis of international relations (1983) may also be interpreted as accentuating the gap between international reality governed by a slow move towards a Kantian pax liberala and the Hobbesian description of the state of nature.

In a world in which there is liberal hegemony, Brilmayer argues, the unequal distribution of power between states can benefit, rather than hamper, the establishment of a just world order. When a liberal state acquires hegemony in global affairs and feels secure enough to 'afford the luxury of attending to principles', then hegemony can create an 'opportunity for political morality' (1996: 224).

The analogy of international relations and the Hobbesian state of nature thus seems to rely on a flimsy theory. As a result, the Hobbesian argument for skepticism does not carry over to international relations (Beitz 1979: 49). Western social science, Susan Strange argues, 'and especially social science directed at the world system . . . had overemphasized both the role of the state and the violent conflict between states as the core problematique of the system' (1995: 70). A more balanced and accurate view would be to take not the Hobbesian but the Lockian state of nature as the starting point of the discussion. States are therefore to be seen as agents found in a state of perfect freedom to order their actions and dispose of their possessions as they think fit 'within the bounds of the law of nature' (Locke 1924: 119). In such a state of nature, the formation of cooperation and voluntary associations is not impossible; the parties do not lack the moral language that would allow them to negotiate, bargain and reach agreements that promote their interests. This description fits much better the international reality in which, despite the absence of a sovereign power, cooperation and association are common phenomena.

Preferring a Lockian description to a Hobbesian one changes the normative balance between the state and the international arena. According to the Hobbesian description, moral discourse can develop only within the boundaries of sovereign states. States, then, are seen as islands of morality floating in an international ocean which is condemned, by definition, to lack moral lever that would restrict its inherent brutality. National politics must therefore be preferred and defended. But if a Lockian description is accepted, then, *a priori*, there is no reason to assume that international politics would be more brutal or selfish than national politics. There is, then, no reason to prefer the latter over the former, and a global state may emerge as an option.

False harmony

One may claim that even if the international scene is found in a Lockian state of nature, a global state cannot be established, as the plurality of incommensurable and incompatible moral conceptions found on the international scene prevents the formation of a moral consensus which would legitimize and guide global institutions. In the lack of such a consensus, a state may indeed be created, but it would not be able to function as it will have no agreed moral code on which to draw.

This is a serious problem which must haunt political and international theory alike, but here again the asymmetry between the description of the national and the international scene is quite astonishing; while political theory fosters a far too harmonious view of the state, international theory emphasizes the disharmonious nature of the international scene. Consequently, the fact that in recent decades the international and national scenes have grown more alike than ever before is commonly neglected. States no longer are the homogeneous political units both liberalism and nationalism (each for its own reasons) aspired them to be. Their multi-national, multicultural nature becomes more apparent every day. The present world, Stanley Hoffmann writes, is full of Austria-Hungaries: states which look more like miniature international communities among whose members there is little unity or agreement (1981: 581).

The sharp distinction drawn between the kind of pluralism found within states and within the international arena leads to the conclusion that unan-imous agreement necessary to support the legitimacy of political institutions can be reached within states but not within a global setting. If this des-cription is an adequate one, then both the likelihood of establishing international institutions and the legitimacy of existing ones are severely undermined. The sovereign state, then, remains the only legitimate polit-ical framework. If, however, the difference between the international and internal scene is much smaller than is usually assumed, and if unanimous consent cannot be reached on either scene, then the state loses its theo-retical advantage.

It is important to pause for a moment and analyse the role played by the idea of unanimous consent, as this idea is often used to legitimize state sovereignty and delegitimize international institutions. In modern liberal political theory, the legitimacy of political institutions depends on the ability to achieve unanimous consent of the governed regarding the formation of the political system and the principles of justice which would govern its institutions. Such a consent cannot be reached among individuals who do not share common norms and values.

To justify a conception of justice to someone, John Rawls says, is to give him a proof, and yet 'a proof simply displays logical relations between propositions. But proofs become justifications once the starting points are mutually recognized' (1971: 581). A theory of justice thus starts from shared intuitions, norms, and judgments. Moreover, as all parties involved in the construction of a conception of justice are assumed to hold reasonable conceptions of the good (Rawls 1995: 59), the existence of a certain degree of overlap between these conceptions is presupposed. Consequently, the issue of disagreement is never raised. We are therefore left ignorant as to how those who hold unreasonable doctrines should be treated: are we to assume that these individuals are unreasonable, irrational, and should therefore be treated as either minors or feeble-minded individuals whose consent we need not seek?[12] Should it be presupposed that individuals must have adopted these doctrines, not from a position of freedom and therefore see them as if they were forced to hold such views and 'free' them by imposing on them liberal values,[13] hoping that they will develop a taste for them in years to come?

Liberal political theory has little to say about these issues. Even though in *Political Liberalism*, Rawls acknowledged the fact of reasonable pluralism (reasonable being a key concept in this discussion, as by its very definition it sets the grounds for an overlapping consensus), he ignored the issue of thick pluralism (which includes reasonable and unreasonable conceptions of the good) until he started reflecting on 'The law of peoples'. Only then, when looking at the international scene, did Rawls start to grapple with the implication of thick pluralism on his theory.

This late revelation is not coincidental; it befits the liberal to disregard matters of internal disagreement that might undermine the legitimacy of political institutions, but what is true of the international setting is also true, in a miniature scale, for the national one. Think for a moment about Rawls' own society, which includes not only liberal subcultures but also decent hierarchical ones (like the Protestant church), less decent ones that do not respect the right of women (such as the Amish) and have no consultation hierarchy (like the ultra-Orthodox community of Kyrias Yoel), as well as group that could be seen as outlaws and likely to 'refuse to comply' with political liberalism (Moslem and Jewish fundamentalists or militant militia). This kind of pluralism is far thicker than a liberal or a reasonable one.

If most, if not all, modern societies are characterized by thick pluralism, and if the moral status of the state and its stability derive from the fact that its regime is neither imposed nor coerced but wins support 'by addressing each citizen's reason' (Rawls 1971: 143), then difficulties raised by the existence of illiberal groups that cannot be coopted into an overlapping consensus must frustrate not only the legitimacy of international institutions but also of national ones. One must then cope with the political and theoretical consequence of the impossibility of reaching voluntary, reasonable consent. I do not intend to try and cope with this question here, but in view of the growing diversity within states, the lack of serious discussion of these matters seems quite surprising.

What goes unnoticed on the internal scene is excessively emphasized on the international scene: when discussing international affairs, the fact that a voluntary agreement over the principles of justice cannot be reached is taken as a proof that legitimate international institutions cannot be constructed.

I could end the discussion here, making a negative claim, namely that neither states nor international institutions can draw their legitimacy from consent; there is then no reason to award the state theoretical privileges, but taking into account the significance of consent-based theories leads me to take the argument one step further.

Can an agreement be reached under conditions of thick pluralism, and can that agreement be seen as a source of political legitimization? In order to answer this question, it is worthwhile to follow Rawls' attempt to sketch a law of peoples which will be globally acceptable. In order to achieve this goal, Rawls develops the notion of well-ordered hierarchical societies which are peaceful and gain their legitimate aims through diplomacy and trade; their system of law is guided, sincerely an not unreasonably, by a common conception of justice; their institutions include a reasonable consultation hierarchy; their citizens are seen as responsible members who can recognize their moral duties and obligations and play a part in social life; they admit a measure of human rights and of liberty of conscience and freedom of thought, even if these freedoms are not generally equal for all members. Such societies, Rawls argues, are reasonable (Rawls 1971: 78). He admits, though, that in comparison to *Political Liberalism*, the criteria of reasonableness have been 'relaxed'.

In *Political Liberalism*, reasonableness related to the exercise of theoretical reason and the power and burden of judgment. This implies that a doctrine is deemed reasonable if the deliberations that lead individuals to endorse it are of a particular kind. In 'The law of peoples', no reference is made to the grounds on which the different societies choose to endorse doctrines that qualify them as 'well-ordered hierarchical societies' (Rawls 1994: 43). In this case, then, reasonableness seems to be measured by the endorsement of some social norms and practices, rather than by the kind of justifications that lead to their endorsement.

This is a welcome move, as it allows the incorporation of societies that follow certain norms and practices for a variety of reasons: they may respect some measures of public consultation, rights, and free expression, due to a particular religious doctrine that sees individuals as created in God's image and therefore as worthy of respect; or to some conception of efficiency that sees open public dialogue as the best means of formulating effective policies and urging the public to pursue them; or to a traditionalist attempt to preserve a participatory tradition and customary collective decision-making procedures; or even to mere prudential considerations. What kind of overlapping consensus could be founded among such a diverse group of peoples? Failing overlapping consensus over principles, we may still reach overlapping consensus over practices. This suggests that convergence of practices may support the legitimate exercise of power and enforcement of these practices.

Can there be an agreement between the different political societies inhabiting our world on practices protecting the right of women, on children's rights or religious rights, on the right to protection, to due process or to political participation? One simple, perhaps simplistic answer is to draw attention to international charters such as the Universal Declaration of Human Rights, the two Covenants on civil and political rights and on economic, social and cultural rights, and the establishment of institutions such as the European Commission and Court of Human Rights, and the Inter-American Commission on Human Rights, and claim that these testify that agreement on issues of human rights can be achieved. This does not imply that there would not be permanent disagreement as to how these rights should be interpreted, or what counts as a violation of a particular right, but such controversies, severe as they may be, are based on a shared perception regarding the importance and primacy of rights.[14] This claim does not rest on an illusion that rights language is a universal language; it is quite clear that it is well grounded in a comprehensive moral theory which is a product of a particular time and place. Maximal substantive morality always precedes a minimal one, Walzer argues. The way to detect the latter is to 'acknowledge the great diversity of historical processes, and look for similar or overlapping outcomes; locate communality and the end point of diversity' (1994: 15). There is no moral Esperanto, no neutral, inexpressive moral language, he argues, but we can list our moral responses and make a catalogue of the moral behavior to which we object.

> Perhaps the end product of this effort will be a set of standards to which all societies can be held – negative injunctions, most likely, rules against murder, deceit, torture, oppression, and tyranny. Among ourselves, late-twentieth century Americans or Europeans, these standards will probably be expressed in the language of rights, which is the language of our own moral maximalism. But that is not a bad way of talking about injuries and wrongs that no one should have to endure, and I assume it is translatable.
>
> (ibid.: 10)

Needless to say, not all societies share a commitment to human rights in theory or in practice. What are we to do about these societies? When discussing the international scene, Rawls is ready to openly endorse a practice which goes unnoticed in internal politics: the imposition of liberal principles. Why is it better to impose liberal values on internal dissenters than on external ones? The answer cannot be given in terms of autonomy; after all, the autonomy of societies to preserve their values is derived from the autonomy of individuals, and if the latter can be overruled under certain circumstances, why not the former?

Imposing a just world order

Once we remove the illusion of unanimous consent and accept the fact the within every political framework the imposition of some principles on some individuals is inevitable, the question of legitimacy may be left unsolved, but a global state can no longer be ruled out due to the lack of agreement.

If unanimous consent can no longer be used to justify a political arrangement, the justice of the arrangement might serve as a source of legitimization. However, some fear that a global state that may be formed will necessarily be an unjust one. This is one of Thomas Pogge's concerns; a global state, he argues, will necessarily reflect the existing, unjust, distribution of power. Statesmen and citizens will then be left 'without a moral reason for wanting their state to support this order, which is seen as merely the crystallization of the momentary balance of power' (Pogge 1988: 128). This again, is a deficiency shared by all forms of social contracts, which could either take the actual distribution of powers as their starting point, thus perpetuating existing injustice and inequalities but making the agreement truly advantageous to all parties, or rather start from a moral ideal – that of the equality of all parties – thus making the contract advantageous for the weak parties and risking the compliance of the stronger ones. It could then be claimed that a just social agreement – whether national or international – cannot be achieved, as the strong parties will not join an agreement which will force them to surrender some of their powers, even if they have contrived this power unjustly. An unjust agreement could, however, be achieved, as the weak parties might join an agreement which improves their condition but leaves them in an inferior position.[15] As only an unjust agreement could be reached, it is better not to reach one at all.

This conclusion should not surprise us; it is inherent in the attempt to ground social contract in self-interest alone. Once moral motivations are introduced, the situation changes, as we have no reason to assume that the strong parties will be less motivated by moral arguments than the weak ones. This is especially true in a world in which the hegemony is a liberal state. What sort of arrangements between such a hegemony and all other parties are plausible and justified?[16] Lea Brilmayer looks at four kinds of consent, each allowing the actual will of states to play a less important role than the previous one:

1   *Actual contemporaneous consent* is the least problematic type of consent as it reflects the actual will of the states involved.
2   *Actual* ex ante *consent* is 'also highly dependent on consent because the existence of norms depends on prior agreement by the states' (Brilmayer 1996: 154). And yet it is less deferential to the autonomy of weak states because the are bound by pre-existing norms, many of which have been laid down by the hegemony itself is bound by the norms it enforces.
3   *Hypothetical consent* is more problematic, as it is based not on what actual states want but on what reasonable states, placed in their position, would hypothetically consent to.
4   The theory least attentive to the actual preferences of states is that which is based on substantive morality. According to this approach, what matters is moral correctness, not state's will.

If the actual will of the states involved is the criterion according to which an agreement should be evaluated, then agreements grounded in contemporaneous consent are the most defensible ones; if the normative content of the agreement is what counts, then substantive morality is the theory to follow.

Brilmayer rightly points to a possible combination between the different kinds of consent: one should follow actual consent when the agreement does not violate basic moral standards, and give priority to moral considerations when such issues are at stake. This suggests that exchanges of commodities and services should be based on contemporaneous consent or *ex ante* consent, reflecting, as closely as possible, the will of the parties to the agreement, while questions of human rights cannot be decided this way.[17]

We can conceive, then, of a global state which imposes a thin layer of human rights and leaves a wide range of autonomy to the different groups to govern their own lives and coordinate a wide range of exchanges between themselves. Such a state will intervene in the autonomy of groups only in order to stop oppression and protect human rights.

The need to intervene in the life of a community in order to protect human rights is not peculiar to the international scene; it can also occur within state borders. After all, the intensity of a clash of cultures does not depend on the size of the cultural groups involved.

One may therefore conclude than no actual political framework can draw its legitimacy from the unanimous consent of the governed. A measure of coercion cannot be avoided. Coercion must, however, be restricted to normative issues only; all other issues must be decided on the basis of consent. In this respect, there is no escape from imposing one normative view on all participants. This is as much true within each state as it is in the international arena.

The need to balance the rights of individuals versus the right of a community to retain its identity and traditions raises a whole set of difficult issues which I cannot possibly discuss here. It is, however, a feature of the disproportionate importance attributed to the state that intervention that violates state sovereignty is seen as much more problematic morally than intervention in the affairs of national and local communities.

Note however that the moral reasons for non-intervention are grounded in the autonomy of individuals and their right to retain their traditions, and are independent of the institutional framework within which these rights are implemented. Hence, there seems to be little reason to prefer the autonomy of states over that of individuals or local communities. Giving priority to the autonomy of states raises not only theoretical problems but also political ones. By giving undue priorities to the autonomy of states, one privileges members of cultural communities who managed to establish a state of their own. This attitude creates a situation whereby members of such communities cannot protect their interests, lest they establish a state of their own – a reality that unnecessarily intensifies national struggles.

Walzer disagrees with the position offered here: the existence of 'oppressive communities, 'islands of tyranny in a sea of indifference,' is preferable to the centralized tyranny (of a world state) that would be necessary to end oppression' (1997: 106). But why assume that only a tyrannical global state will be able to end oppression within its member states? And if this conclusion can be theoretically and politically supported, why not assume that only tyrannical states can intervene in the lives of their communities in order to end intracommunal oppression? Must we then reach the para-doxical conclusion that only tyrannical states can protect their members' rights and defend them from oppression? There is no escape but to conclude that this whole line of argument is misleading.

Who needs a global state?

One must admit, then, to a certain measure of hypocrisy embedded in claims made against the idea of a global state in the name of the reluc-tance to impose a thin moral agreement on dissenters, be they states or communities. Liberal states regularly pursue such measures. Through inter-national covenants and treaties as well as by means of economic and political sanctions, the present international community also imposes moral standards, but it does so in a process in which influence is one-sided. If a global state were to be established, there is a better chance that influence will flow both ways. The establishment of such a state may then result in a democratic gain.

The establishment of a global state can also lead to a gain in the enforce-ment of law and order. As Pogge (1988) rightly claims, the present disregard and cynicism about international law may be attributed to the weakness of existing international mechanisms of adjudication and enforcement. As long as international laws and treaties are rarely enforced, he admits, governments are tempted to violate, abrogate, or reinterpret the laws and treaties so as to serve their interests. This behavior, in turn, influences the behavior of even those governments that are strongly committed to the ideal of a law-governed world order, as no government is ready to sacri-fice its interests unilaterally.

Furthermore, in the absence of a global state, intervention to reduce persecution and suffering is less likely to occur. International tolerance has its limits and humanitarian intervention is morally and legally allowed, Walzer argues, but the requirement is an imperfect duty he adds, 'which is to say, no one's duty in particular, so in fact the brutalities and oppres-sion of international society are more often denounced than interdicted' (1997: 107). Would it not be better, then, if we had international author-ities authorized, or even obliged, to intervene in such cases? Would not the future of the citizens of the former Yugoslavia or the citizens of Rwanda be better if decisions concerning intervention had been easier to make and implement.

Protecting human lives and defending human rights might be the most important moral role of a global state, but it is certainly not the only one. Pogge (1988) enumerates four justifications for transcending the bound-aries of existing states: preserving peace and security, reducing oppression, advancing global economic justice, and lessening ecological damages. Due to limitations of space, I cannot follow his argument step by step and demonstrate that in each of these spheres regionalism, rather than globalism, will enhance insecurity and inequality. A new world order which would stop short of a global state might lead to the formation of some very powerful trans-state alliances in Europe, North America and Southeast Asia and some very poor ones in Africa, Southeast Asia, Eastern Europe and South America. Those in greatest need will then have to face conglomerates of wealthy states which have no interest in sharing their fortune with the weak and needy. Consequently, social gaps will grow larger and more dangerous. Left to cope with unmanageable problems, such as starvation, disease, illiteracy, and unemployment, the less well-off states are doomed to failure; these problems may lead to massive destabilization of these states and unmanageable waves of immigration. There is a danger, then, 'of regional "blocs" becoming a platform for new forms of exclusive nationalism, which undermine globalization and lay basis for conflict' (Cable 1995: 42). It thus appears that if the transcendence of state boundaries is necessary, as indeed it is, moral and practical considerations would oblige us not to stop short of a global state.

So why is the idea of a global state alarming rather than appealing? One of the main reasons is the fear that such a state will obliterate the possibility of exit. This argument overemphasizes the importance of the ability to exit other social, cultural communities. There is no reason to assume that this emphasis is justified. While states have much more elaborate means of oppression, small scale communities also have ways of exerting pressure which can be devastating. Who can weigh which kind of oppression is more destructive?

A second reason why the idea of a global state seems alarming is the fear that such a state might concentrate too much power. The division of power between sovereign states, so it is argued, safeguards us from global tyranny, 'just as a domestic division of powers safeguards us from lesser tyrannies' (O'Neil 1992: 2). The opposite argument can, however, also be made: the fear of tyranny is more real in the present world order in which militarily strong and economically affluent states unilaterally influence the future of smaller, less potent states. The establishment of a global state might consolidate such influences, but it will also open channels of influence for weaker states, stateless nations, and individuals united in non-governmental organizations. In this sense, a democratic global state will reduce the risk of tyranny, open new political channels, new modes of influence and participation and will vitalize the political discourse, rather than annihilate it.

A democratic global state would aspire to delegate as much authority as possible to smaller units. It would want to allow cultural groups to preserve their uniqueness, voluntary associations to pursue their interests, religious groups to practice their religion, neighborhoods to determine their specific character, and the like. It would also aspire that political, economic or ecological problems which could be solved at lower levels will be dealt with at these levels. Hence, a global state can foster at once both centralization and decentralization.

The fact that authority is decentralized, that some governmental agencies, local organizations, or even federated states are sovereign in certain respects does not imply that there is no sovereign. It is a mistake to identify absolute sovereignty with centralized government. The amount of decisions that emanate from the political center reveals the degree of decentralization, not the extent of 'absoluteness' of the sovereign.

In fact, the main role of an absolute global authority would be to decide which policy should be determined at what level and by what authoritative bodies. Some authority must do the weighing and allocate decisions to the most suitable institutions. Such decisions are not permanent ones; as Pogge rightly acknowledges, 'nothing definite can be said about the ideal number of levels or the exact distribution of legislative, executive and judicial functions over them. These matters might vary in space and time, depending on the prevailing empirical facts' (1992: 69). If we are to avoid permanent conflicts over the allocation of authority, some superior power should have the authority to take such decisions and enforce them.

One might object that such a functionalist vision contradicts nationalist aspirations. I beg to differ. Even if a global state were ever to be formed, it is likely to be divided into a plurality of national units. Emphasizing a thin layer of common values need not undermine the desire to retain national distinctiveness. As Plamenatz (1967) rightly argued, national feelings are intensified when several nations, sharing the same values and the same perceptions of progress, become aware of their cultural uniqueness and attempt to preserve it.

The ability to preserve and renew national identities need not be hampered by institutional unification. In a global state, minorities would feel less marginalized and deprived than in a national framework, as the traditional concepts of 'majority' and 'minority' will no longer apply. A global state will be genuinely multinational. In such a multinational framework, national minorities will not have to secede from existing nation–states in order to protect their rights; they will be equal partners in a global political, economic, and strategic system. Their size and location will be of little importance. Moreover, the formation of a global state may allow for the formation of international institutions which will grant national groups political status and means of self-representation. Note that in the present world order, only states have recognized political standing. Any change in global order should find a way to secure the equal standing of stateless nations. This implies an institutional dissociation of states and nations.

The basic idea behind the concept of liberal nationalism, which I have developed elsewhere (Tamir 1993), is that there is no sense in replacing the nation–state by a new type of alliance between states and nations, as suggested by supporters of civic nationalism; too much misery and insecurity have been instigated by the attempt to fuse the two. We need to free these two social structures from each other and allow states to join the process of globalization without fearing that this will force their citizens to assimilate into a shallow global culture, and we must allow nations to struggle to retain their identity without fearing that this will force on them economic, strategic or political isolation.

States are becoming increasingly hollow, or defective, institutions.

> To outward appearances unchanged, the inner core of their authority in society and over economic transactions within their defined territorial borders is seriously impaired. They are like old trees, hollow in the middle, showing signs of weakness and vulnerability to storm, drought, or disease, yet continuing to grow leaves, new shoot and branches.
>
> (Strange 1994: 57)

In the twenty-first century, states are going to grow even weaker. No state will be able to be autonomous, and only trans-national organizations will be able to allow their members the security and well-being they aspire to achieve. If we must transcend both the state and the nation, we ought to construct new political forms, why exclude the possibility of forming a global state?

I do not claim that the idea of a global state is faultless or feasible, but think it should be taken more seriously than ever before. True, it embodies as many dangers as hopes, but this is a feature of all known political arrangements. We should not look then for perfect solutions, but for better ones. There is no better way to end this chapter but to quote the words of C. Day Lewis (1992: 335):

> It is the logic of our times
> No subject of immortal verse
> That those who lived by honest dreams
> Defend the bad against the worst.

Acknowledgements

This chapter was written while I was a visiting scholar at the Center for Jewish Political Thought of the Shalom Hartman Institute for Advanced Judaic Studies in Jerusalem. I wish to thank the Institute and especially its director, Prof. David Hartman for the generous support. Menachem Lorberbaum and Susan Neiman were kind enough to dedicate time to discuss the issues of this chapter with me time and again. I am deeply appreciative of their help and support. My greatest debt though is to Lili Galili; without her help, support and common sense, this chapter would not have been written.

Notes

1 The analysis depends on a cultural historical interpretation of the term 'nation', which dissociates it from the state. I have developed this interpretation in Tamir (1993: Chapters 2 and 3).

2 I am well aware of the fact that we have grown accustomed to thinking that nationalism justifies comprehensive sovereignty, a habit which has been reinforced by the use of the term 'national' to define the activities of states; for example we use terms such as 'national health service', or 'national resources', in order to define that which belongs to the state and is administrated by its institutions. This creates the false impression that national justifications can account for state ownership of these services and goods. The truth of the matter is that the term 'nation' is used here as a synonym of state in a way that has little to do with nationalist ideas. I have discussed some of these issues in greater detail in Tamir (1993: Chapter 3).

3 The emphasis is mine.

4 I have discussed this issue in greater detail in Liberal Nationalism, Chapter 3; see also Margalit and Raz (1990).

5 This is also the inevitable conclusion of Nozick's justification for the establishment of sovereign states in *Anarchy, State and Utopia* (1989).

6 This claim does not apply to Hobbes's theory, as it draws on the need to protect only one kind of interest: that of self-preservation.

7 Note that the term 'realism' is used in very different ways in moral philosophy, international relations and common language. In philosophy realism is the doctrine that universals exist outside the mind (as opposed to nominalism), or the objects of sense perception are real in their own right, existing independently of their being known. In international theory, the term refers to the Hobbesian state of nature which dooms states to remain in the state of nature. In common language the term is used to denote a preoccupation with reality as opposed to idealistic, speculative or sentimental attitudes. In this section I use the third meaning of the term realism.

8 This might be a result of the division of labor between political science, which deals with institutions, and political theory, which deals with theories of right and justice.

9 As in other theoretical spheres, in the case of political theory, the relation between facts and values is rather complex: 'Though we do not logically derive our values from what we know (or think we know) about ourselves and our social environment, we do change them as we change our minds about the facts' (Hampshire 1989: 58).

10 One reason nationalism was an attractive theory for liberal and democratic states to endorse was the fact that it allowed states to pretend that they are natural.

11 See, for example, Cohen's discussion of this issue (1984: 322).

12 Should we accept Mill's claim that liberal doctrines are meant to apply

> only to human beings in the maturity of their faculties. We are not speaking of . . . those who are still in a state to require being taken care of by others, must be protected against their own actions as well as against external injury. For the same reason, we may leave out of consideration those back-

ward states of society in which the race itself may be considered as in its
non-age.

(Mill 1975: 15)

13 This suggests that the criterion of reciprocity, implying that the parties must
enter the agreement as free and equal and not as dominated or manipulated,
or under the pressure of an inferior political or social position, is therefore
compromised.

14 A compromise between liberal and illiberal cultures which is based on respect
for human rights must be grounded in a *rights-based* liberalism which takes the
rights of individuals to be paramount, without conceiving of those rights as
grounded in autonomy entitlement and choice prerogatives. Hence it can express
not only toleration but also respect for decent illiberal cultures which do not
foster the ideal of personal autonomy, but which do respect their members'
rights and allow them some means of participation and social influence. On this
view, respect for illiberal, reasonable communities which are valued by their
members, even if they fail to provide (or even prevent) the chance to develop
autonomous lives, is derived from respect for the right of individuals to live
according to their values, traditions and preferences, as long as they do not
involve harm to others.

15 Nash has convincingly shown that in the process of negotiations it would be
rational for weak parties to surrender some of their interests in order to achieve
an agreement, if that agreement improves their conditions. See Barry (1989:
12–24).

16 Note that if the obligation to respect agreements is necessarily undermined by
the inequality of the negotiating parties, then there is a reason to discard most
actual agreements among states as well as among individuals.

17 This is somewhat of an untidy compromise, as trade relations and human rights
are not wholly separated, but untidy compromises are all one can aspire for in
the real world.

Bibliography

Ackerman, B. A. (1980) *Social Justice in a Liberal State*, New Haven, CN: Yale University Press.

Agnew, J. A. and Corbridge, S. (1995) *Mastering Space: Hegemony, Territory, and International Political Economy*, London: Routledge.

Ahmed, I. (1996) *State, Nation and Ethnicity in Contemporary South Asia*, London: Frances Pinter.

Al-Azm, S. (1993) 'Islamic fundamentalism reconsidered: a critical outline of problems, ideas and approaches, part I', *South Asia Bulletin* 13, 1+2: 93–121.

Anderson, B. (1983) *Imagined Communities: Reflections on the Origins and Spread of Nationalism*, London: Verso.

Anderson, B. (1991) *Imagined Communities: Reflections on the Origins and Spread of Nationalism* (revised and extended edition), London: Verso.

Anderson, P. (1997) 'Under the sign of the interim', in P. Gowan and P. Anderson (eds) *The Question of Europe*, London: Verso.

Ангелов, В. (1997a) 'Малко ивестии и иеивестни протестни документи за денационализаторската политика на БРП(к) в Пиринса Македония' (1946–48г) [Little known and unknown documents protesting against the policy of denationalization of the Bulgarian Workers Party (Communists) in Pirin Macedonia (1946–1948)] *Минало. Тримесечно списание за историа*, 4, 1, pp. 59–76.

Ангелов, В. (1997b) 'Решенията на X разширен пленум на ЦК на БРП(к) по македонския въпрос от 9–10. VIII. 1946 г'. [Resolutions of the Tenth Broad Plenary Session of the Central Committee of the Bulgarian Workers Party (Communists) on the Macedonian question, 9–10. VIII 1946] *Минало. Тримесечно списание за историа*, 4, 3–4, pp. 67–83.

Anonymous. (1971) 'USSR and the politics of Polish anti-Semitism 1956 69', *Soviet Jewish Affairs* 1, 1: 19–39.

Appadurai, A. (1996a) *Modernity at Large: Cultural Dimensions of Globalization*, Minneapolis, MN: University of Minnesota Press.

Appadurai, A. (1996b) 'Sovereignty without territoriality', in P. Yeager (ed.) *The Geography of Identity*, Ann Arbor, MI: University of Michigan Press, pp. 40–58.

Appadurai, A. (1998a) 'Dead certainty: ethnic violence in the era of globalization', *Public Culture*, 10, 2, pp. 225–47.

Appadurai, A. (1998b) 'Full attachment' *Public Culture* 10, 2: 443–50.

Arendt, H. (1967) *The Origins of Totalitarianism*, rev. edn, London: George Allen & Unwin.

Audard, C. (1996) 'Political liberalism, secular republicanism: two answers to the challenges of pluralism', in D. Archard (ed.) *Philosophy and Pluralism*, Cambridge: Cambridge University Press, pp. 163–76.

Balibar, E. (1991) 'The nation form: history and ideology' in E. Balibar and I. Wallerstein (eds) *Race, Nation, Class*, London: Verso, pp. 86–106.

Banuazizi, A. and Weiner, M. (eds) (1994) *The New Geopolitics of Central Asia and its Borderlands*, London: I.B. Taurus.

Barry, B. (1989) *Theories of Justice*, London: Harvester Wheatsheaf.

Barry, B. (1991) *Essays in Political Theory, Vol.1 Democracy and Power*, Oxford: Clarendon Press.

Barry, B. (1992) 'The quest for consistency: a skeptical view', in B. B. and R. Goodin (eds) *Free Movement: Ethical Issues in the Transnational Migration of People and of Money*, University Park, PA: The Pennsylvania State University Press, pp. 279–87.

Barth, F. (1959) *Political Leadership among Swat Pathans*, London School of Economics Monographs No. 19 London: The Athlone Press.

Barth, F. (1969) 'Introduction', in F. Barth (ed.) *Ethnic Groups and Boundaries*, Oslo: Universitetsforlaget.

Barth, F. (1975) *Ritual and Knowledge among the Baktaman of New Guinea*, Oslo: Universitetsforlaget.

Barth, F. (1985) *The Last Wali of Swat*, Oslo: Universitetsforlaget.

Bartosz, A. (1994) *Nie bój się Cygana* [Don't be afraid of a gypsy], Sejny: Pogranicze.

Basch, L., Glick Schiller, N. and Szanton Blanc, C. (1994) *Nations Unbound: Transnational Projects, Postcolonial Predicaments and Deterritorialized Nation–states*, Amsterdam: Gordon and Breach Publishers.

Bauböck, R. (1994) *Transnational Citizenship: Membership and Rights in International Migration*, Aldershot: Edward Elgar.

Bauböck, R. (2000) 'Why stay together? A pluralistic approach to secession and federation', in W. Kymlicka and W. Norman (eds) *Citizenship in Diverse Societies*, Oxford: Oxford University Press, pp. 366–94.

Beitz, C. (1979) *Political Theory and International Relations*, Princeton, NJ: Princeton University Press.

Bełdzikowski, R. (1994) 'Żydowskie dylematy ná Dolnym Śląsku w 1956 r' [The Jewish dilemmas in Lower Silesia in 1956], *Słowo Żydowskie* 3, 7: 10–23.

Beran, H. (1984) 'A liberal theory of secession', *Political Studies* 32: 21–31.

Beran, H. (1988) 'More theory of secession: a response to Birch', *Political Studies* 36: 316–23.

Bereciartu, G. J. (1994) *Decline of the Nation–state*, Reno, NV: University of Nevada Press.

Berkok, I. (1958) *Tarihte Kafkasya*, Istanbul: Istanbul Matbaasi.

Bernier, O. (1989) *Words of Fire, Deeds of Blood: The Mob, the Monarchy, and the French Revolution*, Boston, MA: Little, Brown.

Billig, M. (1995) *Banal Nationalism*, London: Sage.

Blanch, L. (1960) *The Sabres of Paradise*, New York: The Viking Press.

Boeckenfoerde, E. W. (1995) 'Die Nation: Identität in Differenz', *Universitas* 50: 974.

Borkowski, J. (1974) 'O społeczeństwie Drugiej Rzeczypospolitej' [On the society of the Second Republic]. *Przegląd Humanistyczny* 18, 7: 107–35.

Bourne, K. (1970) *The Foreign Policy of Victorian England, 1830–1902*, Oxford: Clarendon Press.

Breuilly, J. (1993) *Nationalism and the State*, 2nd edn, Manchester: Manchester University Press.

Brilmayer, L. (1991) 'Secession and self-determination: a territorial interpretation', *Yale Journal of International Law* 16: 177–202.

Brilmayer, L. (1996) *American Hegemony*, New Haven, CT: Yale University Press.

Brown, M. (1993) 'Causes and implications of ethnic conflict', in M. E. Brown (ed.) *Ethnic Conflict and International Security*, Princeton, NJ: Princeton University Press: 3–26.

Brubaker, W. Rogers (1996) *Nationalism Reframed: Nationhood and the National Question in the New Europe*, Cambridge: Cambridge University Press.

Buchanan, A. (1991) *Secession: The Morality of Political Divorce from Fort Sumter to Lithuania and Quebec*, Boulder, CO: Westview Press.

Buchanan, A. (1997a) 'Theories of secession', *Philosophy and Public Affairs* 26, 1: 31–61.

Buchanan, A. (1997b) 'Self-determination, secession, and the rule of law', in R. McKim and J. McMahan (eds) *The Morality of Nationalism*, Oxford: Oxford University Press: 301–32.

Bull, H. (1997) *The Anarchical Society*, London: Macmillan.

Bunce, V. (1985) 'The empire strikes back: the evolution of the eastern bloc from a Soviet asset to a Soviet liability', *International Organization* 39: 1–46.

Cable, V. (1995) 'The diminished nation–state: a study in the loss of economic power', *Daedalus: What Future for the State?* 124, 2: 23–53.

Canovan, M. (1996) 'The skeleton in the cupboard: nationhood, patriotism and limited loyalties', in S. Caney, D. George and P. Jones (eds) *National Rights, International Obligations*, Boulder, CO: Westview Press, pp. 69–85.

Carens, J. (ed.) (1995) *Is Quebec Nationalism Just? Perspectives from Anglophone Canada*, Montreal: McGill-Queen's University Press.

Cartabia, M. (1995) 'Cittadinanza Europea', in *Enciclopedia Giuridica*, Rome: Istituto della Enciclopedia Italiana.

Černy, B., Křen, V., Jan, K. and Otáhal, M. (eds) (1990) *Češi Němci odsun. Diskuse nezávislých historiků* [Czechs, Germans, expulsion: a debate of independent historians], Prague: Academia.

Češi a Němci historická tabu. Tschechen und Deutsche historische Tabus (1995) Prague: Nadace Bernarda Bolzana, Ackermann-Gemeinde.

Chatterjee, P. (1993) *The Nation and Its Fragments: Colonial and Postcolonial Histories*, Princeton, NJ: Princeton University Press.

Chatterjee, P. (1986) *Nationalist Thought and the Colonial World: A Derivative Discourse?*, London: Zed Books.

Chwaszcza, C. (1998) 'Selbstbestimmung, Sezession und Souveräntität. Überlegungen zur normativen Bedeutung politischer Grenzen', in W. Kersting and C. Chwaszcza (eds) *Philosophie der Internationalen Beziehungen*, Frankfurt: Suhrkamp, pp. 467–501.

Clifford, J. (1994) 'Diasporas', *Cultural Anthropology* 9, 3: 302–38.

Closa, C. (1992) 'The concept of citizenship in the treaty on European union', *Common Market Law Review* 29, 6: 1137–69.

Closa, C. (1995) 'Citizenship of the union and nationality of the member states', *Common Market Law Review* 32, 2: 487–518.

Cohen, H. (1995) *Religion der Vernunft aus den Quellen Judentums*, 3rd edn, Wiesbaden: Fourier Verlag.

Cohen, M. (1984) 'Moral skepticism and international relations', *Philosophy and Public Affairs* 13: 299–346.

Colley, L. (1992) *Britons*, New Haven, CT: Yale University Press.

Commins, D. (1994) 'Hasan al-Banna', in A. Rehnema (ed.) *Pioneers of Islamic Revival*, London: Zed Books: 125–53.

Connolly, W. E. (1991) *Identity/Difference: Democratic Negotiations and Political Paradox*, Ithaca, NY: Cornell University Press.

Connor, W. (1990) 'When is a nation?', *Ethnic and Racial Studies* 13, 1: 92–104.

Curtin, D. (1993) 'The constitutional structure of the union: a Europe of bits and pieces', *Common Market Law Review* 30, 1: 17–69.

Чашуле, В. (ed.) (1970) *Од признавање до негирање (бугарски ставови за македонското прашање)* [From recognition to negation. Bulgarian sources on the Macedonian question]. Skopje: Kultura.

Dahrendorf, R. (1983) 'Reflection on social theory and political practice', in C. Lloyd (ed.) *Social Theory and Political Practice*, Oxford: Oxford University Press: 25–38.

Das, V. (1995) 'Communities as political actors', in *Critical Events: An Anthropological Prospective on Contemporary India*, Delhi: Oxford University Press: 84–117.

Day Lewis, C. (1992) 'Where are the war poets?', in Word All Over, in *The Complete Poems of C. Day Lewis*, London: Sinclair-Stevenson, pp. 335.

Дзюбина, С. (1995) *И стверди дило рук наших. Спогады.* Видавництво Укрїнськый Архів [And confirm the work of our hands. Reminiscences] Варшава: Видавництво Укрїнськый Архів.

De Certeau, M. (1984) *The Practice of Everyday Life*, Berkeley, CA: University of California Press.

de Swan, A. (1997), 'Widening circles of disidentification: on the psycho- and socio-genesis of the hatred of distant strangers. Reflections on Rwanda', *Theory, Culture and Society* 14, 2: 105–22.

De Witte, B. (1991) 'Community law and national constitutional values', *Legal Issues of European Integration* 1991/1: 1–22.

D'Oliveira, J. H. U. (1993) 'European citizenship: its meaning, its potential', in J. Monar, W. Ungerer and W. Wessels (eds) *The Maastricht Treaty on European Union*, Brussels: European Interuniversity Press: 81–106.

Downs, A. (1957) *An Economic Theory of Democracy*, New York: Harper & Row.

Doyle, M. W. (1983) 'Kant, liberal legacies and foreign affairs', *Philosophy and Public Affairs* 12: 205–35.

Doyle, M. W. (1986) 'Liberalism and world politics', *American Political Science Review* 80, 4: 1151–70.

Drakulic, S. (1993) *The Balkan Express: Fragments from the Other Side of the War*, New York: W. W. Norton.

Dworkin, R. (1976) *Taking Rights Seriously*, Cambridge, MA: Harvard University Press.

Dziubina, S. (1997) 'Jak dziady pod kościo[łem. Z księdzem mitratem Stefanem Dziubiną rozmawia Ireneusz Cieślik' [As beggars at church's steps: an interview with Rev. Stephen Dziubina] *Tygodnik Powszechny* 51, 2: 6–7.

The Economist (1990) 'The state of the nation state', 22 December, pp. 43–6.

Eisler, J. (1991) *Marzec 1968. Geneza. Przebieg. Konsekwencje* [March 1968. Origin. Course. Consequences] Warsaw: Państwowe Wydawnictwo Naukowe.

Etzioni, A. (1993) 'The evils of self-determination', *Foreign Policy* 89: 21–35.

Evans, A. (1995) 'Union citizenship and the equality principle', in E. Antola and A. Rosas (eds) *A Citizens' Europe: In Search of a New Order*, London: Sage, pp. 85–112.

Fearon, J. D. and Laitin, D. D. (1996) 'Explaining interethnic cooperation', *American Political Science Review* 90, 4: 715–34.

Feldman, A. (1991) *Formations of Violence: The Narrative of the Body and Political Terror in Northern Ireland*, Chicago: University of Chicago Press.

Ficowski, J. (1989) *Cyganie w Polsce: dzieje i obyczaje* [Gypsies in Poland: history and customs], Warsaw: Wydawnictwo Interpress.

Fitzgerald B. (1996) 'The future of belief', *First Things* 63: 23–7.

Fukuyama, F. (1989) 'The end of history?', *National Interest* Summer: 3–18.

Fuller, G. E. (1994) 'The new geopolitical order', in A. Banuazizi and M. Weiner (eds) *The New Geopolitics of Central Asia and its Borderlands*, London: I.B. Tauris: 19–43.

Garlicki, A. and Paczkowski, A. (eds) (1995) *Zaciskanie pętli. Tajne dokumenty dotyczące Czechosłowacji 1968 r.* [Tightening the loop: secret documents on Czechoslovakia in 1968] Warsaw: Wydawnictwo Sejmowe.

Gauthier, D. (1995) 'Breaking up: an essay on secession', *Canadian Journal of Philosophy* 24, 3: 357–72.

Geertz, C. (1963) 'The integrative revolution: primordial sentiments and civil politics in the new states', in C. Geertz (ed.) *Old Societies and New States*, New York: Free Press, pp. 105–57.

Gellner, E. (1983) *Nations and Nationalism*, Oxford: Blackwell.

Glover, J. (1997) 'Nations, identity, and conflict', in R. McKim and J. McMahan (eds) *The Morality of Nationalism*, Oxford: Oxford University Press, pp. 11–30.

Gluckman, M. (1965) *The Ideas in Barotse Jurisprudence*, New Haven, CT: Yale University Press.

Goldenberg, S. (1994) *Pride of Small Nations: The Caucasus and Post-Soviet Disorder*, London: Zed Books.

Goldgeier, J. and McFaul, M. (1992) 'A tale of two worlds: core and periphery in the post-Cold War era', *International Organization* 46, 1: 467–92.

Goldmann, K. (1994) *The Logic of Internationalism: Coercion and Accommodation*, London: Routledge.

Goldmann, K. (1997) 'Nationalism and internationalism in post-Cold War Europe', *European Journal of International Relations* 3, 3: 259–90.

Gotlieb, G. (1993) *Nation Against State: A New Approach to Ethnic Conflicts and the Decline of Sovereignty*, New York: Council of Foreign Relations Press.

Gowan, P. and Anderson, P. (eds) (1997) *The Question of Europe*, London: Verso.

Grabowska, A. (1996) 'Porządek na własnym podwórku' [Tidy our own backyard], *Rzeczpospolita* 15, 239 (12–13 X), 16.

Greenfeld, L. (1985) 'Nationalism and class struggle: two forces or one?', *Survey* 29, 3: 153–74.

Greenfeld, L. (1992) *Nationalism: Five Roads to Modernity*, Cambridge, MA: Harvard University Press.

Greenfeld, L. (1993) 'Nationalism and democracy: the nature of the relationship and the cases of England, France, and Russia', *Research in Democracy and Society* 1: 327–52.

Grey, T. (1980) 'The disintegration of property', in J. R. Pennock and J. W. Chapman (eds) *Property*, New York: New York University Press, pp. 69–85.

Grimm, D. (1995) 'Does Europe need a constitution?', *European Law Journal* 1, 3: 282–302.

Gross, J. (1992) (ed.) *Muslims in Central Asia*, Durham, NC: Duke University Press.

Gurr, T. R. (1996) 'Minorities, nationalists, and ethnopolitical conflict', in C. A. Crocker and F. O. Hampson (eds) *Managing Global Chaos: Sources and Responses to International Conflict*, Washington, DC: United States Institute for Peace Press, pp. 53–77.

Haas, E. B. (1997) *Nationalism, Liberalism and Progress*, vol. 1, Ithaca, NY: Cornell University Press.

Habermas, J. (1992) 'Citizenship and national identity', *Praxis International* 12, 1: 1–19.

Habermas, J. (1995) 'Comment on the paper by Dieter Grimm: does Europe need a constitution?', *European Law Journal* 1, 3: 303–29.

Habermas, J. (1996) *Die Einbeziehung des Anderen: Studien zur politischen Theorie*, Frankfurt: Suhrkamp.

Habermas, J. (1998) 'The European nation–state: on the future of sovereignty and citizenship', *Public Culture* 10, 2: 397–416.

Hallowell, A. I. (1955) 'The nature and function of property as a social institution', in A. I. Hallowell *Culture and Experience*, Philadelphia, PA: University of Pennsylvania Press: 236–49.

Hampshire, S. (1989) *Innocence Experience*, Cambridge, MA: Harvard University Press.

Hannerz, U. (1996) *Transnational Connections: Culture, People, Places*, London: Routledge.

Hannerz, U. and Löfgren, O. (eds) (1993) 'Defining the national', *Ethnos* 58: 3–4.

Hannerz, U. and Löfgren, O. (1994) 'The nation in the global village', *Cultural Studies* 8: 198–207.

Harbeson, J. W., Rothchild, D. and Chazan, N. (1994) (eds) *Civil Society and the State in Africa*, London: Lynne Rienner.

Hardin, R. (1995) *One for All: The Logic of Group Conflict*, Princeton, NJ: Princeton University Press.

Harvey, D. (1989) *The Condition of Postmodernity*, Oxford: Blackwell.

Heller, M. (1998) 'The tragedy of the anti-commons: property in the transition from Marx to markets', *Harvard Law Review* 111, 3: 621–88.

Heraclides, A. (1990) 'Secessionist minorities and external involvement', *International Organization* 44, 3: 341–78.

Heraclides, A. (1997) 'Ethnicity, secessionist conflict and the international society: towards a normative paradigm shift', *Nations and Nationalism*, 3, 4: 493–520.

Hesse, C. (1991) *Publishing and Cultural Politics in Revolutionary Paris, 1789–1810*, Berkeley, CA: University of California Press.

Hinsley, F. H. (1963) *Power and the Pursuit of Peace*, Cambridge: Cambridge University Press.

Hobbes, T. (1651/1962) *Leviathan*, ed. M. Oakeshott, London: Collier.

Hobbes, T. (1949) *Leviathan*, London: Everyman.

Hobsbawm, E. (1990) *Nations and Nationalism since 1780*, Cambridge: Cambridge University Press.

Hobsbawm, E. and Ranger, T. (eds) (1983) *The Invention of Tradition*, Cambridge: Cambridge University Press.

Hoffmann, S. (ed.) (1960) *Contemporary Theory in International Relations*, Englewood Cliffs, NJ: Prentice Hall.

Hoffmann, S. (1981) *Duties Beyond Borders: On the Limits and Possibilities of Ethical International Politics*, Syracuse, NY: Syracuse University Press.

Hoffmann, S. (1992) 'Delusions of world order', *New York Review of Books*, 9 April.

Hoffmann, S. (1995a) 'The crisis of liberal internationalism', *Foreign Policy* Spring: 159–77.

Hoffmann, S. (1995b) 'The politics and ethics of military intervention', *Survival*, Winter: 29–51.

Hoffmann, S. (1997) *The Ethics and Politics of Humanitarian Intervention*, Notre Dame, IN: Notre Dame University Press.

Holsti, K. J. (1992) 'Governance without government: polyarchy in nineteenth-century European international politics', in J. N. Rosenau and E.-O. Czempiel (eds) *Government without Governance: Order and Change in World Politics*, Cambridge: Cambridge University Press: 30–57.

Holsti, K. J. (1996) *The State, War, and the State of War*, Cambridge: Cambridge University Press.

Holsti, K. J. (1997) *The Political Sources of Humanitarian Emergencies*, Research for Action Monograph #36, Helsinki: United Nations University/World Institute for Economics Development Research.

Hooson, D. (1994) 'Ex-Soviet identities and the return of geography', in D. Hooson (ed.) *Geography and National Identity*, Oxford: Blackwell: 134–40.

Horowitz, D. L. (n.d.) (ed.) *Incentives and Behavior in the Ethnic Politics of Sri Lanka and Malaysia*, Durham, NC: Asian/Pacific Studies Institute, Duke University.

Horowitz, D. L. (1997) 'Self-determination: politics, philosophy, and law', in W. Kymlicka and I. Shapiro (eds) *Ethnicity and Group Rights*, New York: New York University Press, pp. 421–62.

Huntington, S. (1993) 'The clash of civilizations?', *Foreign Affairs* 72, 3: 22–49.

Huntington, S. P. (1996) *The Clash of Civilizations and the Remaking of World Order*, New York: Simon & Schuster.

Hurwic, J. (1996) *Wspomnienia i refleksje. Szkic autobiograficzny* [Reminiscences and thoughts. Autobiographical essays], Toruń: 'Comer'.

Ignatieff, M. (1993) *Blood and Belonging: Journeys into the New Nationalism*, Toronto: Penguin Books.

Ingram (1995) 'Separating state and nation', in *State and Nation, IUSEF No. 15*, Oslo: Scandinavian University Press: 33–52.

IOM, UNHCR and OSCE (1996) *CIS Conference on Refugees and Migrants*, Geneva: UNHCR Public Information Section.

Iskandar, F. (1983) *Sandro of Chegem*, New York: Vintage Books.

Kant, I. (1984) *Zum ewigen Frieden*, Stuttgart: Reclam Universal-Bibliothek.

Kaplan, R. D. (1994) 'The coming anarchy', *The Atlantic Monthly*, February: 44–76.

Kaplan, R. D. (1996) *The Ends of the Earth: A Journey at the Dawn of the 21st Century*, New York: Random House.

Karpat, K. (1972) 'Ottoman immigration policies and settlement in Palestine' in I. Abu-Lughod and B. Abu-Laban (eds) *Settler Regimes in Africa and the Arab World*, Wilmette, IL: Medina University Press International: 57–72.

Karpat, K. (1985) *Ottoman Population 1830–1914: Demographic and Social Characteristics*, Madison, WI: University of Wisconsin Press.

Karpat, K. (1990) 'The hijra from Russia and the Balkans: the process of self-definition in the late Ottoman state', in D. F. Eickelman and J. Piscatori (eds) *Muslim Travellers: Pilgrimage, Migration, and the Religious Imagination*, London: Routledge: 131–52.

Keohane, R. O. and Nye Jr., J. S. (1977) *Power and Interdependence: World Politics in Transition*, Boston, MA: Little, Brown.

Kersten, K. (1992) *Polacy Żydzi Komunizm. Anatomia półprawd 1939–68* [Poles, Jews, Communism: an anatomy of half-truths], Warsaw: Niezależna Oficyna Wydawnicza.

Kobylińska, E., Lawaty, A. and Stephan, R. (eds) (1992) *Deutsche und Polen. 100 Schlüsselbegriffe*, Munich: Piper.

Koessler, M. (1946) 'Subject, citizen, national, and permanent allegiance', *Yale Law Journal* 56: 58–76.

Koneczny, F. (1995) *Cywilizacja żydowska*, Warsaw: Wydawnictwo Ojczyzna.

Kornai, J. (1992) *The Socialist System*, Princeton, NJ: Princeton University Press.

Kościół Katolicki o swoich korzeniach (1995) [The Catholic Church about its roots], Warsaw: Polska Rada Chrześcijan i Żydów.

Kozik, Z. (1988) 'O wydarzeniach marcowych 1968 r' [On the March events of 1968], *Nowe Drogi*, 42, 2: 60–75.

Królikowski, P. (1993) 'Jewish culture, religion and history in the teaching and religious instruction of the Catholic Church in Poland', in *The Presentation of Jewish Religion, Culture and History in the New Educational Systems in Central Europe. Proceedings. Strategy Meeting 26–29 April 1993*, Weilrod: Martin Buber House: 15–38.

Krzepkowski, A. (1985) *Umierający i zmartwychwstali. Apokryf współczesny* [Dying and resurrected: a contemporary apocryph], Warsaw: Słowo.

Kymlicka, W. (1992) 'Review of James Buchanan (1991) Secession', *Political Theory* 20, 3: 527–32.

Kymlicka, W. (1995) *Multicultural Citizenship: A Liberal Theory of Minority Rights*, Oxford: Oxford University Press.

Ladeur, K.-H. (1997) 'Towards a legal theory of supranationality: the viability of the network concept', *European Law Journal* 3, 1: 33–54.

Lange, C. L. (1919) *Histoire de l'internationalisme*, Kristiania: Aschehoug.

Lee, S. (1997) 'Not a one-time event: environmental change, ethnic rivalry, and violent conflict in the Third World', *Journal of Environment and Development* 6, 4: 365–96.

Lesch, A. M. (1994) 'Prolonged conflict in the Sudan', in K. P. Magyar and C. P. Danopoulos (eds) *Prolonged Wars: A Post-Nuclear Challenge*, Boulder, CO: Air Force University Press, pp. 99–130.

Lévi-Strauss, C. (1976) *Structural Anthropology*, vol. 2, New York: Basic Books.

Linz, J. J. (1993) 'State building and nation building', *European Review* 1, 4: 355–69.

Locke, J. (1924) *Two Treatises of Civil Government*, London: Everyman's Library.

Lowie, R. (1928) 'Incorporeal property in primitive society', *Yale Law Journal* 37: 551–63.

Ludden, D. E. (1996) *Contesting the Nation: Religion, Community, and the Politics of Democracy in India*, Philadelphia, PA: University of Pennsylvania Press.

Lustick, I. (1993) *Unsettled States/Disputed Lands: Britain and Ireland, France and Algeria, Israel and the West Bank–Gaza*, Ithaca, NY: Cornell University Press.

McClure, K. (1996) *Judging Rights: Lockean Politics and the Limits of Consent*, Ithaca, NY: Cornell University Press.

MacCormick, D. N. (1993) 'Beyond the sovereign state', *Modern Law Review* 56, 1: 1–18.

MacCormick, D. N. (1995a) 'Sovereignty, democracy and subsidiarity', in R. Bellamy, V. Bufacchi and D. Castiglione (eds) *Democracy and Constitutional Culture in the Union of Europe*, London: Lothian Foundation: 95–104.

MacCormick, D. N. (1995b) 'The Maastricht-Urteil: sovereignty now', *European Law Journal* 1, 3: 259–66.

McKim, R. and McMahan, J. (eds) (1997) *The Morality of Nationalism*, Oxford: Oxford University Press.

Madajczyk, P. (1994) *Na drodze do pojednania. Wokół orędzia biskupów polskich do biskupów niemieckich z 1965 roku* [On the way towards reconciliation: on the message of Polish bishops to the German bishops of 1965], Warsaw: Wydawnictwo Naukowe PWN.

Malinowski, B. (1935) *Coral Gardens and Their Magic*, London: Allen & Unwin.

Malkki, L. (1992) 'National geographic: the rooting of peoples and the territorialization of national identity among scholars and refugees', *Cultural Anthropology* 7, 1: 22–44.

Margalit, A. and Raz, J. (1990) 'National self-determination', in J. Raz (1994) *Ethics in the Public Domain: Essays in the Morality of Law and Politics*, Oxford: Clarendon Press, pp. 125–45.

Marko, J. (1995) *Autonomie und Integration. Rechtsinstitute des Nationalitätenrechts im funktionalen Vergleich*, Vienna: Böhlau Verlag.

Masselos, J. (1994) 'The Bombay riots of January 1993: the politics of urban conflagration', *South Asia* 17: 70–95.

Mazrui, A. (1972) *Cultural Engineering and Nation-Building in East Africa*, Evanston, IL: Northwestern University Press.

Meehan, E. (1993) *Citizenship and the European Community*, London: Sage.

Meyer, J. W., Boli, J., Thomas, G. M. and Ramirez, F. O. (1997) 'World society and the nation–state', *American Journal of Sociology* 103: 144–81.

Migdal, J. (1988) *Strong States and Weak Societies: State-Society Relations and State Capabilities in the Third World*, Princeton, NJ: Princeton University Press.

Mill, J. S. (1972) *Utilitarianism, Liberty, Representative Government*, H. B. Acton (ed.), London: Everyman's Library.

Mill, J. S. (1975) *On Liberty. Representative Government. The Subjection of Women: Three Essays*, Oxford: Oxford University Press.

Miller, D. (1995) *On Nationality*, Oxford: Oxford University Press.

Miller, D. (1998) 'Secession and the principle of nationality', in M. Moore (ed.) *National Self-Determination and Secession*, Oxford: Oxford University Press: 62–78.

Minc, A. (1993) *Le Nouveau Moyen Age*, Paris: Gallimard.

Misiło, E. (1996) *Repatriacja czy deportacja. Przesiedlenie Ukraińców z Polski do USRR 1944–46. Tom 1. Dokumenty 1944–45* [Repatriation or deportation: displacement of Ukrainians from Poland to USSR 1944–46. Vol. 1. Documents 1944–45], Warsaw: Oficyna Wydawnicza Archiwum Ukraińskie.

Mitchell, R. P. (1969) *The Society of the Muslim Brothers*, London: Oxford University Press.

Moczulski, L. (1978–9) *Zarys historii PRL* [An outline of the history of the Polish People's Republic], Part 1, 2 Warsaw: Wydawnictwo Polskie.

Moore, M. (1997) 'On national self-determination', *Political Studies* 45: 900–13.

Mráček, P. K. (1995) *Příručka církevních dějin* Prague: Krystal.

Myers, F. (1989) 'Burning the truck and holding the country', in E. N. Wilmsen (ed.) *We Are Here: Politics of Aboriginal Land Tenure*, Berkeley, CA: University of California Press: 15–42.

Myrdal, G. (1957) *Rich Lands and Poor*, New York: Harper and Row.

Napiórkowski, S. C. (ed.) (1997) *A bliźniego swego ... Materiały z sympozjum 'Św. Makysymilian Maria Kolbe – Żydzi – Masoni'* [And your neighbour ... the papers from the symposium 'St Maximilian Maria Kolbe – Jews – Freemasons'], Lublin: Redakcja Wydawnictw Katolickiego Uniwersytetu Lubelskiego.

Nielsen, K. (1993) 'Secession: the case of Quebec', *Journal of Applied Philosophy*, 10: 29–43.

Norman, W. (1994) 'Towards a philosophy of federalism', in J. Baker (ed.) *Group Rights*, Toronto: University of Toronto Press: 79–100.

Norman, W. (1998) 'The ethics of secession as the regulation of secessionist politics', in M. Moore (ed.) *National Self-Determination and Secession*, Oxford: Oxford University Press, pp. 34–61.

Nozick, R. (1989) *Anarchy, State and Utopia*, New York: Basic Books.

Offe, C. (1985) *Disorganized Capitalism: Contemporary Transformations of Work and Politics*, Cambridge, MA: MIT Press.

O'Keeffe, D. O. (1993) 'Union citizenship', in D. O'Keeffe and P. Twomey (eds) *Legal Issues of the Maastricht Treaty*, London: Chancery Press: 87–107.

Olcott, M. B. (1995) 'Soviet nationality studies between past and future', in D. Orlovsky (ed.) *Beyond Soviet Studies*, Washington, DC: The Woodrow Wilson Center Press: 135–48.

O'Leary, S. (1984) 'Nationality and citizenship: a tale of two unhappy bedfellows', *Yearbook of European Law* 12: 353–84.

O'Leary S. (1996) *The Evolving Concept of European Citizenship*, London: Kluwer.

Olszewski, J. (1997) 'Skrajności są wszędzie. Jan Olszewski w rozmowie z Jarosławem Kurskim' [The extremes are everywhere: an interview with Jan Olszewski], *Gazeta Wyborcza* 9, 59, 12 III: 14–15.

O'Neil, O. (1992) 'Justice, gender and international boundaries', in R. Attfield and B. Wilkins (eds) *International Justice and the Third World: Studies in the Philosophy of Development*, London: Routledge, pp. 50–76.

Ortega Y Gasset, J. (1996) *El Hombre y la Gente*, Madrid: Allianza Editorial.

Østerud, Ø. (1997a) 'Nasjon', in Ø. Østerud, K. Goldmann and M. N. Pedersen (eds) *Statsvitenskapelig leksikon*, Oslo: Universitetsforlaget, pp. 169–70.

Østerud, Ø. (1997b) 'The narrow gate: entry to the club of sovereign states', *Review of International Studies* 23, 2: 167–84.

Padaonkar, D. (ed.) (1993) *When Bombay Burned*, New Delhi: UBS Publishers.

Pandey G. (ed.) (1993) *Hindus and Others: The Question of Identity in India*, New York: The Viking Press.

Pascal, R. (1967) *The German Sturm und Drang*, Manchester: Manchester University Press.

Patel, S. and Thorner, A. (eds) (1995) *Bombay: Metaphor for Modern India*, Bombay: Oxford University Press.

Philpott, D. (1995) 'In defense of self-determination', *Ethics* 105, 2: 352–85.

Plamenatz, J. (1967) 'The use of political theory', in A. Quinton (ed.) *Political Philosophy*, Oxford: Oxford University Press: 19–31.

Plamenatz, J. (1976) 'Two types of nationalism', in E. Kamenka (ed.) *Nationalism: The Nature and Evolution of an Idea*, London: Edward Arnold, pp. 22–36.

Podgórska, J. (1997) 'Toruń dla Polaków' [Toruń for Poles], *Polityka* 41, 17: 28, 30.

Pogge, T. (1988) *Realizing Rawls*, Ithaca, NY: Cornell University Press.

Pogge, T. (1992) 'Cosmopolitanism and sovereignty', *Ethics* 103, 1: 48–75.

Pogge, T. (1997) 'Group rights and ethnicity', in I. Shapiro and W. Kymlicka (eds) *Ethnicity and Group Rights*, New York: New York University Press: 187–221.

Poradowski, M. (1993) *Talmud czy Biblia? Gdzie są 'korzenie' Chrześcijaństwa: w judaizmie czy w mozaizmie? W Talmudzie czy w Biblii?* [Talmud or Bible? Where are the roots of Christianity: in Judaism or in Mosaic tradition? In the Talmud or in the Bible?], Warsaw: Oficyna Wydawnicza 'Fulmen'.

Preuss, U. K. (1995) 'Problems of a concept of European citizenship', *European Law Journal* 1, 3: 267–81.

Rahnema, A. (ed.) *Pioneers of Islamic Revival*, London: Zed Books.

Raina, P. (1994) *Kościół – Państwo w świetle akt Wydziałów do Spraw Wyznań 1967–68. Próby kontroli Kościoła. Wydarzenia marcowe. Interwencja sierpniowa w Czechosłowacji* [Church – State in the light of files of the Departments of Denomination 1967–8: Attempts at controlling the Church; The March events; August intervention in Czechoslovakia], Warsaw: Wydawnictwo Książka Polska.

Rawls, J. (1971) *A Theory of Justice*, Oxford: Oxford University Press.

Rawls, J. (1994) 'The law of peoples' in S. Shute and S. Hurley (eds) *On Human Rights*, New York: Basic Books, pp. 41–82.

Rawls, J. (1995) *Political Liberalism*, New York: Columbia University Press.

Renan, E. (1882/1947) 'Qu'est-ce qu'une nation?' in *Œuvres Complètes de Ernest Renan*, vol. 1, Paris: Calman-Lévy: 887–906.

Rex, J. (1985) *The Concept of a Multicultural Society. Occasional Papers in Ethnic Relations*, 3 Warwick: Centre for Research in Ethnic Relations.

Richardson, J. L. (1997) 'Contending liberalisms: past and present', *European Journal of International Relations* 3: 5–33.

Robertson, R. (1992) *Globalization*, London: Sage.

Rose, C. (1994) *Property and Persuasion: Essays on the History, Theory, and Rhetoric of Ownership*, Boulder, CO: Westview Press.

Rosenau, J. N. and Holsti, O. R. (1983) 'U.S. leadership in a shrinking world: The breakdown of consensus and the emergence of conflicting belief systems', *World Politics* 35, 3: 368–92.

Rothchild, D. (1997) *Managing Ethnic Conflict in Africa: Pressures and Incentives for Cooperation*, Washington, DC: Brookings Institution Press.

Rudawski, M. (1996) *Mój obcy kraj?* [My alien country?], Warsaw: Agencja Wydawnicza Tu.

Rummel, R. J. (1994) *Death by Government*, New Brunswick, NJ: Transaction Books.

Said, E. (1978) *Orientalism*, New York: Vintage Books.

Sampson, S. (1996) 'The social life of projects: importing civil society to Albania', in C. Hann and E. Dunn (eds) *Civil Society: Challenging Western Models*, London: Routledge: 121–42.

Sassen, S. (1991) *The Global City: New York, London, Tokyo*, Princeton, NJ: Princeton University Press.

Sayari, S. (1994) 'Turkey, the Caucasus and Central Asia', in A. Banuazizi and M. Weiner (eds) *The New Geopolitics of Central Asia and its Borderlands*, London: I. B. Taurus: 175–96.

Scharf, R. F. (1996) 'Cum ira et studio', in R. F. Scharf *Co mnie i tobie Polsko . . . Eseje bez uprzedzeń* [Poland, what have I to do with thee. Essays without prejudice], Kraków: Fundacja Judaica.

Schnapper, D. (1997) 'The European debate on citizenship', *Daedalus* 126, 3: 207–20.

Schumpeter, J. A. (1950) *Capitalism, Socialism and Democracy*, 3rd edn, New York: Harper Torchbooks.

Shami, S. (1995) 'Disjuncture in ethnicity: negotiating Circassian identity in Jordan, Turkey and the Caucasus', *New Perspectives on Turkey* 12: 79–95.

Shami, S. (1996) 'Transnationalism and refugee studies: rethinking forced migration and identity in the Middle East', *Journal of Refugee Studies* 9, 1: 3–26.

Shami, S. (1998) 'Circassian encounters: the self as other and the production of the homeland in the North Caucasus', *Development and Change* 29, 4: 617–46.

Shami, S. (1999) 'Islam in the Post-Soviet Space: Imaginative Geographies of the Caucasus and Central Asia', *Bulletin of the Royal Institute for Inter-Faith Studies*, 1, 1 (Spring): 181–95.

Shapiro, M. J. (1994) 'Moral geographies and the ethics of post-sovereignty', *Public Culture* 6, 3: 479–502.

Shaw, J. (1997) *Citizenship of the Union: Towards Post National Membership?*, Harvard Jean Monnet Working Paper 6/97 www.law.harvard.edu/Programs/Jean Monnet/

Shotter, J. (1993) 'Psychology and citizenship: identity and belonging', in J. S. Turner (ed.) *Citizenship and Social Theory*, London: Sage Publications: 115–38.

Sidgwick, H. (1897) *The Elements of Politics*, 2nd edn, London: Macmillan.

Singer, M. and Wildavsky, A. (1993) *The Real World Order: Zones of Peace/Zones of Conflict*, Chatham, NJ: Chatham House Publishers.

Sław, A. (1958) 'O rozwinięcie walki z przejawami nacjonalizmu' [For the development of a struggle against symptoms of nationalism], *Nowe Drogi* 12, 5: 28–39.

Śliwa, M. (1997) *Obcy czy swoi? Z dziejów poglądów na kwestię żydowską w Polsce w XIX i XX* [Aliens or our own? From the history of views on the Jewish question in Poland in the XIXth and XXth centuries], Kraków: Wydawnictwo Naukowe WSP.

Smith, A. D. (1986) *The Ethnic Origins of Nations*, Oxford: Blackwell.

Smith, A. D. (1992) 'National identity and the idea of European unity', *International Affairs* 68, 1: 55–76.

Smith, A. D. (1995) 'Gastronomy or geology? The role of nationalism in the reconstruction of nations', *Nations and Nationalism* 1, 1: 3–23.

Smith, M. J. (1986) *Realism from Weber to Kissinger*, New Orleans, LA: Louisiana State University Press.

Soledad G. (1993) (ed.) *European Identity and the Search for Legitimacy*, London: Pinter.

Staniszkis, J. (1991) '"Political Capitalism" in Poland', *East European Politics and Societies* 5 1: 127–41.

Stark, D. (1996) 'Recombinant property in East European capitalism', *American Journal of Sociology* 101, 4: 993–1027.

Stasiak, A. (1975) 'Społeczeństwo Polski międzywojennej' [Society of inter-war Poland], *Ideologia i Polityka* 6, 1: 112–6.

Stasiński, M. (1997) 'Jak Polak z Ukraińcem' [As a Pole with an Ukrainian], *Gazeta Wyborcza* 9, 94, 22 IV: 12–14.

Staszewski, W. (1996) 'Stronniczy przegląd prasy' [The biased review of the press], *Gazeta Wyborcza* 8, 298, 23 XII, pp. 2.

Steiner, H. (1995) 'Liberalism and nationalism', *Analyse und Kritik* 17, 1: 12–20.

Strange, S. (1995) 'The defective state', *Daedalus: What Future for the State?* 124, 2: 55–74.

Suny, R. B. (1995) 'Rethinking Soviet studies: bringing the non-Russians back in', in D. Orlovsky (ed.) *Beyond Soviet Studies*, Washington DC: The Woodrow Wilson Center Press, pp. 105–34.

Szporluk, R. (1994) (ed.) *National Identity and Ethnicity in Russia and the New States of Eurasia*, Armonk, NY: M. E. Sharpe.

Talmon, J. L. (1991) *Myth of the Nation and Vision of Revolution*, New Brunswick, NJ: Transaction.

Tamir, T. (1993) *Liberal Nationalism*, Princeton, NJ: Princeton University Press.

Teague, E. (1994) 'Center-periphery relations in the Russian federation', in R. Szporluk (ed.) *National Identity and Ethnicity in Russia and the New States of Eurasia*, Armonk, NY: M. E. Sharpe, pp. 21–57.

Tomaszewski, J. (1975) 'W sprawie położenia materialnego Żydów polskich w latach 1918–1939' [On the economic situation of the Polish Jews, 1918–39], *Biuletyn Żydowskiego Instytutu Historycznego* 27, 2: 93–101.

Tomaszewski, J. (1992) 'Studia nad najnowszą historią Białorusinów w Polsce' [Studies on the contemporary history of Beloruses in Poland], in *Polska – Polacy – mniejszości narodowe* [Poland – Poles – national minorities], Wrocław: Zakład Narodowy im. Ossolińskich Wydawnictwo, pp. 225–31.

Tomaszewski, J. (1996) 'O tym, co w Polsce jest dozwolone' [What is allowed in Poland], *Słowo Żydowskie* 5, 18: 18.

Tomaszewski, J. (1997) 'Bić Żydów!' [Beat the Jews!], *Słowo Żydowskie* 6, 18: 16.

Urban, T. (1994) *Niemcy w Polsce. Historia mniejszości w XX wieku* [Germans in Poland: a history of a minority in the XXth century], Opole: Wydawnictwo Instytut Śląski Sp. z o.o.

Van der Veer, P. (1994) *Religious Nationalism: Hindus and Muslims in India*, Berkeley, CA: University of California Press.

Verdery, K. (1991) *National Ideology under Socialism: Identity and Cultural Politics in Ceaucescu's Romania*, Berkeley, CA: University of California Press.

Verdery, K. (1996) *What Was Socialism, and What Comes Next?*, Princeton, NJ: Princeton University Press.

Walzer, M. (1977) *Just and Unjust Wars*, New York: Basic Books.

Walzer, M. (1994) *Thick and Thin: Moral Argument at Home and Abroad*, Notre Dame, IN: Notre Dame University Press.

Walzer, M. (1997) 'Responses to Kukathas', in I. Shapiro and W. Kymlicka (eds) *Ethnicity and Group Rights*, New York: New York University Press, pp. 105–11.

Weiner, A. (1992) *Inalienable Possessions: The Paradox of Keeping-While-Giving*, Berkeley, CA: University of California Press.

Wellman, C. H. (1995) 'A defense of secession and political self-determination', *Philosophy and Public Affairs* 24, 2: 142–71.

Wells, C. (1995) *Law and Citizenship in Early Modern France*, Baltimore, MD: Johns Hopkins University Press.

Werblan, A. (1968) 'Przyczynek do genezy konfliktu' [A contribution to the origin of the conflict], *Miesięcznik Literacki* 3, 6: 61–71.

Westin, C. (1998) 'Temporal and spatial aspects of multiculturality: reflections on the blurred boundaries of multicultural societies', in R. Bauböck and J. Rundell (eds) *Blurred Boundaries: Migration, Ethnicity, Citizenship*, Aldershot: Ashgate.

Wikan, U. (1980) *Life Among the Poor in Cairo*, London: Tavistock.

Wikan, U. (1997) *Tomorrow, God Willing*, Chicago: University of Chicago Press.

Wilczak, J. (1996) 'Przemyśl: była kopuła – została dziura' [Przemyśl: there was a dome – remained a hole], *Polityka* 40, 49: 30–2.

Woodward, S. (1995) *The Balkan Tragedy: Chaos and Dissolution After the Cold War*, Washington, DC: The Brookings Institution.

Wrona, Z. (1991) 'Kościół wobec pogromu Żydów w Kielcach w 1946 roku' [The Church's attitude towards the pogrom of Jews in Kielce in 1946], in *Pamiętnik Świętokrzyski. Studia z dziejów kultury chrześcijańskiej. Praca zbiorowa* [Memorial book of Święty Krzyż. Studies on the history of the Christian culture. Collective work], Kielce: Kieleckie Towarzystwo Naukowe: 281–303.

Yeager, P. (ed.) (1996) *The Geography of Identity*, Ann Arbor, MI: University of Michigan Press.

Yenal, D. H. (1998) 'Globalization from below: the transnational market between Turkey and the CIS and Istanbul's role as a node', paper presented to the American Anthropological Association's Annual Meeting, Philadelphia, December 1998.

Żarnowski, J. (1973) *Społeczeństwo Drugiej Rzeczypospolitej 1918–1939* [Society of the Second Republic 1918–1939] Warsaw: Państwowe Wydawnictwo Naukowe.

Żarnowski, J. (1977) 'W sprawie książki Społeczeństwo Drugiej Rzeczypospolitej' [On the Book Society of the Second Republic], *Historyczny* 84, 3: 659–77.

Zubaida, S. (1993) *Islam, the People and the State*, London: I. B. Tauris.

Index